THE ORCHARD

BOOK *of* POEMS

THE ORCHARD
BOOK *of* POEMS

Chosen by ADRIAN MITCHELL

Illustrated by CHLOE CHEESE

ORCHARD BOOKS

This book is especially for my beloved extra daughter

Boty Goodwin and in happy memory of her real mother and father —

Pauline Boty and Clive Goodwin.

ORCHARD BOOKS
96 Leonard Street, London EC2A 4RH
Orchard Books Australia
14 Mars Road, Lane Cove, NSW 2066
ISBN 1 85213 316 3 (hardback)
ISBN 1 86039 268 7 (paperback)
First published in Great Britain 1993
First paperback publication 1996
Selection © Adrian Mitchell 1993
Illustrations © Chloe Cheese 1993
The right of Adrian Mitchell to be identified as the compiler and
Chloe Cheese as the illustrator of this work has been asserted by them in
accordance with the Copyright, Designs and Patents Act, 1988.
A CIP catalogue record for this book is available
from the British Library.
Printed in Great Britain by the Bath Press

CONTENTS

1. THE PALACE OF PEOPLE

2. THE BURNING DESERT AND THE COOL ORCHARD

CONTENTS

3. THE VALLEY OF ANIMALS

4. THE DAZZLING CITY

5. THE CRAZY RIVER

6. THE ROAD TO JEOPARDY

CONTENTS

7. THE SPELLBOUND MOUNTAIN

Welcome to Poetry

Poetry began in the days when everyone lived in caves or forests. Long before writing was invented, people would make up poems — love poems, hate poems, poems to make the crops grow or the rain fall. These poems were usually sung and danced by tribes. Every tribe made up its own poems. They all needed poetry.

Nowadays some people live without poetry. They're missing just as much as people who live without music.

I began to love poetry when I was about two. My Mother and Father would tuck me up in bed and read me poems or sing me songs with one arm around me. So poetry made me feel safe and warm and loved.

At the age of eight I recited a poem in public for the first time. It was the ballad of Sir Patrick Spens, which you'll find in this book. I borrowed my Father's Scottish accent for the performance which thrilled me twice as much as the audience.

I started writing poems and plays at the age of nine, and nobody has been able to stop me. At about the same age I was given the Golden Treasury, a wonderful anthology of poems which I read endlessly. I didn't understand all the poems, but I could enjoy their music.

Pick a poem, any poem, and read it to yourself. If you like it, try reading it aloud. If it sounds good, learn it by heart. It'll stay in your heart and you can use that poem whenever you need it.

When I chose the poems for the book I thought of poetry as an exciting island, with valleys full of animals and palaces packed with people. Maybe it's a slightly foreign island, sometimes dangerous, sometimes magical or ridiculous — poetry is a wild island well worth exploring.

The Orchard Book of Poems includes poems of all kinds — old ones, new ones, mild ones, happy ones, sad ones, daft ones, rough ones and gentle ones. Some of them rhyme and some of them don't — but they all have rhythm and they all have a touch of magic which excites me. A few of them were written specially for children. But most of them were written for everybody. They'll last you a lifetime. The same poem may mean one thing when you're nine, another thing when you're nineteen and yet another thing when you're ninety-nine.

*Reader: But what **is** Poetry?*
Adrian:

Poetry is a beautiful mud-pie
Washed down with a glassful of stars.

Poetry is one of the best ways
Of singing to the whole wide world
Or whispering in the ear of your best friend.

Poetry tunnels you out of your dungeon.
Poetry captures the three-headed dragon.
And teaches it Ludo and Frisbee-throwing.

Poetry is a Mammoth in a shopping mall,
A beggar with no legs in Disneyland,
A chocolate bicycle,
A truthburger with French flies
And the Moon's own telephone.

Poetry is your mind dancing
To the drumbeat of your heart.

Adrian Mitchell

The Palace of People

Births and Deaths   Love and Friendship

Youth and Age

Crimson Curtains

Crimson curtains round my mother's bed,
   Silken soft as may be;
Cool white curtains round about my bed,
   For I am but a baby.

Christina Rossetti

Motherless Baby

Motherless baby and babyless mother,
Bring them together to love one another.

Christina Rossetti

I Remember, I Remember

I remember, I remember,
The house where I was born,
The little window where the sun
Came peeping in at morn;
He never came a wink too soon,
Nor brought too long a day,
But now, I often wish the night
Had borne my breath away!

I remember, I remember,
The roses, red and white,
The violets, and the lily-cups,
Those flowers made of light!
The lilacs where the robin built,
And where my brother set
The laburnum on his birthday –
The tree is living yet!

I remember, I remember,
Where I was used to swing,
And thought the air must rush as fresh
To swallows on the wing;
My spirit flew in feathers then,
That is so heavy now,
And summer pools could hardly cool
The fever on my brow!

I remember, I remember,
The fir trees dark and high;
I used to think their slender tops
Were close against the sky:
It was a childish ignorance,
But now 'tis little joy
To know I'm farther off from Heav'n
Than when I was a boy.

Thomas Hood

First Day at School

A millionbillionwillion miles from home
Waiting for the bell to go. (To go where?)
Why are they all so big, other children?
So noisy? So much at home they
must have been born in uniform
Lived all their lives in playgrounds
Spent the years inventing games
that don't let me in. Games
that are rough, that swallow you up.

And the railings.
All around, the railings.
Are they to keep out wolves and monsters?
Things that carry off and eat children?
Things you don't take sweets from?
Perhaps they're to stop us getting out
Running away from the lessins. Lessin.
What does a lessin look like?
Sounds small and slimy.
They keep them in glassrooms.
Whole rooms made out of glass. Imagine.

I wish I could remember my name
Mummy said it would come in useful.
Like wellies. When there's puddles.
Yellowwellies. I wish she was here.
I think my name is sewn on somewhere
Perhaps the teacher will read it for me.
Tea-cher. The one who makes the tea.

Roger McGough

21

The School-Boy

I love to rise in a summer morn
When the birds sing on every tree;
The distant huntsman winds his horn,
And the sky-lark sings with me:
O, what sweet company!

But to go to school in a summer morn,
O! it drives all joy away;
Under a cruel eye outworn
The little ones spend the day
In sighing and dismay.

Ah! then at times I drooping sit,
And spend many an anxious hour;
Nor in my book can I take delight,
Nor sit in learning's bower,
Worn through with the dreary shower.

How can the bird that is born for joy
Sit in a cage and sing?
How can a child when fears annoy
But droop his tender wing,
And forget his youthful spring?

O! Father and Mother, if buds are nipped,
And blossoms blown away,
And if the tender plants are stripped
Of their joy in the springing day
By sorrow and care's dismay,

How shall the summer arise in joy
Or the summer fruits appear?
Or how shall we gather what griefs destroy
Or bless the mellowing year,
When the blasts of winter appear?

William Blake

1945

The news was of inhumanity,
Of crimes, obscenities,
Unspeakable insanity
And bestial atrocities.

Somebody turned the radio down.
Nobody said a word.
Auschwitz, Buchenwald, and Belsen:
"It couldn't happen here," they said.

At school the teacher set revision:
Of the princes murdered in the tower,
The Spanish Inquisition,
And Genghis Khan drunk with power;

Of heretics, burnt at the stake,
Refusing to deny a vow;
Mass-murders for religion's sake;
He said, "It couldn't happen now."

"You're next," the school bullies snigger,
"Don't try any silly tricks!"
All through History he tries to figure
A way out of punches and kicks.

At the end of morning school,
They drag him to an air-raid shelter.
Down into darkness, damp and cool,
With Puncher and Kicker and Belter.

They tear off all his clothes
And tread them on the floor.
With obscenities and oaths,
They let him have what-for.

Their tortures are very crude,
Clumsy and unrefined.
With a sudden change of mood
They pretend to be friendly and kind.

They change their tack once more
And punch him black and blue.
He ends, crouched on the floor,
And finally they're through.

With a special parting kick
They warn him not to talk.
He feels wretched, sore and sick,
Gets up, can hardly walk.

It's a beautiful Summer day,
His eyes squint in the sun.
He hears two passing women say,
"Oh, schooldays are such fun."

Words echo in his head:
"Couldn't happen here," they said.
And "Couldn't happen now," they said.
He never breathes a word.

Geoffrey Summerfield

It Was Long Ago

I'll tell you, shall I, something I remember?
Something that still means a great deal to me.
It was long ago.

A dusty road in summer I remember,
A mountain, and an old house, and a tree
That stood, you know,

Behind the house. An old woman I remember
In a red shawl with a grey cat on her knee
Humming under a tree.

She seemed the oldest thing I can remember,
But then perhaps I was not more than three.
It was long ago.

I dragged on the dusty road, and I remember
How the old woman looked over the fence at me
And seemed to know

How it felt to be three, and called out, I remember
"Do you like bilberries and cream for tea?"
I went under the tree

And while she hummed, and the cat purred, I remember
How she filled a saucer with berries and cream for me
So long ago,

Such berries and such cream as I remember
I never had seen before, and never see
Today, you know.

And that is almost all I can remember,
The house, the mountain, the grey cat on her knee,
Her red shawl, and the tree,

And the taste of the berries, the feel of the sun I remember,
And the smell of everything that used to be
So long ago,

Till the heat on the road outside again I remember,
And how the long dusty road seemed to have for me
No end, you know.

That is the farthest thing I can remember.
It won't mean much to you. It does to me.
Then I grew up, you see.

Eleanor Farjeon

Fantasy of an African Boy

Such a peculiar lot
we are, we people
without money, in daylong
yearlong sunlight, knowing
money is somewhere, somewhere.

Everybody says it's a big
bigger brain bother now,
money. Such millions and millions
of us don't manage at all
without it, like war going on.

And we can't eat it. Yet
without it our heads alone
stay big, as lots and lots do,
coming from nowhere joyful,
going nowhere happy.

We can't drink it up. Yet
without it we shrivel when small
and stop for ever
where we stopped,
as lots and lots do.

We can't read money for books.
Yet without it we don't
read, don't write numbers,
don't open gates in other countries,
as lots and lots never do.

We can't use money to bandage
sores, can't pound it
to powder for sick eyes
and sick bellies. Yet without
it, flesh melts from our bones.

Such walled-round gentlemen
overseas minding money! Such
bigtime gentlemen, body guarded
because of too much respect
and too many wishes on them:

too many wishes, everywhere,
wanting them to let go
magic of money, and let it fly
away, everywhere, day and night,
just like dropped leaves in wind!

James Berry

Luchin

Fragile as a kite
over the roofs of Barrancas
little Luchin was playing
his hands blue with cold,
with his rag ball
the cat and the dog
and the horse looked on.

Green light was bathing
in the water of his eyes.
Bare-bummed and in the mud
His little life spent crawling
with the rag ball the cat and the dog
and the horse looked on.

His eyes brimming pools of green,
his brief life spent crawling,
little bare bottom in the mud.

The horse was another toy
in that tiny space
and it seemed that the animal
understood his job,
with the rag ball
the cat and the dog
and with Luchin wet through.

If there are children like Luchin
who are eating earth and worms,
let's open all the cages,
so they can fly away like birds
with the rag ball the cat and the dog
and with the horse as well.

Victor Jara

Fern Hill

Now as I was young and easy under the apple boughs
About the lilting house and happy as the grass was green,
    The night above the dingle starry,
        Time let me hail and climb
    Golden in the heydays of his eyes,
And honoured among wagons I was prince of the apple towns
And once below a time I lordly had the trees and leaves
        Trail with daisies and barley
    Down the rivers of the windfall light.

And as I was green and carefree, famous among the barns
About the happy yard and singing as the farm was home,
    In the sun that is young once only,
        Time let me play and be
    Golden in the mercy of his means,
And green and golden I was huntsman and herdsman, the calves
Sang to my horn, the foxes on the hills barked clear and cold,
        And the sabbath rang slowly
    In the pebbles of the holy streams.

All the sun long it was running, it was lovely, the hay
Fields high as the house, the tunes from the chimneys, it was air
    And playing, lovely and watery
        And fire green as grass.
    And nightly under the simple stars
As I rode to sleep the owls were bearing the farm away,
All the moon long I heard, blessed among stables, the nightjars
        Flying with the ricks, and the horses
        Flashing into the dark.

And then to awake, and the farm, like a wanderer white
With the dew, come back, the cock on his shoulder: it was all
    Shining, it was Adam and maiden,
        The sky gathered again
    And the sun grew round that very day.
So it must have been after the birth of the simple light
In the first, spinning place, the spellbound horses walking warm
    Out of the whinnying green stable
        On to the fields of praise.

And honoured among foxes and pheasants by the gay house
Under the new-made clouds and happy as the heart was long,
    In the sun born over and over,
        I ran my heedless ways,
    My wishes raced through the house high hay
And nothing I cared, at my sky blue trades, that time allows
In all his tuneful turning so few and such morning songs
    Before the children green and golden
        Follow him out of grace,

Nothing I cared, in the lamb white days, that time would take me
Up to the swallow-thronged loft by the shadow of my hand,
    In the moon that is always rising,
        Nor that riding to sleep
    I should hear him fly with the high fields
And wake to the farm forever fled from the childless land.
Oh as I was young and easy in the mercy of his means,
        Time held me green and dying
    Though I sang in my chains like the sea.

Dylan Thomas

About Friends

The good thing about friends
is not having to finish sentences.

I sat a whole summer afternoon with my friend
    once
on a river bank, bashing heels on the baked mud
and watching the small chunks slide into the
    water
and listening to them – plop plop plop.
He said "I like the twigs when they...
    you know...
like that." I said "There's that branch..."
We both said "Mmmm". The river flowed and
    flowed
and there were lots of butterflies, that afternoon.

I first thought there was a sad thing about
    friends
when we met twenty years later.
We both talked hundreds of sentences,
taking care to finish all we said,
and explain it all very carefully,
as if we'd been discovered in places
we should not be, and were somehow ashamed.

I understood then what the river meant by
    flowing.

Brian Jones

Poem For My Sister

My little sister likes to try my shoes,
to strut in them,
admire her spindle-thin twelve-year-old legs
in this season's styles.
She says they fit her perfectly,
but wobbles
on their high heels, they're
hard to balance.

I like to watch my little sister
playing hopscotch, admire the neat hops-and-skips of her,
their quick peck,
never missing their mark, not
overstepping the line.
She is competent at peever.

I try to warn my little sister
about unsuitable shoes,
point out my own distorted feet, the calluses,
odd patches of hard skin.
I should not like to see her
in my shoes.
I wish she should stay
sure-footed,
                sensibly shod.

Liz Lochhead

Byes

it's sad when a person gets off the bus
and looks at the one who stayed on top to wave bye
and for the one on top to be looking elsewhere

it's sad when a person gets off the bus
and doesn't look at the one who stayed on top waving bye
and walks off looking as though miles away

it's great when a person gets off the bus
and peeps at the one who stayed on top
to wave bye
and the one on top peeps down
at the one going along the pavement miles away but half peeping
and they both discover each other and wave bye

it's a bore when a person gets off the bus
and waves bye bye to the one on top who
waves bye bye

are there other possible variations?
(do this for homework)

Mauricio Redoles

First Love

I ne'er was struck before that hour
  With love so sudden and so sweet.
Her face it bloomed like a sweet flower
  And stole my heart away complete.
My face turned pale as deadly pale,
  My legs refused to walk away,
And when she looked "what could I ail?"
  My life and all seemed turned to clay.

And then my blood rushed to my face
  And took my sight away.
The trees and bushes round the place
  Seemed midnight at noonday.
I could not see a single thing,
  Words from my eyes did start;
They spoke as chords do from the string
  And blood burnt round my heart.

Are flowers the winter's choice?
  Is love's bed always snow?
She seemed to hear my silent voice
  And love's appeal to know.
I never saw so sweet a face
  As that I stood before:
My heart has left its dwelling place
  And can return no more.

John Clare

Since First I Saw Your Face

Since first I saw your face, I resolved to honour and renown ye;
If now I be disdained, I wish my heart had never known ye.
What? I that loved and you that liked, shall we begin to wrangle?
No, no, no, my heart is fast, and cannot disentangle.

If I admire or praise you too much, that fault you may forgive me;
Or if my hands had strayed but a touch, then justly might you leave me.
I asked you leave, you bade me love; is't now a time to chide me?
No, no, no, I'll love you still what fortune e'er betide me.

The sun, whose beams most glorious are, rejecteth no beholder,
And your sweet beauty past compare made my poor eyes the bolder;
Where beauty moves and wit delights and signs of kindness bind me,
There, O there, where'er I go I'll leave my heart behind me!

Anon

Without You

Without you every morning would be like going back to work
after a holiday,
Without you I couldn't stand the smell of the East Lancs Road,
Without you ghost ferries would cross the Mersey manned by
skeleton crews,
Without you I'd probably feel happy and have more money
and time and nothing to do with it,
Without you I'd have to leave my stillborn poems on other
people's doorsteps, wrapped in brown paper,
Without you there'd never be sauce to put on sausage butties,
Without you plastic flowers in shop windows would just be
plastic flowers in shop windows,
Without you I'd spend my summers picking morosely over
the remains of train crashes,
Without you white birds would wrench themselves free from
my paintings and fly off dripping blood into the night,
Without you green apples wouldn't taste greener,
Without you Mothers wouldn't let their children play out after tea,
Without you every musician in the world would forget how to
play the blues,
Without you Public Houses would be public again,
Without you the Sunday Times colour supplement would
come out in black-and-white,
Without you indifferent colonels would shrug their shoulders
and press the button,
Without you they'd stop changing the flowers in Piccadilly
Gardens,
Without you Clark Kent would forget how to become
Superman,

Without you Sunshine Breakfast would only consist of
Cornflakes,
Without you there'd be no colour in Magic colouring books,
Without you Mahler's 8th would only be performed by street
musicians in derelict houses,
Without you they'd forget to put the salt in every packet of crisps,
Without you it would be an offence punishable by a fine of up
to £200 or two months' imprisonment to be found in
possession of curry powder,
Without you riot police are massing in quiet sidestreets,
Without you all streets would be one-way the other way,
Without you there'd be no one not to kiss goodnight when we
quarrel,
Without you the first martian to land would turn round and go
away again,
Without you they'd forget to change the weather,
Without you blind men would sell unlucky heather,
Without you there would be
no landscapes/no stations/no houses,
no chipshops/no quiet villages/no seagulls
on beaches/no hopscotch on pavements/no night/no morning/
there'd be no city no country
Without you.

Adrian Henri

She Walks in Beauty

She walks in beauty, like the night
   Of cloudless climes and starry skies;
And all that's best of dark and bright
   Meet in her aspect and her eyes:
Thus mellow'd to that tender light
   Which heaven to gaudy day denies.

One shade the more, one ray the less,
   Had half impair'd the nameless grace
Which waves in every raven tress,
   Or softly lightens o'er her face;
Where thoughts serenely sweet express
   How pure, how dear their dwelling-place.

And on that cheek, and o'er that brow,
   So soft, so calm, yet eloquent,
The smiles that win, the tints that glow,
   But tell of days in goodness spent,
A mind at peace with all below,
   A heart whose love is innocent!

Lord Byron

Meeting at Night

The grey sea and the long black land;
And the yellow half-moon large and low;
And the startled little waves that leap
In fiery ringlets from their sleep,
As I gain the cove with pushing prow,
And quench its speed i' the slushy sand.

Then a mile of warm sea-scented beach;
Three fields to cross till a farm appears;
A tap at the pane, the quick sharp scratch
And blue spurt of a lighted match,
And a voice less loud, thro' its joys and fears,
Than the two hearts beating each to each!

Robert Browning

Like a Flame

Raising up
from my weeding
of ripening cane

my eyes
make four
with this man

there ain't
no reason
to laugh

but
I laughing
in confusion

his hands
soft his words
quick his lips
curling as in
prayer

I nod

I like this man

Tonight
I go to meet him
like a flame

Grace Nichols

How Long Blues

How long, baby, how long
Has that even' train been gone?
How long? How long? I say, How long?
Standin' at the station watchin' my baby leave town,
Sure am disgusted – for where could she be gone –
For how long? How long? I say, how long?

I can hear the whistle blowin' but I cannot see no train
And deep down in my heart I got an ache and pain
For how long? How long? I say, how long?

Sometimes I feel so disgusted and I feel so blue
That I hardly know what in this world it's best to do
For how long, how long, how long?

If I could holler like I was a mountain jack
I'd go up on the mountain and call my baby back.
For how long, how long, how long?

If some day she's gonna be sorry that she done me wrong
Baby, it will be too late then – for I'll be gone
For so long, so long, so long!

My mind gets to rattling, I feel so bad
Thinkin' 'bout the bad luck that I have had
For so long, so long, so long.

How long? Baby, how long?
Baby, how long?
How long?

Anon

The Enchanted Mistress

I met brightness of brightness upon the path of loneliness;
Plaiting of plaiting in every lock of her yellow hair.
News of news she gave me, and she as lonely as she was;
News of the coming back of him that owns the tribute of the king.

Folly of follies I to go so near to her,
Slave I was made by a slave that put me in hard bonds.
She made away from me then and I following after her
Till we came to a house of houses made by Druid enchantments.

They broke into mocking laughter, a troop of men of enchantments,
And a troop of young girls with smooth-plaited hair.
They put me up in chains, they made no delay about it –
And my love holding to her breast an awkward ugly clown.

I told her then with the truest words I could tell her,
It was not right for her to be joined with a common clumsy churl;
And the man that was three times fairer than the whole race of the Scots
Waiting till she would come to him to be his beautiful bride.

At the sound of my words her pride set her crying,
The tears were running down over the kindling of her cheeks.
She sent a lad to bring me safe from the place I was in.
She is the brightness of brightness I met in the path of loneliness.

Lady Gregory

I Gave My Love a Cherry

I gave my love a cherry without a stone;
I gave my love a chicken without a bone;
I gave my love a ring without an end;
I gave my love a baby with no crying.

How can there be a cherry without a stone?
How can there be a chicken without a bone?
How can there be a ring without an end?
How can there be a baby with no crying?

A cherry, when it's blooming, it has no stone;
A chicken, when it's pipping, it has no bone;
A ring, when it's rolling, it has no end;
A baby, when it's sleeping, has no crying.

Anon

Donall Oge

It is late last night the dog was speaking of you,
The snipe was speaking of you in her deep marsh.
It is you are the lonely bird throughout the woods,
And that you may be without a mate until you find me.

You promised me and you said a lie to me,
That you would be before me where the sheep are flocked.
I gave a whistle and three hundred cries to you,
And I found nothing there but a bleating lamb.

You promised me a thing that was hard for you,
A ship of gold under a silver mast,
Twelve towns and a market in all of them,
And a fine white court by the side of the sea.

You promised me a thing that is not possible,
That you would give me gloves of the skin of a fish,
That you would give me shoes of the skin of a bird,
And a suit of the dearest silk in Ireland.

My mother said to me not to be talking with you,
Today or tomorrow or on the Sunday.
It was a bad time she took for telling me that,
It was shutting the door after the house was robbed.

You have taken the east from me, you have taken the west from me,
You have taken what is before me and what is behind me;
You have taken the moon, you have taken the sun from me,
And my fear is great you have taken God from me.

Lady Gregory

A Red, Red Rose

O my Luve's like a red, red rose
    That's newly sprung in June:
O my Luve's like the melodie
    That's sweetly play'd in tune!

As fair art thou, my bonnie lass,
    So deep in luve am I:
And I will luve thee still, my dear,
    Till a' the seas gang dry:

Till a' the seas gang dry, my dear,
   And the rocks melt wi' the sun;
I will luve thee still, my dear,
   While the sands o' life shall run.

And fare thee weel, my only Luve,
   And fare thee weel a while!
And I will come again, my Luve,
   Tho' it were ten thousand mile.

Robert Burns

A Ditty

My true-love hath my heart, and I have his,
By just exchange one to the other given:
I hold his dear, and mine he cannot miss,
There never was a better bargain driven:
   My true-love hath my heart, and I have his.

His heart in me keeps him and me in one,
My heart in him his thoughts and senses guides:
He loves my heart, for once it was his own,
I cherish his because in me it bides:
   My true-love hath my heart, and I have his.

Sir Philip Sidney

A Poison Tree

I was angry with my friend:
I told my wrath, my wrath did end.
I was angry with my foe:
I told it not, my wrath did grow.

And I water'd it in fears,
Night and morning with my tears;
And I sunned it with smiles,
And with soft deceitful wiles.

And it grew both day and night,
Till it bore an apple bright;
And my foe beheld it shine,
And he knew that it was mine,

And into my garden stole
When the night had veil'd the pole:
In the morning glad I see
My foe outstretch'd beneath the tree.

William Blake

Love's Farewell

Since there's no help, come let us kiss and part –
Nay I have done, you get no more of me;
And I am glad, yea, glad with all my heart,
That thus so cleanly I myself can free;

Shake hands for ever, cancel all our vows,
And when we meet at any time again,
Be it not seen in either of our brows
That we one jot of former love retain.

Now at the last gasp of love's latest breath,
When his pulse failing, passion speechless lies,
When faith is kneeling by his bed of death,
And innocence is closing up his eyes,

– Now if thou woulds't, when all have given him over,
From death to life thou might'st him yet recover!

Michael Drayton

Helen of Kirconnell

I wish I were where Helen lies;
Night and day on me she cries;
O that I were where Helen lies
    On fair Kirconnell lea!

Curst be the heart that thought the thought,
And curst the hand that fired the shot,
When in my arms burd Helen dropt,
    And died to succour me!

O think na but my heart was sair
When my Love dropt down and spak nae mair!
I laid her down wi' meikle care
    On fair Kirconnell lea.

As I went down the waterside,
None but my foe to be my guide,
None but my foe to be my guide,
    On fair Kirconnell lea;

I lighted down my sword to draw,
I hackéd him in pieces sma',
I hackéd him in pieces sma',
    For her sake that died for me.

O Helen fair, beyond compare!
I'll make a garland of thy hair
Shall bind my heart for evermair
    Until the day I die.

O that I were where Helen lies!
Night and day on me she cries;
Out of my bed she bids me rise,
    Says, "Haste and come to me!"

O Helen fair! O Helen chaste!
If I were with thee, I were blest,
Where thou lies low and takes thy rest
    On fair Kirconnell lea.

I wish my grave were growing green,
A winding-sheet drawn ower my een,
And I in Helen's arms lying,
    On fair Kirconnell lea.

I wish I were where Helen lies;
Night and day on me she cries;
And I am weary of the skies,
    Since my Love died for me.

Anon

A Birthday

My heart is like a singing bird
   Whose nest is in a water'd shoot;
My heart is like an apple tree
   Whose boughs are bent with thick-set fruit;
My heart is like a rainbow shell
   That paddles in a halcyon sea;
My heart is gladder than all these,
   Because my love is come to me.

Raise me a daïs of silk and down;
   Hang it with vair and purple dyes;
Carve it in doves and pomegranates,
   And peacocks with a hundred eyes;
Work it in gold and silver grapes,
   In leaves and silver fleurs-de-lys;
Because the birthday of my life
   Is come, my love is come to me.

Christina Rossetti

So We'll Go No More A Roving

So, we'll go no more a roving
   So late into the night,
Though the heart be still as loving,
   And the moon be still as bright.

For the sword outwears its sheath,
   And the soul wears out the breast,
And the heart must pause to breathe,
   And love itself have rest.

Though the night was made for loving,
   And the day returns too soon,
Yet we'll go no more a roving
   By the light of the moon.

Lord Byron

Warning

When I am an old woman I shall wear purple
With a red hat which doesn't go, and doesn't suit me.
And I shall spend my pension on brandy and summer gloves
And satin sandals, and say we've no money for butter.
I shall sit down on the pavement when I'm tired
And gobble up samples in shops and press alarm bells
And run my stick along the public railings
And make up for the sobriety of my youth.
I shall go out in my slippers in the rain
And pick the flowers in other people's gardens
And learn to spit.

You can wear terrible shirts and grow more fat
And eat three pounds of sausages at a go
Or only bread and pickle for a week
And hoard pens and pencils and beermats and things in boxes.

But now we must have clothes that keep us dry
And pay our rent and not swear in the street
And set a good example for the children.
We must have friends to dinner and read the papers.

But maybe I ought to practise a little now?
So people who know me are not too shocked and surprised
When suddenly I am old, and start to wear purple.

Jenny Joseph

53

Happiest Girl

Mrs Mary Leighton's 89-year-old body was as frail as a wigwam:
A house of bone she lived in, covered only by a stretch of skin
And a faint white dusting of talcum powder.
Somewhere in her body grew a rebellion of cells –
The ranks of mutiny silently waiting to erupt.
Oblivious, she laughed for me and said
"Ee, luv, I'm th' appiest girl in th' world!"
I was glad it was true.

And there I stood in my white coat and blue trousers,
Wanting to be a friend rather than an Efficiency –
I didn't want to Organise her.
How I wished I could banish her threat of pain
With pink carnations, or the sun, or a song,
As I watched her head with the old, old mist of hair around
And helped her climb the stairs towards home.

Beautiful, wonderful Mary!
(How my throat hurt as she patted my hand)
"What would I do without you?" she said, and laughed.
I tried to laugh too (if only from duty).
Only my white coat and blue trousers stopped me
From hugging her to me and crushing the cancer
And climbing each stair for her, taking her back
To her pink carnations.

She is the sun and a song and pink carnations.
She was the truth when she told me of luck and of fortune,
And of the happiest girl in the world.

Frances Clewlow

Grandad

Grandad's dead
And I'm sorry about that.

He'd a huge black overcoat.
He felt proud in it.
You could have hidden
A football crowd in it.
Far too big –
It was a lousy fit
But Grandad didn't
Mind a bit.
He wore it all winter
With a squashed black hat.

Now he's dead
And I'm sorry about that.

He'd got twelve stories.
I'd heard every one of them
Hundreds of times
But that was the fun of them:
You knew what was coming
So you could join in.
He'd got big hands
And brown, grooved skin
And when he laughed
It knocked you flat.

Now he's dead
And I'm sorry about that.

Kit Wright

As I Was Going Down Treak Street

As I was going down Treak Street
For half a pound of treacle,
Who should I meet but my old friend Micky Thumps.
He said to me, "Wilt thou come to our wake?"
I thought a bit,
I thought a bit,
I said I didn't mind:
So I went.

As I was sitting on our doorstep
Who should come by but my old friend Micky Thumps' brother.
He said to me, "Wilt thou come to our house?
Micky is ill."
I thought a bit,
I thought a bit,
I said I didn't mind:
So I went.

And he were ill:
He were gradely ill.
He said to me,
"Wilt thou come to my funeral, mon, if I die?"
I thought a bit,
I thought a bit,
I said I didn't mind:
So I went.

And it *were* a funeral.
Some stamped on his grave:
Some spat on his grave:
But I scraped my eyes out for my old friend Micky Thumps.

Anon

A Child Said, "What is the grass?"

(from *Song of Myself*)

A child said, "What is the grass?" fetching it to me with full hands;
How could I answer the child? I do not know what it is, any more than he.

I guess it must be the flag of my disposition, out of hopeful green stuff woven.

Or I guess it is the handkerchief of the Lord,
A scented gift and remembrancer, designedly dropt,
Bearing the owner's name someway in the corner, that we may see and
 remark, and say, Whose?

Or I guess the grass is itself a child, the produced babe of the vegetation.

Or I guess it is a uniform hieroglyphic;
And it means, Sprouting alike in broad zones and narrow zones,
Growing among black folks as among white;
Kanuck, Tuckahoe, Congressman, Cuff, I give them the same, I receive them
 the same.

And now it seems to me the beautiful uncut hair of graves.

Tenderly will I use you, curling grass;
It may be you transpire from the breasts of young men;
It may be if I had known them I would have loved them;
It may be you are from old people, and from women, and from offspring
 taken soon out of their mothers' laps;
And here you are the mothers' laps.

This grass is very dark to be from the white heads of old mothers;
Darker than the colourless beards of old men;
Dark to come from under the faint red roofs of mouths.

O I perceive after all so many uttering tongues!
And I perceive they do not come from the roofs of mouths for nothing.

I wish I could translate the hints about the dead young men and women,
And the hints about old men and mothers, and the offspring taken soon out
   of their laps.

What do you think has become of the young and old men?
And what do you think has become of the women and children?

They are alive and well somewhere;
The smallest sprout shows there is really no death;
And if ever there was, it led forward life, and does not wait at the end to arrest
   it,
And ceas'd the moment life appear'd.

All goes onward and outward – nothing collapses;
And to die is different from what any one supposed, and luckier.

Has any one supposed it lucky to be born?
I hasten to inform him or her, it is just as lucky to die, and I know it.

Walt Whitman

Fear No More the Heat o' the Sun

Fear no more the heat o' the sun,
   Nor the furious winter's rages;
Thou thy worldly task hast done,
   Home art gone, and ta'en thy wages;
Golden lads and girls all must,
As chimney-sweepers, come to dust.

Fear no more the frown o' the great,
   Thou art past the tyrant's stroke:
Care no more to clothe and eat;
   To thee the reed is as the oak;
The sceptre, learning, physic, must
All follow this, and come to dust.

Fear no more the lightning-flash,
   Nor the all-dreaded thunder-stone;
Fear not slander, censure rash;
   Thou hast finish'd joy and moan:
All lovers young, all lovers must
Consign to thee, and come to dust.

No exorciser harm thee!
Nor no witchcraft charm thee!
Ghost unlaid forbear thee!
Nothing ill come near thee!
Quiet consummation have;
And renowned be thy grave!

William Shakespeare

In Painswick Churchyard

"Is this where people are buried?
I will not let them bury you"

He picnics among tombs
– pours imaginary tea,
a yew tree his kitchen

"You will live with me in my house"

Oh could I believe the living and dead inhabit one house under
the sky and you my child run into your future for ever

Frances Horovitz

The Song of Wandering Aengus

I went out to the hazel wood,
Because a fire was in my head,
And cut and peeled a hazel wand,
And hooked a berry to a thread,
And when white moths were on the wing,
And moth-like stars were flickering out.
I dropped the berry in a stream
And caught a little silver trout.

When I had laid it on the floor
I went to blow the fire a-flame
But something rustled on the floor,
And someone called me by my name:

It had become a glimmering girl
With apple blossoms in her hair
Who called me by my name and ran
And faded through the brightening air.

Though I am old with wandering
Through hollow lands and hilly lands,
I will find out where she has gone,
And kiss her lips and take her hands;
And walk among long dappled grass,
And pluck till time and times are done,
The silver apples of the moon,
The golden apples of the sun.

W. B. Yeats

Requiem

Under the wide and starry sky
　　Dig the grave and let me lie:
Glad did I live and gladly die,
　　And I laid me down with a will.

This be the verse you grave for me:
Here he lies where he long'd to be;
Home is the sailor, home from sea,
　　And the hunter home from the hill.

Robert Louis Stevenson

Yes

Last night I dreamt again of Adam returning
To the Garden's scented, bubbling cauldron.

Eve was beside him,
Their shadows were cut adrift
And the hum of bees was in their blood,

And the world was slow and good and all
The warm and yawning newness of their flesh
Was fixed for ever in the glow of "Yes".

Brian Patten

The Burning Desert and the Cool Orchard

Bad Times, Good Times
Food and Drink
War and Peace
Fun and Games

Centrifugalised in Finsbury Park

Hey I just had a go on one of them
things! Didn't notice it had a name,
but anyone could see what it was going to do to you –

something like a giant-size round biscuit-tin without a lid
made of wire-netting, and all around the inside,
niches, like for statues, 30 or so, like coffins, only
upright, and open of course with the kind of lattice –
with a padded red heart at head-height.

Paid some money, got myself a niche, and stood and waited
with a little chain dangling across my hips,
until it was full, the gate shut, the music started
and the thing began to whirl.

It wasn't the stomach, it was what to do with the head:
no good looking down, but if you let your head back
it felt as if it was going to go on going back, or off –
a bit peculiar, shut my eyes to get through that.

And as it whirled, the whole thing turned on end,
more or less vertical – well, I'd seen that right from
the park gates and couldn't believe it, which was why –
and opening my eyes again then, just found myself
lying there – lying down face up, lying up face down
over the whole fairground!

And it didn't make you scream like the top of the Big
Wheel, but smile – look up and everyone else is standing there,
hanging there, smiling, look down and you might as well be a lazy
bird on the wind, though I did forget I could let go,

and the only strange feeling was,
every time you were on the down side hurtling up again,
you left the skin of your face behind for a second.
You know I've never dared try anything quite like that
before, and it was just very nice!

And when it slowed down and sank down, and all of us
were ordinary upright, and unhitched our little chains,
I only staggered a couple of times, disappearing
on ground level into the dark – and nobody was sick.

Libby Houston

Reggae Sounds

Shock-black bubble-doun-beat bouncing
rock-wise tumble-doun sound music;
foot-drop find drum, blood story,
bass history is a moving
          is a hurting black story.

Thunda from a bass drum sounding
lightening from a trumpet and a organ,
bass and rhythm and trumpet double-up,
team-up with drums for a deep doun searching.

Rhythm of a tropical electrical storm
(cooled doun to the pace of the struggle),
flame-rhythm of historically yearning
flame-rhythm of the time of turning,
measuring the time for bombs and for burning.

Slow drop. make stop. move forward.
dig doun to the root of the pain;
shape it into violence for the people,
they will know what to do, they will do it.

Shock-black bubble-doun-beat bouncing
rock-wise tumble-doun sound music;
foot-drop find drum, blood story,
bass history is a moving
          is a hurting black story.

Linton Kwesi Johnson

Where Poems Came From

They came, I supposed, from London.
Or from somewhere in England – Heaven,
most likely: wasn't God, after all, a bit
chalky – the grey suit and silver hair,
the underwear somewhat neglectful –
wasn't he the sort, in his spare time,
    to be spinning out rhymes
    on the prettiness of things?

Journeys they claimed –
    over hills and vales,
    through moonlit doors,
    down the last furlong
    from Ghent to Aix –
        but they reached us
too heavy for words with chalk-dust.
They were chalk-dust and the tired eye,
they were trembling knees when all went
speechless at the eager end of Friday.
They were paper and they were
    words, books of them
yellowed in the classroom cupboard –
the place that poems truly came from.

Yet truly they came,
behind my back they talked
to me, though I heard no words,
their coming was not to do
with words.

    It was in the laughter of dogs
    way across the snow. I could smell it
    in freshly painted rooms, taste it warmer
    in the cream than the milk. In the tricks
    that skies played with stone I found it,
    I found it in my body when first
    I discovered its emptying joy
    and wanted, afraid, to share it.

They came too in forgotten
things, in the thing wholly strange –
        that I recognised.
And one mart-day they came,
in a farmer's voice as he sat
drinking tea,
    explaining to himself, trying
    to explain the world to himself.

But not in the words of his explanation,
not from the names did they come.
    For there's a space
    in things, a gap between
    the words for it and a wave's
    movement, its infinite motion.

As I stood,
     a baby, at the sea's edge
     I began to wail – for no misery,
     no joy that I could name –
     lost, quite lost for words

to be facing there our world's great noise,
     to be facing there its silence.

Nigel Jenkins

Motherless Child

Sometimes I feel like a motherless child,
Sometimes I feel like a motherless child,
Sometimes I feel like a motherless child,
A long ways from home,
A long ways from home.

Sometimes I feel like I'm almost gone,
Sometimes I feel like I'm almost gone,
Sometimes I feel like I'm almost gone,
A long ways from home,
A long ways from home.

Sometimes I feel like a feather in the air,
Sometimes I feel like a feather in the air,
Sometimes I feel like a feather in the air,
And I spread my wings and I fly,

I spread my wings and I fly.

Anon

Lean Out of the Window

Lean out of the window,
    Goldenhair,
I heard you singing
    A merry air.

My book is closed,
    I read no more,
Watching the fire dance
    On the floor.

I have left my book:
    I have left my room:
For I heard you singing
    Through the gloom,

Singing and singing
    A merry air.
Lean out of the window,
    Goldenhair.

James Joyce

Hard Times Ain't Gone Nowhere

Peoples' raving 'bout hard times, tell me what it's all about.
Peoples' raving 'bout hard times, tell me what it's all about.
Hard times don't worry me, I was broke when they first started out.

Friends, it could be worser, you don't seem to understand.
Friends, it could be worser, you don't seem to understand.
Some is crying with a sack of gold under each arm and a loaf of
    bread in each hand.

Peoples' raving 'bout hard times, I don't know why they should.
Peoples' raving 'bout hard times, I don't know why they should.
If some people was like me, they didn't have no money when
    times were good.

Lonnie Johnson

Winter

When icicles hang by the wall,
   And Dick the shepherd blows his nail,
And Tom bears logs into the hall,
   And milk comes frozen home in pail,
When blood is nipp'd and ways be foul,
Then nightly sings the staring owl,
                     Tu-who;
Tu-whit, tu-who – a merry note,
While greasy Joan doth keel the pot.

When all aloud the wind doth blow,
   And coughing drowns the parson's saw,
And birds sit brooding in the snow,
   And Marian's nose looks red and raw,
When roasted crabs hiss in the bowl,
Then nightly sings the staring owl,
                     Tu-who;
Tu-whit, tu-who – a merry note,
While greasy Joan doth keel the pot.

William Shakespeare

The Warm and the Cold

Freezing dusk is closing
    Like a slow trap of steel
On trees and roads and hills and all
    That can no longer feel.
        But the carp is in its depth
            Like a planet in its heaven.
        And the badger in its bedding
            Like a loaf in the oven.
        And the butterfly in its mummy
            Like a viol in its case.
        And the owl in its feathers
            Like a doll in its lace.

Freezing dusk has tightened
    Like a nut screwed tight
On the starry aeroplane
    Of the soaring night.
        But the trout is in its hole
            Like a chuckle in a sleeper.
        The hare strays down the highway
            Like a root going deeper.
        The snail is dry in the outhouse
            Like a seed in a sunflower.
        The owl is pale on the gatepost
            Like a clock on its tower.

Moonlight freezes the shaggy world
    Like a mammoth of ice –
The past and the future
    Are the jaws of a steel vice.
        But the cod is in the tide-rip
            Like a key in a purse.

The deer are on the bare-blown hill
Like smiles on a nurse.
The flies are behind the plaster
Like the lost score of a jig.
Sparrows are in the ivy-clump
Like money in a pig.

Such a frost
The flimsy moon
Has lost her wits.

A star falls.

The sweating farmers
Turn in their sleep
Like oxen on spits.

Ted Hughes

To a Poor Old Woman

munching a plum on
the street a paper bag
of them in her hand

They taste good to her
They taste good
to her. They taste
good to her

You can see it by
the way she gives herself
to the one half
sucked out in her hand

Comforted
a solace of ripe plums
seeming to fill the air
They taste good to her

William Carlos Williams

Rotting Song

old green cheese
old green cheese
you'll never get another chance —

Green cheese sits in the airtight tin
wondering just how those mites got in,
crosses off the minutes to the sinking knife —
hasn't found out he's in prison for life

Cold meat sweats on the larder plate
a wet flesh target, doesn't have to wait,
in dive the black flies, drop their eggs —
drive him crazy those hairy legs

Dud plum squashed on the kitchen floor
can't see what he's been put there for,
knows he's going soft but he can't stir —
old age buries him deep in fur

Dud plum, cold meat, old green cheese
rot in your own time at your ease,
nobody minds, nobody cares —
moved out their lives and gone downstairs

Libby Houston

Greedyguts

I sat in the café and sipped at a Coke.
There sat down beside me a WHOPPING great bloke
Who sighed as he elbowed me into the wall:
"Your trouble, my boy, is your belly's too small!
Your bottom's too thin! Take a lesson from me:
I may not be nice, but I'm GREAT, you'll agree,
And I've lasted a lifetime by playing this hunch:
The bigger the breakfast, the larger the lunch!

The larger the lunch, then the huger the supper.
The deeper the teapot, the vaster the cupper.
The fatter the sausage, the fuller the tea.
The MORE on the table, the BETTER for ME!"

His elbows moved in and his elbows moved out,
His belly grew bigger, chins wobbled about,
As forkful by forkful and plate after plate,
He ate and he ate and he ate and he ATE!

I hardly could breathe, I was squashed out of shape,
So under the table I made my escape.

"Aha!" he rejoiced, "when it's put to the test,
The fellow who's fattest will come off the best!
Remember, my boy, when it comes to the crunch:
The bigger the breakfast, the larger the lunch!

The larger the lunch, then the huger the supper.
The deeper the teapot, the vaster the cupper.
The fatter the sausage, the fuller the tea.
The MORE on the table, the BETTER for ME!"

A lady came by who was scrubbing the floor
With a mop and a bucket. To even the score,
I lifted that bucket of water and said,
As I poured the whole lot of it over his head:

"*I've* found all my life, it's a pretty sure bet:
The FULLER the bucket, the WETTER you GET!"

Kit Wright

Figgie Hobbin

Nightingales' tongues, your majesty?
   Quails in aspic, cost a purse of money?
Oysters from the deep, raving sea?
   Grapes and Greek honey?
Beads of black caviare from the Caspian?
   Rock melon with corn on the cob in?
Take it all away! grumbled the old King of Cornwall.
   Bring me some figgie hobbin!

Devilled lobster, your majesty?
   Scots kail brose or broth?
Grilled mackerel with gooseberry sauce?
   Cider ice that melts in your mouth?
Pears filled with nut and date salad?
   Christmas pudding with a tanner or a bob in?
Take it all away! groused the old King of Cornwall.
   Bring me some figgie hobbin!

Amber jelly, your majesty?
   Passion fruit flummery?
Pineapple sherbet, milk punch or Pavlova cake,
   Sugary, summery?

Carpet-bag steak, blueberry grunt, cinnamon crescents?
    Spaghetti as fine as the thread on a bobbin?
Take it all away! grizzled the old King of Cornwall.
    Bring me some figgie hobbin!

So in from the kitchen came figgie hobbin,
    Shining and speckled with raisins sweet,
And though on the King of Cornwall's land
    The rain it fell and wind it beat,
As soon as a forkful of figgie hobbin
    Up to his lips he drew,
Over the palace a pure sun shone
    And the sky was blue.
THAT'S what I wanted! he smiled, his face
    Now as bright as the breast of the robin.
To cure the sickness of the heart, ah –
    Bring me some figgie hobbin!

Charles Causley

Porridge

Why is there no monument
    To Porridge in our land?
If it's good enough to eat
    It's good enough to stand!

On a plinth in London
    A statue we should see
Of Porridge made in Scotland
    Signed "Oatmeal, O.B.E."
        (By a young dog of three)

Spike Milligan

I Hear an Army Charging

I hear an army charging upon the land,
    And the thunder of horses plunging, foam about their knees:
Arrogant, in black armour, behind them stand,
    Disdaining the reins, with fluttering whips, the charioteers.

They cry unto the night their battle-name:
    I moan in sleep when I hear afar their whirling laughter.
They cleave the gloom of dreams, a blinding flame,
    Clanging, clanging upon the heart as upon an anvil.

They come shaking in triumph their long, green hair:
    They come out of the sea and run shouting by the shore.
My heart, have you no wisdom thus to despair?
    My love, my love, my love, why have you left me alone?

James Joyce

The Field of Waterloo

Yea, the coneys are scared by the thud of hoofs,
And their white scuts flash at their vanishing heels,
And swallows abandon the hamlet-roofs.

The mole's tunnelled chambers are crushed by wheels,
The lark's eggs scattered, their owners fled;
And the hedgehog's household the sapper unseals.

The snail draws in at the terrible tread,
But in vain; he is crushed by the felloe-rim;
The worm asks what can be overhead,

And wriggles deep from a scene so grim,
And guesses him safe; for he does not know
What a foul red flood will be soaking him!

Beaten about by the heel and toe
Are butterflies, sick of the day's long rheum,
To die of a worse than the weather-foe.

Trodden and bruised to a miry tomb
Are ears that have greened but will never be gold,
And flowers in the bud that will never bloom.

Thomas Hardy

Tommy

I went into a public-'ouse to get a pint o' beer,
The publican 'e up an' sez, "We serve no red-coats here."
The girls be'ind the bar they laughed an' giggled fit to die,
I outs into the street again an' to myself sez I:
  O it's Tommy this, an' Tommy that, an' "Tommy, go away";
  But it's "Thank you, Mister Atkins," when the band begins to play –
  The band begins to play, my boys, the band begins to play,
  O it's "Thank you, Mister Atkins," when the band begins to play.

I went into a theatre as sober as could be,
They gave a drunk civilian room, but 'adn't none for me;
They sent me to the gallery or round the music-'alls,
But when it comes to fightin', Lord! they'll shove me in the stalls!
  For it's Tommy this, an' Tommy that, an' "Tommy, wait outside";
  But it's "Special train for Atkins" when the trooper's on the tide –
  The troopship's on the tide, my boys, the troopship's on the tide,
  O it's "Special train for Atkins" when the trooper's on the tide.

Yes, makin' mock o' uniforms that guard you while you sleep
Is cheaper than them uniforms, an' they're starvation cheap;
An' hustlin' drunken soldiers when they're goin' large a bit
Is five times better business than paradin' in full kit.
>   Then it's Tommy this, an' Tommy that, an' "Tommy, 'ow's yer soul?"
>   But it's "Thin red line of 'eroes" when the drums begin to roll –
>   The drums begin to roll, my boys, the drums begin to roll,
>   O it's "Thin red line of 'eroes" when the drums begin to roll.

We aren't no thin red 'eroes, nor we aren't no blackguards too,
But single men in barricks, most remarkable like you;
An' if sometimes our conduck isn't all your fancy paints,
Why, single men in barricks don't grow into plaster saints;
>   While it's Tommy this, an' Tommy that, an' "Tommy, fall be'ind,"
>   But it's "Please to walk in front, sir," when there's trouble in the wind –
>   There's trouble in the wind, my boys, there's trouble in the wind,
>   O it's "Please to walk in front, sir," when there's trouble in the wind.

You talk o' better food for us, an' schools, an' fires, an' all:
We'll wait for extry rations if you treat us rational.
Don't mess about the cook-room slops, but prove it to our face
The Widow's Uniform is not the soldier-man's disgrace.
>   For it's Tommy this, an' Tommy that, an' "Chuck him out, the brute!"
>   But it's "Saviour of 'is country" when the guns begin to shoot;
>   An' it's Tommy this, an' Tommy that, an' anything you please;
>   An' Tommy ain't a bloomin' fool – you bet that Tommy sees!

Rudyard Kipling

Johnny, I Hardly Knew Ye

While going the road to sweet Athy,
    Hurroo! hurroo!
While going the road to sweet Athy,
    Hurroo! hurroo!
While going the road to sweet Athy,
A stick in my hand and a drop in my eye,
A doleful damsel I heard cry –
    "Och, Johnny, I hardly knew ye!
With drums and guns and guns and drums,
    The enemy nearly slew ye,
    My darling dear, you look so queer,
    Och, Johnny, I hardly knew ye!

"Where are your eyes that looked so mild?
    Hurroo! hurroo!
Where are your eyes that looked so mild?
    Hurroo! hurroo!
Where are your eyes that looked so mild
When my poor heart you first beguiled?
Why did you run from me and the child?
    Och, Johnny, I hardly knew ye!
With drums and guns and guns and drums,
    The enemy nearly slew ye,
    My darling dear, you look so queer,
    Och, Johnny, I hardly knew ye!

"Where are the legs with which you run?
    Hurroo! hurroo!
Where are the legs with which you run?
    Hurroo! hurroo!
Where are the legs with which you run,
When you went to carry a gun?

Indeed, your dancing days are done!
  Och, Johnny, I hardly knew ye!
With drums and guns and guns and drums,
  The enemy nearly slew ye,
  My darling dear, you look so queer,
  Och, Johnny, I hardly knew ye!

"It grieved my heart to see you sail,
  Hurroo! hurroo!
It grieved my heart to see you sail,
  Hurroo! hurroo!
It grieved my heart to see you sail,
Though from my heart you took leg bail –
Like a cod you're doubled up head and tail.
  Och, Johnny, I hardly knew ye!
With drums and guns and guns and drums,
  The enemy nearly slew ye,
  My darling dear, you look so queer,
  Och, Johnny, I hardly knew ye!

"You haven't an arm and you haven't a leg,
  Hurroo! hurroo!
You haven't an arm and you haven't a leg,
  Hurroo! hurroo!
You haven't an arm and you haven't a leg,
You're an eyeless, noseless, chickenless egg;
You'll have to be put in a bowl to beg;
  Och, Johnny, I hardly knew ye!
With drums and guns and guns and drums,
  The enemy nearly slew ye,
  My darling dear, you look so queer,
  Och, Johnny, I hardly knew ye!

"I'm happy for to see you home,
    Hurroo! hurroo!
I'm happy for to see you home,
    Hurroo! hurroo!
I'm happy for to see you home,
All from the island of Sulloon,
So low in flesh, so high in bone,
    Och, Johnny, I hardly knew ye!
With drums and guns and guns and drums,
    The enemy nearly slew ye,
    My darling dear, you look so queer,
    Och, Johnny, I hardly knew ye!

"But sad as it is to see you so,
    Hurroo! hurroo!
But sad as it is to see you so,
    Hurroo! hurroo!
But sad as it is to see you so,
And to think of you now as an object of woe,
Your Peggy'll still keep ye on as her beau;
    Och, Johnny, I hardly knew ye!
With drums and guns and guns and drums,
    The enemy nearly slew ye,
    My darling dear, you look so queer,
    Och, Johnny, I hardly knew ye!"

Anon

How Much Longer?

Day after day after day it goes on
and no one knows how to stop it or escape.
Friends come bearing impersonal agonies,
I hear our hopeless laughter, I watch us drink.

War is in everyone's eyes, war is made
in the kitchen, in the bedroom, in the car at stoplights.
A marriage collapses like a burning house
and the other houses smoulder. Old friends
make their way in silence. Students stare
at their teachers, and suddenly feel afraid.
The old people are terrified like cattle
rolling their eyes and bellowing, while the young
wander in darkness, dazed, half-believing
some half-forgotten poem, or else come out
with their hearts on fire, alive in the last days.
Small children roam the neighbourhoods armed
with submachineguns, gas masks and riot sticks.
Excavations are made in us and slowly
we are filled in with used-up things: knives
too dull to cut bread with, bombs that failed to go off,
cats smashed on the highway, broken pencils,
slivers of soap, hair, gristle, old TV sets
that hum and stare out blindly like the insane.
Bridges kneel down, the cities billow and plunge
like horses in their smoke, the tall buildings
open their hysterical burning eyes at night,
the leafy suburbs look up at the clouds and tremble –
and my wife leaves her bed before dawn, walking
the icy pasture, shrieking her grief to the cows,
praying in tears to the softening blackness. I hear her
outside the window, crazed, inconsolable,
and go out to fetch her. Yesterday she saw
a photograph, Naomi our little girl
in a ditch in Viet Nam, half in the water,
the rest of her, beached on the mud, was horribly burned.

Robert Mezey

A Hard Rain's A-Gonna Fall

Oh, where have you been, my blue-eyed son?
Oh, where have you been, my darling young one?
I've stumbled on the side of twelve misty mountains,
I've walked and I've crawled on six crooked highways,
I've stepped in the middle of seven sad forests,
I've been out in front of a dozen dead oceans,
I've been ten thousand miles in the mouth of a graveyard,
And it's a hard, and it's a hard, it's a hard, and it's a hard,
And it's a hard rain's a-gonna fall.

Oh, what did you see, my blue-eyed son?
Oh, what did you see, my darling young one?
I saw a newborn baby with wild wolves all around it,
I saw a highway of diamonds with nobody on it,
I saw a black branch with blood that kept drippin',
I saw a room full of men with their hammers a-bleedin',
I saw a white ladder all covered with water,
I saw ten thousand talkers whose tongues were all broken,
I saw guns and sharp swords in the hands of young children,
And it's a hard, and it's a hard, it's a hard, it's a hard,
And it's a hard rain's a-gonna fall.

And what did you hear, my blue-eyed son?
And what did you hear, my darling young one?
I heard the sound of a thunder, it roared out a warnin',
Heard the roar of a wave that could drown the whole world,
Heard one hundred drummers whose hands were a-blazin',
Heard ten thousand whisperin' and nobody listenin',
Heard one person starve, I heard many people laughin',
Heard the song of a poet who died in the gutter,
Heard the sound of a clown who cried in the alley,
And it's a hard, and it's a hard, it's a hard, it's a hard,
And it's a hard rain's a-gonna fall.

Oh, who did you meet, my blue-eyed son?
Who did you meet, my darling young one?
I met a young child beside a dead pony,
I met a white man who walked a black dog,
I met a young woman whose body was burning,
I met a young girl, she gave me a rainbow,
I met one man who was wounded in love,
I met another man who was wounded with hatred,
And it's a hard, it's a hard, it's a hard, it's a hard,
It's a hard rain's a-gonna fall.

Oh, what'll you do now, my blue-eyed son?
Oh, what'll you do now, my darling young one?
I'm a-goin' back out 'fore the rain starts a-fallin',
I'll walk to the depths of the deepest black forest,
Where the people are many and their hands are all empty,
Where the pellets of poison are flooding their waters,
Where the home in the valley meets the damp dirty prison,
Where the executioner's face is always well hidden,
Where hunger is ugly, where souls are forgotten,
Where black is the colour, where none is the number,
And I'll tell it and think it and speak it and breathe it,
And reflect it from the mountain so all souls can see it,
Then I'll stand on the ocean until I start sinkin',
But I'll know my song well before I start singin',
And it's a hard, it's a hard, it's a hard, it's a hard,
It's a hard rain's a-gonna fall.

Bob Dylan

Starting to Make a Tree

First we carried out the faggot of steel stakes; they varied in
length, though most were taller than a man.

We slid one free of the bundle and drove it into the ground, first
padding the top with rag, that the branch might not be injured
with leaning on it.

Then we took turns to choose stakes of the length we wanted,
and to feel for the distances between them. We gathered to
thrust them firmly in.

There were twenty or thirty of them in all; and when they
were in place we had, round the clearing we had left for the
trunk, an irregular radial plantation of these props, each with
its wad of white at the tip. It was to be an old, downcurving tree.

This was in keeping with the burnt, chemical blue of the soil,
and the even hue of the sky which seemed to have been washed
with a pale brownish smoke;

another clue was the flatness of the horizon on all sides except
the north, where it was broken by the low slate or tarred
shingle roofs of the houses, which stretched away from us for
a mile or more.

This was the work of the morning. It was done with care, for
we had no wish to make revisions;

we were, nonetheless, a little excited, and hindered the women
at their cooking in our anxiety to know whose armpit and
whose groin would help us most in the modelling of the bole,
and the thrust of the boughs.

That done, we spent the early dusk of the afternoon gathering
materials from the nearest houses; and there was plenty:

a great flock mattress; two carved chairs; cement; chicken-
wire; tarpaulin, a smashed barrel; lead piping; leather of all
kinds; and many small things.

In the evening we sat late, and discussed how we could best
use them. Our tree was to be very beautiful.

Roy Fisher

Shalom Bomb

I want a bomb, my own private bomb, my shalom bomb.
I'll test it in the morning, when my son awakes,
hot and stretching, smelling beautiful from sleep. Boom! Boom!

Come my son dance naked in the room.
I'll test it on the landing and wake my neighbours,
the masons and the whores and the students who live downstairs.

Oh I must have a bomb and I'll throw open windows and
count down as I whizz around the living room,
on his bike, with him flying angels on my shoulder;
and my wife dancing in her dressing gown.
I want a happy family bomb, a do-it-yourself bomb,
I'll climb on the roof and ignite it there about noon.
My improved design will gong the world and we'll all eat lunch.

My pretty little bomb will play a daytime lullaby and
thank you bomb for now my son falls fast asleep.
My love come close, close the curtains, my lovely bomb, my darling.

My naughty bomb. Burst around us, burst between us, burst within us.

Light up the universe, then linger, linger
while the drone of the world recedes.

Shalom bomb

I want to explode the breasts of my wife.
and wake everyone,
to explode over playgrounds and parks, just as children
come from schools. I want a laughter bomb,
filled with sherbet fountains, licorice allsorts, chocolate kisses,
candy floss,
tinsel and streamers, balloons and fireworks, lucky bags,
bubbles and masks and false noses.

I want my bomb to sprinkle the earth with roses.
I want a one-man-band bomb. My own bomb.

My live long and die happy bomb. My die peacefully of old age bomb
in my own bed bomb.
My Om Mane Padme Aum Bomb, My Tiddly Om Pom Bomb.
My goodnight bomb, my sleeptight bomb,
my see you in the morning bomb.
I want my bomb, my own private bomb, my Shalom bomb.

Bernard Kops

The Lake Isle of Innisfree

I will arise and go now, and go to Innisfree,
And a small cabin build there, of clay and wattles made;
Nine bean rows will I have there, a hive for the honey bee,
   And live alone in the bee-loud glade.

And I shall have some peace there, for peace comes dropping slow,
Dropping from the veils of the morning to where the cricket sings;
There midnight's all a glimmer, and noon a purple glow,
   And evening full of the linnet's wings.

I will arise and go now, for always night and day
I hear lake water lapping with low sounds by the shore;
While I stand on the roadway, or on the pavements grey,
   I hear it in the deep heart's core.

W. B. Yeats

Freedom

This mountain standing in the sun.
Out of the light into the heat
out of the heat into the wind
out of the wind into the sun.
Out of the rock onto the snow
out of the shadow of the rock
onto the rock below the peak,
off the rock into shadow.
Freedom cannot be ended.
Out of the snow onto the grass
out of the grass onto the face
out of the grass onto the snow.

93

Freedom cannot be ended.
Out of the cold into the light
out of the heat into the snow
out of the snow onto the grass
and off the grass into the trees
among the trees in the shadow
out of the trees onto the rock.
This mountain standing in the sun.

Peter Levi

Galway Races

It's there you'll see confectioners with sugar sticks and dainties,
The lozenges and oranges, lemonade and the raisins;
The gingerbread and spices to accommodate the ladies,
And a bit crubeen for threepence to be picking while you're able.

It's there you'll see the gamblers, the thimbles and the garters,
And the sporting Wheel of Fortune with the four and twenty quarters.
There was others without scruple pelting wattles at poor Maggy,
And her father well contented and he looking at his daughter.

It's there you'll see the pipers and fiddlers competing,
And the nimble-footed dancers and they tripping on the daisies.
There was others crying segars and lights, and bills of all the races,
With the colour of the jockeys, the prize and horses' ages.

It's there you'd see the jockeys and they mounted on most stately,
The pink and blue, the red and green, the Emblem of our nation.
When the bell was rung for starting, the horses seemed impatient,
Though they never stood on ground, their speed was so amazing.

There was half a million people there of all denominations,
The Catholic, the Protestant, the Jew and Prespetarian.
There was yet no animosity, no matter what persuasion,
But *failte* and hospitality, inducing fresh acquaintance.

Anon

When I Went to the Circus

When I went to the circus that had pitched on the waste lot
it was full of uneasy people
frightened of the bare earth and the temporary canvas
and the smell of horses and other beasts
instead of merely the smell of man.

Monkeys rode rather grey and wizened
on curly plump piebald ponies
and the children uttered a little cry –
and dogs jumped through hoops and turned somersaults
and then the geese scuttled in a little flock
and round the ring they went to the sound of the whip
then doubled, and back, with a funny up-flutter of wings –
and the children suddenly shouted out.

Then came the hush again, like a hush of fear.

The tight-rope lady, pink and blonde and nude-looking, with a few gold spangles
footed cautiously out on the rope, turned prettily, spun round
bowed, and lifted her foot in her hand, smiled, swung her parasol
to another balance, tripped round, poised, and slowly sank
her handsome thighs down, down, till she slept her splendid body on the rope.
When she rose, tilting her parasol, and smiled at the cautious people
they cheered, but nervously.

The trapeze man, slim and beautiful and like a fish in the air
swung great curves through the upper space, and came down like a star
– And the people applauded, with hollow, frightened applause.

The elephants, huge and grey, loomed their curved bulk through the dusk
and sat up, taking strange postures, showing the pink soles of their feet
and curling their precious live trunks like ammonites
and moving always with soft slow precision
as when a great ship moves to anchor.
The people watched and wondered, and seemed to resent the mystery
    that lies in beasts.

Horses, gay horses, swirling round and plaiting
in a long line, their heads laid over each other's necks;
they were happy, they enjoyed it;
all the creatures seemed to enjoy the game
in the circus, with their circus people.

But the audience, compelled to wonder
compelled to admire the bright rhythms of moving bodies
compelled to see the delicate skill of flickering human bodies
flesh flamey and a little heroic, even in a tumbling clown,
they were not really happy.
There was no gushing response, as there is at the film.

When modern people see the carnal body dauntless and flickering gay
playing among the elements neatly, beyond competition
and displaying no personality,
modern people are depressed.

Modern people feel themselves at a disadvantage.
They know they have no bodies that could play among the elements.
They have only their personalities, that are best seen flat, on the film,
flat personalities in two dimensions, imponderable and touchless.

And they grudge the circus people the swooping gay weight of limbs
that flower in mere movement,
and they grudge them the immediate, physical understanding they have
    with their circus beasts,
and they grudge them their circus-life altogether.

Yet the strange, almost frightened shout of delight that comes now and then
    from the children
shows that the children vaguely know how cheated they are of their birthright
in the bright wild circus flesh.

D. H. Lawrence

Lord Beginner's Victory Calypso, Lord's Cricket Ground, 1950

Cricket, lovely cricket,
At Lord's where I saw it;
Cricket, lovely cricket,
At Lord's where I saw it;
Yardley tried his best
But Goddard won the Test.
They gave the crowd plenty fun;
Second Test and West Indies won.

Chorus: With those two little pals of mine
Ramadhin and Valentine.

The King was there well attired,
So they started with Rae and Stollmeyer;
Stolly was hitting balls around the boundary,
But Wardle stopped him at twenty.

Rae had confidence,
So he put up a strong defence;
He saw the King was waiting to see,
So he gave him a century.

Chorus: With those two little pals of mine
Ramadhin and Valentine.

West Indies first innings total was three-twenty-six
Just as usual.
When Bedser bowled Christiani
The whole thing collapsed quite easily,
England then went on,
And made one-hundred-fifty-one;
West Indies then had two-twenty lead,
And Goddard said, 'That's nice indeed.'

Chorus: With those two little pals of mine
Ramadhin and Valentine.

Yardley wasn't broken-hearted
When the second innings started;
Jenkins was like a target
Getting the first five into his basket.
But Gomez broke him down,
While Walcott licked them around;
He was not out for one-hundred and sixty-eight,
Leaving Yardley to contemplate.

Chorus: The bowling was super-fine
Ramadhin and Valentine.

West Indies was feeling homely,
Their audience had them happy.
When Washbrook's century had ended,
West Indies' voices all blended.
Hats went in the air.
They jumped and shouted without fear;
So at Lord's was the scenery
Bound to go down in history.

Chorus: After all was said and done,
Second Test and West Indies won!

Egbert Moore
(*'Lord Beginner'*)

The Dance

In Breughel's great picture, The Kermess,
the dancers go round, they go round and
around, the squeal and the blare and the
tweedle of bagpipes, a bugle and fiddles
tipping their bellies (round as the thick-
sided glasses whose wash they impound)
their hips and their bellies off balance
to turn them. Kicking and rolling about
the Fair Grounds, swinging their butts, those
shanks must be sound to bear up under such
rollicking measures, prance as they dance
in Breughel's great picture, The Kermess.

William Carlos Williams

Surfers

Couched in a recess from the wind I've seen
ravens fly back and forth to this cliff-ledge,
and watched the sea returning, and its sheen

turn bluebottle-blue flecked with indigo,
as though ink dropped into an abalone
accounted for that darkening. The flow

is rapid, and surf blazes across flats
burnished a hard gold by the wind, ribbed sand
planed level as a sheet of glass. In hats

and beach shorts, the surfing crowd congregate
beneath the sea wall, and out of the wind,
absorb the sun's fierce energies, the slate-

like textures of their bodies oiled to bear
both sea and sun. Up here I watch those birds
drop down through a blue crystal of sea air

and comb beached drifts of wrack dried by the heat
to fossil strands where flies fester. Each wave
asserts a resonance – a drumming beat

communicated to the group who tan,
awaiting a heavier lift of surf
to call them to their boards. I watch a man

squat down, his pulse picking up the rhythm
of each new smoking wall of surf that gains
momentum, shot through with light by the sun

to subside with a mulling poker's hiss.
He's like a sentry in his black peaked cap,
maintaining vigil, and at his raised fist

the word is out, and down the beach they race
these tiny figures running with their boards
into the wind and the blue rim of space.

Jeremy Reed

Seven Activities for a Young Child

Turn on the tap for straight and silver water in the sink,
Cross your finger through
The sleek thread falling

    – *One.*

Spread white sandgrains on a tray,
And make clean furrows with a bent stick
To stare for a meaning

    – *Two.*

Draw some clumsy birds on yellow paper,
Confronting each other and as if to fly
Over your scribbled hill

    – *Three.*

Cut rapid holes into folded paper, look
At the unfolded patterns, look
through the unfolded pattern

— Four.

Walk on any square stone of the pavement,
Or on any crack between, as long
As it's with no one or with someone

— Five.

Throw up a ball to touch the truest brick
Of the red, brick wall,
Catch it with neat, cupped hand

— Six.

Make up in your head a path, and name it,
Name where it will lead you,
Walk towards where it will lead you

— Seven.

One, two, three, four, five, six, seven:
Take-up-the-rag-doll-quietly-and-sing-her-to-sleep.

Alan Brownjohn

The Valley of Animals

Birds and Beasts

I Think I Could Turn and Live with Animals

(from Song of Myself)

I think I could turn and live with animals, they are so placid and self-contained;
I stand and look at them long and long.
They do not sweat and whine about their condition;
They do not lie awake in the dark and weep for their sins;
They do not make me sick discussing their duty to God;
Not one is dissatisfied – not one is demented with the mania of owning things;
Not one kneels to another, nor to his kind that lived thousands of years ago;
Not one is respectable or industrious over the whole earth.

Walt Whitman

From 'Auguries of Innocence'

To see a World in a grain of sand,
And a Heaven in a wild flower,
Hold Infinity in the palm of your hand,
And Eternity in an hour.

A robin redbreast in a cage
Puts all Heaven in a rage.
A dove-house fill'd with doves and pigeons
Shudders Hell thro' all its regions.
A dog starv'd at his master's gate
Predicts the ruin of the State.
A horse misus'd upon the road
Calls to Heaven for human blood.
Each outcry of the hunted hare
A fibre from the brain does tear.
A skylark wounded in the wing,
A cherubim does cease to sing.
The game-cock clipt and arm'd for fight
Does the rising sun affright.
Every wolf's and lion's howl
Raises from Hell a Human soul.
The wild deer, wandering here and there,
Keeps the Human soul from care.
The lamb misus'd breeds public strife,
And yet forgives the butcher's knife.
The bat that flits at close of eve
Has left the brain that won't believe.
The owl that calls upon the night
Speaks the unbeliever's fright.
He who shall hurt the little wren
Shall never be belov'd by men.

He who the ox to wrath has mov'd
Shall never be by woman lov'd.
The wanton boy that kills the fly
Shall feel the spider's enmity.
He who torments the chafer's sprite
Weaves a bower in endless night.
The caterpillar on the leaf
Repeats to thee thy mother's grief.
Kill not the moth nor butterfly,
For the Last Judgement draweth nigh.
He who shall train the horse to war
Shall never pass the polar bar.
The beggar's dog and widow's cat,
Feed them, and thou wilt grow fat.

William Blake

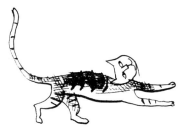

Poem

As the cat
climbed over
the top of

the jamcloset
first the right
forefoot

carefully
then the hind
stepped down

into the pit of
the empty
flowerpot

William Carlos Williams

Skimbleshanks: the Railway Cat

There's a whisper down the line at 11.39
When the Night Mail's ready to depart,
Saying "Skimble where is Skimble has he gone to hunt the thimble?
We must find him or the train can't start."
All the guards and all the porters and the stationmaster's daughters
They are searching high and low,
Saying "Skimble where is Skimble for unless he's very nimble
Then the Night Mail just can't go."
At 11.42 then the signal's overdue
And the passengers are frantic to a man –
Then Skimble will appear and he'll saunter to the rear:
He's been busy in the luggage van!
    He gives one flash of his glass-green eyes
        And the signal goes "All Clear!"
    And we're off at last for the northern part
        Of the Northern Hemisphere!

You may say that by and large it is Skimble who's in charge
Of the Sleeping Car Express.
From the driver and the guards to the bagmen playing cards
He will supervise them all, more or less.
Down the corridor he paces and examines all the faces
Of the travellers in the First and in the Third;
He establishes control by a regular patrol
And he'd know at once if anything occurred.

He will watch you without winking and he sees what you are thinking
And it's certain that he doesn't approve
Of hilarity and riot, so the folk are very quiet
When Skimble is about and on the move.
    You can play no pranks with Skimbleshanks!
      He's a Cat that cannot be ignored;
    So nothing goes wrong on the Northern Mail
      When Skimbleshanks is aboard.

Oh it's very pleasant when you have found your little den
With your name written up on the door.
And the berth is very neat with a newly folded sheet
And there's not a speck of dust on the floor.
There is every sort of light – you can make it dark or bright:
There's a button that you turn to make a breeze.
There's a funny little basin you're supposed to wash your face in
And a crank to shut the window if you sneeze.
Then the guard looks in politely and will ask you very brightly
"Do you like your morning tea weak or strong?"
But Skimble's just behind him and was ready to remind him,
For Skimble won't let anything go wrong.
    And when you creep into your cosy berth
      And pull up the counterpane,
    You ought to reflect that it's very nice
    To know that you won't be bothered by mice –
    You can leave all that to the Railway Cat,
      The Cat of the Railway Train!

In the watches of the night he is always fresh and bright;
Every now and then he has a cup of tea
With perhaps a drop of Scotch while he's keeping on the watch,
Only stopping here and there to catch a flea.
You were fast asleep at Crewe and so you never knew
That he was walking up and down the station;
You were sleeping all the while he was busy at Carlisle,
Where he greets the stationmaster with elation.
But you saw him at Dumfries, where he summons the police
If there's anything they ought to know about:
When you get to Gallowgate there you do not have to wait –
For Skimbleshanks will help you to get out!
    He gives you a wave of his long brown tail
        Which says: "I'll see you again!
    You'll meet without fail on the Midnight Mail
        The Cat of the Railway Train."

T. S Eliot

A Dog in San Francisco

Sitting in an empty house
with a dog from the Mexican Circus!
O Daisy, embrace is my only pleasure.
Holding and hugging my friends. Education.

A wave of eucalyptus. Warm granite.
These are the things I have in my heart.
Heart and skills, there's nothing else.

I usually don't like small dogs but you
like midwestern women take over the air.
You leap into the air and pivot
a diver going up! You are known
to open the fridge and eat when you wish
you can roll down car windows and step out
you know when to get off the elevator.

I always wanted to be a dog
but I hesitated
for I thought they lacked certain skills.
Now I want to be a dog.

Michael Ondaatje

Today I Saw the Dragon-fly

Today I saw the dragon-fly
Come from the wells where he did lie.

An inner impulse rent the veil
Of his old husk: from head to tail
Came out clear plates of sapphire mail.

He dried his wings: like gauze they grew;
Through crofts and pastures wet with dew
A living flash of light, he flew.

Alfred, Lord Tennyson

Praise of a Collie

She was a small dog, neat and fluid –
Even her conversation was tiny:
She greeted you with *bow*, never *bow-wow*.

Her sons stood monumentally over her
But did what she told them. Each grew grizzled
Till it seemed he was his own mother's grandfather.

Once, gathering sheep on a showery day,
I remarked how dry she was. Pollóchan said, "Ah,
It would take a very accurate drop to hit Lassie."

She sailed in the dinghy like a proper sea-dog.
Where's a burn? – she's first on the other side.
She flowed through fences like a piece of black wind.

But suddenly she was old and sick and crippled . . .
I grieved for Pollóchan when he took her a stroll
And put his gun to the back of her head.

Norman MacCaig

Blackbird

Blackbird singing in the dead of night
Take these broken wings and learn to fly.
All your life
You were only waiting for this moment to arise.
Blackbird singing in the dead of night
Take these sunken eyes and learn to see.
All your life
You were only waiting for this moment to be free.

Blackbird fly, Blackbird fly
Into the light of the dark black night.
Blackbird fly, Blackbird fly
Into the light of the dark black night.
Blackbird singing in the dead of night
Take these broken wings and learn to fly.
All your life
You were only waiting for this moment to arise
You were only waiting for this moment to arise
You were only waiting for this moment to arise

Paul McCartney

Byron's Dog, Boatswain

When Lord Byron's favourite dog died, the poet had
a marble monument erected to his memory, with this inscription:

NEAR THIS SPOT

ARE DEPOSITED THE REMAINS OF ONE

WHO POSSESSED BEAUTY WITHOUT VANITY,

STRENGTH WITHOUT INSOLENCE,

COURAGE WITHOUT FEROCITY,

AND ALL THE VIRTUES OF MAN WITHOUT HIS VICES.

THIS PRAISE, WHICH WOULD BE UNMEANING

FLATTERY IF INSCRIBED OVER HUMAN ASHES,

IS BUT A JUST TRIBUTE TO THE MEMORY OF

BOATSWAIN, A DOG,

WHO WAS BORN AT NEWFOUNDLAND, MAY 1803,

AND DIED AT NEWSTEAD ABBEY, NOV. 18, 1808.

Lord Byron

Ode to a Nightingale

My heart aches, and a drowsy numbness pains
　My sense, as though of hemlock I had drunk,
Or emptied some dull opiate to the drains
　One minute past, and Lethe-wards had sunk:
'Tis not through envy of thy happy lot,
　But being too happy in thine happiness, –
　　That thou, light-winged Dryad of the trees,
　　　In some melodious plot
Of beechen green, and shadows numberless,
　　Singest of summer in full-throated ease.

O, for a draught of vintage! that hath been
　Cool'd a long age in the deep-delved earth,
Tasting of Flora and the country green,
　Dance, and Provençal song, and sunburnt mirth!
O for a beaker full of the warm South,
　Full of the true, the blushful Hippocrene,
　　With beaded bubbles winking at the brim,
　　　And purple-stained mouth;
That I might drink, and leave the world unseen,
　And with thee fade away into the forest dim:

Fade far away, dissolve, and quite forget
　What thou among the leaves hast never known,
The weariness, the fever, and the fret
　Here, where men sit and hear each other groan;
Where palsy shakes a few, sad, last grey hairs,
　Where youth grows pale, and spectre-thin, and dies;
　　Where but to think is to be full of sorrow
　　　And leaden-eyed despairs,
Where Beauty cannot keep her lustrous eyes,
　Or new Love pine at them beyond to-morrow.

Away! away! for I will fly to thee,
   Not charioted by Bacchus and his pards,
But on the viewless wings of Poesy,
   Though the dull brain perplexes and retards:
Already with thee! tender is the night,
   And haply the Queen-Moon is on her throne,
     Cluster'd around by all her starry Fays;
       But here there is no light,
   Save what from heaven is with the breezes blown
     Through verdurous glooms and winding mossy ways.

I cannot see what flowers are at my feet,
   Nor what soft incense hangs upon the boughs,
But, in embalmed darkness, guess each sweet
   Wherewith the seasonable month endows
The grass, the thicket, and the fruit-tree wild;
   White hawthorn, and the pastoral eglantine;
     Fast fading violets cover'd up in leaves;
       And mid-May's eldest child,
   The coming musk-rose, full of dewy wine,
     The murmurous haunt of flies on summer eves.

Darkling I listen; and, for many a time
   I have been half in love with easeful Death,
Call'd him soft names in many a mused rhyme,
   To take into the air my quiet breath;
Now more than ever seems it rich to die,
   To cease upon the midnight with no pain,
     While thou art pouring forth thy soul abroad
       In such an ecstasy!
   Still wouldst thou sing, and I have ears in vain –
     To thy high requiem become a sod.

Thou wast not born for death, immortal Bird!
No hungry generations tread thee down;
The voice I hear this passing night was heard
In ancient days by emperor and clown:
Perhaps the self-same song that found a path
Through the sad heart of Ruth, when, sick for home,
She stood in tears amid the alien corn;
The same that oft-times hath
Charm'd magic casements, opening on the foam
Of perilous seas, in faery lands forlorn.

Forlorn! the very word is like a bell
To toll me back from thee to my sole self!
Adieu! the fancy cannot cheat so well
As she is fam'd to do, deceiving elf.
Adieu! adieu! thy plaintive anthem fades
Past the near meadows, over the still stream,
Up the hill-side; and now 'tis buried deep
In the next valley-glades:
Was it a vision, or a waking dream?
Fled is that music: – Do I wake or sleep?

John Keats

Magpies

One for sorrow
Two for joy
Three for a girl
Four for a boy

Five for silver
Six for gold
Seven for all the joys untold.

Anon

The Common Cormorant

The common cormorant or shag
Lays eggs inside a paper bag
The reason you will see no doubt
It is to keep the lightning out.
But what these unobservant birds
Have never noticed is that herds
Of wandering bears may come with buns
And steal the bags to hold the crumbs.

Anon

The Eagle

He clasps the crag with crooked hands;
Close to the sun in lonely lands,
Ring'd with the azure world, he stands.

The wrinkled sea beneath him crawls;
He watches from his mountain walls,
And like a thunderbolt he falls.

Alfred, Lord Tennyson

Lizard

A lizard ran out on a rock and looked up, listening
no doubt to the sounding of the spheres.
And what a dandy fellow! the right toss of a chin for you
and swirl of a tail!

If men were as much men as lizards are lizards
they'd be worth looking at.

D. H. Lawrence

Don't Call Alligator Long-Mouth till You Cross River

Call alligator long-mouth
call alligator saw-mouth
call alligator pushy-mouth
call alligator scissors-mouth
call alligator raggedy-mouth
call alligator bumpy-bum
call alligator all dem rude word
but better wait
            till you cross river.

John Agard

To a Mouse, On Turning Her Up in Her Nest, With the Plough, November 1785

WEE, sleekit, cow'rin', tim'rous beastie,
O, what a panic's in thy breastie!
Thou need na start awa sae hasty,
   Wi' bickering brattle! scamper
I wad be laith to rin an' chase thee,
   Wi' murd'ring pattle!

I'm truly sorry Man's dominion
Has broken Nature's social union,
An' justifies that ill opinion,
   Which makes thee startle
At me, thy poor, earth-born companion,
   An' fellow-mortal!

I doubt na, whyles, but thou may thieve;
What then? poor beastie, thou maun live!
A daimen icker in a thrave
   'S a sma' request:
I'll get a blessin' wi' the lave,
   An' never miss't!

Thy wee-bit housie, too, in ruin!
It's silly wa's the win's are strewin'!
An' naething, now, to big a new ane,
   O' foggage green!
An' bleak December's winds ensuin',
   Baith snell an' keen!

Thou saw the fields laid bare an' waste,
An' weary Winter comin' fast,
An' cozie heare, beneath the blast,

Thou thought to dwell,
Till, crash! the cruel coulter past
    Out thro' thy cell.

That wee-bit heap o' leaves an' stibble
Has cost thee mony a weary nibble!
Now thou's turn'd out, for a' thy trouble,
    But house or hald,
To thole the Winter's sleety dribble,
    An' cranreuch cauld!

But, Mousie, thou art no thy lane,
In proving foresight may be vain:
The best-laid schemes o' Mice an' Men
    Gang aft a-gley, ·
An' lea'e us nought but grief an' pain,
    For promis'd joy!

Still thou art blest, compar'd wi' me!
The present only toucheth thee:
But, och! I backward cast my e'e
    On prospects drear!
An' forward, tho' I canna see,
    I guess an' fear!

Robert Burns

*Laith means loath; a pattle is a plough-staff; whyles means
sometimes; a daimen icker in a thrave means an odd ear of corn;
the lave means the sheaves of corn; silly here means feeble;
big means to build; foggage is moss; baith snell means biting;
the coulter is a blade attached to the plough; stibble is
stubble; a hald is a holding; to thole means to endure; cranreuch
is hoar frost; no thy lane means not alone; a-gley means awry.*

After Prévert

We are going to see the rabbit,
We are going to see the rabbit.
Which rabbit, people say?
Which rabbit, ask the children?
Which rabbit?
The only rabbit,
The only rabbit in England,
Sitting behind a barbed-wire fence
Under the floodlights, neon lights,
Sodium lights,
Nibbling grass
On the only patch of grass
In England, in England
(Except the grass by the hoardings
Which doesn't count.)
We are going to see the rabbit
And we must be there on time.

First we shall go by escalator,
Then we shall go by underground,
And then we shall go by motorway
And then by helicopterway,
And the last ten yards we shall have to go
On foot.

And now we are going
All the way to see the rabbit,
We are nearly there,
We are longing to see it,
And so is the crowd

Which is here in thousands
With mounted policemen
And big loudspeakers
And bands and banners,
And everyone has come a long way.
But soon we shall see it
Sitting and nibbling
The blades of grass
On the only patch of grass
In – but something has gone wrong!
Why is everyone so angry,
Why is everyone jostling
And slanging and complaining?

The rabbit has gone,
Yes, the rabbit has gone.
He has actually burrowed down into the earth
And made himself a warren, under the earth,
Despite all these people.
And what shall we do?
What *can* we do?

It is all a pity, you must be disappointed,
Go home and do something else for today,
Go home again, go home for today.
For you cannot hear the rabbit, under the earth,
Remarking rather sadly to himself, by himself,
As he rests in his warren, under the earth:
"It won't be long, they are bound to come,
They are bound to come and find me, even here."

Alan Brownjohn

Epitaph on a Hare

Here lies, whom hound did ne'er pursue,
　　Nor swifter greyhound follow,
Whose foot ne'er tainted morning dew,
　　Nor ear heard huntsman's halloo,

Old Tiney, surliest of his kind,
　　Who, nurs'd with tender care,
And to domestic bounds confin'd,
　　Was still a wild Jack-hare.

Though duly from my hand he took
　　His pittance ev'ry night,
He did it with a jealous look,
　　And, when he could, would bite.

His diet was of wheaten bread,
　　And milk, and oats, and straw;
Thistles, or lettuces instead,
　　With sand to scour his maw.

On twigs of hawthorn he regal'd,
　　On pippins' russet peel,
And, when his juicy salads fail'd,
　　Slic'd carrot pleas'd him well.

A Turkey carpet was his lawn,
　　Whereon he lov'd to bound,
To skip and gambol like a fawn,
　　And swing his rump around.

His frisking was at ev'ning hours,
　　For then he lost his fear,
But most before approaching show'rs,
　　Or when a storm drew near.

Eight years and five round-rolling moons
　　He thus saw steal away,
Dozing out all his idle noons,
　　And ev'ry night at play.

I kept him for his humour's sake,
　　For he would oft beguile
My heart of thoughts, that made it ache,
　　And force me to a smile.

But now beneath his walnut shade
　　He finds his long last home,
And waits in snug concealment laid,
　　Till gentler Puss shall come.

He still more aged feels the shocks,
　　From which no care can save,
And, partner once of Tiney's box,
　　Must soon partake his grave.

William Cowper

The Badger

When midnight comes a host of dogs and men
Go out and track the badger to his den,
And put a sack within the hole and lie
Till the old grunting badger passes bye.
He comes and hears – they let the strongest loose.
The old fox hears the noise and drops the goose.
The poacher shoots and hurries from the cry,
And the old hare half-wounded buzzes bye.
They get a forked stick to bear him down
And clap the dogs and take him to the town,
And bait him all the day with many dogs,
And laugh and shout and fright the scampering hogs.
He runs along and bites at all he meets;
They shout and hollo down the noisy streets.
He turns about to face the loud uproar
And drives the rebels to their very door.
The frequent stone is hurled where e'er they go;
When badgers fight, then everyone's a foe.
The dogs are clapt and urged to join the fray;
The badger turns and drives them all away.
Though scarcely half as big, demure and small,
He fights with dogs for bones and beats them all.
The heavy mastiff, savage in the fray,
Lies down and licks his feet and turns away.
The bulldog knows his match and waxes cold,
The badger grins and never leaves his hold.
He drives the crowd and follows at their heels
And bites them through – the drunkard swears and reels.

The frightened women take the boys away,
The blackguard laughs and hurries on the fray.
He tries to reach the woods, an awkward race,
But sticks and cudgels quickly stop the chase.
He turns agen and drives the noisy crowd
And beats the many dogs in noises loud.
He drives away and beats them every one,
And then they loose them all and set them on,
He falls as dead and kicked by boys and men,
Then starts and grins and drives the crowd agen;
Till kicked and torn and beaten out he lies
And leaves his hold and cackles, groans, and dies.

John Clare

Maninagar Days

They are always there
just as pigeons or flies
can be *always there*
and the children have to fight them off,
especially during those hot May afternoons
when they dare to jump down from the trees
into the cool shaded spots, the corners between
the canna flower beds
still moist from the mornings watering.

Monkeys in the garden –
I'm talking about rhesus monkeys
the colour of dirt roads and khaki
        and sometimes even of honey.
Rhesus monkeys that travel in small groups,
extended families; constantly feuding brothers, sisters,
uncles, aunts, cousins screaming through
the trees – while the grandmother sits farther away
sadly, holding on to the sleepy newborn.
Somehow they manage to make peace
before every meal.

Now and then a solitary langur:
the Hanuman-monkey, crossing the terrace
with the importance of someone going to the airport.
A lanky dancer's steps
with black hands, black feet
sharp as black leather gloves and black leather shoes
against the soft grey body.
Sharp
and yet delicate
as if they were brush-stroked in
with a Japanese flourish.
And black-faced too,
with thick tufts of silver grey eyebrows,
a bushy chin. So aloof
he couldn't be bothered
with anyone.

Some people live with rhesus monkeys
and langurs in their gardens.
To these children
the monkeys are as normal and common as dogs.
And yet, the monkeys remain magical.

The children feel closer
to the monkeys, although they never
really play together, although the monkeys
probably hate the children:
those three children, two girls and a boy
who are all a bit afraid
of the full-grown-to-their-prime males
that stretch themselves and stretch themselves
to the height of wisdom and fatherly wit.

The monkeys are not at all cuddly like toys.
No.
They are lean twirls, strong tails, fast shadows
abrupt with yellow teeth.
The monkeys are not so innocent
the elders warn,
not so content with their daily routine
for they are turning
into urban thieves, imitating
and even outdoing the crows:

One day a tall monkey leaped down on the clothesline
and stole a blinding white shirt.
Another day, a very muscular monkey
bounded out of the neighbour's house
with a huge rock of golden *gur*, solid raw sugar.
The boy was impressed. His mother
would have difficulty carrying such a load.
Still, the children treat the monkeys
as if they were children newly arrived from a foreign
country, unable to speak the language yet.

And the children's grandmother comes out
to the front door from time to time.
Just awakened from her afternoon nap, now
she readjusts her thin white sari
readjusts her thin white sari
and squints against the sun
watching over them all –
And the faint May breeze that struggles
through the monkey crowded branches
is Hanuman's breath.
How could you know it, how could you miss it
unless you had lived
in such a garden.

Monkeys in the garden.
They are always there,
usually in the gulmuhore trees
chewing on the sour rubbery leaves
and the even more delicious bright
scarlet-orange flowers: petals
sparkling as sliced blood oranges,
water-plump green stems . . .

The monkeys have become everything
to the children, although
the children are not aware of it yet,
and one summer the children can't help
learning everything from them:
their noise, their shadows, their defiant stare,
the way they shake their heads,
the curve of their elbows
their weight on the trees . . .
In fact, without the monkeys
the trees begin to look a little barren
to the children.

Oh there are days when the monkeys refuse
to come down from the gulmuhore trees
and that makes the children jealous
and unhappy.
Oh there are days when the monkeys
never intrude, never interfere
with the children's favourite hide-outs.
Peaceful days, one would think
with the monkeys chatter-reclining and nibbling,
dozing and basking, jabbering and
lice-picking safe above in the gulmuhore trees
while the children run about exhausting
one game after another right below.
Peaceful hours one would think.
But the children are jealous
for they too love to eat
the gulmuhore flowers and leaves.

Invariably they try
to convince the monkeys to throw some flowers down
and then, that failing,
invariably they try to persuade the monkeys
to come down into their garden
(maybe with some flowers)
and then, that failing,
they are simply angry, so angry
at the monkeys, they terrify them off
into the neighbouring gardens.

Oh with monkeys like that
the children believe in Hanuman.
In their secret wishes the children reinvent
the perfect monkey: Hanuman,
wild and fierce and loyal and gentle . . .

One day the boy defended his sisters
single-handedly with a stick like a sword
he chased the whole band of monkeys
not up the trees but to the back of the house:
a complete disappearance.
Then there was such silence
the girls were afraid – where
had all the birds gone? And the neighbour's dog?
A few minutes later the boy returned
running, chased by the monkeys,
and the stick like a sword was in the hand
of the angry leader . . .

Monkeys in the garden.
Some people have monkeys
in their dreams, monkeys in their nightmares,
monkeys crossing their shadows
long after they have stopped being children
long after they have left such a garden.

Sujata Bhatt

A Small Dragon

I've found a small dragon in the woodshed.
Think it must have come from deep inside a forest
because it's damp and green and leaves
are still reflecting in its eyes.

I fed it on many things, tried grass,
the roots of stars, hazel-nut and dandelion,
but it stared up at me as if to say, I need
foods you can't provide.

It made a nest among the coal,
not unlike a bird's but larger,
it is out of place here
and is quite silent.

If you believed in it I would come
hurrying to your house to let you share my wonder,
but I want instead to see
if you yourself will pass this way.

Brian Patten

Cow

The Cow comes home swinging
Her udder and singing:

"The dirt O the dirt
It does me no hurt.

And a good splash of muck
Is a blessing of luck.

O I splosh through the mud
But the breath of my cud

Is sweeter than silk.
O I splush through manure

But my heart stays as pure
As a pitcher of milk."

Ted Hughes

Blind Horse

He snuffles towards
pouches of water in the grass
and doesn't drink
when he finds them.

He twitches listlessly
at sappy grass stems and stands
stone still, his hanging head
caricatured with a scribble
of green whiskers.

Sometimes that head swings high,
ears cock – and he stares
down a long sound,
he stares and whinnies
for what never comes.

His eyes never close,
not in the heat of the day
when his leather lip droops and
he wears blinkers of flies.

At any time of the night
you hear him in his dark field
stamp the ground, stamp
the world down, waiting impatiently
for the light to break.

Norman MacCaig

The Lion

Strange spirit with inky hair,
   Tail tufted stiff in rage,
I saw with sudden stare
   Leap on the printed page.

The stillness of its roar
   From midnight deserts torn
Clove silence to the core
   Like the blare of a great horn.

I saw the sudden sky;
   Cities in crumbling sand;
The stars fall wheeling by;
   The lion roaring stand:

The stars fall wheeling by,
   Their silent, silver stain,
Cold on his glittering eye,
   Cold on his carven mane.

The full-orbed Moon shone down,
   The silence was so loud,
From jaws wide-open thrown
   His voice hung like a cloud.

Earth shrank to blackest air;
   That spirit stiff in rage
Into some midnight lair
   Leapt from the printed page.

W. J. Turner

The Lion and Albert

There's a famous seaside place called Blackpool,
   That's noted for fresh air and fun,
And Mr and Mrs Ramsbottom
   Went there with young Albert, their son.

A grand little lad was young Albert,
   All dressed in his best; quite a swell
With a stick with an 'orse's 'ead 'andle,
   The finest that Woolworth's could sell.

They didn't think much to the Ocean:
    The waves, they was fiddlin' and small,
There was no wrecks and nobody drownded,
    Fact, nothing to laugh at at all.

So, seeking for further amusement,
    They paid and went into the Zoo,
Where they'd Lions and Tigers and Camels,
    And old ale and sandwiches too.

There were one great big Lion called Wallace;
    His nose were all coverd with scars –
He lay in a somnolent posture
    With the side of his face on the bars.

Now Albert had heard about Lions,
    How they was ferocious and wild –
To see Wallace lying so peaceful,
    Well, it didn't seem right to the child.

So straightway the brave little feller,
    Not showing a morsel of fear,
Took his stick with its 'orse's 'ead 'andle
    And poked it in Wallace's ear.

You could see that the Lion didn't like it,
    For giving a kind of a roll,
He pulled Albert inside the cage with 'im,
    And swallowed the little lad 'ole.

Then Pa, who had seen the occurrence,
    And didn't know what to do next,
Said "Mother! Yon Lion's 'et Albert,"
    And Mother said "Well, I am vexed!"

Then Mr and Mrs Ramsbottom –
  Quite rightly, when all's said and done –
Complained to the Animal Keeper
  That the Lion had eaten their son.

The keeper was quite nice about it;
  He said "What a nasty mishap.
Are you sure that it's *your* boy he's eaten?"
  Pa said "Am I sure? There's his cap!"

The manager had to be sent for.
  He came and he said "What's to do?"
Pa said "Yon Lion's 'et Albert,
  And 'im in his Sunday clothes, too."

Then Mother said, "Right's right, young feller;
  I think it's a shame and a sin
For a lion to go and eat Albert,
  And after we've paid to come in."

The manager wanted no trouble,
  He took out his purse right away,
Saying "How much to settle the matter?"
  And Pa said "What do you usually pay?"

But Mother had turned a bit awkward
  When she thought where her Albert had gone.
She said "No! someone's got to be summonsed" –
  So that was decided upon.

Then off they went to the P'lice Station,
  In front of the Magistrate chap;
They told 'im what happened to Albert,
  And proved it by showing his cap.

The Magistrate gave his opinion
   That no one was really to blame
And he said that he hoped the Ramsbottoms
   Would have further sons to their name.

At that Mother got proper blazing,
   "And thank you, sir, kindly," said she.
"What, waste all our lives raising children
   To feed ruddy Lions? Not me!"

Marriott Edgar

The Kraken

Below the thunders of the upper deep;
Far, far beneath in the abysmal sea,
His ancient, dreamless, uninvaded sleep
The Kraken sleepeth: faintest sunlights flee
About his shadowy sides: above him swell
Huge sponges of millennial growth and height;
And far away into the sickly light,
From many a wondrous grot and secret cell
Unnumber'd and enormous polypi
Winnow with giant arms the slumbering green.
There hath he lain for ages and will lie
Battening upon huge seaworms in his sleep,
Until the latter fire shall heat the deep;
Then once by man and angels to be seen,
In roaring he shall rise and on the surface die.

Alfred, Lord Tennyson

The Lamb

Little Lamb who made thee
Dost thou know who made thee
Gave thee life & bid thee feed,
By the stream & o'er the mead;
Gave thee clothing of delight,
Softest clothing wooly bright;
Gave thee such a tender voice,
Making all the vales rejoice:
Little Lamb who made thee
Dost thou know who made thee

Little Lamb I'll tell thee,
Little Lamb I'll tell thee;
He is called by thy name,
For he calls himself a Lamb:
He is meek & he is mild,
He became a little child:
I a child & thou a lamb,
We are called by his name.
Little Lamb God bless thee,
Little Lamb God bless thee.

William Blake

The Tyger

Tyger Tyger, burning bright,
In the forests of the night;
What immortal hand or eye,
Could frame thy fearful symmetry?

In what distant deeps or skies,
Burnt the fire of thine eyes?
On what wings dare he aspire?
What the hand, dare sieze the fire?

And what shoulder, and what art,
Could twist the sinews of thy heart?
And when thy heart began to beat,
What dread hand? and what dread feet?

What the hammer? what the chain,
In what furnace was thy brain?
What the anvil? what dread grasp,
Dare its deadly terrors clasp?

When the stars threw down their spears
And water'd heaven with their tears:
Did he smile his work to see?
Did he who made the Lamb make thee?

Tyger Tyger burning bright,
In the forests of the night:
What immortal hand or eye,
Dare frame thy fearful symmetry?

William Blake

Caring for Animals

I ask sometimes why these small animals
With bitter eyes, why we should care for them.

I question the sky, the serene blue water,
But it cannot say. It gives no answer.

And no answer releases in my head
A procession of grey shades patched and whimpering,

Dogs with clipped ears, wheezing cart horses
A fly without shadow and without thought.

Is it with these menaces to our vision
With this procession led by a man carrying wood

We must be concerned? The holy land, the rearing
Green island should be kindlier than this.

Yet the animals, our ghosts, need tending to.
Take in the whipped cat and the blinded owl;

Take up the man-trapped squirrel upon your shoulder.
Attend to the unnecessary beasts.

From growing mercy and a moderate love
Great love for the human animal occurs.

And your love grows. Your great love grows and grows.

Jon Silkin

The Dazzling City

Work and Machinery
Towns and Cities

Sparkles from the Wheel

Where the city's ceaseless crowd moves on, the live-long day,
Withdrawn, I join a group of children watching – I pause aside with them.

By the kerb, toward the edge of the flagging,
A knife-grinder works at his wheel, sharpening a great knife;
Bending over, he carefully holds it to the stone – by foot and knee,
With measured tread, he turns rapidly – As he presses with light but firm
hand,
Forth issue, then, in copious golden jets,
Sparkles from the wheel.

The scene, and all its belongings – how they seize and affect me!
The sad, sharp-chinned old man, with worn clothes, and broad shoulder
band of leather;
Myself, effusing and fluid – a phantom curiously floating – now here
absorb'd and arrested;

The group (an unminded point, set in a vast surrounding);
The attentive, quiet children – the loud, proud, restive base of the streets;
The low, hoarse purr of the whirling stone – the light-press'd blade,
Diffusing, dropping, sideways-darting, in tiny showers of gold,
Sparkles from the wheel.

Walt Whitman

The Sand Artist

On the damp seashore
above dark rainbows of shells, seaweed, seacoal,
the sandman wanders, seeking for a pitch.

Ebb tide is his time. The sands are lonely,
but a few lost families
camp for the day on its Easter emptiness.

He seeks the firm dark sand of the retreating waves.
– With their sandwiches and flasks of tea, they
lay their towels on the dry slopes of dunes.

From the sea's edge he draws his pail
of bitter brine, and bears it carefully
towards the place of first creation.

There he begins his labours. Silent,
not looking up at passing shadows
of curious children, he moulds his dreams.

Not simple sandcastles, melting as they dry,
but galleons, anchors, dolphins, cornucopias of fish,
mermaids, Neptunes, dragons of the deep.

With a piece of stick, a playing card
and the blunt fingers of a working man
the artist resurrects existence from the sea.

And as the returning tide takes back its gifts,
he waits in silence by his pitman's cap
for pennies from the sky.

James Kirkup

Big Wind

Where were the greenhouses going,
Lunging into the lashing
Wind driving water
So far down the river
All the faucets stopped? –
So we drained the manure-machine
For the steam plant,
Pumping the stale mixture
Into the rusty boilers,
Watching the pressure gauge
Waver over to red,
As the seams hissed
And the live steam
Drove to the far
End of the rose-house,
Where the worst wind was,
Creaking the cypress window-frames,
Cracking so much thin glass
We stayed all night,
Stuffing the holes with burlap;
But she rode it out,
That old rose-house,
She hove into the teeth of it,
The core and pith of that ugly storm,
Ploughing with her stiff prow,
Bucking into the wind-waves
That broke over the whole of her,
Flailing her sides with spray,
Flinging long strings of wet across the roof-top,
Finally veering, wearing themselves out, merely

Whistling thinly under the wind-vents;
She sailed until the calm morning,
Carrying her full cargo of roses.

Theodore Roethke

Song: Lift-Boy

Let me tell you the story of how I began:
I began as the boot-boy and ended as the boot-man,
With nothing in my pockets but a jack-knife and a button,
With nothing in my pockets but a jack-knife and a button,
With nothing in my pockets.

Let me tell you the story of how I went on:
I began as the lift-boy and ended as the lift-man,
With nothing in my pockets but a jack-knife and a button,
With nothing in my pockets but a jack-knife and a button,
With nothing in my pockets.

I found it very easy to whistle and play
With nothing in my head or my pockets all day,
With nothing in my pockets.

But along came Old Eagle, like Moses or David,
He stopped at the fourth floor and preached me Damnation:
"Not a soul shall be savèd, not one shall be savèd.
The whole First Creation shall forfeit salvation:
From knife-boy to lift-boy, from ragged to regal,
Not one shall be savèd, not you, not Old Eagle,
No soul on earth escapeth, even if all repent –"
So I cut the cords of the lift and down we went,
With nothing in our pockets.

Robert Graves   **147**

Go to Ahmedabad

Go walk the streets of Baroda,
go to Ahmedabad,
go breathe the dust
until you choke and get sick
with a fever no doctor's heard of.
Don't ask me
for I will tell you nothing
about hunger and suffering.

As a girl I learned
never to turn anyone away
from our door. Ma told me
give fresh water, good food,
nothing you wouldn't eat.
Hunger is when your mother
tells you years later
in America the doctor says
she is malnourished,
her bones are weak
because there was never enough
food for the children,
hers and the women who came
to our door with theirs.
The children must always be fed.
Hunger is when your mother is sick
in America because she wanted you
to eat well. Hunger is
when you walk
down the streets of Ahmedabad
and instead of handing out
coins to everyone
you give them tomatoes, cucumbers,

and go home with your mouth
tasting of burnt eucalyptus leaves
because you've lost
your appetite.
And yet, I say nothing
about hunger, nothing.

I have friends everywhere.
This time we met after ten years.
Someone died.
Someone got married.
Someone just had a baby.
And I hold the baby
because he's crying,
because there's a strange rash
all over his chest.
And my friend says
do you have a child? Why not?
When will you get married?
And the bus arrives
crowded with people hanging
out the doors and windows.
And her baby cries
in my arms, cries
so an old man wakes up and yells
at me: How could I let
my child get so sick?
Luckily, just then
someone tells a good joke.

I have friends everywhere.
This time we met after ten years.
And suffering is
when I walk around Ahmedabad
for this is the place

I always loved
this is the place
I always hated
for this is the place
I can never be at home in
this is the place
I will always be at home in.
Suffering is
When I'm in Ahmedabad
after ten years
and I learn for the first time
I will never choose
to live here. Suffering is
living in America
and not being able
to write a damn thing
about it. Suffering is
not for me to tell you about.

Go walk the streets of Baroda,
go to Ahmedabad
and step around the cow-dung
but don't forget
to look at the sky.
It's special in January,
you'll never see kites like these again.
Go meet the people if you can
and if you want to know
about hunger, about suffering,
go live it for yourself.
When there's an epidemic,
when the doctor says
your brother may die soon,
your father may die soon –

don't ask me how it feels.
It does not feel good.
That's why we make
tea with tulsi leaves,
that's why there's always someone
who knows a good story.

Sujata Bhatt

If I Were Walking

If I were walking along the canal
I would look in at me reading by the window
and think – I wish I was reading
by that window overlooking the canal
instead of walking along here by the canal
in the rain
and I would look in at all the other windows
and see the pictures on their walls
and the televisions they talk to
and perhaps even the different kinds of tea
moving from hand to hand
each in his own kind of room
and I would feel the damp
rise from the green leaves
where it had just sunk
and all along the walls
the leaves would die an inch more tonight
if I were walking there
looking in at me.

Michael Rosen

White Child Meets Black Man

She caught me outside a London
suburban shop, I like a giraffe
and she a mouse. I tried to go
but felt she stood
lovely as light on my back.

I turned with hello
and waited. Her eyes got
wider but not her lips.
Hello I smiled again and watched.

She stepped around me
slowly, in a kind of dance,
her wide eyes searching
inch by inch up and down:
no fur no scales no feathers
no shell. Just a live silhouette,
wild and strange
and compulsive
till mother came horrified.

"Mummy is his tummy black?"
Mother grasped her and swung
toward the crowd. She tangled
mother's legs looking back at me.
As I watched them birds were singing.

James Berry

Comprehensive

Tutumantu is like hopscotch, Kwani-kwani is
  like hide-and-seek.
When my sister came back to Africa she could
  only speak
English. Sometimes we fought in bed because
  she didn't know
what I was saying. I like Africa better than
  England.
My mother says You will like it when we get
  our own house.
We talk a lot about the things we used to do
in Africa and then we are happy.

Wayne. Fourteen. Games are for kids. I support
the National Front. Paki-bashing and pulling
  girls'
knickers down. Dad's got his own mini-cab.
  We watch
the video. I Spit on Your Grave. Brilliant.
I don't suppose I'll get a job. It's all them
coming over here to work. Arsenal.

Masjid at 6 o'clock. School at 8. There was
a friendly shop selling flour. They kneaded
  it at home
to make the evening nan. Families face Mecca.
There was much more room to play than here
  in London.
We played in an old village. It is empty now.
We got a plane to Heathrow. People wrote to us
that everything was easy here.

It's boring. Get engaged. Probably work in
   Safeways
worst luck. I haven't lost it yet because I want
respect. Marlon Frederic's nice but he's a bit dark.
I like Madness. The lead singer's dead good.
My mum is bad with her nerves. She won't
let me do nothing. Michelle. It's just boring.

Ejaz. They put some sausages on my plate.
As I was going to put one in my mouth
a Moslem boy jumped on me and pulled.
The plate dropped on the floor and broke. He
   asked me in Urdu
if I was a Moslem. I said Yes. You shouldn't
   be eating this.
It's a pig's meat. So we became friends.

My sister went out with one. There was murder.
I'd like to be mates, but they're different from us.
Some of them wear turbans in class. You can't
   help
taking the piss. I'm going in the Army.
No choice really. When I get married
I might emigrate. A girl who can cook
with long legs. Australia sounds all right.

Some of my family are named after the Moghul
   emperors.
Aurangzeb, Jehangir, Babur, Humayun. I was
   born
thirteen years ago in Jhelum. This is a hard
   school.

A man came in with a milk crate. The teacher
   told us
to drink our milk. I didn't understand what
   she was saying,
so I didn't go to get any milk. I have hope
   and am ambitious.
At first I felt as if I was dreaming, but I wasn't.
Everything I saw was true.

Carol Ann Duffy

Casey Jones

Come, all you rounders, if you want to hear
A story 'bout a brave engineer.
Casey Jones was the rounder's name
On a six-eight wheeler, boys, he won his fame.
The caller called Casey at a half past four,
Kissed his wife at the station door,
Mounted to the cabin with his orders in his hand
And he took his farewell trip to the promised land:
   Casey Jones, mounted to the cabin,
   Casey Jones, with his orders in his hand,
   Casey Jones, mounted to the cabin,
   And he took his farewell trip to the promised land.

"Put in your water and shovel in your coal,
Put your head out the window, watch them drivers roll,
I'll run her till she leaves the rail
'Cause I'm eight hours late with the western mail."
He looked at his watch and his watch was slow,
He looked at the water and the water was low,
He turned to the fireman and then he said,
"We're goin' to reach Frisco but we'll all be dead":

Casey Jones, goin' to reach Frisco,
Casey Jones, but we'll all be dead,
Casey Jones, goin' to reach Frisco,
"We're goin' to reach Frisco, but we'll all be dead."

Casey pulled up that Reno Hill,
He tooted for the crossing with an awful shrill,
The switchman knew by the engine's moan
That the man at the throttle was Casey Jones.
He pulled up within two miles of the place
Number Four stared him right in the face,
He turned to the fireman, said, "Boy, you better jump,
'Cause there's two locomotives that's a-goin' to bump":
Casey Jones, two locomotives,
Casey Jones, that's a-goin' to bump,
Casey Jones, two locomotives,
"There's two locomotives that's a-goin' to bump."

Casey said just before he died,
"There's two more roads that I'd like to ride."
The fireman said what could they be?
"The Southern Pacific and the Santa Fe."
Mrs Casey sat on her bed a-sighin',
Just received a message that Casey was dyin'.
Said, "Go to bed, children, and hush your cryin',
'Cause you got another papa on the Salt Lake Line":
Mrs Casey Jones, got another papa,
Mrs Casey Jones, on that Salt Lake Line,
Mrs Casey Jones, got another papa,
"And you've got another papa on the Salt Lake Line."

Anon

156

Take This Hammer

Take this hammer – huh!
And carry it to the captain – huh!
You tell him I'm gone – huh!
Tell him I'm gone – huh!

If he asks you – huh!
Was I runnin' – huh!
You tell him I was flyin' – huh!
Tell him I was flyin' – huh!

If he asks you – huh!
Was I laughin' – huh!
You tell him I was cryin' – huh!
You tell him I was cryin' – huh!

Anon

The Song of the Banana Man

Touris, white man, wipin his face,
Met me in Golden Grove market place.
He looked at m'ol' clothes brown wid stain,
An soaked right through wid de Portlan rain,
He cas his eye, turn up his nose,
He says, "You're a beggar man, I suppose?"
He says, "Boy, get some occupation,
Be of some value to your nation."
   I said, "By God and dis big right han
   You mus recognise a banana man.

"Up in de hills, where de streams are cool,
An mullet an janga swim in de pool,
I have ten acres of mountain side,
An a dainty-foot donkey dat I ride,
Four Gros Michel, an four Lacatan,
Some coconut trees, and some hills of yam,
An I pasture on dat very same lan
Five she-goats an a big black ram,
    Dat, by God an dis big right han
    Is de property of a banana man.

"I leave m'yard early-mornin time
An set m'foot to de mountain climb,
I ben m'back to de hot-sun toil,
An m'cutlass rings on de stony soil,
Ploughin an weedin, diggin an plantin
Till Massa Sun drop back o John Crow mountain,
Den home again in cool evenin time,
Perhaps whistling dis likkle rhyme,
    (*Sung*) Praise God an m'big right han
    I will live an die a banana man.

"Banana day is my special day,
I cut my stems an I'm on m'way,
Load up de donkey, leave de lan
Head down de hill to banana stan,
When de truck comes roun I take a ride
All de way down to de harbour side –
Dat is de night, when you, touris man,
Would change your place wid a banana man.
    Yes, by God, an m'big right han
    I will live an die a banana man.

"De bay is calm, an de moon is bright
De hills look black for de sky is light,
Down at de dock is an English ship,
Restin after her ocean trip,
While on de pier is a monstrous hustle,
Tallymen, carriers, all in a bustle,
Wid stems on deir heads in a long black snake
Some singin de songs dat banana men make,
  Like, (*Sung*) Praise God an m'big right han
  I will live an die a banana man.

"Den de payment comes, an we have some fun,
Me, Zekiel, Breda and Duppy Son.
Down at de bar near United Wharf
We knock back a white rum, bus a laugh,
Fill de empty bag for further toil
Wid saltfish, breadfruit, coconut oil.
Den head back home to m'yard to sleep,
A proper sleep dat is long an deep.
  Yes, by God, an m'big right han
  I will live an die a banana man.

"So when you see dese ol clothes brown wid stain,
An soaked right through wid de Portlan rain,
Don't cas your eye nor turn your nose,
Don't judge a man by his patchy clothes,
I'm a strong man, a proud man, an I'm free,
Free as dese mountains, free as dis sea,
I know myself, an I know my ways,
An will sing wid pride to de end o my days
  (*Sung*) Praise God an m'big right han
  I will live an die a banana man."

Evan Jones

All Over the World

women are knitting
in Ireland they are knitting thick
creamy cables each with their special stitch
so when their man is dragged out of the sea
with his face bloated purple
they will know him

in New York they are knitting on subways
with bright orange yarn stitch after
stitch and folding up their needles
tucking them into the plastic bag inside
a flowered plastic tote
in time to the train wheels as
the subway stops and they get off

in England they are knitting in airports
not only the English the Indians
the Pakistani the Americans they are
all sitting in Heathrow Airport knitting
long indecipherable scarves for persons
unknown

in Italy they are knitting black sweaters
for the saints with the methodical care
they perform upon their rosaries

women in Wales are knitting the dawn into
peat bog afghans girls in Ghana are
knitting tribal chieftans into unimagined
legends women in Chile are knitting
blood into the stockpile of tourniquets
waiting for the next round young women

in Istanbul are knitting far into the future
which is a replica of the past and it keeps
shrinking the closer they move into tomorrow

women in Iran are knitting insignias of the
oil companies to be sewn into the
covers for the coffins women in Ethiopia
are knitting green and white and red ribbons
to be worn around the hearts of those who
will not recognise the outcome

women in Russia are knitting peaceful parables
that will win the Nobel Prize
with long slavonic colours of melancholy
and hearty despair

women in Kansas are knitting according to the
latest catalogue in yellow and white
they are knitting strands of wheat into their
needles and they will
fill their kitchens with the abundance
that smiles because Kansas has not been bloody
since the time of the fierce old man John Brown

women in Amsterdam are knitting blue and white
porcelain doilies that are brittle and break
quickly unless purchased by tourists
their daughters are knitting with the
precision of an etching deep brown
quilts to cover themselves and their
lovers against the piercing sky

women in Paris are knitting bright Picasso
sweaters that they will never wear because
even now they do not know what makes them
choose those colours

women in the swamps and rivers of Indochina
are knitting the reeds and nettles into the
steel of machine gun bullets that will
explode with warmth into the bodies of
the men that are cold with the ignorance
of trespassing and long for comfort

girls in vacant towns
inbetween cities inbetween rivers on
maps are knitting their hopes in
small stitches echoing into each other
like muffled mirrors the needles
click smoothly in the language all
of the same word over and over
that no one can read the
same word over and over

Christina Starobin

Miners

There was a whispering in my hearth,
    A sigh of the coal,
Grown wistful of a former earth
    It might recall.

I listened for a tale of leaves
    And smothered ferns:
Frond-forests; and the low, sly lives
    Before the fawns.

My fire might show steam-phantoms simmer
    From Time's old cauldron,
Before the birds made nests in summer,
    Or men had children.

But the coals were murmuring of their mine,
    And moans down there
Of boys that slept wry sleep, and men
    Writhing for air.

And I saw white bones in the cinder-shard.
    Bones without number;
For many hearts with coal are charred
    And few remember.

I thought of some who worked dark pits
    Or war, and died
Digging the rock where Death reputes
    Peace lies indeed.

Comforted years will sit soft-chaired
    In rooms of amber;
The years will stretch their hands, well-cheered
    By our lives' ember.

The centuries will burn rich loads
    With which we groaned,
Whose warmth shall lull their dreaming lids
    While songs are crooned.
But they will not dream of us poor lads
    Lost in the ground.

Wilfred Owen

The Lincolnshire Poacher

When I was bound apprentice, in famous Lincolnshire,
Full well I served my master for more than seven year,
Till I took up to poaching, as you shall quickly hear:
Oh, 'tis my delight on a shining night, in the season of the year.

As me and my companions were setting of a snare,
'Twas then we spied the gamekeeper, for him we did not care.
For we can wrestle and fight, my boys, and jump out anywhere;
Oh, 'tis my delight on a shining night, in the season of the year.

As me and my companions were setting four or five,
And, taking on 'em up again, we caught a hare alive.
We took the hare alive, my boys, and through the wood did steer:
Oh, 'tis my delight on a shining night, in the season of the year.

I threw him on my shoulder, and then we trudgèd home,
We took him to a neighbour's house and sold him for a crown,
We sold him for a crown, my boys, but I did not tell you where:
Oh, 'tis my delight on a shining night, in the season of the year.

Success to every gentleman that lives in Lincolnshire,
Success to every poacher that wants to sell a hare,
Bad luck to every gamekeeper that will not sell his deer:
Oh, 'tis my delight on a shining night, in the season of the year.

Anon

The Justice of the Peace

Distinguish carefully between these two,
   This thing is yours, that other thing is mine.
You have a shirt, a brimless hat, a shoe
   And half a coat. I am the Lord benign
Of fifty hundred acres of fat land
To which I have a right. You understand?

I have a right because I have, because,
   Because I have – because I have a right.
Now be quite calm and good, obey the laws,
   Remember your low station, do not fight
Against the goad, because, you know, it pricks
Whenever the uncleanly demos kicks.

I do not envy you your hat, your shoe.
   Why should you envy me my small estate?
It's fearfully illogical in you
   To fight with economic force and fate.
Moreover, I have got the upper hand,
And mean to keep it. Do you understand?

Hilaire Belloc

Heaven-Haven
A Nun Takes the Veil

I have desired to go
    Where springs not fail,
To fields where flies no sharp and sided hail
    And a few lilies blow.

And I have asked to be
    Where no storms come,
Where the green swell is in the havens dumb,
    And out of the swing of the sea.

Gerard Manley Hopkins

Old Shepherd's Prayer

Up to the bed by the window, where I be lyin',
Comes bells and bleat of the flock wi' they two children's clack.
Over, from under the eaves there's the starlings flyin',
And down in yard, fit to burst his chain, yapping out at Sue I do hear
    young Mac.

Turning around like a falled-over sack
I can see team ploughin' in Whithy-bush field and meal carts startin' up
    road to Church-Town;
Saturday arternoon the men goin' back
And the women from market, trapin' home over the down.

Heavenly Master, I wud like to wake to they same green places
Where I be know'd for breakin' dogs and follerin' sheep.
And if I may not walk in th' old ways and look on th' old faces
I wud sooner sleep.

King of the Road

Trailer for sale or rent,
Rooms to let fifty cents,
No phone, no pool, no pets,
I ain't got no cigarettes.
Ah, but two hours of pushing broom buys a
Eight-by-twelve four-bit room
I'm a man of means by no means
King of the Road.

Third box car midnight train
Destination Bangor, Maine,
Old worn-out suit and shoes,
I don't pay no union dues.
I smoke old stogies I have found,
Short but not too big around.
I'm a man of means by no means
King of the Road.

I know every engineer on every train
All of the children and all of their names
And every handout in every town
And every lock that ain't locked when no one's around.

I sing, "Trailer for sale or rent,
Rooms to let fifty cents,"
No phone, no pool, no pets,
I ain't got no cigarettes.
Ah, but two hours of pushing broom buys a
Eight-by-twelve four-bit room
I'm a man of means by no means
King of the Road.

Roger Miller   **167**

Things Men Have Made —

Things men have made with wakened hands, and put soft life into
are awake through years with transferred touch, and go on glowing
for long years.
And for this reason, some old things are lovely
warm still with the life of forgotten men who made them.

Things Made by Iron —

Things made by iron and handled by steel
are born dead, they are shrouds, they soak life out of us.
Till after a long time, when they are old and have steeped in our life
they begin to be soothed and soothing: then we throw them away.

New Houses, New Clothes —

New houses, new furniture, new streets, new clothes, new sheets
everything new and machine-made sucks life out of us
and makes us cold, makes us lifeless
the more we have.

Whatever Man Makes —

Whatever man makes and makes it live
lives because of the life put into it.
A yard of India muslin is alive with Hindu life.
And a Navajo woman, weaving her rug in the pattern of her dream
must run the pattern out in a little break at the end
so that her soul can come out, back to her.

But in the odd pattern, like snake-marks on the sand
it leaves its trail.

168   **D. H. Lawrence**

Spectator Ab Extra

As I sat at the café I said to myself,
They may talk as they please about what they call pelf,
They may sneer as they like about eating and drinking,
But help it I cannot, I cannot help thinking,
    How pleasant it is to have money, heigh-ho!
    How pleasant it is to have money.

I sit at my table *en grand seigneur*,
And when I have done, throw a crust to the poor;
Not only the pleasure, one's self, of good living,
But also the pleasure of now and then giving.
    So pleasant it is to have money, heigh-ho!
    So pleasant it is to have money.

They may talk as they please about what they call pelf,
And how one ought never to think of one's self,
How pleasures of thought surpass eating and drinking –
My pleasure of thought is the pleasure of thinking
    How pleasant it is to have money, heigh-ho!
    How pleasant it is to have money.

Arthur Hugh Clough

Job Hunting

On the wasteland that stretches
From here to the river
My children play a game.
It is called job hunting.
They blacken their faces,
And with knives and imitation guns
They go stalking among
The lichen-coated ruins
Of broken machinery and cranes.
It is an exciting game.
Sometimes they come back exhausted,
Clutching objects they have prised
From the earth –
Nuts, bolts, the broken vizor
Of a welder's mask.
"Daddy," they ask, "Daddy,
Is this a job? Can we keep it?"

Brian Patten

The Crazy River

Riddles and Utter Nonsense

The Frog

What a wonderful bird the frog are.
When he sit he stand almost.
When he hop he fly almost.
He ain't got no sense hardly.
He ain't got no tail hardly neither
Where he sit almost.

Anon

What's in There?

What's in there?
Gold and money.
Where's my share of it?
The moosie ran awa' wi't.
Where's the moosie?
In her hoosie.
Where's her hoosie?
In the wood.
Where's the wood?
The fire burnt it.
Where's the fire?
The water quenched it.
Where's the water?
The broon bull drank it.
Where's the broon bull?
Back o' Burnie's hill.
Where's Burnie's hill?
A'clad wi' snaw.
Where's the snaw?
The sun melted it.
Where's the sun?
High, high, up i' the air!

Anon

What Is Pink?

What is pink? a rose is pink
By the fountain's brink.
What is red? a poppy's red
In its barley bed.
What is blue? the sky is blue
Where the clouds float thro'
What is white? a swan is white
Sailing in the light.
What is yellow? pears are yellow,
Rich and ripe and mellow.
What is green? the grass is green,
With small flowers between.
What is violet? clouds are violet
In the summer twilight.
What is orange? why, an orange,
Just an orange!

Christina Rossetti

Snow and Sun

White bird, featherless,
Flew from Paradise,
Pitched on the castle wall;
Along came Lord Landless,
Took it up handless,
And rode away horseless to the King's white hall.

Anon

Sensitive, Seldom and Sad

Sensitive, Seldom and Sad are we,
As we wend our way to the sneezing sea,
With our hampers full of thistles and fronds
To plant round the edge of the dab-fish ponds;
Oh, so Sensitive, Seldom and Sad –
Oh, *so* Seldom and Sad.

In the shambling shades of the shelving shore,
We will sing us a song of the Long Before,
And light a red fire and warm our paws
For it's chilly, it is, on the Desolate shores,
For those who are Sensitive, Seldom and Sad,
For those who are Seldom and Sad.

Sensitive, Seldom and Sad we are,
As we wander along through Lands Afar,
To the sneezing sea, where the sea-weeds be,
And the dab-fish ponds that are waiting for we
Who are, Oh, so Sensitive, Seldom and Sad,
Oh, *so* Seldom and Sad.

Mervyn Peake

I Cannot Give the Reasons

I cannot give the reasons,
I only sing the tunes:
the sadness of the seasons
the madness of the moons.

I cannot be didactic
or lucid, but I can
be quite obscure and practically marzipan

In gorgery and gushness
and all that's squishified.
My voice has all the lushness
of what I can't abide

And yet it has a beauty
most proud and terrible
denied to those whose duty
is to be cerebral.

Among the antlered mountains
I make my viscous way
and watch the sepia fountains
throw up their lime-green spray.

Mervyn Peake

A is for Parrot

A is for Parrot which we can plainly see

B is for glasses which we can plainly see

C is for plastic which we can plainly see

D is for Doris

E is for binoculars I'll get it in five

F is for Ethel who lives next door

G is for orange which we love to eat when we can get
   them because they come from abroad

H is for England and (Heather)

I is for monkey we see in the tree

J is for parrot which we can plainly see

K is for shoetop we wear to the ball

L is for Land because brown

M is for Venezuela where the oranges come from

N is for Brazil near Venezuela (very near)

O is for football which we kick about a bit

T is for Tommy who won the war

Q is a garden which we can plainly see

R is for intestines which hurt when we dance

S is for pancake or whole-wheat bread

U is for Ethel who lives on the hill

P is arab and her sister will

V is for me

W is for lighter which never lights

X is for easter – have one yourself

Y is a crooked letter and you can't straighten it

Z is for Apple which we can plainly see

This is my story both humble and true

Take it to pieces and mend it with glue

John Lennon

The White Knight's Song

I'll tell thee everything I can;
    There's little to relate.
I saw an aged aged man,
    A-sitting on a gate.
"Who are you, aged man?" I said,
    "And how is it you live?"
And his answer trickled through my head
    Like water through a sieve.

He said "I look for butterflies
    That sleep among the wheat:
I make them into mutton-pies,
    And sell them in the street.
I sell them unto men," he said,
    "Who sail on stormy seas;
And that's the way I get my bread –
    A trifle, if you please."

But I was thinking of a plan
    To dye one's whiskers green,
And always use so large a fan
    That they could not be seen.
So, having no reply to give
    To what the old man said,
I cried "Come, tell me how you live!"
    And thumped him on the head.

His accents mild took up the tale:
  He said "I go my ways,
And when I find a mountain-rill,
  I set it in a blaze;
And thence they make a stuff they call
  Rowland's Macassar-Oil –
Yet twopence-halfpenny is all
  They give me for my toil."

But I was thinking of a way
  To feed oneself on batter,
And so go on from day to day
  Getting a little fatter.
I shook him well from side to side,
  Until his face was blue:
"Come, tell me how you live," I cried,
  "And, what it is you do!"

He said "I hunt for haddocks' eyes
  Among the heather bright,
And work them into waistcoat-buttons
  In the silent night.
And these I do not sell for gold
  Or coin of silvery shine,
But for a copper halfpenny,
  And that will purchase nine.

"I sometimes dig for buttered rolls,
  Or set limed twigs for crabs;
I sometimes search the grassy knolls
  For wheels of Hansom-cabs.
And that's the way" (he gave a wink)
  "By which I get my wealth –
And very gladly will I drink
  Your Honour's noble health."

I heard him then, for I had just
   Completed my design
To keep the Menai bridge from rust
   By boiling it in wine.
I thanked him much for telling me
   The way he got his wealth,
But chiefly for his wish that he
   Might drink my noble health.

And now, if e'er by chance I put
   My fingers into glue,
Or madly squeeze a right-hand foot
   Into a left-hand shoe,
Or if I drop upon my toe
   A very heavy weight,
I weep, for it reminds me so
Of that old man I used to know –
Whose look was mild, whose speech was slow,
Whose hair was whiter than the snow,
Whose face was very like a crow,
With eyes, like cinders, all aglow,
Who seemed distracted with his woe,
Who rocked his body to and fro,
And muttered mumblingly and low,
As if his mouth were full of dough,
Who snorted like a buffalo –
That summer evening long ago
   A-sitting on a gate.

Lewis Carroll

He Thought He Saw an Elephant

He thought he saw an Elephant,
   That practised on a fife:
He looked again, and found it was
   A letter from his wife.
"At length I realise," he said,
   "The bitterness of Life!"

He thought he saw a Buffalo
   Upon the chimney-piece:
He looked again, and found it was
   His Sister's Husband's Niece.
"Unless you leave this house," he said,
   "I'll send for the Police!"

He thought he saw a Rattlesnake
   That questioned him in Greek:
He looked again, and found it was
   The Middle of Next Week.
"The one thing I regret," he said,
   "Is that it cannot speak!"

He thought he saw a Banker's Clerk
   Descending from the bus:
He looked again, and found it was
   A Hippopotamus:
"If this should stay to dine," he said,
   "There won't be much for us!"

He thought he saw a Kangaroo
   That worked a coffee-mill:

He looked again, and found it was
  A Vegetable-Pill.
"Were I to swallow this," he said,
  "I should be very ill!"

He thought he saw a Coach-and-Four
  That stood beside his bed:
He looked again and found it was
  A Bear without a Head.
"Poor thing," he said, "Poor silly thing!
  "It's waiting to be fed!"

He thought he saw an Albatross
  That fluttered round the lamp:
He looked again, and found it was
  A Penny-Postage-Stamp.
"You'd best be getting home," he said:
  "The nights are very damp!"

He thought he saw a Garden-Door
  That opened with a key:
He looked again, and found it was
  A Double Rule of Three:
"And all its mystery," he said,
  "Is clear as day to me!"

He thought he saw an Argument
  That proved he was the Pope:
He looked again, and found it was
  A Bar of Mottled Soap.
"A fact so dread," he faintly said,
  "Extinguishes all hope!"

Lewis Carroll

Scorflufus
By a well-known National Health Victim
No. 3908631

There are many diseases,
That strike people's kneeses,
Scorflufus! is one by name
It comes from the East
Packed in bladders of yeast
So the Chinese must take half the blame.

There's a case in the files
Of Sir Barrington-Pyles
While hunting a fox one day
Shot up in the air
And *remained hanging there!*
While the hairs on his socks turned grey!

Aye! Scorflufus had struck!
At man, beast and duck.
And the knees of the world went Bong!
Some knees went Ping!
Other knees turned to string
From Balham to old Hong-Kong.

Should you hold your life dear,
Then the remedy's clear,
If you're offered some yeast – don't eat it!
Turn the offer down flat –
Don your travelling hat –
Put an egg in your boot – and beat it!

Spike Milligan

Look Ahead

Our toes are ahead of us – they have grown out of us

Our nails are ahead of our toes – we can't reach to cut them

Our hammers are ahead of our nails – they strike
   like underpaid lightning

Our sickles are ahead of our hammers – shape of our hammer toes

Our televisions are ahead of our cinemas – our films are because
   we don't use good toothpaste
   state and church fight tooth and nail
   whilst producers forge ahead of viewers

Our commercials are ahead of our patrons –
   all is peddled

Our cycles are ahead of our tricycles and our trickles are
   our fashionable works of art
   trickled by cyclists on paint

Our best cyclists are our worst painters and

Our best painters are worse than our worst cyclists –

Our worst cyclists are ahead of all our painters
   put together – save the painters become cyclists
   and that's what they've done –
   every day more painters are taking up cycling
   and daily they are discovered
   biking up the strand –

sponsored they swerve through swirls of paint
dribble ahead of trolleys trams trombones –
start brushing their feet with toothpaste
that the Tour de France is gunged to a standstill
whilst cinemas clean up with the masses at bingo
and the backsliding punter lies down with the telly –

Our piledriver toes hammer furiously on motorcycles
but the hammers are sliced by sickles
struck hard by

Our frames our nails catch up with our toes till at last
we're in –
we find our – teeth
fully grown

footballers

Michael Horovitz

Self-Portrait of the Laureate of Nonsense

How pleasant to know Mr Lear!
　Who has written such volumes of stuff!
Some think him ill-tempered and queer,
　But a few think him pleasant enough.

His mind is concrete and fastidious,
　His nose is remarkably big;
His visage is more or less hideous,
　His beard it resembles a wig.

He has ears, and two eyes, and ten fingers,
Leastways if you reckon two thumbs;
Long ago he was one of the singers,
But now he is one of the dumbs.

He sits in a beautiful parlour,
With hundreds of books on the wall;
He drinks a great deal of Marsala,
But never gets tipsy at all.

He has many friends, laymen and clerical;
Old Foss is the name of his cat;
His body is perfectly spherical,
He weareth a runcible hat.

When he walks in a waterproof white,
The children run after him so!
Calling out, "He's come out in his night-
Gown, that crazy old Englishman, oh!"

He weeps by the side of the ocean,
He weeps on the top of the hill;
He purchases pancakes and lotion,
And chocolate shrimps from the mill.

He reads but he cannot speak Spanish,
He cannot abide ginger-beer:
Ere the days of his pilgrimage vanish,
How pleasant to know Mr Lear!

Edward Lear

The Pobble Who Has No Toes

The Pobble who has no toes
   Had once as many as we;
When they said, "Some day you may lose them all" –
   He replied, "Fish fiddle de-dee!"
And his Aunt Jobiska made him drink,
Lavender water tinged with pink,
For she said, "The World in general knows
There's nothing so good for a Pobble's toes!"

The Pobble who has no toes,
   Swam across the Bristol Channel;
But before he set out he wrapped his nose,
   In a piece of scarlet flannel.
For his Aunt Jobiska said, "No harm
Can come to his toes if his nose is warm;
And it's perfectly known that a Pobble's toes
Are safe – provided he minds his nose."

The Pobble swam fast and well
   And when boats or ships came near him
He tinkledy-binkledy-winkled a bell
   So that all the world could hear him.
And all the Sailors and Admirals cried,
When they saw him nearing the further side –
"He has gone to fish, for his Aunt Jobiska's
Runcible Cat with crimson whiskers!"

But before he touched the shore,
   The shore of the Bristol Channel,
A sea-green Porpoise carried away
   His wrapper of scarlet flannel.
And when he came to observe his feet

Formerly garnished with toes so neat
His face at once became forlorn
On perceiving that all his toes were gone!

And nobody ever knew
   From that dark day to the present,
Whoso had taken the Pobble's toes,
   In a manner so far from pleasant.
Whether the shrimps or crawfish gray,
Or crafty Mermaids stole them away –
Nobody knew; and nobody knows
How the Pobble was robbed of his twice five toes!

The Pobble who has no toes
   Was placed in a friendly Bark,
And they rowed him back, and carried him up,
   To his Aunt Jobiska's Park.
And she made him a feast at his earnest wish
Of eggs and buttercups fried with fish –
And she said, "It's a fact the whole world knows,
That Pobbles are happier without their toes."

Edward Lear

Hallelujah!

"Hallelujah!" was the only observation
That escaped Lieutenant-Colonel Mary Jane,
When she tumbled off the platform in the station,
And was cut in little pieces by the train.
   Mary Jane, the train is through yer:
   Hallelujah, Hallelujah!
We will gather up the fragments that remain.

A. E. Housman

Alternative Endings to an Unwritten Ballad

I stole through the dungeons, while everyone slept,
    Till I came to the cage where the Monster was kept.
There, locked in the arms of a Giant Baboon,
    Rigid and smilling, lay . . . MRS RAVOON!

I climbed the clock tower in the first morning sun
    And 'twas midday at least 'ere my journey was done;
But the clock never sounded the last stroke of noon,
    For there, from the clapper, swung MRS RAVOON!

I hauled in the line, and I took my first look
    At the half-eaten horror that hung from the hook.
I had dragged from the depths of the limpid lagoon
    The luminous body of MRS RAVOON.

I fled in the storm, the lightning and thunder,
    And there, as a flash split the darkness asunder,
Chewing a rat's-tail and mumbling a rune,
    Mad in the moat squatted MRS RAVOON!

I stood by the waters so green and so thick,
    And I stirred at the scum with my old, withered stick;
When there rose through the ooze, like a monstrous balloon,
    The bloated cadaver of MRS RAVOON.

Facing the fens, I looked back from the shore
    Where all had been empty a moment before;
And there by the light of the Lincolnshire moon,
    Immense on the marshes, stood . . . MRS RAVOON!

Paul Dehn

The Road to Jeopardy

Dangerous Journeys
Desperate Criminals
and Life on the High Seas

Thoughts of a Module

It is black so. There is that dust.

My ladder in light. What are my men.

One is foot down. That is pack drill.

Black what is vizor. A hiss I heard.

The talks go up. Clump now but float.

Is a jump near. A camera paced out.

I phase another man. Another man is second.

Second last feet on. The dust I think.

So some soles cross. Is a flag near.

No move yon flag. Which voice comes down.

White house thanks all. Command module man not.

Is kangaroo hop around. I think moon dance.

Or white bird is. Good oxygen I heard.

Earth monitors must be. Is it too pressing.

Trained man is gay. Fail safe is gay.

The black I see. What instruments are lonely.

Sharp is a shadow. A horizon goes flat.

All rock are samples. Dust taken I think.

Is bright my leg. In what sun yonder.

An end I think. How my men go.

The talks come down. The ladder I shake.

To leave that bright. Space dark I see.

Is my men last. Men are that first.

That moon is there. They have some dust.

Is home they know. Blue earth I think.

I lift I see. It is that command.

My men go back. I leave that there.

It is bright so.

Edwin Morgan

Stars and Planets

Trees are cages for them: water holds its breath
To balance them without smudging on its delicate meniscus.
Children watch them playing in their heavenly playground;
Men use them to lug ships across oceans, through firths.

They seem so twinkle-still, but they never cease
Inventing new spaces and huge explosions
And migrating in mathematical tribes over
The steppes of space at their outrageous ease.

It's hard to think that the earth is one –
This poor sad bearer of wars and disasters
Rolls-Roycing round the sun with its load of gangsters,
Attended only by the loveless moon.

Norman MacCaig

Uphill

Does the road wind uphill all the way?
    Yes, to the very end.
Will the day's journey take the whole long day?
    From morn to night, my friend.

But is there for the night a resting-place?
    A roof for when the slow, dark hours begin.
May not the darkness hide it from my face?
    You cannot miss that inn.

Shall I meet other wayfarers at night?
    Those who have gone before.
Then must I knock, or call when just in sight?
    They will not keep you waiting at that door.

Shall I find comfort, travel-sore and weak?
    Of labour you shall find the sum.
Will there be beds for me and all who seek?
    Yea, beds for all who come.

Christina Rossetti

Message from the Border

A messenger,
>bald, his skin burnt onto his bones, he appears on the skyrim
>walking, not slowly nor fast, just walking: his bones move,
>his toe-joints grip the ground: he has been on his way,
>he will soon arrive,

We see him approach,
>we will see him arrive, we are his arrival: we will see
>how he opens his mouth, we will say: no! first – drink this!
>we will see how the water runs down into this sun-crumpled hide,
>filling out a few wrinkles,

And he will open his mouth
>and deliver the message: what will he say?

He will say what the one before him said,
>and the one before that one – he will tell us! The dancers! –
>the dancers – they – are surrounded! by the burning –

So simple it hurts . . . and always the same.
What else could it be?
What else could the messenger say
>these days? The dancers, in the midst of the burning . . .
>>this
>is the messenger's voice, the sound of his horn, abandoned
>for lightness, and speed, now it lies on the sand
>cracked by the heat, blackened – soon charred
>by the black
>heat

Anselm Hollo

The Jungle Husband

Dearest Evelyn, I often think of you
Out with the guns in the jungle stew
Yesterday I hittapotamus
I put the measurements down for you but they got lost in
    the fuss
It's not a good thing to drink out here
You know, I've practically given it up dear.
Tomorrow I am going alone a long way
Into the jungle. It is all grey
But green on top
Only sometimes when a tree has fallen
The sun comes down plop, it is quite appalling.
You never want to go in a jungle pool
In the hot sun, it would be the act of a fool
Because it's always full of anacondas, Evelyn, not looking
    ill-fed
I'll say. So no more now, from your loving husband,
    Wilfred.

Stevie Smith

Ozymandias

I met a traveller from an antique land
Who said: Two vast and trunkless legs of stone
Stand in the desert . . . Near them, on the sand,
Half sunk, a shattered visage lies, whose frown,
And wrinkled lip, and sneer of cold command,
Tell that its sculptor well those passions read
Which yet survive, stamped on these lifeless things,
The hand that mocked them, and the heart that fed:
And on the pedestal these words appear:
"My name is Ozymandias, king of kings:
Look on my works, ye Mighty, and despair!"
Nothing beside remains. Round the decay
Of that colossal wreck, boundless and bare
The lone and level sands stretch far away.

Percy Bysshe Shelley

Frankie looked over the transom,
Oh, what a sight met her eye.
Down on a couch sat Johnny,
Making up to Nelly Bly.
    He was her man,
    He was doing her wrong.

Frankie pulled back her kimono,
Took out her little forty-four.
Rooty-toot-toot three times she shot
Right through that hardwood door.
    She shot her man
    'Cause he done her wrong.

"Roll me over easy,
Roll me over slow.
Roll me over on my left side
For your bullets are hurting me so.
    I was your man
    Though I done you wrong."

Johnny he was a gambler,
He gambled for the gain.
The very last words he ever said were:
"High-low Jack and the game."
    He was her man,
    But he done her wrong.

The first shot, Johnny staggered.
The second shot, he fell.
The third shot, Frankie fired at him.
Then was a new man's face in Hell.
   He was her man,
   But he done her wrong.

Frankie she went to the river,
She looked from bank to bank.
"Do all you can for a gambling man
But you will get no thanks.
   He was my man,
   But he done me wrong."

Frankie she looked down Main Street,
Far as the eye could see.
All she could hear was a one-string guitar
Playing 'Nearer O My God to Thee'.
   He was her man,
   But he done her wrong.

"Bring round your rubber-tyred hearses.
Bring round your rubber-tyred hack.
I'm taking my man to the boneyard
And I ain't gonna bring him back.
   He was my man,
   Though he done me wrong."

"Bring round a thousand policemen,
Bring 'em round today.
Oh, lock me up in a dungeon cell
And throw the key away.
   I shot my man,
   But he done me wrong.

"Yes, put me down in that dungeon,
Lock me up in that cell.
Put me where the north wind blows
From the south-east corner of Hell.
   I shot my man
   When he done me wrong."

The Judge he said to Frankie:
"Explain it if you can."
Frankie looked him straight in the eye,
Said: "I shot my lovin' man.
   He was my man,
   But he done me wrong."

Now it wasn't murder in the second degree,
Was not murder in the third.
Frankie simply shot her man
Like a hunter drops a bird.
   He was her man,
   But he done her wrong.

Now the last time I saw Frankie
She was sitting in the 'lectric chair.
She was crying out for Johnny
And the sparks were in her hair.
   She shot her man,
    But he done her wrong.

This story has no moral,
This story has no end.
This story only goes to show
That there ain't no good in men.
   He was her man,
    But he done her wrong.

Anon

My Bonny Black Bess

Let the lover his mistress's beauty rehearse,
And laud her attractions in languishing verse;
Be it mine in rude strain but with truth to express
The love that I bear to my Bonny Black Bess.

From the West was her dam, from the East was her sire;
From the one came her swiftness, the other her fire;
No peer of the realm better blood can possess
Than flows in the blood of my Bonny Black Bess.

Look! Look! how that eyeball glows bright as a brand,
That neck proudly arching, those nostrils expand;
Mark that wide flowing mane, of which each silky tress
Might adorn prouder beauties, though none like Black Bess.

Mark that skin sleek as velvet and dusky as night,
With its jet undisfigured by one lock of white,
That throat branched with veins, prompt to charge or caress,
Now is she not beautiful, Bonny Black Bess?

Over·highway and byway, in rough or smooth weather,
Some thousands of miles have we journeyed together;
Our couch the same straw, our meals the same mess,
No couple more constant than I and Black Bess.

By moonlight, in darkness, by night and by day
Her headlong career there is nothing can stay;
She cares not for distance, she knows not distress.
Can you show me a courser to match with Black Bess?

Once it happened in Cheshire, near Durham, I popped
On a horseman alone whom I suddenly stopped;
That I lightened his pockets you'll readily guess –
Quick work makes Dick Turpin when mounted on Bess.

Now it seems the man knew me: "Dick Turpin," said he,
"You shall swing for this job, as you live, d'ye see?"
I laughed at his threats and his vows of redress –
I was sure of an alibi then with Black Bess.

Brake, brook, meadow, and ploughed field Bess fleetly bestrode;
As the crow wings his flight we selected our road.
We arrived at Hough Green in five minutes or less,
My neck it was saved by the speed of Black Bess.

Stepping carelessly forward I lounge on the green,
Taking excellent care that by all I am seen;
Some remarks on time's flight to the squires I address;
But I say not a word of the flight of Black Bess.

I mention the hour – it is just about four,
Play a rubber at bowls, think the danger is o'er,
When athwart my next game like a checkmate in chess
Comes the horseman in search of the rider of Bess.

What matter details? Off with triumph I came.
He swears to the hour and the squires swear the same.
I had robbed him at four, while at four, they profess
I was quietly bowling – all thanks to Black Bess.

Then one halloo, boys, one loud cheering halloo,
For the swiftest of coursers, the gallant, the true,
For the sportsman inborn shall the memory bless
Of the horse of the highwaymen, Bonny Black Bess.

Anon

Lord Randal

"O where hae ye been, Lord Randal, my son?
  O where hae ye been, my handsome young man?"
"I hae been to the wild wood; mother, make my bed soon,
  For I'm weary wi' hunting, and fain wald lie down."

"Where gat ye your dinner, Lord Randal, my son?
  Where gat ye your dinner, my handsome young man?"
"I din'd wi' my true-love; mother, make my bed soon,
  For I'm weary wi' hunting, and fain wald lie down."

"What gat ye to your dinner, Lord Randal, my son?
  What gat ye to your dinner, my handsome young man?"
"I gat eels boil'd in broo; mother, make my bed soon,
  For I'm weary wi' hunting, and fain wald lie down."

"What became of your bloodhounds, Lord Randal, my son?
  What became of your bloodhounds, my handsome young man?"
"O they swell'd and they died; mother, make my bed soon,
  For I'm weary wi' hunting, and fain wald lie down."

"O I fear ye are poisoned, Lord Randal, my son!
  O I fear ye are poisoned, my handsome young man!"
"O yes! I am poison'd; mother, make my bed soon,
  For I'm sick at the heart, and fain wald lie down."

Anon

Henry My Son

"Where have you been all the day,
Henry my son?
Where have you been all the day,
My handsome one?"

"In the woods, dear Mother.
In the woods, dear Mother.
Oh, Mother, be quick
I'm going to be sick
And lay me down to die."

"Oh, what did you do in the woods,
Henry my boy?
What did you do in the woods,
My pride and joy?"

"Ate, dear Mother.
Ate, dear Mother.
Oh, Mother, be quick
I'm going to be sick
And lay me down to die."

"Oh, what did you eat in the woods,
Henry my son?
What did you eat in the woods,
My handsome one?"

"Eels, dear Mother.
Eels, dear Mother.
Oh, Mother, be quick
I'm going to be sick
And lay me down to die."

"Oh, what colour was them eels,
Henry my boy?
What colour was them eels,
My pride and joy?"

"Green and yeller!
Green and yeller!
Oh, Mother, be quick
I'm going to be sick
And lay me down to die."

"Them eels was snakes,
Henry my son.
Them eels was snakes,
My handsome one."

"Yerr-uck! dear Mother.
Yerr-uck! dear Mother.
Oh, Mother, be quick
I'm going to be sick
And lay me down to die."

"Oh, what colour flowers would you like,
Henry my son?
What colour flowers would you like,
My handsome one?"

"Green and yeller.
Green and yeller.
Oh, Mother, be quick
I'm going to be sick
And lay me down to die."

Anon

At the Railway Station, Upway

"There is not much that I can do,
   For I've no money that's quite my own!"
   Spoke up the pitying child –
A little boy with a violin
At the station before the train came in –
"But I can play my fiddle to you,
And a nice one 'tis, and good in tone!"

   The man in the handcuffs smiled;
The constable looked, and he smiled, too,
   As the fiddle began to twang;
And the man in the handcuffs suddenly sang
      With grimful glee:
     "This life so free
     Is the thing for me!"
And the constable smiled, and said no word,
As if unconscious of what he heard;
And so they went on till the train came in –
The convict, and boy with the violin.

Thomas Hardy

Frank Carew Macgraw

The name of Frank Carew Macgraw
Was notorious in the West,
Not as the fastest on the draw
But 'cause he only wore a vest.

Yes just a vest and nothing more!
Through the Wild and Woolly West,
They knew the name of Frank Macgraw
'Cause he only wore a vest.

Oh! His nether parts swung wild and free
As on his horse he sat.
He wore a vest and nothing else –
Oh! except a cowboy hat.

Yes! naked from the waist he rode –
He did not give two hoots!
Frank Macgraw in hat and vest
Oh! and a pair of boots.

But nothing else – no! not a stitch!
As through the cactus he
Rode on his horse, although of course
He did protect his knee

With leather leggings – but that's all!
No wonder that his name
Was infamous throughout the West
And spoken of with shame.

Actually he *did* wear pants
On Sunday, and it's true
He also wore them other days –
And sometimes he wore two!

And often in an overcoat
You'd see him riding by,
But as he went men shook their heads
And ladies winked their eye,

For *everyone* knew Frank Macgraw
Throughout the Old Wild West –
Not because he broke the law
But 'cause he *only* wore a vest!

Terry Jones

The Frivolous Cake

A freckled and frivolous cake there was
　　That sailed on a pointless sea,
Or any lugubrious lake there was,
　　In a manner emphatic and free.
How jointlessly, and how jointlessly
　　The frivolous cake sailed by
On the waves of the ocean that pointlessly
　　Threw fish to the lilac sky.

Oh, plenty and plenty of hake there was
　　Of a glory beyond compare,
And every conceivable make there was
　　Was tossed through the lilac air.

Up the smooth billows and over the crests
　　Of the cumbersome combers flew
The frivolous cake with a knife in the wake
　　Of herself and her curranty crew.

Like a swordfish grim it would bounce and skim
　　(This dinner knife fierce and blue),
And the frivolous cake was filled to the brim
　　With the fun of her curranty crew.

Oh, plenty and plenty of hake there was
　　Of a glory beyond compare –
And every conceivable make there was
　　Was tossed through the lilac air.

Around the shores of the Elegant Isles
　　Where the cat-fish bask and purr
And lick their paws with adhesive smiles

215

And wriggle their fins of fur,
They fly and fly 'neath the lilac sky –
   The frivolous cake and the knife
Who winketh his glamorous indigo eye
   In the wake of his future wife.

The crumbs blow free down the pointless sea
   To the beat of a cakey heart
And the sensitive steel of the knife can feel
   That love is a race apart.
In the speed of the lingering light are blown
   The crumbs to the hake above,
And the tropical air vibrates to the drone
   Of a cake in the throes of love.

Mervyn Peake

Profoundly True Reflections on the Sea

O billows bounding far,
How wet, how wet ye are!

When first my gaze you met
I said "These waves are wet."

I said it, and am quite
Convinced that I was right.

Who saith that ye are dry?
I give that man the lie.

Thy wetness, O thou sea,
Is wonderful to me.

It agitates my heart,
To think how wet thou art.

No object I have met
Is more profoundly wet.

Methinks 'twere vain to try,
O sea, to wipe thee dry.

I therefore will refrain.
Farewell, thou humid main.

A. E. Housman

Stone Speech

Crowding this beach
are milkstones, white
teardrops; flints
edged out of flinthood
into smoothness chafe
against grainy ovals,
pitted pieces, nosestones,
stoppers and saddles;
veins of orange
inlay black beads:
chalk-swaddled babyshapes,
tiny fists, facestones
and facestone's brother
skullstone, roundheads
pierced by a single eye,
purple finds, all
rubbing shoulders:
a mob of grindings,
groundlings, scatterings
from a million necklaces
mined under sea-hills, the pebbles
are as various as the people.

Charles Tomlinson

The King of Quizzical Island

The King of Quizzical Island
Had a most inquisitive mind.
He said, "If I sail to the edge of the world
I wonder what I'll find?"

His fearful people pleaded.
They wept fat tears of woe.
Some said, "Remain!" and some, "Please stay!"
While others said, "Don't go!"

"For it's quite well known, and I've heard it said
By wise men, old and clever,
That those who sail to the edge of the world
Fall off – and fall for ever."

But the King of Quizzical Island
Said, "Tosh!" and "Bosh!" and "Twaddle!
For I can sail to the edge of the world
As sure as a duck can waddle."

So he built himself a singular ship
Made of wood from the Tea-Bag Tree –
And the rigging was a spider's web
And the rudder a bumble-bee.

The ship sailed out of the harbour
And the silken sails unfurled
As the King of Quizzical Island
Set sail for the edge of the world.

He sailed through waves as high as hills
For thirty days or more
Until at last, the ship was cast
On a higgledy-piggledy shore.

He found himself in a Jigsaw Land
Which lay there, all in pieces:
The blue bits might have been sea – or sky –
Or sheep, with ink-stained fleeces . . .

The green bits might have been grass – or leaves –
Or a snake, or a dragon's tail;
And the white bits might have been clouds – or snow –
Or the teeth of a smiling whale . . .

It took the King nine days and nights
To fit those bits in place –
Then he saw before him a river
And a smile lit up his face.

So he sailed up that Jigsaw River
And there, round the final bend,
He found himself in Vertical Land
Where everything stands on end.

The rivers go up like fountains
And the crocodiles stand on their tails
And the meadows tower like mountains
And the trains run on vertical rails.

The King said, "That's *one* way of using
Every inch of space you've got –
But it doesn't look very comfortable . . ."
And the crocodiles said, "It's not!"

So the singular ship sailed upwards
On a river tall and wide
And from the top of the river
It sailed down the other side.

It sailed through Hurricane Harriet
To the Sea of Dreadful Dreams,
Where the waves are forever wailing,
And the Wild Wind sighs and screams,

Where the Sea-Horse turns into a Night-Mare
And prances upon the foam,
And gaggles of ghostly jelly-fish
Wobble their way back home.

"All things ghastly and ghoulish,"
Said the King, "I can put to flight –
They'll all feel extremely foolish
When I wake, and turn on the light."

He rang a hundred alarm-clocks,
And the Sky switched on the Sun,
And the Dreadful Dreams were ended
As quickly as they'd begun.

The wild wind sank to a whisper
And even the waves were shy
And the moon smiled down, benignly,
From the sleeping deeps of the sky.

The King of Quizzical Island
Sailed on, till he sighted land.
And the singular ship was beached upon
A handy, sandy strand.

He looked at the castle before him,
And knew he had seen it before –
And he said, "I've sailed to the edge of the world,
And arrived at my own back door!"

His people rushed out to greet him –
They gave him a rousing cheer:
And he said, "There *is* no edge of the world –
The world is a perfect sphere.

"I sailed out there in my singular ship,
And I'll tell you what I found.
I found I was back at my own back door –
So I've proved that the world is round!"

Everyone cheered and shouted,
They shouted and cheered and kissed.
Their King had come back from the edge of the world,
And proved it didn't exist!

Gordon Snell

O Sailor, Come Ashore

O Sailor, come ashore,
    What have you brought for me?
Red coral, white coral,
    Coral from the sea.

I did not dig it from the ground,
    Nor pluck it from a tree;
Feeble insects made it
    In the stormy sea.

Christina Rossetti

The Owl and the Pussy-cat

The Owl and the Pussy-cat went to sea
   In a beautiful pea-green boat,
They took some honey, and plenty of money,
   Wrapped up in a five-pound note.
The Owl looked up to the stars above,
   And sang to a small guitar,
"O lovely Pussy! O Pussy, my love,
     What a beautiful Pussy you are,
       You are,
       You are!
   What a beautiful Pussy you are!"

Pussy said to the Owl, "You elegant fowl!
   How charmingly sweet you sing!
O let us be married! too long we have tarried:
   But what shall we do for a ring?"
They sailed away, for a year and a day,
   To the land where the Bong-tree grows
And there in a wood a Piggy-wig stood
   With a ring at the end of his nose,
     His nose,
     His nose,
   With a ring at the end of his nose.

"Dear Pig, are you willing to sell for one shilling
　　Your ring?" Said the Piggy, "I will."
So they took it away, and were married next day
　　By the Turkey who lives on the hill.
They dined on mince, and slices of quince,
　　Which they ate with a runcible spoon;
And hand in hand, on the edge of the sand,
　　They danced by the light of the moon,
　　　　The moon,
　　　　The moon,
They danced by the light of the moon.

Edward Lear

A Ballad of John Silver

We were schooner-rigged and rakish, with a long and lissome hull,
And we flew the pretty colours of the cross-bones and the skull;
We'd a big black Jolly Roger flapping grimly at the fore,
And we sailed the Spanish Water in the happy days of yore.

We'd a long brass gun amidships, like a well-conducted ship,
We had each a brace of pistols and a cutlass at the hip;
It's a point which tells against us, and a fact to be deplored,
But we chased the goodly merchant-men and laid their ships aboard.

Then the dead men fouled the scuppers and the wounded filled the chains,
And the paint-work all was spatter-dashed with other people's brains,
She was boarded, she was looted, she was scuttled till she sank.
And the pale survivors left us by the medium of the plank.

O! then it was (while standing by the taffrail on the poop)
We could hear the drowning folk lament the absent chicken-coop;
Then, having washed the blood away, we'd little else to do
Than to dance a quiet hornpipe as the old salts taught us to.

O! the fiddle on the fo'c's'le, and the slapping naked soles,
And the genial "Down the middle, Jake, and curtsey when she rolls!"
With the silver seas around us and the pale moon overhead,
And the look-out not a-looking and his pipe-bowl glowing red.

Ah! the pig-tailed, quidding pirates and the pretty pranks we played,
All have since been put a stop-to by the naughty Board of Trade;
The schooners and the merry crews are laid away to rest,
A little south the sunset in the Islands of the Blest.

John Masefield

Sir Patrick Spens

I. The Sailing

The king sits in Dunfermline town
  Drinking the blude-red wine;
"O whare will I get a skeely skipper
  To sail this new ship o' mine?"

O up and spak an eldern knight,
  Sat at the king's right knee;
"Sir Patrick Spens is the best sailor
  That ever sail'd the sea."

Our king has written a braid letter,
  And seal'd it with his hand,
And sent it to Sir Patrick Spens,
  Was walking on the strand.

"To Noroway, to Noroway,
  To Noroway o'er the faem;
The king's daughter o' Noroway,
  'Tis thou must bring her hame."

The first word that Sir Patrick read
  So loud, loud laugh'd he;
The neist word that Sir Patrick read
  The tear blinded his e'e.

"O wha is this has done this deed
  And tauld the king o' me,
To send us out, at this time o' year,
  To sail upon the sea?

"Be it wind, be it weet, be it hail, be it sleet,
  Our ship must sail the faem;
The king's daughter o' Noroway,
  'Tis we must fetch her hame."

They hoysed their sails on Monenday morn
  Wi' a' the speed they may;
They hae landed in Noroway
  Upon a Wodensday.

II. The Return

"Mak ready, mak ready, my merry men a'!
  Our gude ship sails the morn."
"Now ever alack, my master dear,
  I fear a deadly storm.

"I saw the new moon late yestreen
  Wi' the auld moon in her arm;
And if we gang to sea, master,
  I fear we'll come to harm."

They hadna sail'd a league, a league,
   A league but barely three,
When the lift grew dark, and the wind blew loud,
   And gurly grew the sea.

The ankers brak, and the topmast lap,
   It was sic a deadly storm:
And the waves cam owre the broken ship
   Till a' her sides were torn.

"Go fetch a web o' the silken claith,
   Another o' the twine,
And wap them into our ship's side,
   And let nae the sea come in."

They fetch'd a web o' the silken claith,
   Another o' the twine,
And they wapp'd them round that gude ship's side,
   But still the sea came in.

O laith, laith were our gude Scots lords
   To wet their cork-heel'd shoon;
But lang or a' the play was play'd
   They wat their hats aboon.

And mony was the feather bed
   That flatter'd on the faem;
And mony was the gude lord's son
   That never mair cam hame.

O lang, lang may the ladies sit,
   Wi' their fans into their hand,
Before they see Sir Patrick Spens
   Come sailing to the strand!

And lang, lang may the maidens sit
   Wi' their gowd kames in their hair,
A-waiting for their ain dear loves!
   For them they'll see nae mair.

Half-owre, half-owre to Aberdour,
   'Tis fifty fathoms deep;
And there lies gude Sir Patrick Spens,
   Wi' the Scots lords at his feet!

Anon

*Skeely means skilful; the lift is the sky;
lap means split; flatter'd means floated;
kames are combs.*

A Sea Dirge

Full fathom five thy father lies:
    Of his bones are coral made;
Those are pearls that were his eyes:
    Nothing of him that doth fade,
But doth suffer a sea-change
Into something rich and strange.
Sea-nymphs hourly ring his knell:
Hark! now I hear them –
    Ding, dong, bell.

William Shakespeare

The Jumblies

They went to sea in a Sieve, they did,
    In a Sieve they went to sea:
In spite of all their friends could say,
On a winter's morn, on a stormy day,
    In a Sieve they went to sea!
And when the Sieve turned round and round,
And every one cried, "You'll all be drowned!"
They called aloud, "Our Sieve ain't big,
But we don't care a button! we don't care a fig!
    In a Sieve we'll go to sea!"
      Far and few, far and few,
        Are the lands where the Jumblies live;
        Their heads are green, and their hands are blue,
        And they went to sea in a Sieve.

They sailed away in a Sieve, they did,
   In a Sieve they sailed so fast,
With only a beautiful pea-green veil
Tied with a riband by way of a sail,
   To a small tobacco-pipe mast;
And every one said, who saw them go,
"O won't they be soon upset, you know!
For the sky is dark, and the voyage is long,
And happen what may, it's extremely wrong
   In a Sieve to sail so fast!"
    Far and few, far and few,
      Are the lands where the Jumblies live;
      Their heads are green, and their hands are blue,
      And they went to sea in a Sieve.

The water it soon came in, it did,
   The water it soon came in;
So to keep them dry, they wrapped their feet
In a pinky paper all folded neat,
   And they fastened it down with a pin.
And they passed the night in a crockery-jar,
And each of them said, "How wise we are!
Though the sky be dark, and the voyage be long,
Yet we never can think we were rash or wrong,
   While round in our Sieve we spin!"
    Far and few, far and few,
      Are the lands where the Jumblies live;
      Their heads are green, and their hands are blue,
      And they went to sea in a Sieve.

And all night long they sailed away;
   And when the sun went down,
They whistled and warbled a moony song
To the echoing sound of a coppery gong,
   In the shade of the mountains brown.
"O Timballo! How happy we are,
When we live in a sieve and a crockery-jar,
And all night long in the moonlight pale,
We sail away with a pea-green sail,
   In the shade of the mountains brown!"
    Far and few, far and few,
      Are the lands where the Jumblies live;
      Their heads are green, and their hands are blue,
      And they went to sea in a Sieve.

They sailed to the Western Sea, they did,
   To a land all covered with trees,
And they bought an Owl, and a useful Cart,
And a pound of Rice, and a Cranberry Tart,
   And a hive of silvery Bees.
And they bought a Pig, and some green Jack-daws,
And a lovely Monkey with lollipop paws,
And forty bottles of Ring-Bo-Ree,
   And no end of Stilton Cheese.
    Far and few, far and few,
      Are the lands where the Jumblies live;
      Their heads are green, and their hands are blue,
      And they went to sea in a Sieve.

And in twenty years they all came back,
    In twenty years or more,
And every one said, "How tall they've grown!
For they've been to the Lakes, and the Torrible Zone,
    And the hills of the Chankly Bore";
And they drank their health, and gave them a feast
Of dumplings made of beautiful yeast;
And every one said, "If we only live,
We too will go to sea in a Sieve –
    To the hills of the Chankly Bore!"
    Far and few, far and few,
      Are the lands where the Jumblies live;
    Their heads are green, and their hands are blue,
      And they went to sea in a Sieve.

Edward Lear

The Spellbound Mountain
Golden Dreams and Fiery Nightmares
Magical People and Enchanted Places

Romance

When I was but thirteen or so
   I went into a golden land,
Chimborazo, Cotopaxi
   Took me by the hand.

My father died, my brother too,
   They passed like fleeting dreams.
I stood where Popocatapetl
   In the sunlight gleams.

I dimly heard the Master's voice
   And boys far-off at play,
Chimborazo, Cotopaxi
   Had stolen me away.

I walked in a great golden dream
   To and fro from school –
Shining Popocatapetl
   The dusty streets did rule.

I walked home with a gold dark boy
   And never a word I'd say,
Chimborazo, Cotopaxi
   Had taken my speech away:

I gazed entranced upon his face
　　Fairer than any flower –
O shining Popocatapetl
　　It was thy magic hour:

The houses, people, traffic seemed
　　Thin fading dreams by day,
Chimborazo, Cotopaxi
　　They had stolen my soul away!

Walter James Turner

The Aristocrat

The Devil is a gentleman, and asks you down to stay
At his little place at What'sitsname (it isn't far away).
They say the sport is splendid; there is always something new,
And fairy scenes, and fearful feats that none but he can do;
He can shoot the feathered cherubs if they fly on the estate,
Or fish for Father Neptune with the mermaids for a bait;
He scaled amid the staggering stars that precipice, the sky,
And blew his trumpet above heaven, and got by mastery
The starry crown of God Himself, and shoved it on the shelf;
But the Devil is a gentleman, and doesn't brag himself.

O blind your eyes and break your heart and hack your hand away,
And lose your love and shave your head; but do not go to stay
At the little place in What'sitsname where folks are rich and clever;
The golden and the goodly house, where things grow worse for ever;
There are things you need not know of, though you live and die in vain,
There are souls more sick of pleasure than you are sick of pain;
There is a game of April Fool that's played behind its door,
Where the fool remains for ever and the April comes no more,
Where the splendour of the daylight grows drearier than the dark,
And life droops like a vulture that once was such a lark:
And that is the Blue Devil that once was the Blue Bird;
For the Devil is a gentleman, and doesn't keep his word.

G. K. Chesterton

Kubla Khan

In Xanadu did Kubla Khan
  A stately pleasure-dome decree:
Where Alph, the sacred river, ran
Through caverns measureless to man
  Down to a sunless sea.
So twice five miles of fertile ground
With walls and towers were girdled round:
And there were gardens bright with sinuous rills
Where blossom'd many an incense-bearing tree;
And here were forests ancient as the hills,
Enfolding sunny spots of greenery.

But O, that deep romantic chasm which slanted
Down the green hill athwart a cedarn cover!
A savage place! as holy and enchanted
As e'er beneath a waning moon was haunted
By woman wailing for her demon-lover!
And from this chasm, with ceaseless turmoil seething,
As if this earth in fast thick pants were breathing,
A mighty fountain momently was forced;
Amid whose swift half-intermitted burst
Huge fragments vaulted like rebounding hail,
Or chaffy grain beneath the thresher's flail:
And 'mid these dancing rocks at once and ever
It flung up momently the sacred river.
Five miles meandering with a mazy motion
Through wood and dale the sacred river ran,
Then reach'd the caverns measureless to man,
And sank in tumult to a lifeless ocean:
And 'mid this tumult Kubla heard from far
Ancestral voices prophesying war!

241

The shadow of the dome of pleasure
    Floated midway on the waves;
Where was heard the mingled measure
    From the fountain and the caves.
It was a miracle of rare device,
A sunny pleasure-dome with caves of ice!

A damsel with a dulcimer
    In a vision once I saw:
It was an Abyssinian maid,
    And on her dulcimer she play'd,
Singing of Mount Abora.
Could I revive within me,
    Her symphony and song,
To such a deep delight 'twould win me,
That with music loud and long,
I would build that dome in air,
That sunny dome! those caves of ice!
And all who heard should see them there,
And all should cry, Beware! Beware!
His flashing eyes, his floating hair!
Weave a circle round him thrice,
    And close your eyes with holy dread,
    For he on honey-dew hath fed,
And drunk the milk of Paradise.

Samuel Taylor Coleridge

Science Fiction – Contribution to the Shakespeare Festival

Dragon-lovers with sweet serious eyes
brood in a desert wood thick with bluebells:
the tough, fire-belching curiosities
mate among ugly smoke and pungent smells.

Seal women linger on the wild foreshore
where in the wrack and footprints of green slime
doe-eyed enormous weed-eaters explore
pebbles and sand, and then begin to climb.

I belong to the Monster Society,
they are my only ramshackle heroes,
I really love them, and whenever I see
monster films I cheer them from the back rows.

I like steam tractors and big, broken machines,
have two old coke bottles on my book-shelf,
I sit through Shakespeare mostly for the scenes
where I am Caliban and love myself.

Peter Levi

Jerusalem

And did those feet in ancient time
    Walk upon England's mountains green?
And was the holy Lamb of God
    On England's pleasant pastures seen?

And did the Countenance Divine
    Shine forth upon our clouded hills?
And was Jerusalem builded here
    Among these dark Satanic Mills?

Bring me my bow of burning gold!
    Bring me my arrows of desire!
Bring me my spear! O clouds, unfold!
    Bring me my chariot of fire!

I will not cease from mental fight,
    Nor shall my sword sleep in my hand,
Till we have built Jerusalem
    In England's green and pleasant land.

William Blake

Things

There are worse things than having behaved foolishly in public.
There are worse things than these miniature betrayals,
committed or endured or suspected; there are worse things
than not being able to sleep for thinking about them.
It is 5 a.m. All the worse things come stalking in
and stand icily about the bed looking worse and worse

and worse.

Fleur Adcock

Griffin of the Night

I'm holding my son in my arms
sweating after nightmares
small me
fingers in his mouth
his other fist clenched in my hair
small me
sweating after nightmares

Michael Ondaatje

Imagine

Imagine there's no heaven
It's easy if you try.
No hell below us,
Above us only sky.
Imagine all the people,
Living for today.

Imagine there's no countries
It isn't hard to do,
Nothing to kill or die for
And no religion too.
Imagine all the people
Living life in peace.
You may say I'm a dreamer,
But I'm not the only one.
I hope some day you'll join us
And the world will be as one.

Imagine no possessions
I wonder if you can
No need for greed or hunger
A brotherhood of man.
Imagine all the people
Sharing all the world.
You may say I'm a dreamer,
But I'm not the only one.
I hope some day you'll join us
And the world will live as one.

John Lennon

The Witch! The Witch!

The Witch! the Witch! don't let her get you!
Or your Aunt wouldn't know you the next time
she met you!

Eleanor Farjeon

Alison Gross

O Alison Gross, that lives in yon tow'r,
    The ugliest witch i' the north countrie,
Has trysted me ae day up till her bow'r
    And mony fair speeches she made to me.

She straik'd my head an' she kaim'd my hair,
    An' she set me down saftly on her knee;
Says, "Gin ye will be my lemman sae true,
    Sae mony braw things as I would you gie!"

She show'd me a mantle o' red scarlét,
    Wi' gouden flowers an' fringes fine;
Says, "Gin ye will be my lemman sae true,
    This gudely gift it sall be thine" –

"Awa', awa', ye ugly witch,
    Haud far awa', an' lat me be!
I never will be your lemman sae true,
    An' I wish I were out o' your company."

She neist brought a sark o' the saftest silk,
    Well wrought wi' pearls about the band,
Says, "Gin ye will be my lemman sae true,
    This gudely gift ye sall command."

She show'd me a cup o' the good red gowd,
  Well set wi' jewels sae fair to see;
Says, "Gin ye will be my lemman sae true,
  This gudely gift I will you gie" –

"Awa', awa', ye ugly witch,
  Haud far awa', an' lat me be!
For I wouldna once kiss your ugly mouth
  For a' the gifts that ye could gie."

She's turn'd her right an' roun' about,
  An' thrice she blaw on a grass-green horn;
An' she sware by the moon an' the stars abune
  That she'd gar me rue the day I was born.

Then out has she ta'en a silver wand,
  An' she's turn'd her three times roun' and roun';
She mutter'd sic words till my strength it fail'd,
  An' I fell down senseless upon the groun'.

She's turn'd me into an ugly worm,
  And gar'd me toddle about the tree;
An' ay, on ilka Saturday's night,
  My sister Maisry came to me.

Wi' silver bason an' silver kaim
   To kaim my headie upon her knee;
But or I had kiss'd wi' Alison Gross
   I'd sooner ha' toddled about the tree.

But as it fell out, on last Hallowe'en,
   When the Seely Court was ridin' by,
The Queen lighted down on a gowany bank
   Nae far frae the tree where I wont to lye.

She took me up in her milk-white han',
   An' she's straik'd me three times o'er her knee;
She changed me again to my ain proper shape,
   An' nae mair I toddle about the tree.

Anon

Trysted means invited; a lemman is a sweetheart;
Seely Court is the Happy Court (of the Fairies);
gowany means daisied.

La Belle Dame Sans Merci

O what can ail thee, knight-at-arms,
　Alone and palely loitering?
The sedge has wither'd from the lake,
　And no birds sing.

O what can ail thee, knight-at-arms,
　So haggard and so woe-begone?
The squirrel's granary is full,
　And the harvest's done.

I see a lily on thy brow,
　With anguish moist and fever dew;
And on thy cheeks a fading rose
　Fast withereth too.

I met a lady in the meads,
　Full beautiful – a faery's child;
Her hair was long, her foot was light,
　And her eyes were wild.

I made a garland for her head,
　And bracelets too, and fragrant zone;
She look'd at me as she did love,
　And made sweet moan.

I set her on my pacing steed,
　And nothing else saw all day long;
For sidelong would she bend, and sing
　A faery's song.

She found me roots of relish sweet,
    And honey wild, and manna-dew;
And sure in language strange she said,
    "I love thee true."

She took me to her elfin grot,
    And there she wept and sigh'd full sore:
And there I shut her wild, wild eyes
    With kisses four.

And there she lulled me asleep,
    And there I dream'd – Ah! woe betide.
The latest dream I ever dream'd
    On the cold hill's side.

I saw pale kings and princes too,
    Pale warriors – death-pale were they all;
They cried, "La Belle Dame Sans Merci
    Hath thee in thrall!"

I saw their starv'd lips in the gloam,
    With horrid warning gaped wide;
And I awoke, and found me here
    On the cold hill's side.

And this is why I sojourn here,
    Alone and palely loitering;
Though the sedge is wither'd from the lake,
    And no birds sing.

John Keats

The Woman of Water

There once was a woman of water
Refused a Wizard her hand.
So he took the tears of a statue
And the weight from a grain of sand
And he squeezed the sap from a comet
And the height from a cypress tree
And he drained the dark from midnight
And he charmed the brains from a bee
And he soured the mixture with thunder
And stirred it with ice from hell
And the woman of water drank it down
And she changed into a well.

There once was a woman of water
Who was changed into a well
And the well smiled up at the Wizard
And down down down that old Wizard fell . . .

Adrian Mitchell

Beware : Do Not Read This Poem

tonite, thriller was
abt an ol woman, so vain she
surrounded herself w/
         many mirrors

it got so bad that finally she
locked herself indoors & her
whole life became the
         mirrors

one day the villagers broke
into her house   ,   but she was too
swift for them   .   she disappeared
         into a mirror
each tenant who bought the house
after that   ,   lost a loved one to

         the ol woman in the mirror   :
         first a little girl
         then a young woman
         then   the   young   woman/s   husband

the hunger of this poem is legendary
it has taken in many victims
back off from this poem
it has drawn in yr feet
back off from this poem
it has drawn in yr legs

back off from this poem
it is a greedy mirror
you are into this poem   .   from
              the waist down
nobody can hear you can they?
this poem has had you up to here
            belch
this poem aint got no manners
you cant call out frm this poem
relax now & go w/ this poem

move & roll on to this poem
do not resist this poem
this poem has yr eyes
this poem has his head
this poem has his arms
this poem has his fingers
this poem has his fingertips

this poem is the reader & the
reader this poem

statistic   :   the us bureau of missing persons re-
                    ports that in 1968 over 100,000 people
                    disappeared leaving no solid clues
                              nor trace   only
a space   in the lives of their friends

Ishmael Reed

Warning to Children

Children, if you dare to think
Of the greatness, rareness, muchness,
Fewness of this precious only
Endless world in which you say
You live, you think of things like this:
Blocks of slate enclosing dappled
Red and green, enclosing tawny
Yellow nets, enclosing white
And black acres of dominoes,
Where a neat brown paper parcel
Tempts you to untie the string.
In the parcel a small island,
On the island a large tree,
On the tree a husky fruit.
Strip the husk and pare the rind off:
In the kernel you will see
Blocks of slate enclosed by dappled
Red and green, enclosed by tawny
Yellow nets, enclosed by white
And black acres of dominoes,
Where the same brown paper parcel –
Children, leave the string untied!
For who dares undo the parcel
Finds himself at once inside it,
On the island, in the fruit,
Blocks of slate about his head,
Finds himself enclosed by dappled
Green and red, enclosed by yellow
Tawny nets, enclosed by black
And white acres of dominoes,

With the same brown paper parcel
Still untied upon his knee.
And, if he then should dare to think
Of the fewness, muchness, rareness,
Greatness of this endless only
Precious world in which he says
He lives – he then unties the string.

Robert Graves

Silver

Slowly, silently, now the moon
Walks the night in her silver shoon;
This way, and that, she peers, and sees
Silver fruit upon silver trees;
One by one the casements catch
Her beams beneath the silvery thatch;
Couched in his kennel, like a log,
With paws of silver sleeps the dog;
From their shadowy cote the white breasts peep
Of doves in a silver-feathered sleep;
A harvest mouse goes scampering by,
With silver claws, and silver eye;
And moveless fish in the water gleam,
By silver reeds in a silver stream.

Walter de la Mare

The Old Summerhouse

This blue-washed, old, thatched summerhouse –
Paint scaling, and fading from its walls –
How often from its hingeless door
I have watched – dead leaf, like the ghost of a mouse,
Rasping the worn brick floor –
The snows of the weir descending below,
And their thunderous waterfall.

Fall – fall: dark, garrulous rumour,
Until I could listen no more.
Could listen no more – for beauty with sorrow
Is a burden hard to be borne:
The evening light on the foam, and the swans, there;
That music, remote, forlorn.

Walter de la Mare

The Negro Speaks of Rivers

I've known rivers:
I've known rivers ancient as the world and older than the flow
    of human blood in human veins.

My soul has grown deep like the rivers.

I bathed in the Euphrates when dawns were young.
I built my hut near the Congo and it lulled me to sleep.
I looked upon the Nile and raised the pyramids above it.
I heard the singing of the Mississippi when Abe Lincoln went
    down to New Orleans, and I've seen its muddy bosom turn
    all golden in the sunset.

I've known rivers:
Ancient, dusky rivers.

My soul has grown deep like the rivers.

Langston Hughes

Weeds

Some people are flower lovers.
I'm a weed lover.

Weeds don't need planting in well-drained soil;
They don't ask for fertiliser or bits of rag to scare
    away birds
They come without invitation;
And they don't take the hint when you want them to go.
Weeds are nobody's guests:
More like squatters.

Coltsfoot laying claim to every new-dug clump of clay;
Pearlwort scraping up a living from a ha'porth of
        mortar;
Dandelions you daren't pick or you know what will
        happen;
Sour docks that make a first-rate poultice for nettle-
        stings;
And flat-foot plantain in the back street,
    gathering more dust than the dustmen.

Even the names are a folk-song:
Fat hen, rat's tail, cat's ear, old men's baccy and
        Stinking Billy
Ring a prettier chime for me than honeysuckle or
        jasmine,
And Sweet Cicely smells cleaner than Sweet William
        though
    she's barred from the garden.

And they have their uses, weeds.
Think of the old, worked-out mines –
Quarries and tunnels, earth scorched and scruffy,
　torn-up railways, splintered sleepers,
And a whole Sahara of grit and smother and cinders.

But go in summer and where is all the clutter?
For a new town has risen of a thousand towers,
Sparkling like granite, swaying like larches,
And every spiky belfry humming with a peal of bees.
Rosebay willowherb:
Only a weed!

Flowers are for wrapping in cellophane to present as a
　bouquet;
Flowers are for prize-arrangements in vases and silver
　tea-pots;
Flowers are for plaiting into funeral wreaths.
You can keep your flowers.
Give me weeds!

Norman Nicholson

Arracombe Wood

Some said, because he wud'n spaik
Any words to women but Yes and No,
Nor put out his hand for Parson to shake
He mun be bird-witted. But I do go
By the lie of the barley that he did sow,
And I wish no better thing than to hold a rake
Like Dave, in his time, or to see him mow.

Put up in churchyard a month ago,
"A bitter old soul," they said, but it wadn't so.
His heart were in Arracombe Wood where he'd used to go
To sit and talk wi' his shadder till sun went low,
Though what it was all about us'll never know.
And there baint no mem'ry in the place
Of th' old man's footmark, nor his face;
Arracombe Wood do think more of a crow –
'Will be violets there in the Spring: in Summer time the spider's lace;
And come the Fall, the whizzle and race
Of the dry, dead leaves when the wind gies chase;
And on the Eve of Christmas, fallin' snow.

Charlotte Mew

Blow, Bugle, Blow

The splendour falls on castle walls
And snowy summits old in story:
The long light shakes across the lakes,
And the wild cataract leaps in glory.
Blow, bugle, blow, set the wild echoes flying,
Blow, bugle; answer, echoes, dying, dying, dying.

O hark, O hear! how thin and clear,
And thinner, clearer, farther going!
O sweet and far from cliff and scar
The horns of Elfland faintly blowing!
Blow, let us hear the purple glens replying:
Blow, bugle; answer, echoes, dying, dying, dying.

O love, they die in yon rich sky,
They faint on hill or field or river:
Our echoes roll from soul to soul,
And grow for ever and for ever.
Blow, bugle, blow, set the wild echoes flying,
And answer, echoes, answer, dying, dying, dying.

Alfred, Lord Tennyson

Speak of the North

Speak of the North! A lonely moor
Silent and dark and trackless swells,
The waves of some wild streamlet pour
Hurriedly through its ferny dells.

Profoundly still the twilight air,
Lifeless the landscape; so we deem
Till like a phantom gliding near
A stag bends down to drink the stream.

And far away a mountain zone,
A cold, white waste of snow-drifts lies,
And one star, large and soft and lone,
Silently lights the unclouded skies.

Charlotte Brontë

The Trees Are Down

— and he cried with a loud voice:
Hurt not the earth, neither the sea, nor the trees —
(Revelation)

They are cutting down the great plane trees at the end of the gardens.
For days there has been the grate of the saw, the swish of the branches as they fall,
The crash of trunks, the rustle of trodden leaves,
With the "Whoops" and the "Whoas", the loud common talk, the loud common laughs of the men, above it all.

I remember one evening of a long past spring
Turning in at a gate, getting out of a cart, and finding a large dead rat in the mud of the drive.
I remember thinking: alive or dead, a rat was a god-forsaken thing,
But at least, in May, that even a rat should be alive.

The week's work here is as good as done. There is just one bough
   On the roped bole, in the fine grey rain,
         Green and high
         And lonely against the sky.
            (Down now! –)
         And but for that,
         If an old dead rat
Did once, for a moment, unmake the spring, I might never have thought of
him again.

It is not for a moment the spring is unmade today;
These were great trees, it was in them from root to stem:
When the men with the "Whoops" and the "Whoas" have carted the whole of
the whispering loveliness away
Half the spring, for me, will have gone with them.

It is going now, and my heart has been struck with the hearts of the planes;
Half my life it has beat with these, in the sun, in the rains,
        In the March wind, the May breeze,
In the great gales that came over to them across the roofs from the great seas.
        There was only a quiet rain when they were dying;
        They must have heard the sparrows flying,
And the small creeping creatures in the earth where they were lying –
        But I, all day, I heard an angel crying:
         "Hurt not the trees."

Charlotte Mew

Lucy in the Sky with Diamonds

Picture yourself in a boat on a river,

with tangerine trees and marmalade skies.

Somebody calls you, you answer quite slowly,

a girl with kaleidoscope eyes.

Cellophane flowers of yellow and green,

towering over your head.

Look for the girl with the sun in her eyes,

and she's gone.

Lucy in the sky with diamonds,

Follow her down to a bridge by a fountain

where rocking horse people eat marshmallow pies,

everyone smiles as you drift past the flowers,

that grow so incredibly high.

Newspaper taxis appear on the shore,

waiting to take you away.

Climb in the back with your head in the clouds,

and you're gone.

Lucy in the sky with diamonds,

Picture yourself on a train in a station,

with plasticine porters with looking-glass ties,

suddenly someone is there at the turnstile,

the girl with kaleidoscope eyes.

Lucy in the sky with diamonds.

John Lennon and Paul McCartney

Song in Space

When man first flew beyond the sky
He looked back into the world's blue eye.
Man said: What makes your eye so blue?
Earth said: The tears in the oceans do.
Why are the seas so full of tears?
Because I've wept so many thousand years.
Why do you weep as you dance through space?
Because I am the Mother of the Human Race.

Adrian Mitchell

Autumn

In autumn I cannot believe my eyes the leaves turn yellow and red. The fresh beautiful airy smell I cannot avoid. I hear my steps go crash crunch. Oh why can't autumn be so long. I like the sound of trees in the wind, so sweet are the animals of this park. I dare not pick the high red mushrooms. The squirrels are the King of autumn. The berries hang glowing bright red and no people seem to run about. But autumn is my lucky season. The fire is bright burning red as night-time falls. I like to sit and tell the tale of autumn falling on the rail. Oh please do not let autumn go. That wicked noise of Hallowe'en. Good-bye pretty blue peck birds but no good-bye to autumn fall. That wicked man can say good-bye by falling down in ashes high. The clock goes forward just swing swing swing. I get up and say it's dark dark dark. I like to dream of autumn season. The people get wrapped up warm in scarves and jackets of soft white wool but I wear more than just one thing. I wear three pairs of woolly white socks. The animals hibernate in small brown nests. I pretend to be a little bird just one step in my nest.

Marina Plentl

Pleasant Sounds

The rustling of leaves under the feet in woods and under hedges;

The crumping of cat-ice and snow down wood-rides, narrow
lanes, and every street causeway;

Rustling through a wood or rather rushing, while the wind
halloos in the oak-top like thunder;

The rustle of birds' wings startled from their nests or flying
unseen into the bushes;

The whizzing of larger birds overhead in a wood, such as crows,
puddocks, buzzards;

The trample of robins and woodlarks on the brown leaves, and
the patter of squirrels on the green moss;

The fall of an acorn on the ground, the pattering of nuts on the
hazel branches as they fall from ripeness;

The flirt of the groundlark's wing from the stubbles – how
sweet such pictures on dewy mornings, when the dew
flashes from its brown feathers!

John Clare

Be a Butterfly

Don't be a kyatta-pilla
Be a butterfly
old preacher screamed
to illustrate his sermon
of Jesus and the higher life

rivulets of well-earned
sweat sliding down
his muscly mahogany face
in the half-empty school church
we sat shaking with muffling
laughter
watching our mother trying to save
herself from joining the wave

only our father remaining poker face
and afterwards we always went home to
split peas Sunday soup
with dumplings, fufu and pigtail

Don't be a kyatta-pilla
Be a butterfly
Be a butterfly

That was de life preacher
and you was right

Grace Nichols

Blow the Stars Home

Blow the Stars home, Wind, blow the Stars home
Ere Morning drowns them in golden foam.

Eleanor Farjeon

Night Way

In beauty	may I walk
All day long	may I walk
Through the returning seasons	may I walk
Beautifully will I possess again	
Beautifully birds	
Beautifully joyful birds	
On the trail marked with pollen	may I walk
With grasshoppers about my feet	may I walk
With dew about my feet	may I walk
With beauty	may I walk
With beauty before me	may I walk
With beauty behind me	may I walk
With beauty above me	may I walk
With beauty all around me	may I walk
In old age, wandering on a trail of beauty, lively,	may I walk
In old age, wandering on a trail of beauty, living again,	may I walk
It is finished in beauty	
It is finished in beauty	

Anon

(translated from the Navajo by Jerome K. Rothenberg)

ACKNOWLEDGEMENTS

'Things' by Fleur Adcock from SELECTED POEMS, reprinted by permission of Oxford University Press; By kind permission of John Agard c/o Caroline Sheldon Literary Agency 'Don't Call Alligator Long Mouth Till You Cross River' from SAY IT AGAIN GRANNY published by Cambridge University Press 1986; 'The Justice of the Peace' by Hilaire Belloc reprinted by permission of the Peters Fraser and Dunlop Group Ltd; 'Fantasy of an African Boy' © copyright 1981 James Berry; 'White Child Meets Black Man' from FRACTURED CIRCLES by James Berry, published by New Beacon Books in 1979; 'Go to Ahmedabad' and 'Maninagar Days' by Sujata Bhatt from MONKEY SHADOWS AND BRUNIZEM, published by Carcanet Press Limited; 'After Prevert' and 'Seven Activities for a Young Child' by Alan Brownjohn, reprinted by permission of Rosica Colin Limited; 'Figgie Hobbin' by Charles Causley, from FIGGIE HOBBIN published by Macmillan, reprinted by permission of David Higham Associates; 'Happiest Girl' © copyright 1982 Frances Mary Whittle, née Clewlow; 'Alternative Endings to an Unwritten Ballad' by Paul Dehn from DANCE MACABRE, reprinted by permission of London Management; 'Comprehensive' by Carol Ann Duffy from STANDING FEMALE NUDE, published by Anvil Press Poetry (1985); 'A Hard Rain's a-Gonna Fall' by Bob Dylan, reprinted by permission of Special Rider Music/ Sony Music Publishing, 17/19 Soho Square, London W1V 6HE; 'Lion and Albert' words by George Marriott Edgar copyright © 1968, reproduced by permission of Francis Day and Hunter Ltd, London WC2H 0EA; 'Skimbleshanks: the Railway Cat' by TS Eliot from OLD POSSUM'S BOOK OF PRACTICAL CATS, reprinted by permission of Faber and Faber Limited; 'Blow the Stars Home'. 'It Was Long Ago' and 'The Witch! The Witch!' by Eleanor Farjeon from SILVER, SAND AND SNOW published by Michael Joseph, reprinted by permission of David Higham Associates; 'Starting to Make a Tree' copyright © Roy Fisher 1998. Reprinted from POEMS 1955 – 1987 by Roy Fisher (1988) by permission of Oxford University Press; 'Song: Lift-Boy' and 'Warning to Children' by Robert Graves from COLLECTED POEMS 1975, reprinted by permission of A. P. Watt Ltd on behalf of The Trustees of The Robert Graves Copyright Trust; 'Without You' © Adrian Henri 1986 from COLLECTED POEMS published by Allison and Busby and reprinted by permission of Rogers Coleridge and White Ltd; 'Message From the Border' © 1962, 1992 by Anselm Hollo, originally published in AND IT IS A SONG, Migrant Press, Worcester/England and Ventura/California, 1965' 'In Painswick Churchyard' by Frances Horovitz: COLLECTED POEMS (Bloodaxe Books and Enitharmon Press, 1985); 'Look Ahead' © Michael Horovitz, published in GROWING UP: SELECTED POEMS AND PICTURES 1951-1979 (Allison and Busby 1979); 'Centrifugalized in Finsbury Park' © Libby Houston 1981, reprinted from AT THE MERCY (Allison and Busby 1981) by permission of Libby Houston; 'Rotting Song' © Libby Houston 1971, reprinted from PLAIN CLOTHES (Allison and Busby 1981) by permission of Libby Houston; 'The Negro Speaks of Rivers' by Langston Hughes reprinted from SELECTED POEMS published by Vintage, by permission of David Higham Associates; 'Cow'; by Ted Hughes from THE CAT AND THE CUCKOO, published by and reprinted by permission of Faber and Faber Limited; 'The Warm and the Cold' by Ted Hughes from SEASON SONGS, published by and reprinted by permission of Faber and Faber Limited; 'Where Poems Come From' © Nigel Jenkins, from SONG AND DANCE (Poetry Wales Press 1981) and ACTS OF UNION SELECTED POEMS 1974 – 1989 (Gwasg Gomer, 1990); 'Reggae Sounds' by Linton Kwesi Johnson, reprinted by permission of LKJ Music Publishers Ltd; 'Hard Times Ain't Gone Nowhere' by Lonnie Johnson from BLUES AND THE POETIC SPIRIT by Paul Garon (1975); 'About Friends' by Brian Jones from A SPITFIRE ON THE NORTHERN LINE, published by Chatto and Windus and reprinted by permission of The Random Century Group; 'The Song of the Banana Man' by Evan Jones, reprinted by permission of Blake Friedmann; 'Frank Carew McGraw' © Terry Jones; 'Warning' by Jenny Joseph, reprinted by permission of John Johnson Limited; 'The Sand Artist' © James Kirkup, from TO THE ANCESTRAL NORTH (Asahi Press, Tokyo); 'Shalom Bomb' by Bernard Kops from BARRICADES IN WEST HAMPSTEAD published by Hearing Eye, reprinted by permission of David Higham Associates; 'Blackbird' by Paul McCartney and 'Lucy in the Sky with Diamonds' by John Lennon/Paul McCartney, reprinted by permission of MCA Music Limited: 'Imagine' by John Lennon, © 1989 Lenono Music (administered in the UK and Eire by BMG Music Publishing Ltd); 'Freedom' and 'Science Fiction' by Peter Levi from FRESH WATER SEA WATER, published by and reprinted by permission of Andre Deutsch Limited; 'Poem for my Sister' by Liz Lochhead from DREAMING FRANKENSTEIN AND COLLECTED POEMS, published by and reprinted by permission of Polygon; 'Blind Horse', 'Praise of a Collie' and 'Stars and Planets' by Norman McCaig from COLLECTED POEMS, published by Chatto and Windus and reprinted by permission of The Random Century Group; 'First Day at School' by Roger McGough from YOU TELL ME, published by Penguin and reprinted by permission of the Peters, Fraser and Dunlop Group Ltd; 'How Much Longer' by Robert Mezey from THE DOOR STANDING OPEN, reprinted by permission of Oxford University Press; 'King of the Road' by Roger Miller © 1964 Tree Publishing; 'Porridge' and 'Scorflufus' by Spike Milligan, reprinted by permission of Spike Milligan Productions Ltd; 'Thoughts of a Module' by Edwin Morgan from FROM GLASGOW TO SATURN, published by and reprinted by permission of Carcanet Press Limited; 'Be a Butterfly' by Grace Nichols from THE FAT BLACK WOMEN'S POEMS, published by and reprinted by permission of Virago Press; 'Like a Flame' by Grace Nichols reprinted by permission of Karnak House; 'Weeds' by Norman Nicholson from SEA TO THE WEST published by Faber and Faber (1981) and reprinted by permission of David Higham Associates; 'A Dog in San Francisco' by Michael Ondaatje from SECULAR LOVE, reprinted by permission of Marion Boyars Publishers Ltd; 'Griffin of the Night' by Michael Ondaatje from RAT JELLY, reprinted by permission Marion Boyars Publishers Ltd; 'Yes' and 'Job Hunting' by Brian Patten from STORM DAMAGE, published by and reprinted by permission of HarperCollins Publishers; 'A Small Dragon' by Brian Patten from NOTES TO THE HURRYING MAN, published by and reprinted by permission of HarperCollins Publishers; 'The Terrible Path' by Brian Patten from GARGLING WITH JELLY, © Brian Patten, 1985, published by Viking Kestrel and Puffin Books; 'I Cannot Give the Reason' by Mervyn Peake from A BOOK OF NONSENSE, reprinted by permission of Peter Owen Publishers, London; 'The Frivolous Cake' from TITUS GROAN, published by Methuen and reprinted by permission of David Higham Associates; 'Sensitive, Seldom and Sad' by Mervyn Peake from RHYMES WITHOUT REASON, published by Methuen and reprinted by permission of David Higham Associates; 'Autumn' by Marina Plentl, an award-winning entry in the 1990 W H Smith Young Writers' Competition and was first published in YOUNG WORDS; 'Beware: Do Not Read This Poem' by Ishmael Reed from CATECHISM OF A NEO AMERICAN HOODOO CHURCH, reprinted by permission of Abner Stein; 'Surfers' by Jeremy Reed from BY THE FISHERIES, published by Jonathan Cape and reprinted by permission of The Random Century Group; 'Big Wind' by Theodore Roethke from THE COLLECTED POEMS OF THEODORE ROETHKE, published by and reprinted by permission of

Scholastic Publications Ltd; 'Caring for Animals' by Jon Silkin from SELECTED POEMS published by Routledge, 1988; 'Jungle Husband' by Stevie Smith from THE COLLECTED POEMS OF STEVIE SMITH (PENGUIN 20TH CENTURY CLASSICS) and reprinted by permission of James MacGibbon; 'The King of Quizzical Island' by Gordon Snell, published by and reprinted by permission of John Johnson (authors agent) Limited; 'All Over the World' © Dr Christina Starobin; '1945' by Geoffrey Summerfield from WELCOME, published by Andre Deutsch and reprinted by permission of Scholastic Publications Ltd; 'Fern Hill' by Dylan Thomas from THE POEMS, published by Dent and reprinted by permission of David Higham Associates; 'Stone Speech' by Charles Tomlinson from COLLECTED POEMS (1985), reprinted by permission of Oxford University Press; 'The Lion' and 'Romance' by W J Turner from SELECTED POEMS 1916-36, published by Oxford University Press; 'As the Cat' 'The Dance' and 'To a Poor Old Woman' by William Carlos Williams from THE COLLECTED POEMS, reprinted by permission of Carcanet Press Ltd; 'Grandad' by Kit Wright from RABBITTING ON, published by Fontana Lions, an imprint of HarperCollins Publishers and reprinted by permission of HarperCollins Publishers; 'Greedyguts' by Kit Wright from HOTDOG AND OTHER STORIES copyright © Kit Wright 1981, published by Viking Kestrel and Puffin Books.

Index *of* Poets

INDEX *of* FIRST LINES

Now that you have your European rail pass,
you'll need somewhere to stay!

Whether you are visiting one city or twenty – *roomkey.com* **can help you find the perfect room, in the best location and at a great price.** Booking is quick and easy with over 15,000 European hotels ranging from ultrabudget to ultrachic.

Visit **www.roomkey.com**
to book your accommodations today!

Enjoy your vacation without having to worry about where you're going to stay once you get there. Book your rooms from the comfort of your own home easily and securely with one of Europe's largest accommodation wholesalers.

Britain *by* BritRail

2005

Touring Britain by Train

Twenty-Fifth Edition

written by
LaVerne Ferguson-Kosinski

edited by
Matthew Palma
Adam Price

rail schedules by
Adam Price

The
Globe
Pequot
Press

GUILFORD, CONNECTICUT

Copyright © 1980, 1981, 1982, 1983, 1984, 1985, 1986, 1987, 1988, 1989, 1990, 1991, 1992, 1993, 1994, 1995, 1997, 1998 by George Wright and LaVerne P. Ferguson; 1999 by LaVerne P. Ferguson; 2000, 2001, 2002, 2003, 2004, 2005 by LaVerne P. Ferguson-Kosinski

The author and the publisher gratefully acknowledge the kind permission of Eurostar Passenger Services and its Web site, Deutsche Bahn and its Web site, Brittany Ferries, Hoverspeed UK Limited, Irish Ferries U.K. Limited, P&O Stena Line, SeaFrance Limited, DFDS Seaways, and Stena Line to use their resources in the compilation of the timetables in this text.

Text design: *osprey*design

ISSN 1081-1117
ISBN 0-7627-3437–X

Manufactured in the United States of America
Twenty-Fifth Edition/First Printing

About the Author

LaVerne Ferguson-Kosinski and her former husband, Lt. Col. George Ferguson, first coauthored this unique and comprehensive how-to guide in 1980.

After battling a long illness, George, who was globally and affectionately known as "Mr. Eurail," passed away in 1997 and was buried at Arlington National Cemetery.

LaVerne wanted to ensure that accurate British and European rail travel information would continue to be available. She is devoted to producing comprehensive, practical, yet friendly guidebooks for the independent rail traveler or armchair dreamer. Her technical writing and editorial background, academic education in English, world history, and communications, plus her experience in research and development for an international research institute, have added considerable substance to her twenty-nine years of traveling the rails in Britain and Europe.

Her dream of exploring the world began in third-grade geography class when she first began collecting travel brochures. After attending Ohio State University, LaVerne lived in and traveled throughout Europe. She resides in Fort Myers Beach, Florida, with her husband, Joe "Cool" Kosinski, a structural engineer.

LaVerne thanks her entire family, especially husband, Joe, and son, Matthew Palma, whose expertise and support of her career have been invaluable in enabling her to continue writing both *Britain by BritRail* and *Europe by Eurail*.

Heartfelt thanks and appreciation also go to you, the readers, whose comments, suggestions, and corrections help keep both guidebooks accurate and up to date. Send them directly to:

LaVerne Ferguson-Kosinski
c/o RailPass.com
2737 Sawbury Boulevard
Columbus, OH 43235
E-mail: laverne@railpass.com
Web site: www.railpass.com

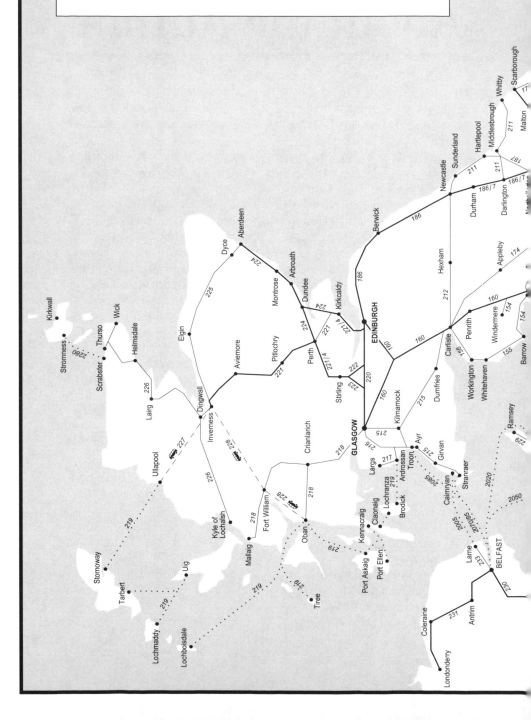

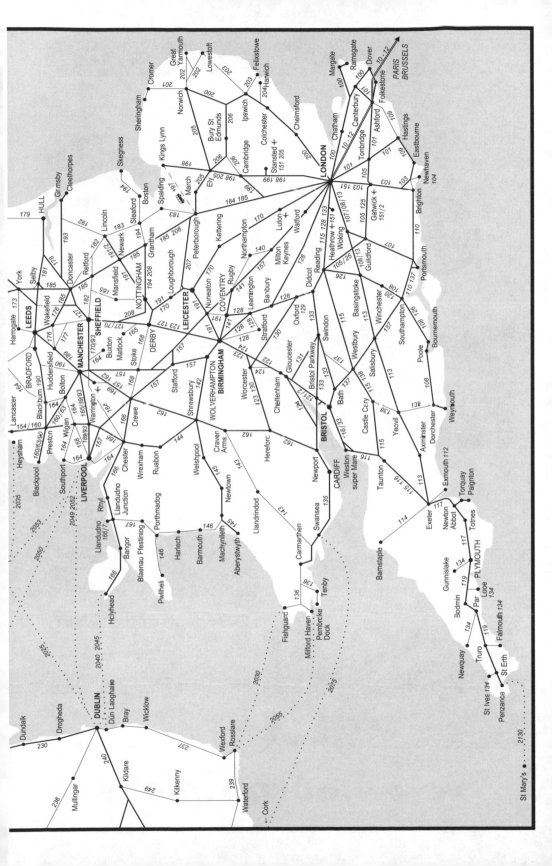

Contents

Scotland 165
Rail Travel in Scotland

Arriving by Air—Arriving by Train—Getting around in Edinburgh—
Enticing Edinburgh—Day Excursions—Train Connections to
Other Base Cities from Edinburgh

Arriving by Air—Arriving by Train—Glasgow Central Station—
Queen Street Station—Glasgow Gazette—Glasgow Connections to Day
Excursions—Train Connections to Other Base Cities from Glasgow

Wales 223
Rail Travel in Wales

Appendix

About RailPass.com

Author LaVerne Ferguson-Kosinski is the founder and former Chief Executive Officer of RailPass.com, previously known as RailPass Express.

An extraordinary small-business success story, what became Rail Pass. com was created in 1980 from a humble beginning in the Fergusons' home—with a couple of desks, a toll-free telephone number, and a singular idea to provide the best customer service for the independent traveler. Incorporated in 1986 by the Fergusons, RailPass.com blossomed into one of the world's largest independent, consumer-focused European railpass sales outlets.

The expertly trained (yes, pun intended) and well-traveled staff at RailPass.com provides the informational resources and travel products necessary to pursue the concepts and itineraries as outlined in the guidebooks. The team of international researchers shares LaVerne's enthusiasm for the exciting world of train travel—its comfort, speed, and continuous adventure—and is devoted to producing a comprehensive, practical-yet-friendly guidebook to touring Britain by train:

Matthew Palma, president of RailPass.com, has long provided valuable input for the guidebooks *Britain by BritRail* and *Europe by Eurail,* as well as strategic business planning to keep RailPass.com on the right track. As LaVerne's son, Matt had the privilege of growing up in the British and European rail travel business and participated in his first group tour of Europe at the age of nine.

Mary Kish, general manager, devotes her excellent managerial and business acuity to RailPass.com. She is instrumental in streamlining operations and keeping RailPass.com moving at high speed while making customer service standards even better.

Lesley Tate, financial assistant, integrates operational systems and procedures and attends to customer service overflow.

Sheila Clowes is the "Lady of the Lines" on the RailPass.com voice-mail system. Originally from London, England, she is our "resident expert" on all things British. Actually, her official title is training coordinator, and we credit her with maintaining the highest-quality customer service standards in our representatives.

Ellen Byrnes heads the train reservations and information department. She has traveled most of Europe and is full of globe-trotting stories and expertise. Assisting her are **Susan Beougher** and **Lesley Tate.** As rail reservation and information specialists, they decipher complicated point-to-point timetables for the best and most convenient trains, schedules, and itineraries. They love to share travel stories while assisting travelers. They also offer tours, including luxury train tours, and group rates and discounts. Visit www.railpass.com on the Internet or call (877) RAILPASS (877–724–5727) toll-free for an enjoyable and easy way to book a tour, to order rail passes or point-to-point tickets, or to make seat and sleeper reservations.

We extend our thanks to Jean Heger of Rail Europe Group; Tim Roebuck, Anthony O'Rawe, and the entire staff of ACP Marketing; Raffaela Essayan, Frank Berardi, David Breuer, Bill Schroeder, and the entire staff of CIT Tours; our many friends in the British Tourist Authority; our travel partner professionals throughout Britain and Europe; and, most of all, the many readers who help to keep us up to date.

In the Beginning

"My heart is warm with the friends I make,
And better friends I'll not be knowing;
Yet there isn't a train I wouldn't take
No matter where it's going."
—Edna St. Vincent Millay

Like thousands of other discerning visitors, you are about to learn that the British rail system offers a delightful way of traveling throughout the length and breadth of Europe's only English-speaking nation—Britain. So welcome aboard *Britain by BritRail!* You are embarking on a unique and rewarding traveling experience.

Train travel is an anomaly for most Americans. Millions of Americans have either forgotten or have never had the opportunity to learn what travel by train can be like. The British and Europeans' outlook on train travel is different. They need trains for transport; thus, they have created trains with the simplest and yet most extravagant amenities of their culture. In so doing, they provide fast, economical, and often elegant modes of transportation.

Britain is a rather compact nation. It's about two-thirds the size of California or approximately one-third larger than the New England area of Maine, Vermont, New Hampshire, Massachusetts, Rhode Island, and Connecticut—the North American area to which Britain has contributed much of its heritage since Colonial days.

This twenty-fifth edition of *Britain by BritRail* encompasses rail travel in England, Scotland, and Wales. Although the Republic of Ireland and Northern Ireland are, of course, a part of the British Isles, Ireland's railways do not accept the BritRail Pass. They do, however, accept the BritRail Pass + Ireland add-on, which provides for rail travel within England, Scotland, Wales, Northern Ireland, and the Republic of Ireland.

The Republic of Ireland also accepts Eurail passes. For rail travel information about the Republic of Ireland, please consult *Europe by Eurail: Touring Europe by Train* or our Web site, www.railpass.com.

In Britain, you'll find more than 18,700 trains traveling to more than 2,500 destinations daily. The service is so frequent that if you miss a train, chances are you won't have to wait more than a half hour to an hour for another. The British frequently seize such an opportunity to nip into a nearby pub for a quick pint and a game of darts. So follow the adage "When in Rome, do as the Romans do." After all, Britain inherited some of Rome's customs too!

Aboard a British train, the driver (that's what the British call their train engineers) takes care of all the driving while you sip a beverage, enjoy an uninterrupted view of the countryside, and stretch out in a comfortable seat. You may even respond to "nature's call" at your own option rather than waiting for the closest petrol (gas) station.

Few places in Britain cannot be reached by train. By employing the base cities of London, England; Edinburgh or Glasgow in Scotland; or Cardiff in Wales, the splendor of Windsor Castle, the legendary Loch Ness Monster, or the natural beauty of Swansea Bay is an easy, comfortable train ride away.

London is a tourist magnet, but despite what other writers say, London is not Britain. A visit to Britain that does not include at least a few days in the countryside is unthinkable. Britain has some of the most beautiful countryside in the world. The mountains may not be a match in size to the Alps, and the seas not azure blue like the Mediterranean, but all of this is offset by a magical quality of green so peaceful and picturesque that, in a mere glance, the visitor becomes aware that he or she is seeing history.

How to Use *Britain by BritRail*

Britain by BritRail is the perfect traveling companion for visitors using the BritRail Pass. This guidebook is written to provide detailed train-related information to readers in a direct, pragmatic manner. *Britain by BritRail* is devoted to the visitor who goes to Britain expecting its train services to provide the necessary transportation for a holiday that is exciting and different. We have gone ahead of you, probed what can be done, and solved the problems of doing it long before you arrive. We personally experience every city and day excursion, and our researchers pledge to constantly recheck and revise subsequent editions. This is accomplished by personal visits and through a British and European network of correspondents.

Britain by BritRail presents a concept for comfortable, unhurried travel by train in Britain. By utilizing the economy of a BritRail Pass, along with the innovative, fully described Base City–Day Excursion method, you really see Britain at its best—by train.

This book helps to introduce and establish the reader in the base cities of London, Edinburgh, Glasgow, and Cardiff. Establish yourself in affordable, comfortable accommodations. Then, when you have finished your sightseeing and shopping in the base city, let *Britain by BritRail* guide you to recommended day excursions. For the most part, these interesting places are based on train schedules and geographic locations that assure your return each night to the same hotel room. With a BritRail Pass and a current copy of this book, you become your own tour guide and avoid the constant packing and unpacking that accompanies most bus tours attempting to cover the same territory. *You* call the shots and set the pace.

Britons and their continental cousins have employed rail services for "holidaymaking" for decades. Train travel is too fast for any possible chance of boredom setting in, yet it is leisurely enough to enjoy fully the constantly changing scene of hills and hamlets, farms and forests, countrysides and cities—everything that forms Britain's fascinating landscape.

Should you pause to ponder why, for example, the English leave their cars at home when they're "off on holiday," you will find the answer very quickly when your train parallels a major highway or flashes across a bridge through the center of a British city. The superhighways—right down to the ancient, narrow streets—are packed with vehicles, all proceeding at a much slower pace than you and your train.

In the chapters describing the base cities and day excursions, *Britain by BritRail* meets you upon arrival at the base-city airport or train station, then leads you step by step to those essential facilities such as tourist information sources, currency exchanges, and hotel accommodations.

Britain by BritRail does not include comprehensive hotel listings, but it does include quaint bed-and-breakfasts and personally selected hotels convenient to the rail services. The primary purpose, insofar as accommodations are concerned, is to point out the most convenient tourist information center or hotel booking (reservations) facility and how to get there.

Restaurants are treated in the same manner. We appreciate good food and good service. With few exceptions, however, the choice of what to eat and where to find it remains the option of the reader perusing the wealth of excellent publications catering to this most worthy pursuit. We do, however, include some of our own personal recommendations.

Each day-excursion section begins with the distance and average train time for the trip, along with the tourist information office location and hours of operation. You'll also find explicit walking or easy transport directions on how to get from the train station to the city tourist information office.

Readers requiring advance information regarding the base cities should contact the closest British Tourist Authority office listed in the Appendix of this edition, or visit the BTA Web site on the Internet at www.visitbritain.com. Country and individual city contacts and Web sites are included in each chapter and in the Appendix.

Train schedules in Britain and those appearing in this edition are shown in twenty-four-hour style. For example, a train departing at 1935 leaves at 7:35 P.M. Schedules between the base cities of London, Edinburgh, Glasgow, and Cardiff are included with each base-city description. This particular information should prove helpful when you are initially planning your BritRail trip.

Train schedules for the day-excursion trips out of the base cities are also provided in the text describing each day excursion. With a few exceptions for overnight excursions, we chose trains departing from the base cities on morning schedules and trains returning from the day excursions usually in the late afternoon or early evening.

Please remember the timetables and schedules appearing in this edition are provided for planning purposes only. Every care has been taken to make the timetables and schedules correct at printing, and the information is checked with authoritative sources up to press time. *Britain by BritRail* and/or its publisher cannot, however, be held responsible for the consequences of either changes or inadvertent inaccuracies.

Current rail schedules are posted in all British rail stations. Timetables from the base cities to each day-excursion point are available free for the asking in the base-city train stations. Please consult them. You may also visit the point-to-point rail schedule pages of www.railpass.com, www.railtrack.co.uk, or www.nationalrail.co.uk, or call (877) RAILPASS (877–724–5727).

Planning a BritRail Trip

A plan is often defined as "a program of action." Plans vary in detail and complexity, according to the nature of the user. We have observed two general types of rail travelers: one conservative, the other adventurous. One traveler may require a detailed, hour-by-hour schedule for each day's activities; another may merely plan to get up in the morning and see what the day brings.

One of the first questions to answer when planning a trip is "When can I go, and how much time can I spend?" In Britain, April through October are the most popular months for tourists and for many events; plus during the Christmas and New Year's holidays, London literally sparkles.

When planning your trip, take British bank holidays into consideration because banks, postal services, and most shops and many attractions are closed, and some transportation services are reduced. Bank holidays include New Year's Day, Good Friday, Easter Sunday, Easter Monday, May Day, Spring Holiday, Queen's Official Birthday, Summer Holiday, Christmas Day, and Boxing Day. (See the "2005 Bank and Public Holidays" section in the Appendix.)

Whether you admit it or not, everyone has a problem budgeting vacation time. Human nature is to try to see as much as possible in as little time as possible. This "sightseers' syndrome" could be dangerous to your vacation. Avoid it by planning an itinerary that allows ample free time. Also, vary the day excursions by going on a short one following a particularly long outing away from the base city. Press too hard by trying to see and do too much and you will return home looking as if you desperately need another vacation.

How long should your BritRail tour be? There are many factors bearing on such a determination. How much annual vacation time do you have? How do you use it—all at one time or in two or more segments? BritRail Passes can accommodate just about anyone's personal needs, with consecutive passes ranging from eight days to one month of travel and flexible passes ranging from four to fifteen days of travel in two months. BritRail Passes permit travel on all scheduled British trains.

Even if you don't have two weeks or more for a grand tour of Britain, travel magazines and the travel sections of the Sunday newspapers are usually loaded with one-week bargain air fares to almost anywhere, Britain and mainland Europe included. By coupling our Base City–Day Excursion mode of easy travel with a four-day BritRail Flexipass, you can maximize the time you do have to spend in Britain.

Once you know how much time you have for your BritRail trip, the next step is to develop a clear idea of where you want to go in Britain, what you want to see, and what you want to do. Develop your objectives well before your departure date. We disagree with those who believe that anticipation of travel is more rewarding than its realization. But we do agree that the planning phase can also be a fun part of your trip. Properly done, this "homework" will pay substantial dividends when your travel actually begins.

To get things started, write to, e-mail, or telephone the British Tourist Authority (BTA) at (800) GO 2 BRIT (800–462–2748) for information. (BTA office addresses in North America are listed in the Appendix.) Be specific. In your request, indicate when you will be going, where you wish to go within Britain, and what in particular you would like to see. If you have any special interests or hobbies, be sure to mention them in your request. By spelling out your information needs, you will obtain better responses.

Don't overlook the Internet and your local library as valuable information sources. Travelers who have computers and access to the Internet can do an incredible amount of research and planning in the comfort of their own homes or offices. The great "information highway" is at your disposal.

You may want to start with some basic Web sites about Britain in general, then do subject-specific searches. For example, to obtain general information on Britain, start with the British Tourist Authority's Web site: www.visitbritain.com. Other sources of information may be found in the Appendix of this edition, including city tourist information sites. If you want to know more about British rail travel and BritRail Passes, or to request a free Info Pack, call toll-free (877) RAILPASS (877–724–5727); or write to RailPass.com, 2737 Sawbury Boulevard, Columbus, OH 43235; or check out the Web site at www.railpass.com.

Seek out friends and neighbors who have been to Britain. No doubt you'll find their experiences flavored by their own likes and dislikes.

Nevertheless, any and all information gathered prior to your trip will eventually find its place in your memory bank. You'll find yourself recalling many of these fragments of information during your own journey.

Now comes the decisive phase of your trip planning—constructing an itinerary. The moment of truth is at hand! Your only limitation during this portion of the planning phase is the lack of more than twenty-four hours in a day.

Draw a blank calendar-style form covering a period from at least one week prior to your departure to a few days following your return. Make extra copies of the form—you'll need them. (Perfection is a long time coming in this project!) Begin to block your itinerary into calendar form, being mindful that the itinerary can be changed, but the number of days in a week remains fixed at all times. Possibly by the third time through the exercise, you'll begin to "see the light at the end of the tunnel." Remember, it is only human to try to cram too many activities into a day, but better to discover planning errors before starting your trip rather than during the middle of it.

With your itinerary in a calendar format, you can determine housing requirements, seat and sleeper reservations, and the other facets of your forthcoming trip. The days blocked out in advance of your departure show your "countdown" items, such as stopping the newspaper, having mail held at the post office, getting prescriptions filled, taking pets to the kennel, shopping, arranging legal documents and credit cards, and so on. Make several copies of your completed itinerary, and leave some behind for the folks with whom you want to stay in touch. Above all, take copies of your itinerary with you—you'll refer to them frequently.

If there have been any break-ins in your neighborhood, you should take steps to ensure it doesn't happen to you while you are gone. Alert the neighbors to keep a watchful eye for suspicious people and their activities. Many professional thieves have been known to park in a driveway in broad daylight with a moving van. The police should be advised regarding your absence. Check with the insurance agency that writes your homeowners policy. Ask the same question they ask in those television commercials: "Am I covered?" You may need additional coverage during your absence. Some travelers have a trusted friend or family member "housesit" while abroad. This option eliminates having to stop the paper and mail, and perhaps even sending Fluffy to the kennel. One final caution: Don't announce your forthcoming vacation or honeymoon plans in the newspapers. Many thieves can read too. Save the social column for your return.

U.S. citizens are required to have a passport to be admitted into Britain; a visa is not necessary. If you do not have a passport or if yours has expired, write immediately to one of the U.S. passport offices listed in the Appendix. Allow about six weeks to obtain your passport. There are ways to expedite the process by going online to **www.passportsand visas.com,** at a substantially higher cost. Passport Services through the U.S. Department of State, Bureau of Consular Affairs offers the brochure *Passports: Applying for Them the Easy Way.* Call the National Passport Information Center (NPIC) at (900) 225–5674 or (888) 362–8668 to request the pamphlet, to receive applications, or to check on passport status or emergency passport procedures. See "Passport Info" in the Appendix.

Travel Economy

"Know before you go," the slogan of the U.S. Customs Service concerning what you may return with, also applies to the financial aspects of vacation planning. The fluctuation of the dollar's purchasing power abroad over the past few years has left a lot of us wondering whether or not we could afford a vacation on the other side of the Atlantic. It is sometimes difficult to determine what effect Britain's inflation will have on your dollars once you're there.

Advance planning pays off. Purchasing most of your vacation needs in advance (particularly transportation) in American dollars is probably the most effective way to combat inflation and price fluctuations. Buy as much of your vacation needs before you go, and plan to limit your out-of-pocket costs paid in foreign currency to a minimum. In this way, you are protected against fluctuating currency values.

Train travel in Britain is one of the best means of effectively stabilizing your travel dollars. Prepayment plans, such as the BritRail Pass, are ideal. Not only do you purchase the pass with American dollars prior to departure, but the BritRail Pass also provides the most inexpensive way to travel in Britain—the quickest too! Order an economical BritRail Pass by calling BritRail's sales outlet, RailPass.com, at (877) RAILPASS (877–724–5727) (secured online ordering address: www.railpass.com).

Most travel agents still have a penchant for wanting to sell a "fly-drive" program to clients who want to vacation in Britain. But, in general, car rentals have one basic flaw—the price you see is not the price you pay; it always seems to be higher. As a general rule, add to the quoted price another 20 percent for personal accident insurance, collision insurance, and taxes. After that, consider fuel costs at about three times that of fuel in the United States. Don't forget about the 17.5 percent value-added tax (VAT). Remember, driving is on the left in Britain.

Accommodations usually account for the greatest share of a traveler's budget. Low-cost air fares and transportation bargains like the BritRail Pass can get the traveler to and around Britain, but the real bite out of the buck comes when the visitor pays for a night's lodging. Attractively priced accommodations packages are being offered by some tour operators, but too few suit the needs of individual itineraries, as is the case for travelers on a BritRail vacation. With advance planning and advance payment, however, you can realize significant savings if you are willing to put forth the extra time and effort to do your homework.

Well ahead of your intended departure date—preferably two months in advance, but no less than six weeks—write, call, or visit the Web sites of one of the British Tourist Authority (BTA) offices listed in the Appendix of this edition, or contact the tourist offices of your specific destination and request information regarding lodging (including the bed-and-breakfasts) in the areas you intend to visit during your BritRail journey. You may make reservations, or "bookings," as the British call them, in a variety of ways.

The best assurance you will have a room waiting upon arrival is to make an advance deposit directly to the hotel, then take care of the balance with the hotel's cashier when checking out. Always ask the hotel to confirm the room rate upon check-in, and be sure to ask what is included in the rate (for example, is breakfast included?). This will avoid delays and possible financial embarrassment when leaving.

One final bit of advice on reducing the cost of accommodations in Britain: Use your BritRail Pass. Too many of us overlook the fact that the BritRail Pass can actually provide exceptional savings in housing costs by permitting you to stay *outside* the base city's center, where hotel rooms, pensions, bed-and-breakfasts, and the like are far less expensive than their in-town counterparts.

London particularly lends itself to such a suburban arrangement because there are many areas outside the city's center that are readily accessible by rail. Anytime downtown accommodations become difficult to find, or too demanding on the budget, tell the housing people you have a BritRail Pass and can easily stay in the suburbs.

Staying in London's northern or western suburbs has other advantages too. From many of the suburban stations, you can board a fast InterCity train for a day excursion without ever going into a London terminus. You can return to the suburbs in the evening, too, without becoming involved in London's rush hours.

Watford Junction, 16 miles from London's Euston Station, is one of the stations in London's suburbs that offers excellent InterCity connections to such day-excursion points as Birmingham and Coventry, as well as the base city of Glasgow. Most InterCity departures from Euston Station on weekday mornings pick up at Watford Junction sixteen minutes later. On weekday evenings, most InterCity trains set down at Watford Junction twenty minutes ahead of their arrival times in Euston Station.

Going to St. Albans, Perth, or the base cities of Edinburgh and

Cardiff, we recommend transferring to King's Cross or Paddington from Euston to continue the trip.

Other rail points in London suburbs are Luton, for direct rail connections to Nottingham and Sheffield; Stevenage, along the main line to Edinburgh via York; and Slough or Reading, for connections to Bath as well as the Welsh cities of Cardiff and Swansea.

There are times when accommodations in the base cities are very limited. Edinburgh, during its annual Military Tattoo and Festival every August, is an excellent example. Lodgings in the suburbs, a la BritRail Pass, can be more economical and just as convenient as those in the base cities. If you have your heart set on lodgings in London, when inquiring as to availability you will be asked the inevitable question "What do you want to be near to?" Naturally, when you're traveling by rail, your response will be, "The rail station." You are in for a surprise: At last count, London had seventeen primary rail stations. Because these terminals rim the vast, sprawling city, a better site-selection statement would be to ask for a hotel near one of the major lines of the Underground (the "Tube").

How to Get There

Transatlantic air traffic is so frequent and varied today that no description of it—short of an entire book—could do it justice. Excursion fares are available in a multitudinous variety. Charter flights are available too, but some excursion rates are less expensive than charters. On a regularly scheduled airliner winging its way to Europe, it is not uncommon to find every passenger in your row of seats paid a different fare for the same flight with the same service.

We refer readers to their travel agents for airline tickets. Since many airlines no longer pay commissions to travel agents, you may have to pay a service fee. If you've dealt with a reputable travel agency over the years, contact it for air-excursion fare options. Or, if you have lots of time, you can call the various airlines' toll-free telephone numbers and ask them for fare information or visit their Web sites. We have listed contact information for a few airlines in the Appendix. Don't be disturbed if you receive a variety of responses. Sift them out until you find what you're looking for. Internet users can search online for those bargain fares with consolidators, travel portals, and the actual airlines as well.

Regarding charter flights, inquire about them but investigate thoroughly before making any final decisions. Here again, get your travel agent involved, even if it's only to obtain the tickets. Even some of the most reputable air-charter carriers still operate on a "Go–No Go" basis. This means that if enough passengers sign up for the flight, it will go as scheduled; if there are not enough passengers booked, the flight will be scrubbed. Look up the airline in your phone book, or dial (800) 555–1212 and tell the operator the name of the airline information office with which you wish to speak, or use the search engines on the Internet to find specific Web addresses.

BritRail Passes

A BritRail Pass provides unlimited train travel for a specified number of days in England, Scotland, and Wales. You don't have to purchase a rail pass to travel by train in Britain; having one, however, is very convenient and economical. For example, with a BritRail Pass, you do not have to purchase a rail ticket every time you want to make a trip somewhere by train. Just board any train going your way and travel whenever, wherever, and as often as you like throughout the period your BritRail Pass is valid.

BritRail Passes are not available in Britain and must be purchased in North America prior to departure. You may order directly from BritRail's U.S. sales agent, RailPass.com, toll-free at (877) RAILPASS (877–724–5727); secured online ordering is available at www.railpass.com. You may also purchase some of the passes through some travel agents. A list of British and European rail passes and their corresponding prices at press time is available in the Appendix.

Visitors to Britain should consider purchasing a BritRail Pass if they plan to travel primarily by train. To help you decide whether or not to purchase a rail pass, we have included a selection of British one-way rail fares in the Appendix. Compare the individual fares for your itinerary with the cost of the type of BritRail Pass best for your trip or go online to **www.railsaver.com.**

Keep in mind when comparing the point-to-point rail fares to the cost of the rail pass that convenience has a value too. Standing in line ("queuing") to purchase train tickets is an inconvenience that can be avoided. With a BritRail Pass, you need do this only once—when you validate your pass at the station.

Even short-time visitors to the British Isles may find it advantageous to purchase a BritRail Pass in lieu of point-to-point tickets. For example, the cost of point-to-point tickets for a circuitous journey—like a quick dash out of London for a look around Edinburgh and Bath—exceeds the cost of an eight-day first-class or standard-class adult BritRail Classic Pass. The economy of the pass becomes immediately apparent when doing such comparisons. Also, consider the London–Edinburgh–Bath–London circuit could be made comfortably in as little as three days, leaving five more days of unlimited rail travel available to the pass holder. Even if you could not extend your stay, you would still save money, in this case, by purchasing a BritRail Pass.

BritRail Passes are available for first- or standard-class rail travel. First-class seats are wider; consequently, first-class coaches are more spacious since they accommodate fewer passengers. BritRail's standard class, however, is also very comfortable. Some trains in Britain have entirely standard-class carriages. One thing in common to both classes is the view. Whether in first or standard class, you can lounge ensconced in comfort while watching the countryside glide by. Expand your horizons—don't leave home without a rail pass!

When traveling in Britain on certain peak days, holidays, or summer Saturdays, seat reservations are recommended. You may make them at most rail stations or at the rail counters in Heathrow, Gatwick, Birmingham, and Manchester Airports by giving destination and departure times of the train (train numbers are not used in Britain). Although you can make seat reservations in the United States after purchasing a BritRail Pass (at least two weeks prior to departure is necessary), it is more economical to make them in Britain.

RailPass.com may book seat reservations for travel trips in Britain of more than two and a half hours. Please call (877) RAILPASS (877–724–5727) for more information. Trips less than two and a half hours and overnight sleeper trains must be booked in Britain directly.

There are two basic types of passes to choose from: BritRail Classic Pass and BritRail Flexipass. Prices are listed in the Appendix.

BritRail Classic Pass. The Classic Pass offers unlimited consecutive-day rail travel in England, Scotland, and Wales. Choose to travel for four, eight, fifteen, or twenty-two days or one month. The BritRail Senior Classic Pass (available to adults age sixty and older) offers a discount off the first-class BritRail Adult Classic Pass. The BritRail Youth Classic Pass is available in standard class only for those age sixteen through twenty-five.

BritRail Flexipass. This pass provides exactly what its name implies: flexibility. Travel on any four, eight, or fifteen days within the two-month validity period in either first or standard class. Unlike the Classic Pass, your travel days need not be consecutive, thus enabling you to stay in your favorite location for several days until you continue your journey.

A BritRail Senior Flexipass (age sixty and older) offers first-class rail travel at a discount off the adult BritRail Flexipass price. A Youth Flexipass (age sixteen through twenty-five) is available in standard class only for any four, eight, or fifteen days of travel within a two-month period.

BritRail Family Pass. With the purchase of one adult or senior pass, one accompanying child (age five through fifteen) gets a pass of the same type and duration free. Passes for additional children may be purchased at a 50 percent discount off the regular adult pass price. Children younger than age five travel free. The BritRail Family Pass program is available with BritRail Classic, BritRail Flexipass, BritRail Senior, BritRail Pass 'n Drive, BritRail Pass + Ireland, and BritRail Party Pass.

BritRail Party Pass. Offers a 50 percent discount on the third and fourth person's pass when parties of three or four passengers are traveling together at all times. Applies to the BritRail Classic and Flexipass, first class, adult and senior only.

BritRail Pass 'n Drive. Although Britain's compactness makes it convenient to take the train and see the sights, there are a few nooks and crannies that cannot be reached by train. Those who want to combine the thrill of driving on the left-hand side of the road with rail travel can opt for the BritRail Pass 'n Drive. Use the fast, comfortable British trains for the longer journeys and the freedom of a rental car to explore the beautiful British countryside.

First, purchase your BritRail Pass 'n Drive voucher from (877) RAIL PASS (877–724–5727) or www.railpass.com. The price includes a BritRail Flexipass for unlimited rail travel (choice of first or standard class) for any two days within a two-month period and car rental vouchers for any three days within the same period. Then, at least seven days prior to departure, telephone Hertz toll-free at (800) 654–3001 to reserve your first car rental date. Be certain to state that you have already purchased a BritRail Pass 'n Drive and mention the program code IT-BRIT. Reservations should be made as soon as possible, particularly if you want a car with an automatic transmission. For the remainder of your car rental reservations, Hertz has rental offices at rail stations throughout England, Scotland, and Wales.

Since your car rental vouchers may be used only during the validity period of your BritRail Flexipass, the most economical way of utilizing them is to arrange for a car to meet your train at a day-excursion point, do your exploring, and return the car to the same station before returning to your base city by train. Prebooked requests for a car to meet your train will be honored seven days a week, but note that some Hertz offices are closed on Sundays.

Each car rental voucher includes a twenty-four-consecutive-hour rental with unlimited mileage, no drop-off charge, and government tax (VAT) of 17.5 percent. The renter is responsible for collision damage, personal accident insurance, gasoline, and road tax. Payment of these charges may be made by credit card or a deposit at the start of each rental period. Aside from gasoline, other additional charges are a minimum of approximately $15 (U.S.) per day. The BritRail Pass 'n Drive option rates are based on two adults per car; the pass for a third or fourth person is offered at a reduced rate.

BritRail Pass + Ireland. For unlimited travel on the rail networks of Britain, Northern Ireland, and Irish Rail, this is the pass for you. The price also includes one round-trip ferry crossing on the Stena ferry services (within the validity of your pass) between Holyhead and Dun Laoghaire, Fishguard and Rosslare, or Stranraer and Belfast. The round-trip sea crossing need not be done from the same port. The BritRail Pass + Ireland is available for any five or ten days of travel within a one-month period in either first or standard class (no senior or youth discounts; children younger than age five travel free; one free child's pass, age five through fifteen, with purchase of adult pass).

BritRail England Consecutive Pass. Valid for unlimited travel on England's rail network for four, eight, fifteen, or twenty-two days or one month in either first or standard class. Includes transportation from Heathrow, Gatwick, or Stansted Airports, but it counts as one day of travel on your pass. Special youth, senior, and family rates.

BritRail England Flexipass. Valid for unlimited four, eight, fifteen, twenty-two, or thirty days of flexible (non-consecutive) rail travel in a two-month period throughout England (Scotland and Wales not included) in either first or standard class. Includes transportation from Heathrow, Gatwick, or Stansted airports, but it counts as one day of travel on your pass. Special youth, senior, and family rates. Youth age sixteen to twenty-five. Senior age sixty and older. Family passes allow one child to travel free with each adult. Party passes allow 50 percent discount for the third or fourth person traveling in a group.

BritRail Days Out of London Pass. Casual, short-term, or business visitors to Britain may benefit from this special flexible rail pass tucked in their pocket before leaving home. The Days Out of London Pass offers unlimited rail travel throughout a large portion of southern England for any two or four days out of an eight-day period or for any seven days within a fifteen-day period. Choose first- or standard-class rail travel; special youth rates are applicable. *The pass is* **not** *valid for travel on London Underground, Heathrow Express, Gatwick Express, or Stansted Express services.* It does not extend to Bath and is not valid on First Great Western Trains services.

The **London Visitor Travelcard** provides access to the London Underground (subway, or "Tube," as the Britons say) and red double-decker buses for three, four, or seven days. The **Central Zone Travelcard** is valid for travel in London's two inner zones; the **All Zone Travelcard** covers all six zones, the Docklands Light Railway, and Heathrow Airport transfers.

Freedom of Scotland Travelpass. The Travelpass offers unlimited rail travel in Scotland on ScotRail's network, including travel to and from Berwick and Carlisle for any four days within an eight-day period or any eight days within a fifteen-day validity period. The pass includes transportation on all Caledonian MacBrayne and Strathclyde ferries to the islands of Scotland and a discount on some P&O ferry routes. No discounts are available for youths or seniors. Children age five through fifteen travel at half the adult fare; younger than age five travel free.

The Great British Heritage Pass. This pass provides entry to more than 600 of Britain's public and privately owned historic sites, castles, homes, and gardens, available in consecutive increments of four, seven, or fifteen days or one month.

Eurostar Plus BritRail Pass. Provides a three-day BritRail Flexipass in combination with a one-way or round-trip open ticket on Eurostar between London and Paris or London and Brussels. First class on Eurostar trains includes spacious reclining seats with meals served at your seat; standard class offers refreshments and snacks in the bar car or from the trolley cart. You receive a Eurostar voucher that must be exchanged for a ticket any time from sixty days to forty-five minutes before the date of travel (depending on availability). Eurostar vouchers may be exchanged in London Waterloo International, Paris Gare du Nord, or Brussels Midi train stations.

Travel Tips

Planning Pays Off. Careful planning is key to every successful thing we do, and planning a rail vacation in Britain is no exception.

For rail travelers, we recommend the *Thomas Cook European Timetable* (www.thomascookpublishing.com), which contains timetables covering major rail routes in Britain honoring the BritRail Pass. Copies can be purchased from RailPass.com (877) RAILPASS (877–724–5727). In Britain, the timetable may be purchased at most Thomas Cook Travel Agencies and Bureaux de Change (money exchange offices). Free rail schedules for Britain may be found online at www.railpass.com, www.railtrack.co.uk, or www.nationalrail.co.uk. Also, free schedules may be obtained at any British rail station. Plus, you may purchase the *Great Britain Railway Passenger Timetable* in rail station book stalls (however, you'll also need to buy a magnifying glass!).

How Much to Take? Half the clothes and twice the money! Obviously, practical advice would be "as little as possible." We usually tend to pack everything we conceivably might use during a vacation, lug it everywhere, use it very little, and return home with longer arms. In these days of wash-and-wear fabrics (and deodorants), this is not necessary. A good rule is to take a shoulder bag and one medium-size suitcase with wheels or two small bags. Hold to this rule, and you will have a more comfortable trip.

Regardless of how comfortable you expect the weather at your destination to be, pack a sweater. Brief cold spells in Britain are not uncommon. Stow a small pocket flashlight in your shoulder bag together with a collapsible umbrella or rain hat in the "unlikely event" that you may need them. Remember where you're going, chap!

Bring a washcloth if you normally use one; washcloths are not frequently found in hotels abroad. Take an electrical converter and adapter plugs for your appliances such as razors and hair dryers. Travel-size dual-voltage hair dryers are convenient; you only need to switch the voltage to the European 220 and add the adapter plug for Britain.

If you must take expensive jewelry with you (which we do not recommend), take a copy of its insurance appraisal as proof of purchase to customs officials upon your return. Same for watches produced by foreign manufacturers. You may have bought that solid-gold Rolex in a Saint Louis pawnshop for a song, but the customs inspector may have you singing a different tune if you can't come up with the paperwork!

If you wear prescription eyeglasses or contact lenses, take a copy of your prescription. The same applies to prescription medications. Even if you use only over-the-counter drug products, we suggest taking an adequate supply of the item in its original container. Many such products may not be available or are sold under a different label or packaging.

Cash, Cards, and Credentials. Don't carry more cash than you can afford to lose; use ATMs (automated teller machines), or carry traveler's checks. You will, of course, need both U.K. and U.S. cash to pay for tips, snacks, refreshments, and taxi fares at your arrival and departure gateways. Distribute your currency around in pockets, briefcase, money clip, and money belt. A money belt is an ideal way to carry the larger notes.

ATMs offer the best exchange rate on foreign currencies, but if you plan to use them, do your homework first. Ask your bank for a list of ATM locations in Britain and whether or not your magnetic imprint needs to be modified to work in foreign ATMs. Be certain to know your PIN number, and inquire if the bank will charge you per overseas cash withdrawal. Although U.S. banks levy surcharges for the luxury of using their machines, these charges do not extend to U.S.–issued cards at machines overseas. Remember, though, that a cash withdrawal on a credit card is like a "temporary miniloan," and there is an interest charge. Get more information online at www.visa.com or www.mastercard.com for Visa and Mastercard charge cards, or contact the issuing institution of your card directly for specific details. For ATM locations, click on www.mastercard.com/atm or www.visa.com/pd/atm.

You can avoid interest charges by using a debit card (cash withdrawals and purchases are deducted from your checking account). You probably will still pay a fee of around $2.00 per withdrawal.

If you do carry traveler's checks, cash them at the branch-bank facilities located in or near railway stations and airports. Banks and official currency-exchange services are government supervised and are required to pay the official exchange rates. Hotels and stores seldom give you the full exchange value and often add substantial service fees. Credit cards are handy for paying the larger expenses such as hotels and restaurants. The charge is converted into dollars at the applicable exchange rate on the date the charge is posted.

Make a list of credit card, traveler's check, rail pass, and airline ticket numbers that you plan to take. Leave a copy at home, and pack one in your suitcase or carry-on bag. When purchasing your BritRail Pass, inquire about Pass Protection, a type of optional travel insurance covering any unused portion of the pass in case of loss or theft while abroad. Make two copies of your passport. Leave one copy at home, and take the other one with you. Carry a certified copy of your birth certificate and a few extra passport photos. Taking the time to do this will save you days of delay on your trip if your passport is lost or stolen. If your passport is lost or stolen, report it to the local police and contact the nearest U.S. embassy or consulate.

Cameras and Film. If you plan to take an expensive foreign-made camera purchased in the United States, take the sales slip with you. Otherwise, go to a U.S. Customs Office before leaving the country and register your equipment. Carry a copy of the sales slip or the registration form with your passport, and keep a spare copy tucked away in the camera case or your shoulder bag.

Despite what airport officials tell you, electronic luggage-checking devices could fog your film. The best way to avoid it is to not have film in your camera when you go through airport security, and place unboxed film in clear plastic bags. Ask that your cameras and film be inspected by hand. Above all, do not pack film in your check-through luggage. Although special lead-lined bags are available at most camera stores, luggage is subjected to a high level of radiation, and the film may still be damaged.

The cost of color film in Britain is usually more expensive than at home. Solution? Take all the film you'll need with you. If traveling with digital cameras, the same principle applies: Bring enough disks to last your trip. If you will be taping your British adventures, bring a spare battery or two along with enough videocassettes. Not wanting to miss a shot, we found it a stress-reliever to carry the extra battery and to recharge overnight.

En Route Tips

With all the luxuries of flight that modern airplanes offer, there is still something about flying that makes it more demanding than a similar amount of time spent at home or in the office. A transatlantic trip with a minimum of incidents and inconveniences is what we're after. Here are some suggestions we've found helpful.

In-Flight Comfort. If you plan to catch some shut-eye en route, ask for a seat alongside a bulkhead. Bulkheads don't mind being leaned on, but passengers do. If you need more legroom, sit in an emergency exit row, but be prepared to accept the responsibility for being physically capable of standing and opening the exit hatch if necessary. Also, be sure your seat reclines. On some planes, the seats forward of the emergency exits do not recline. Opt for seats in the forward section of the airplane; passengers in the forward section generally experience less vibration and engine noise.

Wear loose clothing. Unfasten your shoes, but don't take them off. Your feet will swell following several hours of immobility. The best remedy is to walk the length of the aisle in the airplane every hour or so. Try deep knee bends. To reduce swelling, consider wearing elastic stockings.

Flying dehydrates your body. Drink lots of water, and watch what you mix with it—alcohol dehydrates too. Special meals for special diets are no problem with the airlines, but requests should be made at the same time as reservations.

Tax-Free Purchases. Tax-free shopping in Europe was abolished in 1999 between European Union (EU) countries. This change has little if any effect on U.S. and other non–EU travelers as long as travel is to or from a non–EU destination. The EU consists of Austria, Belgium, Cyprus, Czech Republic, Denmark, Estonia, Finland, France, Germany, Greece, Hungary, Ireland, Italy, Latvia, Lithuania, Luxembourg, Malta, Poland, Portugal, Slovakia, Slovenia, Spain, Sweden, The Netherlands, and the United Kingdom. Every international airport, as well as many ferry ports and train stations, has a "tax-free" shopping service. The routine is generally the same. You select your purchases, pay for them and add them to your carry-on luggage, find safe storage for them during the flight, then haul them off the airplane. There are variations.

For example, at JFK in New York, you select the items from a sample or catalog. The items are then delivered "for your convenience" to your departure gate for pickup. The hazards of this system are many. If the delivery person gets things mixed up and fails to make the right gate at the right time, you'll be off into the wild blue yonder sans purchases. Or, if you are late passing the pickup point, sometimes an unknown "benefactor" tries to help by taking your purchases on board the plane ahead of you. Finding this so-called benefactor can prove to be difficult.

Solution? Buy your "booty" aboard the airplane while en route. Most international airlines carry aboard a good stock of tax-free items, which you may purchase from the cabin crew. It's always best to check at the airline counter, however, to be certain that this in-flight service will be available on your particular flight.

Many airports have created specialty shopping outlets to compensate for revenue losses. Look for the British Airport Authority to be a trendsetter in this area. "Tax free," by the way, is a misused term. Many items, with the exception of alcohol and tobacco, normally may be purchased cheaper in the arrival city. The U.K. can be a bit pricey, so you may wish to purchase prior to departure. If taking any Eurostar or channel-crossing trips while abroad, the taxes are lower in Belgium and France than in Britain.

Keep in mind everything you purchase, "tax free" or otherwise, is subject to customs duty when returning home. Items shipped are processed separately. Consequently, know your quotas, and attempt to stay within them to avoid paying duty and the ensuing delays involved. Remember, honesty is always the best policy.

Prior to Landing. Fill out all the customs forms your flight attendant gives to you, and keep them with your passport and airline ticket. Keep this packet handy, but secure, until your credentials are required by the customs officials at the airport.

What to Do about Jet Lag

For North Americans, it usually takes an entire day to reach Britain by air and an entire day to return. Although the flying time aboard most jet airplanes ranges from seven to eight hours, airport to airport, it will be day two before you arrive in Britain. *Most* eastbound transatlantic flights depart at night and arrive the following morning. There is, however, limited daytime service on some airlines. The idea is to find a flight that will get you to your European destination as close as possible to bedtime according to the clock in your arrival city. Westward bound, try to get a flight as late as possible so you can go straight to bed when you arrive home in North America.

During the flight, you will be exposed to a cocktail hour, a dinner hour, a break for an after-dinner drink, followed by a full-length feature movie. In the morning, as the sun rises in the east over Britain, you'll be awakened for breakfast an hour or so before landing.

Add up the time consumed by all the scheduled events while en route, and you'll quickly conclude that your night spent in the sky over the Atlantic Ocean consisted of many things—except sleep. Even if you did manage to sleep during the entire trip instead of eating, drinking, and watching movies, your body and all its functions will be arriving in Britain a few hours after midnight by North American time. You will crave adjustment to the phenomenon known as "jet lag," which will try its best to interrupt your plans for a carefree vacation.

The following explanation of what jet lag is and some means to combat it should prove helpful to any traveler undergoing four or more hours of time change.

The human body has numerous rhythms; sleep is one of them. Even in a cave without sunlight, your body will still maintain a twenty-four-hour wake/sleep cycle. The heart rate falls to a very low ebb in the early hours of the morning, when you are usually asleep. Body temperature, which affects the mental processes, also drops during this time. Consequently, if an air traveler is transported rapidly to a time zone five or six hours ahead of that of the departure point, even though it may be eight or nine o'clock in the morning at the arrival point in local time, the traveler's body functions are at a low ebb. The result is a subpar feeling that can persist for as long as two or three days unless something corrects it.

To cope effectively with jet lag, start varying your normal sleep–eat–work pattern a week or so before your departure. If you are normally up by 7:00 A.M. and in bed around 11:00 P.M. or so, get up earlier and go to bed later for a few days. Then reverse the procedure by sleeping in a bit in the morning and going to bed ahead of your normal time. Vary your mealtimes, possibly putting off breakfast until lunchtime. This will condition your body to begin accepting changes in routines. In turn, when the big transatlantic change comes, it won't be as much of a shock on your system.

To lessen the effects of jet lag en route, avoid excessive drinking and eating. Set your watch to local time at your destination as you depart on your flight. By doing this, you subconsciously accelerate your adjustment to the new time zone in advance. For example, how many times have you looked at your watch and then realized you were hungry? After your arrival, exercise the first day by taking a vigorous walk, followed by a long nap. Then take it easy for the rest of your arrival day, and begin doing everything you normally do back home according to the new local time.

Some seasoned transatlantic travelers take even stronger precautions to avoid jet lag. They follow the rule of "no coffee, tea, food, wine, beer, or liquor" on the day of the flight to Europe. They do, however, advocate lots of fruit juices, vegetable juices, and water (no carbonated drinks). This method follows the theory that your body clock will then go on hold, waiting for you to restart it with breakfast the day you arrive in Europe. We emphasize slow and easy the first day to avoid personal crash and burn.

Resist the temptations of the airlines up to the point of breakfast and try to get some sleep. Some current studies have shown the hormone melatonin to be useful in combating jet lag, but as with any other over-the-counter drug, you should first consult your physician. And then there's the "light theory"—using a blue light source behind your elevated knee caps. Regardless of which remedies you choose, respect jet lag by taking some precautions, and you'll enjoy your vacation.

Train Travel Tips

Arriving in Britain for the first time, you may experience a confusion of terminology and learn too late that what you sought was really available throughout your visit. The problem may have merely been not knowing where to look or what to call the desired object. The following information may further ease and enhance the pleasure of your BritRail adventures.

Handicapped Travel. First know that the British rail system is a leader in providing facilities and accessibility in its stations and aboard its trains for the disabled and the handicapped. Rail travel therefore has become an increasingly chosen method of transportation and recreation for disabled persons. Many aids for the handicapped have been incorporated into rail-station design. Trains are designed with wider doors for wheelchair access; some even have a removable seat to make room for a wheelchair. Spaces for wheelchairs are at no extra charge and should be prearranged with the railway. Ramp access to toilets, buffets, and other facilities is provided. Folding wheelchairs are also available at main stations so occupants may be transferred to a regular seat once aboard the train.

Stationlink provides ramp-equipped, low-floor buses between the rail terminals and Victoria Coach Station. *Tel:* (020) 7918 4300; *E-mail:* lt.vdp@ltbuses.co.uk. Just follow the signs in the main concourse of the rail station to board. Stationlink circular service operates in both directions and honors the London Visitor Travelcard.

The railways of Britain are most eager to provide as comfortable a journey as possible for the disabled passenger. To do this, prior notice of intended travel plans helps both the traveler and the authorities.

Those readers who want to learn more about this innovative approach should write to the Royal Association for Disability and Rehabilitation (RADAR), 12 City Forum, 250 City Road, London, England EC1V 8AF for details, or call from the United States 011 44 20 7250 3222; *Fax:* 011 44 20 7250 0212; *E-mail:* radar@radar.org.uk; *Web site:* www.radar.org.uk. The association publishes *Cross the Boundaries* and *Motoring with a Wheelchair.*

In the United States, contact Mobility International USA, P.O. Box 10767, Eugene, OR 97440; *Tel:* (541) 343–1284; *Web site:* www.mi usa.org for information about services and referrals to international affiliates. The organization produces the booklet *A World of Options: A Guide to International Educational Exchange, Community Service and Travel for Persons with Disabilities.*

If you plan to travel in Britain with a handicapped person, call the British National Rail Enquires at (0845) 748 4950 (from the United States, dial 011 44 845 748 4950) for information on the train company you will be using (British Train-Operating Companies are listed in the Appendix), or contact one of the British Tourist Agency (BTA) offices as soon as you establish your itinerary and begin making arrangements. For example, call Virgin Trains Journey Care at (0845) 744 3367 or West Anglia Great Northern Services at (0845) 712 5988 if traveling on their lines. Many others will prearrange assistance as well for those with any special needs or requirements. Sleeper services offer compartments efficiently designed for the traveler in a pushchair (wheelchair) regardless if traveling with or without a companion.

The same applies to the airline you'll be using for your transatlantic flight. Provide all the details of your itinerary, the nature of the disability, and any other information that will help them help you, such as if a wheelchair is needed at departures and arrivals. Specifically, tell them about special diets, medications, and toilet and medical-attention requirements. With these details attended to, you can look forward to a pleasant journey.

Baggage Carts. Many otherwise able train visitors to Britain impose a severe disadvantage upon themselves by arriving with more luggage than three men and a small boy could possibly carry. Train porters are nearly an extinct species, and their demise was expedited by the luggage trolley—Britain's version of our baggage cart—an elusive device that, whatever your position on the train platform, haunts the extreme opposite end and requires insertion of £1.00 sterling (coin) to use.

Our number one trip tip to all train travelers is to "go lightly." At most, take one medium-size suitcase with wheels, or two small bags, augmented by a modest shoulder bag. There still will be times when you will wish you could discard your suitcase. Pack lightly and leave room for souvenirs, or you might just need to purchase another piece of luggage for gifts.

If you have purchased a suitcase with built-in wheels, it usually will follow at your heels like a well-trained dog as you apply minimum pulling power. Unlike a dog, the wheeled suitcase cannot climb stairs, so be prepared to lift it on and off the train, and up and down the steps of stations without lifts (elevators).

Rather than relying on the trolleys in the train stations, consider investing in your own baggage cart to take with you if your suitcase does not have built-in wheels. There are many types available.

When loading your luggage onto a baggage cart or station trolley, keep the load as narrow as possible. You may need to pass through rather narrow ticket barriers to and from the trains. A Samsonite suitcase loaded sideways on a baggage cart or one of the station's trolleys will just clear, but a wardrobe case is trouble each and every time.

The trolleys provided by the station should not be taken aboard the train, although we've seen it tried. Again, if you are taking your own cart with you, fold it before boarding. If you don't, you may spend an embarrassing ten minutes or so on the station platform extracting a hapless fellow traveler from it as your train eases out of the station without you.

Using the Lifts (Elevators). The greatest problem in using the train station's luggage trolleys (or your own baggage cart) is traversing the station hall to the platform area, because practically every station has stairs. You can overcome this problem by using the station's lift (elevator). This polite announcement is found posted in most British rail stations: LIFTS ARE AVAILABLE FOR PASSENGERS WHO HAVE DIFFICULTY IN USING THE STAIRS. PLEASE CONTACT STATION STAFF IF ASSISTANCE IS REQUIRED.

In searching for a lift, don't always look for a modern, automatic-door elevator brightly lit with soft music playing. Instead, sometimes you will find the old-fashioned, double-door, manually operated freight elevator, large enough to hold a Mack truck and usually illuminated with a single, bare light bulb—but it works. As the sign says, STATION STAFF WILL ASSIST YOU.

If you use lifts frequently, however, you will develop the knack of handling them all by yourself. A note of caution: Lifts will not operate until both barriers (usually a door and a gate) have been closed securely. Furthermore, the lift will be left inoperative if you fail to close the doors after you have used it. Be considerate of other passengers and the station staff by making certain all doors are secure.

Porter Services. Porter service is on the wane but still available in some train stations, particularly in the larger ones. We found Virgin Train personnel provided the best service and assistance, particularly with luggage. The best way to locate a porter is to inquire at the Left Luggage (baggage storage) area or at the station's incoming taxi stand. Waterloo, Gatwick, and Liverpool Street Stations have left-luggage areas; some stations may offer luggage lockers, but most have stopped this service and even removed trash containers for security reasons.

If your luggage has been checked in at the station, there will be a handling charge, but the tip remains a personal item between you and the porter. We suggest £1.50 minimum per bag as a reasonable gratuity. Most porters will take your bags to the train and place them aboard in the luggage racks over your seats. Porters are rather scarce on arrival platforms. If you must have assistance, approach the stationmaster's office or the train conductor prior to departure with the request that a porter be asked to meet your train upon arrival at your destination.

If you are transferring between base cities or changing hotels from one city to another, you can request the hall porter at the hotel you are leaving to arrange for the arriving hotel's hall porter to meet your train upon arrival. A small tip should arrange everything.

A Few More Train Tips. The following train travel tips should make your trip more enjoyable:

• "Mind the gap!" when boarding and disembarking.

• Show your BritRail Pass or rail ticket upon request, and in the case of the rail pass, have your passport handy should the conductor ask to see it.

• Don't place your feet on the seats of the train unless you have removed your shoes or have provided a protective covering for the seat.

• Place your luggage in the overhead racks or the racks at the ends of the carriages provided for that purpose—not on the seats so other passengers won't be able to crowd you.

• Observe smoking/nonsmoking areas and rules. Rather stiff fines are imposed for those smokers who violate nonsmoking rules.

• Observe seat reservations. They are usually marked by a ticket inserted at the top of the seat. Even though it is apparent that a seat is unoccupied, if there are other passengers seated opposite, ask if the seat is open—it will avoid embarrassment later if the person holding the reservation happens to return.

• Arrange for dining-car reservations on long-distance trains soon after boarding. Inquire with the guard (train conductor). If he or she cannot make them for you, a member of the dining-car crew will do so. Generally, they pass through the train prior to the first seatings for that purpose. There are usually two seatings, so be prepared to select the one to your liking. You can also inquire about the menu at the same time. The second seating is scheduled so that the dining-car crew has time to tidy up before the train reaches its destination. Therefore, the first seating is preferred by many because it does not seem to be as rushed.

• If you plan an overnight journey on a sleeper, ask the attendant to explain how the equipment in your compartment operates. For example, many sleeping cars have electric shades. A push of the button and they open; another push of the same button and they close. If you did not know the button's function, you just might try pushing the button while the train is standing in a station and you are not dressed for the occasion! Tip attendants for their services; the proper time to do so is when they serve breakfast.

Safety Tips

Picking pockets is an art that is practiced seemingly throughout the world. Don't carry anything valuable in hip pockets. Money belts, holster wallets, or pouches that can be hidden are the safest way to carry cash and other valuables.

A concealable money belt or pouch is a good investment. Also, women should place the straps of their purses across their chests and carry the purses in front, not on the side with the straps only on the shoulder. Be mindful of the placement of your passport and money in backpack-style purses as well. Thieves on motorcycles can grab the purse from your shoulder very easily. You can modify the inside pocket of a coat or jacket with a zipper or Velcro. Or sew a medium-size button both above and below the pocket opening. Loop a piece of shoestring or other strong string around the buttons when carrying valuables.

Don't leave cash, cameras, or other valuables in the hotel room or locked up in a suitcase. Take them with you, or leave them in the hotel safe. We advocate leaving expensive jewelry at home, but if you must take it with you, leave it in the hotel safe when you're not wearing it.

Don't dangle your camera from around your neck or wrist; keep it in an inexpensive-looking camera bag.

Don't designate one individual to carry everyone's passports or other valuables, and don't carry all of your own valuables in one place. Split up documents and money in various safe holding locations.

Stay alert. Pickpocketing most commonly occurs in crowded public areas. Be leery of being bumped or someone causing a distracting incident. For all that, don't be alarmed—just be aware and take proper precautions.

For further peace of mind, we suggest reviewing the Web pages at www.travel.state.gov/asafetripabroad.html for insightful tips and suggestions for "A Safe Trip Abroad." This site contains ideas on what to bring and leave behind and what to learn and arrange before you go and also contains helpful tips for public transport safety.

Remember, visitors are always subject to the law of the land; therefore, it may be helpful to pay attention to media reports and research some of the local laws and customs prior to departing for a foreign country. Also consider visiting the U.S. State Department's Internet site, www.state.gov, which contains up-to-date information on foreign affairs. You can contact the U.S. Department of State Consular's Office for information on travel warnings and public announcements by calling (202) 647–5225, faxing (202) 647–3000, or visiting www.travel.state.gov.

Arriving in Britain

That big moment is about to happen. Years of dreaming, months of planning, and weeks of anticipation are about to become a reality. The FASTEN SEAT BELTS sign has been illuminated, and the cabin attendants advise that the aircraft will be landing at your destination in just a few minutes.

For most of us, there is an inexplainable thrill about arriving in a foreign country. Enjoy the emotion; it's part of the reason for your journey—to experience the adventure of travel, to probe beyond the normal confines of your familiar environment, to meet other people, and to enjoy a bit more of the world than you had before the FASTEN SEAT BELTS sign came on.

The Airports

Within Britain, there are six international airports servicing traffic from the United States: Gatwick, Heathrow, and Stansted in the London area, Birmingham and Manchester in central England, and Glasgow in Scotland. For more information, visit www.baa.co.uk.

Gatwick–London: There are two terminals: the North Terminal and the South Terminal. *Tel:* (0870) 000 2468. The Gatwick Express (www.gatwickexpress.co.uk) dedicated rail service departs every fifteen minutes from 0650 to 2050 and every thirty minutes from 0520 to 0650 and from 2050 to 0050 from the South Terminal for London's Victoria Station. The last train departs Gatwick at 0135. Approximate journey time is thirty minutes. Gatwick Express Information: (0845) 850 1530; Express Class Fare: £11.00 one way; £21.50 round-trip.

Heathrow–London: There are four terminals (a fifth one is planned to open in spring 2008)—Terminals 1, 2, 3, and 4—with courtesy coaches operating between the terminals on a regular basis. The high-speed

Heathrow Express service departs every fifteen minutes from the airport, reaching London Paddington Station in only fifteen minutes (eight minutes more from Terminal 4), and runs from 0510 to 2330. Express Class Fare: £13 one way; £25 round-trip. For further information, call the Care Line at (0845) 600 1515 or visit www.heathrowexpress.co.uk.

Heathrow Shuttle by Airbus takes one hour, forty minutes. Two routes serve twenty-three stops with extended operating hours. Adults: £10.00; £15.00 round-trip. Children age three to fifteen: £4.00; £6.00 round-trip. Children younger than age three: Free if they do not require a seat. Airbus A2 goes to King's Cross and Euston Station.

For more detailed information on Gatwick, Heathrow, and Stansted Airports, please consult the chapter on London.

Pick up the free guide *Central London by Tube,* which is available at the travel information centers and tube stations at Heathrow Airport. The guide is full of information on the Underground network, shopping in the West End, and train connections to other towns and cities within Britain.

Stansted: Continental Airlines provides nonstop service between New York (Newark) and London's Stansted Airport. Stansted Express rail station is located beneath the terminal. Trains run to London's Liverpool Street Station every fifteen minutes from 0800 to 1730 weekdays and every thirty minutes during early morning, evening weekdays, and weekends. Journey time is about forty-five minutes. Express Class one-way fare is £13.80; round-trip is £24. *Internet:* www.stanstedexpress .com; *Tel:* (0845) 8500 150.

Airbus A6 departures connect with London's Victoria Station half hourly during the day and hourly at night. *Tel:* (0870) 580 80 80 (U.K. only); *Internet:* www.nationalexpress.com.

Birmingham: Birmingham International Station is right next to the airport and offers direct service to London (Euston Station, about one hour, fifty minutes), Brighton, Edinburgh, Glasgow, Leeds, Liverpool, Manchester, Oxford, and York. *Tel:* (0121) 767 5511.

Manchester: There are three terminals: Terminal 1 Domestic, Terminal 1 International, and Terminal 2. *Tel:* (0161) 489 3000. The airport rail station is linked to Terminal 1 by a covered escalator and to Terminal 2 by a twenty-four-hour shuttle bus service. Up to six trains per hour depart from the airport station for Manchester Piccadilly railway station (twenty to twenty-five minutes).

Glasgow: One terminal, no rail connection at the airport, direct coach service connects with Paisley Gilmor Street station (2 miles from the airport). *Tel:* (0141) 997 1111. Scottish Citylink service 905 operates from Glasgow Airport to the Buchanan Bus Station in the city center about every fifteen to twenty-five minutes. *Tel:* (0870) 550 5050; *Internet:* www.citylink.co.uk.

Clearing Customs

The customs-information cards given to you by the flight attendants before landing will expedite your clearance through arrival formalities. Actually, you will go through two processes—customs and immigration—although they appear to be integrated. Immigration officials will want to examine your passport, usually at a barrier gate en route to the baggage-claim area in the airport. After collecting the checked baggage, you should proceed to the customs-inspection area, where you will find two color-coded lanes: green for NOTHING TO DECLARE and red for TO DECLARE.

Everyone has some apprehension about passing through customs. For the most part, the apprehension is based on the question "Am I doing it properly?" In Britain this consists of going straight through the Nothing to Declare channel (unless you are asked to stop by an officer) and moving through into the airport's general-assembly area.

If customs officials want to examine your luggage, they will indicate so as you approach them. Don't go through the To Declare lane unless you have brought amounts of tobacco or liquor that exceed the allowable limits or have purchased a gift with a value exceeding £145 (£75 for gifts bought in the EU) that you will be leaving in Britain.

The type and amount of duty-free goods that you may bring into Britain vary with your point of departure—a European Common Market country or otherwise. For transatlantic passengers, the limit is 200 cigarettes or 50 cigars; a liter bottle of liquor or two bottles of sparkling wine or two bottles of still wine; and 60 ml of perfume or 250 ml of toilet water. You will have plenty of advance advice on duty-free imports posted in your departing airport, and you can check with the cabin attendants on the airplane as well. Customs prohibits and regulates pornography, firearms, drugs, plants, fruits, and goods made from protected species. Know before you go, and the clearing procedures in Britain will present no problem.

This also applies to your return to North America. The U.S. Treasury Department publishes an informative booklet containing customs hints for returning residents. Write to the Department of the Treasury, Washington, DC 20229 for the *Know Before You Go* booklet. For U.S. Customs information while in London, telephone the American embassy at (020) 7499 9000; *Fax:* (020) 7499 1212. *Internet:* www.usembassy.org.uk.

British Currency

British currency is based on the pound sterling. The pound (£) is divided into one hundred pence (p), just as the U.S. dollar is divided into one hundred cents. Paper notes are issued in values of £50.00, £20.00, £10.00, and £5.00. Coins are issued in values of £2.00, £1.00, 50p, 20p, 10p, 5p, 2p, and 1p. The British pound sterling is used in England, Scotland, and Wales. Scottish currency is also legal tender in England and Wales. If you encounter problems using it there, the banks will exchange it free of charge.

Banks in Britain are usually open Monday through Friday from 0930 to 1700, with some operating Saturday mornings as well from 0930 to 1200. Check the Appendix for bank holiday closings.

British paper notes, like the majority of world currencies, vary in size according to their value, and a variety of them can wreak havoc on the orderliness of a North American's wallet. Certain notes, the £10 and £20 in particular, will require folding before they will fit into a wallet designed to hold dollars. Use discretion when engaged in this folding process, especially in public.

We proudly pointed out to one of our British friends how neatly organized our American wallets are because the U.S. dollar is the same size whether it's a $100.00 note or a $1.00 note. "Yes, that's quite neat," she stated, "but what do your blind people do?"

Although the European Union maintains that Europe is now one market, sort of the "United States of Europe," the British are not fond of relinquishing their pounds sterling to the new "one-Europe" currency, the eurodollar or euro. At press time the United Kingdom still uses the pound sterling. For more information on the euro, visit http://europa .eu.int/euro/.

British Telephones

The public coin-box telephones are simple—with a bit of explanation, that is. Basic differences still exist between British telephones and ours, particularly in the signals they make. A ringing signal is two short rings, followed by a pause. The busy signal sounds the same—only busier. An all-circuits-busy signal is a rapid series of high-low tones, but when you have reached a telephone number not in use, a high-pitched continuous tone is heard.

Public coin-operated telephones are identified by a red stripe across the phone booth door; some of the traditional solid red booths may still be found in smaller towns. They operate much like ours, except that a series of rapid pips will signal more coins must be deposited or your call will be terminated. Keep an eye on the window at the top of the phone box that displays the amount you deposited. The amount decreases as time passes during your call. Have more coins ready so you won't lose your connection midconversation.

Phonecard pay phones are identified by a green stripe across the door. They require the use of a credit card or a prepaid Phonecard. The cards are sold at post offices and wherever the distinctive green British Telecom (BT) Phonecard sign is displayed. If you are planning on doing a bit of telephoning, it pays to shop around for the best rates of Phonecards. Instructions for the use of Phonecards are posted inside each booth, or you can ask an information office for the pamphlet *How to Call Home from the UK.*

When dialing Britain from the United States, use the international calling code **011** followed by the country code **44.** Useful phone numbers are listed in the Appendix. All area codes within Britain begin with 0, which is dropped when calling from the United States. If you need assistance telephoning while in Britain, the national directory is 192, international directory is 153, and for an emergency of any kind dial 999. Free calls within Britain begin with 0800 or 0808; the exchange 0845 is charged as a local call anywhere within Britain. Following are the exchanges for the base cities mentioned in this book: London (inner), (020) 7xxx xxxx; London (outer), (020) 8xxx xxxx; Edinburgh, (0131); Glasgow, (0141); Cardiff, (029) 20xx xxxx.

British Traditions

Some visitors entering Britain for the first time may find some of the British traditions, customs, and way of life a little difficult to understand. Perhaps what follows may assist in the transition.

If an Englishman from London, a Scot from Edinburgh, and a Welshman from Cardiff were traveling together in North America, they would describe themselves as being "British" or "Brits." But among themselves, they would be English, Scottish, and Welsh. These three nationalities, joined by the Ulstermen of Northern Ireland, make up what we refer to as the United Kingdom. Since the BritRail Pass is not accepted for rail travel in Northern Ireland, references in this book are to Britain rather than the United Kingdom, and the term *British* refers to the peoples of England, Scotland, and Wales.

Those who plan to add Northern Ireland and the Republic of Ireland to their rail itinerary should consider the BritRail Pass + Ireland (see Appendix for pass prices).

The British character will wear well on you after a few days. They are generally a well-disciplined and polite people. If anyone is at fault, more than likely it is the visitor, not the host. Visitors are not advised to get into controversial conversations of opinion—especially in a pub! Although the British can face crises and keep their cool, most maintain a fierce loyalty to Her Majesty, Queen Elizabeth II. You'll also learn very quickly that the British queue is the quintessence of "first-come, first-served."

On the surface, Britons may seem reserved, even humorless. In fact, many Britons enjoy some very bold and bawdy humor, as their tabloids will attest. Once their facade is penetrated, you will find them capable of the highest mark of humor—they can laugh at themselves. This becomes most evident in their observations regarding their weather. "The way to ensure summer in England," snapped Horace Walpole, "is to have it framed and glazed in a comfortable room." Byron's observation was perhaps terser: "The English winter—ending in July to recommence in August." Britain does have a tendency to be damp at times. You won't regret taking a small folding umbrella or a rain hat or purchasing authentic British ones once there.

The Language Barrier

George Bernard Shaw once said America and Britain are "two nations divided by a common language." Terminology, more so than pronunciation, appears to be the problem whenever an American and a Briton cannot communicate effectively. *British/American Language Dictionary,* by Norman Moss (1991, Passport Books), or *Divided by a Common Language,* by Christopher Davies and Jason Murphy (1998, Mayflower Press), can be most helpful during an initial visit to Britain.

Reading daily newspapers, listening to the British Broadcasting Corporation (BBC), or watching the telly (television) are quick remedial methods for learning the language (try BBC America). These media communicate through a more or less middle-of-the-road lexicon.

Regional and local dialects can be extremely difficult to comprehend on occasion; even the Brits admit they sometimes have difficulty understanding each other. It has been said that if a Glaswegian (resident of Glasgow) and a Cockney (Londoner) were locked together in the same room, neither would be able to converse with the other—even after being properly introduced.

One of the first things a visitor from "the Colonies" (America) will notice is the manner in which directions are given. Americans geographically locate a point within a city by referring to the number of blocks distant from the point of inquiry, for example, "two blocks down the street." Britain's early road builders, however, never thought too much about a grid system and permitted their streets to wander along the easiest gradient. Consequently, directions given by a constable or someone on the street will usually be linear, that is, "Straight away for 100 meters," "A kilometer or two," and so on. Visual objects are employed as well: "Straight away to the pub," "Keep walking till you come to the third traffic light," and the like. Cabbies (taxi drivers) are good sources for directional information and advice. Every cabby carries a street map in his taxi and usually will be glad to assist you.

Nuances in the American/British vocabulary can sometimes lead to trouble. In a public place, such as a train station, those in search of toilet facilities will do well to employ the term *lavatory* in their quest. The WC (water closet) seems to be losing its effectiveness in Britain, although it still brings direct results when used in continental Europe. However, if you want to be up on British expressions, you might ask for the *loo*—that's where those in the know go to "spend a penny." (Many public loos charge a few pence for admission.) Requesting directions to the *bathroom*, particularly in a train station, might lead you to the public showers. So take our advice and stick with *lavatory* or *loo*.

When a Brit asks you for a *rubber*, don't be offended; just hand him an eraser. If you want a cookie, ask for a *biscuit*; french fries are *chips*, and potato chips are called *crisps*.

Terminology in a train station should not present much of a problem. The baggage room is *left luggage*, and *lost property* translates easily into lost and found. Elevators are labeled *lifts*, but *subway* means a pedestrian underground street crossing. The *Underground*, or *Tube*, is the British version of our subway.

A *carriage* is a (rail) coach, and a *coach* is a long-distance bus. Should you hear the term *goods wagon* or *goods train*, that translates to a freight car or a freight train in American. Aboard a train, the conductor usually is referred to as the *guard*; the engineer becomes the train *driver*.

The British measure body weight in *stones*—a stone being a unit of fourteen pounds. A person weighing fourteen stone six pounds would be 202 pounds avoirdupois. A popular measurement of time is a *fortnight*, meaning fourteen days or two weeks. Britain's conversion to a decimal currency system has not changed the slang for the pound sterling—it's still a *quid*—and then there's the *guinea*. Anyway, before long you'll notice yourself picking up a few words or phrases along the way. *Cheerio!*

British Pubs

The pub is a uniquely British phenomenon. The ingredient that makes a true "public house" is not its construction, architecture, furniture, or the spirits it dispenses—it is the clientele. The term *public house* means just that. Everyone is welcome, even Americans and Australians.

The *local*, as most British pubs are lovingly referred to, is an organic part of the community, ranking in importance along with the local postal office and the town hall—perhaps even higher. The locals who support it generally prefer to stand when they imbibe, for pub etiquette must be observed at all times. Pub etiquette dictates you pay for the "round" when served and if you accept a drink, you are expected to buy a round in return.

To accommodate differences in the drinking etiquette of their visitors, most pubs have a second bar area, identified as a lounge or a saloon. There are more seats, and usually the drinks cost a bit more.

When are the pubs open? Licensing hours generally permit English pubs to remain open anywhere from 1100 to 2300 Monday through Saturday and Sundays from 1200 to 1500 and 1900 to 2230 in England and

Wales; 1230 to 1430 and 1830 to 2300 in Scotland; times are essentially up to the individual pub owner or barkeep. You must be age eighteen or older to buy or consume alcoholic beverages in a pub. Children age fourteen and older may be admitted legally and may consume nonalcoholic drinks. Children of all ages are usually admitted to licensed restaurants; they are also admitted to "beer gardens" and family rooms, which many pubs have.

A pub is usually rated by the congeniality of its owner, and unless "on holiday," he or she is usually found on the premises during operating hours. An entrepreneurial lot, many owners offer "pub grub" in their establishments. Visitors find it a good alternative to Wendy's or McDonald's for a snack or a lunch because a Frosty can never really compete with a good pint of ale or porter.

The personality of a pub greets you at the door. You can tell in an instant whether or not it's your kind of place. If its ambience reaches out to you, enter. No doubt a local or two will note your entrance with a friendly nod as the bartender beams at you and asks, "What'll you have?" When advised, the bartender will then indicate with a slight directional nod that it will be served in the lounge area. Pay when served. Never tip the owner if he or she brings the drinks to the table to bid you welcome. The owner is the host; you are the guest. Later, you might join the locals at the bar; but remember, remain standing and pay for a round when it's your turn to buy. Who knows, the locals might suggest you drop 'round again.

British Passenger Trains

The British rail network has come a long way—with yet longer to go. There is still a discernible difference between the operating speeds and passenger comforts of the trains of continental Europe and those of Britain. With privatization, the once cumbersome and bureaucratic British Rail was split into twenty-six train-operating companies that run the passenger services in specific regions. (See the Appendix for a list of the train-operating companies.) Network Rail is responsible for maintaining and improving Britain's rail infrastructure. *Internet:* www .networkrail.co.uk.

The light at the end of the tunnel appears to be growing brighter. Network Rail plans to spend £10 billion on rail network improvements during this decade. Thameslink 2000, the massive five-year project to improve London's existing railway infrastructure, will increase the number of trains passing through central London from eight trains per hour to twenty-four per hour in each direction during peak times and eighteen in off-peak times. The new cross-London services will greatly improve access to the Southeast of England. The longer twelve-car trains will increase seating capacity, and the new Channel Tunnel Rail Link Station adjacent to the existing St. Pancras Station provides easy interchange for Eurostar services.

InterCity 125 trains provide the majority of long-distance services, and they are shrinking journey times on many of the main routes out of London. From King's Cross Station, for example, the InterCity 125 covers the 393 miles between London and Edinburgh in four hours flat—an average of 98 miles per hour—and that includes a station stop at York and Newcastle in England prior to crossing into Scotland. The trains are powered by two 2,250-horsepower diesel-electric engines, one at each end of the train. The coaches are identified by letter (A, B, C, etc.), and the stations they serve have the platform positions marked accordingly. By InterCity 125 service from London, you can reach Cardiff, Wales, in only one hour and fifty-five minutes and Glasgow, Scotland, in only five hours, seventeen minutes.

A number of the older trains still in service on many of Britain's intermediate rail routes show more than a fair amount of wear and tear. Some of the train-operating companies are refurbishing the rail carriages, and others, such as Virgin, are building brand-new ones. Nevertheless, it may be a while before the "generation gap" in British rolling stock is overcome.

There are many types of railcars, including sleeping, restaurant, buffet, and Pullman cars, along with the standard passenger carriages. British Pullman cars differ from the Pullmans of North America in that they do not convert at night to provide sleeping accommodations. Instead, British Pullmans are the elite of the line, the best in daytime comfort, and exclusively first class.

This luxury service operates on the London-to-Manchester/Liverpool route. Basically, it is designed to offer the businessperson morning and afternoon services between England's capital and its leading commercial center. In London, the Pullman trains depart from Euston Station. They are well worth the experience, but we suggest you dress appropriately for the occasion if you want to engage in tycoon-to-tycoon conversations or afternoon tea with other passengers. Reservations may be required; if not, check with the conductor for arrangements. Reservations may be made in advance through EuropeanVacation. Call toll-free in North America (877) RAILPASS (877–724–5727).

First-class sleeping cars have single-berth compartments; standard-class sleepers have two-berth compartments. Sleeping-car charges are economical: £29 per berth in standard class and £35 per berth first class; there is no discounted rate for children. The sleeping cars are equipped with fresh bedding, washing basins with soap and towels, and a shaver outlet. Sleeping-car passengers are served morning tea or coffee and biscuits free of charge, and they generally can remain in the sleeping cars at their destination for an hour after arrival. The charge is standard for all destinations regardless of the distance.

With such attractive prices, an overnight trip aboard a sleeper may outweigh the alternative of seeking a night's lodging in a city and an early morning departure in order to make your destination on time. Consider the sleeping cars for excursions from London to Inverness, Penzance, and Plymouth; available daily, except Saturday. Sleeper services also operate between London and Aberdeen, Edinburgh, Glasgow, and Fort William. Reservations for sleeper accommodations need to be made at the rail stations in Britain.

An overnight service is available on Caledonian Sleepers between

London's Euston Station and Aberdeen, Edinburgh, Fort William, Glasgow, and Inverness. This "seated coach," as ScotRail terms it, provides comfortable reclining seats with footrests, tray table, individual reading lights, and air-conditioning. You can snooze in your comfortable recliner or get up and stretch your legs by going to the buffet car to buy drinks and snacks. Sweet dreams!

Most long-distance trains haul restaurant cars. If not, there usually is a buffet car where you can obtain snacks and beverages. Aboard the InterCity fleet, restaurant cars offer a wide range of freshly prepared traditional dishes. Silver Standard restaurant service is available on many 125s and on selected "business" trains—the Manchester/Liverpool Pullman, for example. Passengers holding first-class tickets who wish to take meals can reserve seats in the restaurant car or in adjacent coaches. Breakfast aboard British trains has always been a great attraction. It's hearty, generally very good, and, of course, comes with hot tea or coffee.

Some buffet cars offer "grill" meals, which you may enjoy either there or back at your seat. Seating in the buffet cars is not assignable, thereby providing a reasonable opportunity to be seated while you select from the bill of fare. One innovation found aboard many food-service railcars is beer and lager on draft. This, according to many railroad buffs, is an outstanding stride forward in the annals of railroad engineering!

Admittedly, dining aboard a speeding train is an unusual gastronomic experience, but it can be on the expensive side. Although food catering aboard a British train is far more economical than similar services on the trains of the Continent, those seeking less expensive food may want to utilize the food facilities found at most rail stations in Britain. They range in service from complete restaurants serving a variety of hot and cold dishes to a snack bar–type operation. Some have off-license provisions allowing you to purchase alcoholic beverages for consumption elsewhere, but all bars operating in the stations, unlike those on the trains, must observe the local licensing hours for drinks.

The most economical food you may enjoy on a train in Britain is, of course, that which you bring aboard yourself. Many of the station restaurants will prepare box lunches for you to take on your trip. Ask for the "buffet-pack" service. Your hotel or bed-and-breakfast probably can provide similar service with advance notice. Or purchase easy traveling snacks from a convenience store to pack in your bag. Purchase bottled water before you board or from the buffet car. Water from the taps in lavatories aboard trains is not potable.

First Class, Standard Class?

On most British trains you have a choice of first- or standard-class travel. More and more routes are offering strictly standard class or very few first-class carriages. BritRail Passes and Flexipasses are sold for both classes. First-class seats are wider and more spacious. If that is the sort of accommodations you want, then it is worth paying the extra price. Standard class is, however, an excellent standard. All the facilities aboard the trains, such as restaurant and buffet services, are available for both first- and standard-class travelers.

The average British citizen usually travels by standard-class carriage (coach). In fact, it is so much the custom that if you want to purchase a first-class ticket, you must specifically state "first class"; otherwise, you will automatically receive a standard-class ticket.

First class offers extra comfort and is less crowded. First-class accommodations for weekend and holiday travel are particularly desirable. Seats may be reserved in both classes, which is a wise move if your journey is a "must" and the distance is great. "Riding the cases" (sitting on your suitcase for lack of a seat) is not comfortable!

Seat reservations may be made in any major train terminal throughout Britain. Some of the twenty-six operating train companies in Britain offer free seat reservations, some charge a £1.00 to £2.00 fee, and some do not accept seat reservations at all due to frequency of service. Birmingham, Cardiff, Gatwick, Glasgow, Heathrow, Manchester, and Stansted Airports have rail ticket booths where you may make reservations immediately after your arrival. You may obtain advance reservations for treks of more than two and a half hours before arriving in Britain by calling (877) RAILPASS (877–724–5727) for a reservation request form, but it is far more economical to make them once on British soil.

Travelers holding first-class BritRail passes may travel in either first- or standard-class carriages, which is a nice option if the good-looking person you've been yearning to chat with boards the standard-class section. It's a disaster, however, if he or she moves to the first-class section while you're holding a standard-class rail pass.

You will find some single-class trains operating on branch lines. This means that the first-class accommodations are not available aboard that particular train. It is the politely British way of avoiding the somewhat unrefined term, *second class only.*

Similar to those on the Continent, first-class British railcars are marked distinctively by a yellow band running the length of each car above its doors and windows. On other-than-mainline service, where both first- and standard-class accommodations may be provided in the same car, a yellow band will be shown for only the first-class portion of the car. Restaurant cars, buffets, and cars containing other forms of food-catering facilities are identified by a red band above their doors and windows.

Except for those of the InterCity 125s and 225s, it is difficult to determine exactly where the first-class coaches will halt during an en route station stop. The non-English-speaking nations of Europe generally provide a diagram of each train's composition and where it will stop in the station. Not always so in Britain. According to the equipment in use, the first-class section of a British train can be at the head, the rear, or the middle of the train. Through experience, we have devised a system that is relatively effective in determining where the yellow-striped cars will stop.

Position yourself midway on the platform and scan for the yellow band as the train enters the station. Should it pass you, take off to the head of the train; if it doesn't, head in the other direction. Should the yellow-striped car stop directly in front of you, fate has been kind to you this day, but you can bet it won't happen again soon.

There is an increase in the nonsmoking accommodations aboard British trains, reflecting the noticeable change in the public attitude toward smoking. There is a stiff fine for violating the rule. So if you are a smoker, keep your eyes alert for the red nonsmoking signs and smoke only in the areas so designated.

Train Schedules

British timetables are shown in the twenty-four-hour format, and they are generally divided into sections according to the pattern of services provided. A typical two-part division is "Mondays to Saturdays" and "Sundays." You may run across a mix, however, including "Mondays to Fridays," "Mondays to Saturdays," or "Saturdays and Sundays." All days stated are inclusive. In other words, "Mondays to Saturdays" includes all six days. (The schedules appearing in *Britain by BritRail* are noted as to days of operation.)

Always be certain that you look at the correct part of the schedule for the particular day of the week on which you wish to travel, and always double-check departure times and the platform number of the next train you wish to take when you arrive in a station. Sometimes alterations are necessary. Another caution: Services may be modified on days preceding and immediately following bank holidays. The best bet for a "must" trip, a late night return, or an early morning departure is to check your plans with the rail personnel in the station travel centers. Extensive engineering work is often conducted on the rail system on weekends, which frequently affects passengers' schedules. You can also telephone the National Rail Inquiries office at (0845) 748 4950.

You should experience little difficulty in verifying the departure time of your selected train or locating the platform from which it departs once you've made it to the station—providing that in London you've gone to the proper station.

Airport-style digital displays are the usual source for train schedules in most British stations. You will find them in the main station halls and also on the train platforms in many stations. Even the old-fashioned train bulletin boards can still provide the needed information. Augmenting displayed train-departure information are the usual vocal announcements in the station halls and on the platforms. For the most part, they differ from those made by Amtrak because you can understand them. Perhaps it's the accent that makes it possible.

Ask the Guard

Almost all British passenger trains travel with a conductor aboard. As previously explained, his or her official title is *guard*. This person carries with him (or her), in either his handbook or his head, a potpourri of valuable information. If you are required to change trains in order to arrive at your final destination, talk to the guard.

Perhaps en route you learn that the train you are traveling on will be passing a famous British landmark, such as one of the many castles. On which side of the train will it pass? If you are a castle buff, maybe you would like to come back on another day to visit the castle. Is there a local train station near the castle? Is there a local bus to take you there if the castle is beyond walking distance? Is there a pub or inn in the vicinity? You'll probably get responses to all of the above plus a condensed history lesson on the castle and its surroundings—all from the guard.

Crossing the English Channel

he newest method of crossing the English Channel is to go under it via the tunnel (affectionately known as "The Chunnel") connecting England with France and the rest of Europe. Direct rail service from London to Paris or Brussels takes you from city center to city center in only three hours to Paris and in only two hours, forty minutes to Brussels. Even faster schedules will appear within this decade, with the London to Paris journey expected to be reduced to only two hours, twenty-five minutes. High-speed tracks will also be constructed within Britain to allow matching speeds as on the Continent (up from 60 to 80 mph to more than 180 mph).

Other convenient ways of crossing the English Channel between England and France are via the water by Brittany Ferries, Hoverspeed, P&O Stena Line, and SeaFrance. For detailed information about these services, visit the Ferry View pages at the Web site **www.seaview.co.uk.** Since there are various ways of crossing the English Channel and the North Sea en route to Europe, which one should you select? The fastest route from London to Paris or Brussels is through the tunnel under the Channel, utilizing the Eurostar passenger services departing London's Waterloo International Eurostar Terminal.

The "Chunnel" and Eurostar Trains

In 1888, Louis Figuier proclaimed that "linking France and England will meet one of the present-day needs of civilization." On May 6, 1994, England's Queen Elizabeth II and France's President François Mitterrand brought Figuier's words to life and inaugurated a new era in European train travel: the linking of England and France via a 31-mile tunnel that runs underground and beneath the English Channel. More than 17 million tons of earth were moved to build the two rail tunnels (one for north-bound and one for southbound traffic) and one service tunnel.

Three different types of trains utilize the Eurotunnel. Eurotunnel's own trains convey cars, trucks, and buses between the terminals at Folkestone and Calais. Eurostar is the high-speed passenger rail service linking the three capitals of London, Paris, and Brussels, operated by the national railways of Belgium and France and by Eurostar (U.K.) Limited.

Travel times from London to Paris are reduced from as much as nine and a half hours to three hours; Brussels is only two hours and forty minutes away, thus making a European Capitals tour nothing more than an exciting day excursion. Trains arrive and depart from Waterloo International Station in London, Gare du Nord in Paris, and the Brussels-Midi terminal.

The sleek Eurostar trains offer three classes of service:

• **Standard Class:** Comfort for value. Snacks and refreshments are available at reasonable prices in the bar car, or you can select from the roving trolley cart as it rolls right to your seat.

• **First Class:** Relax and recline in your first-class seat as you imbibe complimentary food and beverages. Complimentary newspapers are available upon request.

• **Premium Class** (available London–Paris route only): At a step above first class, this is the ultimate in Eurostar comfort and service. It includes fast check-in service at Waterloo International Station in London/Gare du Nord Station in Paris, use of the Eurostar executive lounges (the Club-house in Waterloo and Ashford and Salon Eurostar in Gare du Nord and Brussels Midi/Zuid), a four-course meal (choice of two main dishes) with complimentary wines, and champagne (on trains departing between 1100 and 1700; breakfast is served on trains departing up to 1100). You can also obtain a voucher to reserve a complimentary taxi/executive car transfer upon arrival at your destination station. Make your reservation at the departure station's Eurostar executive lounge. (This service is not available at Ashford International Station.)

Each train can carry 766 passengers (182 in first class and 560 in standard class, plus 24 premium first-class seats) and reach speeds of 186 miles per hour in Europe, with speeds of 100 miles per hour through the Chunnel. Eurostar zooms through the Channel tunnel in only nineteen minutes. The train is based primarily on the TGV (Train à Grande Vitesse) but was redesigned to accommodate the three different voltage types encountered en route. The trains are accessible to handi-capped passengers and those with special needs. Arrangements must be made forty-eight hours prior to departure by calling Eurostar Complimentary Assistance Service, (020) 7928 0660; *Fax:* (020) 7922 6018. Sufficient storage for luggage is provided.

Those taking advantage of a trip to Paris or Brussels from London on a Eurostar train are in for a treat. The trains offer the comfort and amenities comparable to few trains in the world. From the moment of departure you're in for a smooth, quiet ride, and even when you enter the tunnel the only noticeable change is the sudden darkness outside the windows. Those concerned with changes in air pressure needn't worry. Air flow through the tunnel is regulated to minimize changes in pressure, and few, if any, passengers are uncomfortable.

Families traveling with children may opt for coaches 1 or 18, where baby-changing facilities are offered and flip-up seats allow more room for kids. Ask the train manager for a children's pack of things to do while traveling.

Eurostar staff members are multilingual and are available to provide assistance from the minute you enter the terminal to the minute you exit the platform. You'll notice them right away, with their stylish dark gray uniforms with yellow accents. If you have any questions, don't be shy—they're there to serve you, and serve you they do.

Given the frequency of rail service and the speed of travel, it's easy to see how a "quick trip" to Paris, Brussels, or any continental destination can be accomplished. See the schedule for Eurostar trains running between London and Paris, and between London and Brussels.

Notes
- Reservations are mandatory.
- Be certain to check in at your departure station at least twenty minutes prior to departure.
- Holders of BritRail Pass, Eurail pass, France Rail pass, and Benelux Tourrail Pass receive discounts on Eurostar services.
- BritRail Passes cannot be used for rail travel in continental Europe.
- Smokers take note: All Eurostar trains are nonsmoking.

To purchase one-way or round-trip Eurostar tickets or for scheduling information on trains to other cities, call toll-free (877) RAILPASS (877–724–5727), fax (614) 764–0711, or visit the Web site **www.rail pass.com/eurostar.**

EUROSTAR SCHEDULES

Crossing the English Channel

Depart London Waterloo International	Arrive Paris Gare du Nord	Train Number	Notes
0534	0923	9078	Mon-Fri
0634	1023	9002	Mon-Sat
0801	1153	9088	Sun only
0812	1147	9008	Mon-Sat
0904	1253	9012	Sun only
0909	1253	9012	Mon-Sat
1034	1417	9018	Sun only
1039	1417	9018	Mon-Sat
1209	1559	9024	Mon-Sat
1341	1723	9030	Mon-Sat
1511	1853	9036	Daily
1612	1947	9040	Except Sat
1709	2059	9044	Daily
1742	2117	9046	Except Sat
1811	2153	9048	Sat & Sun
1842	2223	9050	Mon-Fri
1939	2323	9054	Sat
1942	2323	9054	Mon-Fri

Depart Paris Gare du Nord	Arrive London Waterloo International	Train Number	Notes
0637	0826	9005	Mon-Fri
0716	0856	9007	Mon-Fri
0743	0926	9009	Sat only
0813	0951	9011	Mon-Fri
0910	1102	9015	Daily
1019	1154	9019	Mon-Sat
1143	1329	9025	Daily
1304	1454	9031	Daily
1437	1627	9037	Daily
1607	1757	9043	Daily
1710	1857	9047	Daily
1743	1925	9049	Mon-Fri
1816	1958	9051	Daily
1919	2054	9055	Daily
2043	2228	9061	Except Fri, Sun
2113	2257	9063	Fri & Sun only

Depart London Waterloo International	Arrive Brussels Midi	Train Number	Notes
0743	1058	9112	Mon-Fri
0834	1210	9116	Sun only
0839	1210	9116	Mon-Sat
1234	1610	9132	Sun only
1239	1610	9132	Mon-Sat
1639	2010	9148	Daily
1811	2137	9154	Mon-Fri

Depart Brussels Midi	Arrive London Waterloo International	Train Number	Notes
0725	0859	9111	Sat only
0813	0928	9113	Mon-Fri
1258	1425	9133	Daily
1756	1928	9153	Daily
2026	2156	9163	Daily

EUROSTAR FARES

London—Paris or Brussels

Eurostar fares are provided in U.S. dollars, one-way in either direction and are subject to change at the discretion of the railways. For tickets, schedules, and group rates, and for other cities serviced, including Ashford, Lille, Calais-Fethun, Marne-la-Vallee, and Paris Disneyland, contact RailPass.com toll-free at 877–RAILPASS (877–724–5727); *Fax:* (614) 764–0711; *Internet:* www.railpass.com.

Fare Type	First Class	Standard Class	Conditions
Passholder*	$135	$ 75	Valid on Eurostar routes in countries covered by pass
Full Fare	$345	$249	Refundable up to 2 months after travel date
Premium First	$425	NA	Refundable up to 2 months after travel date; exchangeable
Leisure 1**	$170	$120	Std. Class valid Mon–Thurs *only*
Leisure 2***	$142	$90	1st Class: min 1 night stay; Std. Class: valid Mon–Thurs 1100–1500 *only*

Leisure 3***	$95	$75	1st Class: valid Mon–Thurs 1100–1500 *only*; Std. Class: min 1 night stay
Leisure 4***	NA	$60	Valid Mon–Thurs *only*; min 1 night stay
Leisure 5***	NA	$45	Valid Mon–Thurs 1100–1500 *only*; min 1 night stay
Leisure Day Trip***	$95	47	Same-day return ticket required
Leisure Flexi 1****	$255	$195	
Leisure Flexi 2****	$209	$150	Limited availability
Senior	$180	$90	Age 60 and older
Youth	$142	$75	Younger than age 26 on day of travel; nonrefundable
Youth Off Peak	$105	$60	Younger than age 26; 1st Class: valid Mon–Thurs 1100–1500 *only*; Std. Class: 1100–1500 *only* all week
Youth Off Peak 2	NA	$45	Younger than age 26; valid 1100–1500 Mon–Thurs *only*; nonrefundable; can exchange once in Europe
Child	$75	38	Age 4–11
Wheelchair Adult†	$58	NA	
Wheelchair Companion†	$58	NA	
Wheelchair Child†	$49	NA	

- Seat reservations are mandatory on all European trains
- Tickets issued include reservation on the same voucher (inclusive price)
- 1st Class includes meal served at your seat

*Holders of Eurail, BritRail, France, Benelux Tourrail and Eurail Benelux–Germany Passes. Nonrefundable; may be exchanged once prior to departure; exchange only in Europe.
**Limited availability; nonrefundable; nonexchangeable.
***Limited availability; nonrefundable; nonexchangeable and return ticket must be purchased in same fare type.
****Limited availability; 25% refundable up to 3 days prior to travel date; fare may be exchanged once prior to departure; exchange only in Europe.
†100% refundable up to 2 months after travel date; exchangeable.

Other Channel Crossings to France

For those who prefer to skim over the Channel to France rather than ride the Eurostar trains under it, Britain's ferry and ship operators present a delightful alternative. Contact the companies listed below for detailed sailings schedules, fares, reservations, and other information.

Brittany Ferries
Millbay, Plymouth, Devon PL1 3EW
Tel: (0870) 536 0360; *Fax:* (0870) 901 1100
Internet: www.brittany-ferries.co.uk (bookings available online)

Routes and Journey Times to France

Route	Journey Time	Frequency
Plymouth–Roscoff	6 hrs	1–3 daily
Poole–Cherbourg	4 hrs 15 min	1–2 daily May–Sept.
Portsmouth–St. Malo	8 hrs 45 min (day)	1–2 daily
	10 hrs 45 min (night)	
Portsmouth–Caen	6 hrs (day)	2–3 daily
	6 hrs 45 min (night)	
Portsmouth–Cherbourg	5 hrs 45 min	Varies—check sched.
Cork–Roscoff	13 hrs 30 min	Saturday only

Each of Brittany Ferries' luxury cruise-ferries offers restaurant facilities, boutiques, and cabin/berth accommodations. Check in at least 45 min in advance.

Hoverspeed UK Limited

International Hoverport, Marine Parade
Dover, Kent CT17 9TG
Tel: (0870) 240 8070; *Fax:* (0870) 460 7102
Internet: www.hoverspeed.co.uk (bookings available online, 2 percent discount)

Routes and Journey Times to France

Route	Journey Time	Frequency
Dover–Calais	40 min via Superseacat	4–6 daily
	45 min via Seacat	
Newhaven–Dieppe	2 hrs via Superseacat	2–3 daily

Hoverspeed operates a fleet of high-speed Seacat catamarans and Superseacat monohulls. The 100-meter Superseacat began operating on the Dover–Calais route in 2001 at an in-service cruising speed of 37 knots. It can carry up to 674 passengers and 148 vehicles on a separate vehicle deck. The 81-meter Seacat can carry 654 passengers and 140 vehicles. Approximately 64 trains daily travel between London's Victoria Station and Dover Priory (Dover's main station).

Boat trains depart London's Charing Cross (some also call at Waterloo East) for direct service to the pier at Folkestone Harbour.

P&O European Ferries (Portsmouth)
Peninsular House, Wharf Road
Portsmouth PO2 8TA
Tel: (0870) 600 0613 or (0239) 230 1000; *Fax:* (0239) 230 1134, or
(561) 563–2856 in the U.S.
Internet: www.poportsmouth.com (bookings available online)

Routes and Journey Times to France

Route	Journey Time	Frequency
Portsmouth–Le Havre	5 hrs 30 min (day)	3 daily
	7 hrs 30 min (night)	
Portsmouth–Cherbourg		
Fastcraft	2 hrs 45 min	4–6 daily
Conventional ferry	5 hrs (day)	2 daily
	7 hrs (night)	

Trains depart from London's Waterloo Station for Portsmouth Harbour rail station. Use the bus service between the Portsmouth Harbour Rail Station and the Portsmouth Continental Ferry Port.

P&O Stena Line
Channel House, Channel View Road
Dover, Kent CT17 9TJ
Tel: (0870) 520 2020 (reservations); *Fax:* (01304) 863 884
Information line: (0870) 600 0611
Internet: www.poferries.com (bookings available online)

Routes and Journey Times to France

Route	Journey Time	Frequency
Dover–Calais	75 min	30–35 daily

The *Aquitaine,* P&O Stena Line's state-of-the-art "super" ferry, has a 2,000-passenger and 600-vehicle carrying capacity and is one of the largest vessels on the Dover–Calais route.

The seven P&O Stena Line superferries on the Dover–Calais route offer up to thirty-five return sailings daily. Travel in standard or Club Lounge class. The superferries offer restaurants, cafes, bars, a comfortable lounge area, and shopping. Purchase tickets for the sea crossing online or at the ticket offices in London rail stations.

Both first- and standard-class accommodations are available on the boat trains between London and Dover. The BritRail Pass is accepted for the rail portion of the journey from London to the port (seat reservations are recommended). The term *boat train* applies to those trains departing from London's Charing Cross Station to Dover Priory for direct sailing connections at Dover's Eastern Docks with P&O Stena Line ferries crossing to the French port of Calais. The trains traveling from London to Dover Priory are met by a courtesy bus service to the docks.

SeaFrance Limited

SeaFrance Eastern Docks
Dover, Kent CT16 1JA
Tel: (0870) 571 1711; *Information Line:* 09064 710 777 (60 pence per minute)
Fax: (0191) 296 1540
Internet: www.seafrance.co.uk

Routes and Journey Times to France

Route	Journey Time	Frequency
Dover–Calais	70–75 min	15 daily

SeaFrance's new ship, the *Berlioz,* has an overall length of 185 meters and carries up to 1,900 passengers at speeds of up to 25 knots. Journey time for the *Rondin* and *Berlioz* is 70 minutes; all other vessels, 75 minutes. You will find a variety of French food facilities on SeaFrance vessels: Le Brasserie with waiter service; Le Relais Gourmet, a self-serve restaurant stocked with fine French foods; an English-style pub with snacks; and Le Café.

Crossing the Channel to Other Ports

Route	Operator	Journey Time	Frequency
Dover–Oostende, Belgium	Hoverspeed Seacat	2 hrs	3–5 daily
Harwich–Esbjerg, Denmark	DFDS	19 hrs 30 min	3/week
Harwich–Hamburg, Germany	DFDS	19 hrs	3/week
Harwich–Hoek van Holland	Stena Line HSS	3 hrs 40 min	2 daily

DFDS Seaways (U.K.)

Scandinavia House
Parkeston
Harwich, Essex CO12 4QG
Tel: (0870) 533 3000
Internet: www.dfdsseaways.co.uk

SeaEurope Holidays, Inc.

USA Representatives for: **DFDS Seaways, Silja Line**, and **Gota Canal Cruises**
6801 Lake Worth Road, Suite 103
Lake Worth, Florida 33467
Tel: Reservations, Timetables, and Fares—(800) 533–3755, ext. 113
    Brochures—(800) 533–3755 ext. 147
    Tours and Cruises—(800) 533–3755, ext. 115
Fax: (561) 432–2550
Internet: www.seaeurope.com (for U.S./Canada residents, online booking available)

DFDS Seaways routes also include crossing the North Sea to connect Great Britain with Sweden, Norway, and Holland. Seven modern passenger ships traverse eight routes crossing the Channel and the North Sea.

Stena Line
Charter House, Park Street
Ashford, Kent TN24 8EX
Tel: (0870) 570 7070
Fax: (01233) 202 231
Internet: www.stenaline.com (online booking available)

The Harwich–Hoek van Holland (Hook of Holland) via Stena Line HSS (High-Speed Service) is the most direct sea link between London and Amsterdam. Convenient connections may also be made from Hoek van Holland to Brussels, Belgium. Departure by rail from London to Harwich is from the Liverpool Street Station.

Stena HSS onboard facilities include restaurants ranging from gourmet bill of fare at Maxim's to burgers and fries at McDonald's, several bars, two movie theaters, a casino, and video games.

Notes
• BritRail Passes are *not* accepted for travel on the shipping companies operating on either the English Channel or the North Sea.

• Port-to-port tickets must be purchased for all sea voyages (check with the appropriate shipping company for any qualifying discounts).

• Point-to-point tickets must be purchased for continuing rail travel in continental Europe unless you hold a rail pass (e.g., any variety of Eurail pass or France Rail pass) valid for travel in continental Europe. In this case, you may have your rail pass validated at the rail station of the European port upon arrival, then continue your rail trip without the inconvenience of having to purchase point-to-point tickets.

Crossing the Irish Sea

S ome of the ferry crossings on the continent of Europe involve actually loading the passenger railcars aboard the ferry. When this occurs, the passengers need not even disembark. But at all ferry ports in Britain, passengers are required to leave the train and board the ferry, then board another train after docking. You will find this change of transportation mode is no great hardship. In fact, it can be a very enjoyable experience by including drinks and dinner aboard the ferry, followed by a chat with fellow passengers. The salon of a ferry is a good place for meeting people. Everyone has a common interest in travel, and everyone is going to the same destination.

Crossing the Irish Sea is very much like crossing the English Channel by ferry, except you cannot forward your luggage on to the Republic of Ireland. What you take is what you carry. So "go lightly" when it comes to luggage. Porter service is almost nonexistent at the marine terminals, except by prearrangement. Similar to the experiences in the train stations, it is best not to expect porter service. Furthermore, the trolleys (baggage carts) found in the majority of British rail stations are missing at the piers because their use is impractical on the sloping ramps and gangways to the vessels.

When you visit Ireland, keep in mind that Northern Ireland and the Republic of Ireland are two separate political states. Northern Ireland is part of the United Kingdom, while the Republic is independent. There are no customs to contend with when arriving in Northern Ireland from England, Scotland, or Wales. On the other hand, customs formalities entering the Republic of Ireland should present no problem for the bona fide traveler. The efficient "declare" or "nothing to declare" system is used by Irish customs. The BritRail Pass + Ireland covers the complete network of trains in England, Scotland, Wales, Northern Ireland, and the Republic of Ireland. Choose five or ten days of travel to be completed within one month in first or standard class with this pass.

The pass also includes a round-trip on Stena Line between Holyhead and Dun Laoghaire by HSS (High-Speed Service), between Fishguard and Rosslare by ship or Stena's Lynx catamaran, and between Stranraer and Belfast via ship or HSS fast ferry. The HSS ferries cruise at 40 knots, twice the speed of conventional ferries. For more details, visit www .stenaline.co.uk. For schedules and fares, contact these ferry companies:

Stena Line
Charter House, Park Street
Ashford, Kent TN24 8EX, England
Tel: (0870) 570 7070; *Fax:* (01233) 202 231
Internet: www.stenaline.co.uk

Irish Ferries U.K. Limited
Corn Exchange Building, Ground Floor
Brunswick Street
Liverpool L27 TP
Tel: (0870) 517 1717; *Fax:* (0151) 236 0562
Tel: In the U.S. (561) 563–2856
Internet: www.irishferries.com
E-mail: info@irishferries.co.uk

Hoverspeed UK Limited
International Hoverport, Marine Parade
Dover, Kent CT17 9TG
Tel: (0870) 240 8070; *Fax:* (0870) 460 7102
Internet: www.hoverspeed.co.uk (bookings available online, 2 percent discount)

Sea Links to Ireland/Northern Ireland

Crossing the Irish Sea

Operator	Services Per Day	Approx. Crossing Time	Rail Conn. from London	Rail Journey Time	Trains/ Day

Fishguard–Rosslare
Stena Line

Superferry	2	3 hrs 30 min	Paddington Station	4 hrs 30 min	2
Stena Lynx	2–4	1 hr 39 min			

Crossing to Rosslare is recommended for travelers bound for Cork, Killarney, and Shannon Airport. Train time from Rosslare Harbour into Dublin is three hours; to Limerick for connections to Shannon Airport, three hours twenty-five minutes, and travel time from Limerick to Shannon Airport is about forty-five minutes. Food, beverages, and shopping are available on Stena Line and Stena Lynx vessels.

Pembroke–Rosslare

Irish Ferries	2	3 hrs 45 min	Paddington Station	5 hrs	5

Holyhead–Dublin Port

Stena Line	2–4	3 hrs 30 min	Euston Station	4 hrs 5 min	13

Irish Ferries–

Fast Ferries	4	1 hr 49 min
Irish Ferries	2	3 hrs 15 min

Ferry services are provided by both Stena Line and Irish Ferries (choose cruise ferry or Fast Ferry service). Arriving by train at Holyhead Station, follow the posted directions to the main port terminal. The Dublin Ferryport is about 2 miles from the city center. A shuttle bus provides transport to and from Dublin's main bus station.

Holyhead–Dun Laoghaire

Stena HSS	2–4	1 hr 39 min	Euston Station	4 hrs 5 min	13

Stena Line

Superferry		3 hrs

Dun Laoghaire is a suburb of Dublin. Facilities on the Stena HSS (High-Speed Service) catamaran include restaurants, bars, shopping, and entertainment.

Stranraer, Scotland–Belfast, Northern Ireland
Hoverspeed

Seacat	1	1 hr 30 min	Euston/Kings Cross Stations– Glasgow Central	4 hrs 54 min	14

Stena Line

Superferry	up to 12	3 hrs 15 min	Glasgow– Stranraer	2 hrs 8 min	5
Stena HSS	up to 12	1 hr 45 min			

England

Internet: www.visitengland.com

They came, they saw, and they conquered—Celts, Romans, Anglo-Saxons, Danes, and Normans constitute the major ancestry of the modern-day Briton. From the mysterious megaliths at Stonehenge to the formidable fortress at Hastings, the ancient English proved to be a capable people. Despite the size of their island and its limited resources, the English became a nation of traders fostering not only an exchange of commodities but also of cultures, giving rise to one of the most powerful empires ever in history.

England represents about 57 percent of the total land area of the island, or 130,439 square kilometers (50,363 square miles). We normally think of England as gently rolling green countrysides, but its terrain is diversified—from mountains in the northern and western portions to a deeply indented coastline providing excellent natural harbors.

When we think of England, we automatically think of royalty. Never make the mistake of thinking that Her Royal Majesty Queen Elizabeth II is merely Queen of England; she reigns over many other countries and territories as well. In recent years, the older members of the House of Windsor have been puzzled, then distressed, by the world's fascination with the goings-on of its younger generation. The titillating misadventures of Fergie and Prince Andrew as well as the very public feuding of the Prince and Princess of Wales set the stage for the almost unthinkable divorce of Prince Charles from Princess Diana.

Then one fateful evening in Paris, near the end of August 1997, the world lost Diana, "the People's Princess." Her death affected not only her family and all the British, but also people everywhere, who grieved for this young, vibrant woman. Today all eyes seem to be on her sons,

Princes William and Henry (Harry). We'll have to see what the future brings to these handsome young men. For more information on the British monarchy, visit www.royal.gov.uk.

Rail Travel in England

BritRail Passes are, of course, valid throughout England. (See the chapter "Planning a BritRail Trip—BritRail Passes" for an explanation of the various types of Days Out of London BritRail Passes and the new BritRail England Passes.) The Days Out of London Pass, however, is a special rail pass for those who are limiting their travels to making day excursions from London to the surrounding area in southeastern England. It provides for rail travel in southeastern England as far west as Salisbury and Exeter (but not via Reading), as far east as Dover, Margate, and Harwich, southward to Portsmouth, Brighton, and Hastings, and as far north as Banbury, North Hampton, and Kings Lynn.

Choose from any two or four days of rail travel within an eight-day validity period, or any seven days within a fifteen-day validity period either first class or standard class. Note that many of the trains in the southeast area are standard class only and the Days Out of London Pass is not valid for travel to Bath, nor on the Great Western–operated trains, nor on services via Reading.

BritRail Days Out of London Pass

(prices in U.S. dollars)	First class	Standard class
Any two days in eight	$ 89	$ 59
Any four days in eight	$145	$109
Any seven days in fifteen	$195	$145

BritRail England Consecutive Pass

Unlimited rail travel in England for 4, 8, 15, or 22 days or 1 month. Includes transport to/from Gatwick, Heathrow, and Stansted Airports to London. Prices in U.S. dollars.

	Adult 1st class	Adult Standard class	Youth Standard class	Senior 1st class
4 days	$ 225	$149	$112	$191
8 days	$325	$215	$161	$276
15 days	$485	$325	$244	$412
22 days	$615	$409	$307	$523
1 month	$725	$485	$364	$616

BritRail England Party Pass

Unlimited rail travel in England for 4, 8, 15, or 22 days or 1 month; 50% discount for third to ninth passengers who are traveling together at all times. Prices in U.S. dollars.

1st Class

	3 Adults	4 Adults	5 Adults	6 Adults	7 Adults	8 Adults	9 Adults
4 days	$563	$675	$788	$900	$1,013	$1,125	$1,238
8 days	$813	$975	$1,138	$1,300	$1,463	$1,625	$1,788
15 days	$1,213	$1,455	$1,698	$1,940	$2,183	$2,425	$2,668
22 days	$1,538	$1,845	$2,153	$2,460	$2,768	$3,075	$3,383
1 month	$1,813	$2,175	$2,538	$2,900	$3,263	$3,625	$3,988

Standard Class

	3 Adults	4 Adults	5 Adults	6 Adults	7 Adults	8 Adults	9 Adults
4 days	$373	$447	$522	$596	$671	$745	$820
8 days	$538	$645	$753	$860	$968	$1,075	$1,183
15 days	$813	$975	$1,138	$1,300	$1,463	$1,625	$1,788
22 days	$1,023	$1,227	$1,432	$1,636	$1,841	$2,045	$2,250
1 month	$1,213	$1,455	$1,698	$1,940	$2,183	$2,425	$2,668

Base City:

London

Internet: www.londontown.com
www.londononline.co.uk
www.visitlondon.com

When you visit London, you will experience a wonderful combination of ancient elegance and modern technology, of old traditions and vestiges of the past mingling with contemporary conveniences and a futuristic Ferris wheel right along the Thames River. While plumed guards mount jet-black horses in Whitehall, bankers examine computer printouts on Lombard Street. This mixture provides a provocative, fascinating atmosphere in one of the largest and most sophisticated cities in the world.

Although London is Europe's largest city, most of its historical sights are clustered in a compact area. Central London sits astride the Thames River, about 40 miles inland from its estuary on the North Sea. By strolling through the oldest section of Central London, you'll see its first-century Roman walls, the Tower Bridge and infamous Tower of London, Saint Paul's Cathedral (www.stpauls.co.uk), the second-largest cathedral dome in the world, and the city's financial center.

In the so-called newer section of Central London (it's only about 1,000 years old), you can visit such famous sites as Buckingham Palace, the Houses of Parliament, Palace of Westminster, and Westminster Abbey. This area also includes Trafalgar Square (its north side is now pedestrianized), Soho, and Piccadilly Circus.

Experience London from the top of the British Airways' gigantic Ferris wheel, the "London Eye," for a spectacular view from a height of 135 meters. You'll be able to see the old sights as well as the new ones, including the ten-story IMAX theater at Waterloo and the Tate Modern's collection of international contemporary art. Use London's 335-yard-long Millennium Bridge and its two newest footbridges, Golden Jubilee bridges, for easy and enjoyable exploration of this constantly changing city on foot.

In addition to Central London, the city is composed of thirty-two other boroughs. Since the streets seem to follow no particular pattern, use postal designations appearing with the addresses on maps to identify a particular region.

The British Tourist Authority publishes a very useful monthly guide to London—*London Planner*—with extensive information on events, sightseeing, theater, shopping, where to stay, maps, and much more.

Arriving by Air

London's Heathrow and Gatwick Airports are North America's primary gateways, with Stansted International Airport as well as London City and Luton Airports primarily providing service within continental Europe and Great Britain. *Internet:* www.baa.co.uk.

Heathrow Airport. Information Desk: (020) 8759 4321. Heathrow, the world's busiest international airport, is connected by the **Heathrow Express** train service to Paddington Station in Central London. Journey time: fifteen minutes (8 minutes more from Terminal 4); cost: £13 one-way; £25 round-trip; save 10 percent by purchasing online. Trains depart every fifteen minutes daily 0510– 2330. Hop on at stations in Terminals 1, 2, 3, and 4 direct to Paddington Station. In the United States, tickets may be purchased in advance through 877–RAILPASS (877–724–5727). Tickets are also available in the arrivals hall at Terminals 1 and 4 and in the Heathrow Express Central Station in Heathrow Airport. For more information, *Tel:* (0845) 600 1515; *Internet*: www.railpass.com or www.heathrowexpress.com. Paddington has full luggage transfer service to Heathrow Airport. Check-in facilities are open daily 0500–2100.

Using the **Underground** (the "Tube"), the Piccadilly Line has access to all four terminals. (Terminal 4 has a separate station.) Tube service to Piccadilly Circus and Central London runs about every four to ten minutes 0513–0022 Monday through Saturday; Sundays 0557 to about 2355. Journey time: about 1 hour; cost: £3.70. London Transport information, *Tel:* (020) 7222 1234 (twenty-four hours); *Internet:* www.londontransport.co.uk or www.thetube.com.

AirLinks (Speedlink) operates Airbus (A2) transportation between Heathrow and central London, to and from King's Cross. Adult fare is £8.00 single, £15.00 round-trip. Departures are from all four terminals every 30 minutes; journey time, 1 hour 40 minutes. You can purchase tickets on board. Stops include Hyde Park, Marble Arch, Baker Street, Russell Square, and King's Cross. *Tel:* (0870) 575 7757; *Internet:* www.nationalexpress.com.

Travelers headed directly for London's Waterloo International Station to catch the Eurostar trains can take a bus to Woking train station, which is on the main line to London Waterloo.

Gatwick Airport, about 27 miles south of London, provides easy-to-access, efficient, and swift (thirty minutes) train service to London's Victoria Station aboard the **Gatwick Express.** The express train departs Gatwick's South Terminal rail station every fifteen minutes 0600–2000 and operates every thirty minutes 0430–0600 and 2000–0030. Journey time: 30 minutes. A single fare is £11; round-trip £21.50. Information in London: (0845) 850 1530. Gatwick Express tickets may be purchased in advance in the United States by calling toll-free (877) 724–5727. *Internet:* www.railpass.com or www.gatwickexpress.co.uk.

AirLinks (Speedlink) Airport Services operates Airbus coaches to and from London's Victoria Station and Gatwick Airport. Coaches run from 0515 to 2230 every half hour during the morning and every hour in the afternoon. In addition, there are 0630, 2125, and 2325 departures from Victoria Station. The fare is £17. For information in the United Kingdom, call (0870) 574 7777; for information in the United States, call (310) 568–0009, or fax (310) 338–0708; visit www.speedlink.co.uk or www.nationalexpress.com, or e-mail info@speedlink.co.uk.

Stansted Airport, located about 37 miles northeast of London, has fast and frequent links to London via its **Stansted Express** (*Internet:* www.stanstedexpress.com) train service. From the airport to London's Liverpool Street Station takes about forty minutes, with departures every fifteen minutes Monday through Friday 0800–1730 and every thirty minutes 0600–0730 and 1800–2359; every thirty minutes on Saturday and replacement coach service on Sunday. Liverpool Street Station departures to Stansted Airport are every thirty minutes daily 0500–2300. One-way Express Class fare is £13.80; round-trip £24.

Arriving by Train

London is a hub of rail travel for the Western world and a great introduction to the wonders of European train travel. With speed, little expense, and relative comfort, you can access some of the most stimulating sights in one of the world's most beautiful cities.

London's seventeen primary rail stations provide an abundance of travel opportunities within the city, to other cities, and to the countryside and seasides. New signage, departures and arrivals screens, and printed Station Guides enable the traveler to easily and quickly find station facilities and services. For the readers of *Britain by BritRail,* eight of these stations are well worth knowing:

Victoria Station is an international rail terminal. It also provides easy access to the south and southeast of England. When making sea-rail connections with Belgium and France, use the International Rail Centre next to platform 2. Station facilities include shops, eateries, money exchange, and tourist information, which is located at the London Tourist Office by the main entrance to the station. To reach it, follow the corridor running from platform 15. The Gatwick Express help desk is at the entrance to platforms 13/14. *Hours:* 0700–2000 daily. *Tel:* (0990) 301530 (wheelchair assistance: 020 7922 6206). For taxi service, we have found it more convenient to take the escalator to the upper-level taxi entrance at the Plaza exit in Victoria Place rather than walking to the front of Victoria Station. The entrance to the London Underground (access to the Victoria, District, and Circle lines) is opposite platform 7.

Euston Station is closely grouped with St. Pancras and King's Cross Stations for rail services to northern England, North Wales, and Scotland. Direct trains to Glasgow and a few trains to Edinburgh base cities depart from Euston. This station also serves as the terminal for Stena Line ship and ferry services to Belfast via Stranraer and to Dublin via Holyhead. The Travel Centre is open Monday–Friday 0545–2345, Saturday 0600–2255, and Sunday 0700–2345. Waiting rooms, restaurants, and other conveniences are located on the far side of the station hall from the Travel Centre. For taxis, use the steps adjacent to the LRT kiosk to descend to the level beneath the station. For entrance to the London Underground (access to the Northern and Victoria lines), head down the escalators next to the LRT kiosk.

St. Pancras Station is the departure point for *Britain by BritRail*'s day excursions to St. Albans, Nottingham, and Sheffield. The station is undergoing renovation to provide regional Eurostar passenger service from Glasgow, Edinburgh, Manchester, and Birmingham to Paris and Brussels via the Channel Tunnel. Eurostar service is expected to begin in 2007. Directional signs for the Euston and King's Cross Stations, as well as the London Underground, are prominent throughout the station.

Charing Cross Station is London's rail terminal for direct train service to Folkestone, Hastings, Dover, and other ports for P&O Stena Line Sealink and Hoverspeed services to Boulogne and Calais on the Continent.

Train information can be obtained at the Connex Information Desk located at the entrance to platforms 5 and 6. *Hours:* Monday–Saturday 0700–2130 and Sunday 0715–2115. Taxis are at the front of the station. The Underground entrance is down the stairs or escalators located on the left-hand side of the ticket office (access to Jubilee, Bakerloo, and Northern lines).

King's Cross Station is the London terminal for InterCity 125 train service to Scotland and the northeastern and east of England. The Travel Centre is open Monday–Saturday 0645–2100, Sunday 0745–2100. Full information, reservations, and advance ticketing services are available. A money exchange service is available in the forecourt at the front of the station. Taxis are just outside the main entrance, next to platform 1. There are three entrances to the Underground. Station facilities are undergoing changes due to redevelopment of the King's Cross/St. Pancras Underground Station, scheduled to open in 2006.

Paddington Station serves the west InterCity 125 service through Plymouth and Penzance and into *Britain by BritRail's* base city of Cardiff in Wales. It also is the London terminal for Stena Line Sealink services to Ireland via Fishguard to Rosslare. The Travel Centre is located on the concourse near the entrance to platform 1; open twenty-four hours daily. Taxis are located at the side road adjacent to platform 1.

There are two entrances to the Underground in Paddington Station. To access the Bakerloo, Circle, and District lines, use the entrances on the main concourse near platform 11. To access the Hammersmith & City line, follow platform 8 to the footbridge, then follow the Underground signs. Since its recent renovation, Paddington now includes new lifts for improved accessibility for travelers with mobility difficulties, new platforms, and a new dining, shopping, and waiting area called "The Lawn."

Liverpool Street Station, one of the oldest rail terminals in London, has undergone a £150 million renovation. The main ticket/train information office is located on the main concourse. Pick up a copy of the *Station Guide*, which details station facilities. Seat reservations and bookings may be made in advance 0730–1930 daily. The taxi stand is next to platform 10.

There are four entrances to the London Underground providing access to the Central, Metropolitan, Circle, and Hammersmith & City lines: one at the end of platform 1, one on the main concourse alongside the ticket office, one next to Thorntons, and one outside at the corner of Liverpool Street and Old Broad Street.

This station is the gateway for rail and ship traffic between London and the Netherlands, northern Germany, and Scandinavia. Trains departing Liverpool Street Station proceed to Harwich, where passengers then embark from the Parkeston Quay by ship to Hook of Holland, a small peninsula jutting out into the North Sea. There, trains wait to take them to such destinations as Amsterdam, Hamburg, Berlin, and the Scandinavian capital cities of Copenhagen, Oslo, and Stockholm.

Waterloo Station is primarily for trains to the south of England, including the Isle of Wight and continental Europe. The Travel Centre is opposite platforms 16 and 17 and is open twenty-four hours a day. Taxi stands are at exit 3, through the main arch, on Cab Road. London Underground entrances are located down the steps from platforms 17, 18, and 19; down the escalators near platforms 18/19; down the steps opposite platforms 5 and 14 for access to Bakerloo, Northern, and Waterloo & City lines; and via exit 2 opposite platforms 4/5 to access the Jubilee line.

To access the **Waterloo East Station** for travel to Southeast London,

Kent, and Sussex, use the stairs, escalator, or elevator opposite platforms 11 and 12 located alongside Burger King.

The **Waterloo International Eurostar Terminal** for direct service to Paris or Brussels may be accessed next to platform 19 and occupies platforms 20–24. Eurostar is the passenger service operated by the railways of Belgium (SNCB/NMBS) and France (SNCF) and by Eurostar (U.K.) Limited. More than fifteen passenger trains make nearly one hundred daily runs back and forth through the "Chunnel," providing tourists and business travelers with quick, efficient travel to London, Paris, Brussels, and points east. For more detailed Eurostar or channel-crossings information, please see "Crossing the English Channel."

Getting around in London

London is meant for walking. Charming nooks, side streets, stores, and vistas all await your discovery. Of course, time constraints may force you to consider other options. To orient yourself, first-time visitors especially will find an introductory guided bus tour helpful. London Coaches makes it convenient for you to become familiar with the various sections of the city by operating "The Original London Sightseeing Tour" (www .theoriginaltour.com). The tours run across four different routes and depart every six minutes in summer and every thirty minutes in winter around a 20-mile circular route in about two hours. They pass most of London's major historic and contemporary landmarks and provide commentary in several languages. Board the tour at Haymarket, Marble Arch, Embankment Pier, Trafalgar Square outside Charing Cross Station, Victoria, or Baker Street Underground station locations. Fare: £15 adults, £10 children younger than age fifteen.

For a more personalized, albeit more expensive, introduction to London, hail a taxi. London's taxicab drivers, known as "cabbies," are a special breed. They are not issued a taxi operator's license just because they can drive a car. An extensive knowledge of the city and its history is an important part of their taxi-licensing examination. Cabbies usually have fixed rates for such sightseeing excursions, which can add up quickly.

Another picturesque way to get acquainted with London is via **London River Services.** Tours by river provide a view of London and its surroundings from an entirely different perspective. Boat services link Central London with the North Greenwich Station. Fast Ferry Service plies between Festival Pier and Rotherhithe (Holiday Inn) and calls at several piers, including Embankment (formerly Charing Cross pier), Bankside, Canary Wharf, and London Bridge City. For more information about riverboat services, ask at the tourist offices, or call London Travel Information at (020) 7222 1234 (twenty-four hours). *Internet:* www .londontransport.co.uk/river/. *E-mail:* travinfo@tfl.gov.uk.

After an introductory tour, you will be better able to get around on London's Underground, the Tube. Don't let the enormous size of the Tube overwhelm you—it's really very user-friendly. Composed of eleven basic lines, the Tube's train system provides an easy and fast way to get around London from 0530 until midnight Monday–Saturday and 0730–2330 on Sunday.

If you plan to use the Tube for more than one day, consider the **London Visitor Travelcard** for three, four, or seven consecutive days. The card includes unlimited travel on buses and your choice of all zones on the Tube or the Central Zone. The All Zone Card covers all six zones of the Tube, the Docklands Light Railway, and transfers from Heathrow Airport to any part of London via the Tube. It is *not,* however, valid on the Heathrow Express. The Central Zone Card covers zones 1 and 2 of London's public transport system.

With a London Visitor Travelcard, you are eligible to purchase the **London Pass,** which provides free entry to more than fifty major attractions, such as Buckingham Palace (open August and September), St. Paul's Cathedral, and Windsor Castle. It also includes a 132-page *London Pass Guide Book,* commission-free currency exchange, free offers at several top restaurants, discounted telephone calls, and more. With the London Pass, there's no need to wait in lines to purchase entry tickets. (See the Appendix for pass prices.)

Other combination transport tickets that provide access to the Tube, trains, and buses are available from London Transport offices or tourist offices. Maps of the London Underground and some discount coupons are included with the Travelcard and are posted in all the Underground stations, or obtain them from the BTA or any London tourist office. For more information about London's remarkable transportation system, visit **www.londontransport.co.uk.** When in London, you may obtain up-to-date information on many subjects about the city by dialing London Line, (090) 6866 3344 (60 pence per minute).

The Metropolitan Office forecast for Greater London weather is (09014) 722 051. *Internet:* www.met-office.gov.uk.

London, At Your Service

Professional tourist offices managed by Expotel provide visitors with detailed information about hotel accommodations, points of interest around the city, and a twenty-four-hour information line on using London's extensive transportation network of the Underground, bus, and rail services. *Internet:* www.visitlondon.com.

London Tourist Information Centre locations at your service:

Britain and London Visitor Centre: 1 Regent Street, Piccadilly Circus, SW1Y 4XT. Take the Piccadilly Line to Piccadilly Circus. *Hours:*

0930–1830 Monday, 0900–1830 Tuesday–Friday, 1000–1600 Saturday and Sunday (Saturdays from June until the end of September 0900–1700). *Internet:* www.visitbritain.com; *E-mail:* BLVCinfo@visit britain.org.

Victoria Station: Located off the forecourt, to the left of the ticket office. *Hours:* June–September, Monday–Saturday 0800–2100, Sunday 0800–1800; October–March, 0800–1800 daily; April–May, Monday– Saturday 0800–2000, Sunday 0800–1800.

Liverpool Street Station: Located at the Underground Station Concourse. *Hours:* 0800–1800 daily.

London Visitor Centre: Located at Waterloo International Station's arrivals hall. *Tel:* (020) 7620 1550. *Hours:* 0830–2230 daily.

Heathrow Airport: Located at the "Terminal 1, 2, 3" Underground station. *Hours:* 0800–1800 daily.

Visitlondon.com also operates a telephone accommodations reservations service. *Tel:* (0845) 644 3010. From the United States, 011 44 8456 44 3010.

London Limelights

There are, of course, some "must-sees" in London, particularly if you're a first-time visitor. Even if you've been to London several times, here's an update on some basics.

Buckingham Palace, The Visitor Office, Buckingham Palace, London SW1A 1AA; for tickets and info *Tel:* (020) 7839 1377; *Fax:* (020) 7930 9625; *Internet:* www.royal.gov.uk/output/page555.asp; *E-mail:* bucking hampalace@royalcollection.org.uk. Take the Tube to Victoria, Green Park, or St. James's Park Station.

Tours of the **Palace State Rooms:** £12.95 adult; £6.50 children ages five to sixteen; £11.00 for those age sixty and older. Open every day August 1–September 28, 0930–1630. Tickets, which guarantee entry to the State Rooms at a specific time, may be purchased for any day in person from the Buckingham Palace Ticket Office in Green Park (August and September only); by telephoning the credit-card hotline, (020) 7766 7300; by writing to the Visitor Office at the above address; or e-mailing bookinginfo@royalcollection.org.

Ironically, Queen Victoria's favorite palace was originally built in 1702 on the site of a notorious brothel as the home of the Dukes of Buckingham.

You can visit nineteen of the palace's 661 rooms, including the Royal Ballroom, from early August to the end of September, when the royal family is at Balmoral in Scotland. Same-day tickets for the tour are sold on a first-come, first-served basis from a booth at the end of Green Park, which faces the plaza outside the palace. The ticket booth opens at 0900. Be prepared to stand in line for as long as two hours (unless you have the London Pass). The tour includes the prominent vaulted Picture Gallery, which houses part of the royal collection of 10,000 paintings.

The Queen's Gallery is open every day except April 19 and December 25–26. Tickets: £7.50 adult; £4.00 child.

Changing of the Guard—a military pageantry that has taken place since medieval times—takes place with the New Guard arriving promptly at 1130 daily April–July; every other day August–March. The red-jacketed Old Guard and New Guard line up facing each other to the beat of the Band and Corps of Drums—a stunning sight to see.

Imperial War Museum, Lambeth Road, SE1 6HZ; *Tel:* (020) 7416 5320; *Internet:* www.iwm.org.uk. *Hours:* 1000–1800 daily, except December 24, 25, and 26. Free admission. Take the Tube to Lambeth North, Waterloo, or Elephant and Castle Station. Audio guides are available for £3.00 adults, £2.50 seniors.

Appropriately so, the early-nineteenth-century's most famous lunatic asylum, Bedlam, houses the country's memorial to the two world wars. A rotating clock hand in the basement represents the cost of war in terms of human lives, and the body count exceeds 100 million. Two thought-provoking "experiences" include the Trenches and the Blitz, which portray the horror of war. The D-Day Sixtieth Anniversary Exhibition (April 2004–May 2005) portrays the Allied invasion of Normandy in June 1944—Operation Overlord—the most complex military operation in history.

Cabinet War Rooms, Clive Steps, King Charles Street, SW1A 2AQ; *Tel:* (020) 7930 6961; *Internet:* www.iwm.org.uk/cabinet/index.htm. The entrance is across from St. James's Park. Take the Tube to St. James's Park or Westminster Station. *Hours:* 0930–1800 April–Sepember; 1000–1800 October–March. Admission: £7.50 adult; £6.00 senior or student; free for children. Free headset with commentary.

Few Americans are aware that a memorial to President Franklin Roosevelt is in London's Grosvenor Square; perhaps even fewer are aware that the place where Prime Minister Winston Churchill of Britain held secret telephone conversations with him is open to the public.

In 1936, when the storm clouds of World War II were gathering, the British began building a communications center, or war room, beneath the government offices in Whitehall. Building a 10-foot layer of concrete above a labyrinth of wine cellars and connecting tunnels, workers toiled at night so as not to arouse suspicions of what was being constructed. The Allies' direction of the war was conducted from this virtually bombproof communications center. It is interesting to see the place where some of the most dramatic decisions in the history of humanity were made. The Map Room and Churchill's combined bedroom, office, and broadcasting room remain just as they were during the war, and additional previously hidden chambers opened in 2003; the Churchill Museum is scheduled to open in early 2005.

Jewish Museum, Raymond Burton House, 129–131 Albert Street, London, NW1 7NB; *Tel:* (020) 7284 1997. *Internet:* www.jewish museum.org.uk. *Hours:* Monday–Thursday 1000–1600, Sunday 1000–1700; closed Friday and Saturday. Admission: £3.50 adult, £1.50 child or student, £2.50 senior. Take the Tube to Camden Town Station, then a three-minute walk. There's also a branch at 80 East End Road, N3 2SY (Finchley); *Tel:* (020) 8349 1143.

The refurbished Raymond Burton House, the site of the Jewish Museum, explores the history and religious life of the Jewish community in Britain and beyond. It has one of the finest collections of antique cere-monial art.

Kensington Palace State Apartments, High Street, Kensington, W8 4PX; *Tel:* (0) 870 751 5170; *Internet:* www.royal.gov.uk/output/page563.asp. Take the Tube to Queensway, Nottinghill Gate, or High Street Kensington Station. *Hours:* March–October 1000–1800 daily, November–February 1000–1700 daily. Admission: £10.80 adults; £7.00 children. Order tickets in advance via telephone or Internet for a £1.00 discount. Serving as the last home of Diana, Princess of Wales, the palace has been converted into a memorial to the Princess and a home for a por-tion of the Royal Art Collection.

London Transport Museum, Covent Garden Piazza, WC2E 7BB; *Tel:* (020) 7379 6344; *Internet:* www.ltmuseum.co.uk. *Hours:* Saturday–Thursday 1000–1800, Friday 1100–1800 (last admission 1715). Admis-sion: £5.95 adult, £4.50 student; free for accompanied children younger than age sixteen.

See and hear the exciting story of London's famous transportation system—from the red double-decker buses to the masterpiece Under-ground system, the Tube. Try the Tube train simulator, or practice driving a bus. Full of great exhibits and fun kid zone areas.

Madame Tussaud's, Marylebone Road, NW1; *Tel:* (0870) 400 3000; *Internet:* www.madame-tussauds.com. *Hours:* 0930–1730 weekdays, 0900–1800 weekends. Admission: £19.99 adult; £15.99 child (younger than age sixteen); £16.99 seniors. Purchase tickets in advance if possible. To get there, take the Tube to Baker Street Station.

Here's a place where you can mingle with top celebs and notorious criminals at the same time. Showing her first collection back in 1770 in Paris, Tussaud's waxworks number more than 400 lifelike figures of the famous and the notorious. The figures include the late Princess Diana,

Nicolas Cage, and Whoopi Goldberg. The Queen, of course, is a mainstay. Take in the dazzling "Spirit of London" time-travel ride and the chilling "Chamber Live." (Not suitable for those younger than age twelve, pregnant, or with heart conditions.)

Museum of London, 150 London Wall, EC2Y 5HN; *Tel:* (020) 7600 3699; *Internet:* www.museumoflondon.org.uk. *Hours:* Monday–Saturday 1000–1700, Sunday 1130–1700. Admission is free, except for the exhibition "1920s: the decade that changed London." Adults: £5; younger than age sixteen, free. Take the Tube to Barbican or St. Paul's, or take the Tube/rail to Moorgate.

Visit the London Now Gallery, trace London's history from prehistoric times up to the present day, and relive the Great Fire that destroyed London in 1666. The most comprehensive city museum in the world and one of the most imaginatively designed, the Museum of London should be on your "must-see" list.

Natural History Museum, Cromwell Road, South Kensington, SW7 5BD; *Tel:* (020) 7942 5000; *Internet:* www.nhm.ac.uk. *Hours:* 1000–1750 Monday–Saturday and 1100–1750 Sunday. Entry is free, with a small fee for special exhibits. South Kensington is the nearest Underground station (served by the Circle, District, and Piccadilly lines), and the museum is not far from Victoria Rail Station. This museum is located directly behind the Royal Albert Hall and the Science Museum, and Victoria and Albert Museum is nearby. It houses one of the world's largest collections—more than 68 million pieces (it acquires thirty objects per minute!). The Earth Galleries is a fun interactive alternative for kids of all ages.

London Trocadero, 13 Coventry Street, W1D 7DH; *Tel:* (090) 6888 1100; *Internet:* www.troc.co.uk. Take the Underground to Piccadilly Circus. The Trocadero is a two-acre enclosed entertainment, shopping, and restaurant complex. Attractions include Funland, which is Europe's largest indoor family entertainment center. Rock Circus is the rock and pop version of Madame Tussaud's wax museum. Eateries at the Trocadero include Ed's Easy Diner, Yo! Sushi, and Rainforest Cafe.

The Royal Opera House, built in 1858 and refurbished in 1999, is located in historic Covent Garden, home to the Royal Opera and the Royal Ballet. Visit www.royalopera.org for upcoming events and updates.

Shakespeare's Globe Theatre Tour and Exhibition, New Globe Walk, Bankside, London SE1 9ED; *Tel:* (020) 7902 1500; *Fax:* (020) 7902 1515; *Internet:* www.shakespeares-globe.org. Education Centre (for lectures, workshops, etc.) *Tel:* (020) 7902 1433. *Hours:* May–September 0900–1200 (Theatre Tour and Exhibitions) and 1230–1600 (Exhibition and Virtual Tour); October–April 1000–1700 daily. No access during matinees. Admission: £8.00 adults, £5.50 children, £6.50 seniors.

To get there, take the Underground to Mansion House, or take bus

11, 15, 17, 23, 26, or 76 to Mansion House; cross over the Thames River via Southwark Bridge. The theater is along Bankside about 500 yards to the right of the bridge.

The Globe Theatre was rebuilt as the focal point of the International Shakespeare Globe Centre, an educational, entertainment, and cultural complex. Shakespeare's Globe Exhibition was voted "Best of Europe" by the European Federation of Associations of Tourism Journalists.

If you want to know what an Elizabethan audience would have experienced, find out what a "bodger" is, or learn about "penny stinkards," check out the Education Centre and workshops. A guided tour will bring England's most important theatrical heritage to life. Theater performances are from May through September. Box office *Tel:* (020) 7401 9919. According to Mark Rylance, artistic director of Shakespeare's Globe, "The theatre you will see is, to the best of our abilities, the space in which Shakespeare wanted us to meet his plays. It is unique in the world."

Tate Modern, Bankside, SE1 9TG, is the former Bankside Power Station converted into gallery space for the Tate's collection of international contemporary art. *Tel:* (020) 7887 8000; *Internet:* www.tate.org.uk. *Hours:* Sunday–Thursday 1000–1800, Friday–Saturday 1000–2200. No admission fee.

Tower of London, Tower Hill, EC3N 4AB; *Tel:* (0870) 756 6060; *Internet:* www.hrp.org.uk. *Hours:* March–October: Monday–Saturday 0900–1800, Sunday 1000–1800. November–February: Sunday and Monday 1000–1700, Tuesday–Saturday 0900–1700. Admission: £12.00 adult, £7.80 children younger than age sixteen, £9.00 student/senior. To get there, take the Tube to Southwark (Jubilee line) or Blackfriars (District and Circles lines).

Throughout London's history, the Tower has been a fortress, a palace, and a prison, and it is one of the top travel sites in Britain. Allow two to three hours for your visit. The oldest part of the Tower complex, the White Tower, was begun in 1076 and contains the Chapel of St. John the Evangelist, the oldest church in London. Other main attractions include the Bloody Tower (where twelve-year-old Edward V and his ten-year-old brother were incarcerated by their uncle, the future Richard III), the colorful Yeoman Warders, known as "Beefeaters," and the Jewel House, which houses the Crown Jewels. Visit the Martin Tower's special exhibition, "Crowns & Diamonds: The Making of the Crown Jewels." Five royal crowns that were used between 1715 and 1939 and more than 12,000 diamonds may be viewed.

Victoria and Albert Museum, Cromwell Road, South Kensington, SW7 2RL; *Tel:* (020) 7942 2000; *Internet:* www.vam.ac.uk. Take the Tube to South Kensington Station. *Hours:* 1000–1745 daily (until 2200 Wednesday). Admission is free. The famous Victoria and Albert Museum, informally called the "V&A," is considered the finest decorative-arts museum in the world and includes exquisite collections of jewelry, furniture, and oriental carpets. Principal attractions include the Photography Gallery and Art & Design galleries, with a collection of more than 400 years of European fashion.

Royal Parks. Manicured gardens and pastoral grounds within London's vast Royal Parks, once the hunting and recreational property of the Royal Family, now provide the people of London and their visitors with something few megalopolises have: peace and quiet. The lake of St. James is so serene that it is a breeding ground for birds. Boats cruise the Serpentine River in huge Hyde Park, where there is room for riding trails and open-air concerts. *Internet:* www.royalparks.gov.uk.

Westminster Abbey, Parliament Square, SW1; *Tel:* (020) 7222 7110; *Internet:* www.westminster-abbey.org. Take the Tube to Westminster or St. James's Park Station. *Hours:* Monday–Friday 0900–1645 (last admission 1545), Saturday 0930–1445 (last admission 1345); closed to sightseeing on Sunday. Admission to Royal Chapels and Poets' Corner: £7.50 adult; £5.00 children younger than age sixteen/senior; children younger than age eleven free.

Every king and queen of England since 1066 has been crowned here, and more than 3,000 of the nation's most highly valued figures are buried here. You'll see the Tomb of the Unknown Soldier; Elizabeth I's tomb; the Coronation Chair, in use since 1300; Poets' Corner, commemorating Britain's greatest writers; the Chapter House, containing examples of medieval English sculpture; the eleventh-century Pyx Chamber; and the Abbey Museum.

Shopping

Shopping can be quite traditional—even stuffy—at Harrods in Knightsbridge, where the Royals shop, but the store alone is a sight to see. Even though it's more than 150 years old, Harrods does have online service (www.harrods.com), but the actual experience is much more pleasurable. You will find exclusive leather goods at Asprey's and rare antiques at Sotheby's on Bond Street. Oxford Street and Regent Street shopping is the most diverse and the most crowded, featuring famous London department stores such as Marks & Spencer and traditional British fare at Aquascutum, Austin Reed, and Burberry's. For those who desire a princely wardrobe, visit Gieves & Hawkes at No.1 Savile Row, London.

For a different and memorable eclectic shopping excursion, visit the Piazza near the Covent Garden Underground Station. Replacing the Covent Garden flower and vegetable market, which was in age-old times the convent gardens of the Abbey at St. Peter at Westminster, Covent Garden is now a boisterous compound of antiques, clothing, and craft stores, amid a plethora of indoor and outdoor cafes, pubs, eateries, and clubs.

Portobello Market is one of the more popular markets. Made famous in Julia Roberts and Hugh Grant's film *Notting Hill,* the market is located in the West London suburb of the same name. It's a vital mixture of English, Jamaican, Portuguese, and rich and poor. Their Notting Hill Carnival (August 28 and 29, 2005), attracts more than two million people annually.

Restaurants and Pubs

Several years ago, many visitors to London might have regarded English food as overcooked and boring. Now there are more than 6,000 restaurants, thirty-one of which are Michelin starred, serving more than sixty different cuisines. A wide selection of gourmet cafes and bistros set the trend for the new Soho and West Soho areas, with Carnaby Street at its center. Both areas are bedecked with fashionable boutiques, bookstores, craft shops, and expensive private clubs.

Fans of the syndicated American TV show *Cheers* will feel right at home at the Cheers London Bar & Restaurant. It's located on the ground floor of the Café Royal at 72 Regent Street. Nearest Tube station: Piccadilly Circus. For reservations, call (020) 7494 3322; *Fax:* (020) 7494 2211; *Internet:* www.cheersbarlondon.com.

Rail buffs will enjoy Chez Gerard at 64 Bishopsgate. Nearest Tube station: Liverpool Street. The restaurant is decorated with lamps and luggage racks reminiscent of the golden days of the railways. For reservations, call (020) 7588 1200; *Fax:* (020) 7588 1122; *Internet:* www.santeonline.co.uk.

While in London grab *Time Out* at the newsstand to check out what's happening in the heart of London for the arts, including West End shows, films, gigs, and so on.

Day Excursions

After you've seen London, explore more of this wonderful country where, among its many advantages, everyone speaks English. Well, sort of—dialects do abound. You cannot get to know Britain without experiencing the charms of its other cities and seeing firsthand the lovely rural areas that separate them. Of course, there's no better way to view the passing scene and converse with the British themselves than aboard a train.

Like the road builders of Rome, Britain's rail builders laid their tracks leading to London—or, more properly, out of London. London serves as the center of a somewhat lopsided spiderweb with its radials running east and south to the sea on the short side of the web and the longer extensions running west to Wales and north into Scotland. Thirty-two day excursions from London await your pleasure with three of them (Bath, Penzance, and Plymouth) just as easily done from Cardiff.

As with any knight of old, you may want to sally forth on a short sortie or two before departing on a crusade. In that case, you will find the Greenwich, Windsor, and St. Albans day excursions to your liking. Ranging southeast out of London, Kent beckons with its towns of Canterbury, Dover, Folkestone, and Ramsgate. Southward, rail trails lead along the English Channel to the port/resort towns of Hastings, Brighton, Portsmouth, and Southampton and to the Isle of Wight.

Having whetted your appetite with those excursions, you should now be ready to venture farther afield. Almost everything you plan to see has been there for quite some time—usually at least a century or two—so relax and enjoy your longer travels throughout Britain.

West from London, excursions to Salisbury, Stonehenge, and Gloucester await the train traveler. Or journey to Liverpool, home of the Beatles. With a ticket (or rail pass) to ride, you will find great history and new attractions beckoning from this seaport town beyond the Mersey beat. Day excursions to Bath, Plymouth, and Penzance may be made from *either* Cardiff or London. See the chapter on Cardiff for these day excursions. Schedules from both Cardiff and London are included in the chapter on Cardiff.

In the heart of England, excursions to Birmingham, Stratford-upon-Avon, Coventry, Nottingham, Sheffield, Lincoln, and York await you. Farther west beckons Chester.

Northeast of London is East Anglia, where historic King's Lynn, Bury St. Edmunds, and Ipswich abound in museums and memories of World War II. For academic flavor, visit Cambridge or Oxford; school-tie types will appreciate Eton—a stone's throw away from Windsor—where kings are educated.

Train Connections to Other Base Cities from London

London–Cardiff

DEPART PADDINGTON STATION	ARRIVE CARDIFF CENTRAL STATION	NOTES
0700	0901	M–F
0730	0948	M–F
0800	1000	M–F
0830	1041	M–F, Su
0900	1100 (1107 Su)	Daily

Then hourly service daily until 2100

2345	0300	M–Sa

Reservations recommended for all above-listed trains.

London–Edinburgh

Services shown operate from London's King's Cross via the so-called eastern route to Scotland. Other service is available from London Euston Station using the western route, but most trains stop at Glasgow before continuing to Edinburgh. The eastern route provides faster service to Edinburgh.

DEPART KING'S CROSS STATION	ARRIVE EDINBURGH WAVERLEY STATION	NOTES
0615	1110	M–Sa
0700	1127	M–Sa
0800	1230	Daily
0900	1339	Daily
0930	1421	Su

Daily hourly departures until 1800

1900	0015+1	M–F
2230	0727+1	Su, R, Sleeper
2340*	0656+1	M–F, R, Sleeper

R=Reservation required on sleeper trains. Arrives next morning.

*Departs from Euston Station.

+1=Arrives next day

London–Glasgow

Services shown operate from London Euston only; other service available from King's Cross Station.

DEPART EUSTON STATION	ARRIVE GLASGOW CENTRAL STATION	NOTES
0555	1215	Sa
0625	1215	M–F
0830	1402	Daily
1005	1755	Su

Then hourly at 30 minutes past the hour until 1830

2340 (2320 Su)*	0716+1	M–F, Su, Sleeper

+1=Arrives next day

*Reservation required.

Day Excursion to

Birmingham
Heart of England

Depart from Euston Station
Distance by train: 115 miles (185 km)
Average train time: 1 hour, 30 minutes
Train information and InterCity services: (0845) 748 4950
Tourist information: Tourism Centre and Ticket Shop, The Rotunda, 150 New Street,
    Birmingham B2 4PA; *Tel:* (0121) 202 5099; *Fax:* (0121) 616 1038
Internet: www.beinbirmingham.com
E-mail: callcentre@marketingbirmingham.com
Hours: 0930–1730 Monday–Saturday, 1030–1630 Sunday/bank holidays.
Notes: As you exit the main entrance of New Street Station, follow the left-hand path
    in the direction of the city center. The Tourism Centre and Ticket Shop is on your
    left, at the base of the tall building in front of you, The Rotunda, next to Bullring
    Shopping Centre.

Birmingham has more canals than Venice. This is rather unusual because Birmingham claims to be Britain's "city at the center." Although it is in the approximate geographic midpoint of the British Isles, it was once the hub of England's waterways, which carried most of the nation's industrial traffic. With the development of other forms of transportation, particularly rail, canal transportation dissipated. Most of the canals were developed into recreation areas with walks, pubs, and restored buildings alongside their rights-of-way.

For decades, Birmingham was known internationally as one of the world's great industrial cities. Along with that recognition came the image of a smoke-filled, grimy Victorian sprawl of a city. Since World War II, Birmingham has made spectacular progress in developing a beautiful residential city. The center of the city has been completely rebuilt.

One of the best ways to see Birmingham is on foot. Begin a self-guided tour at **Brindley Place,** the main canalside development situated at the rear of the International Convention Centre. You'll see the old, original canal locks, as well as the newer **Water's Edge.** Your walk will lead you to the **National Sealife Centre,** restaurants of all nationalities, and the **Ikon Gallery.** If you prefer to experience the canals on water, barge trips are available at the rear of the Convention Centre.

Birmingham is said to have several haunted pubs, but plenty of ale flowing. Sample a pint when you join the **Ghost Trail** tour. You'll just die to get on this next tour—the **Graveyard Trail,** guided by Birmingham's most popular corpse, John Baskerville. Prices: £5.00 adults, £3.00 children age 8–14. For more details or to sign up for any of the tours, log onto www.birminghamwalks.co.uk or call (0121) 202 5000.

London–Birmingham–London

Direct service from London Euston Station only; other service is available from Paddington Station via Reading and Oxford.

DEPART EUSTON STATION	ARRIVE NEW STREET STATION	NOTES
0544	0815	M–F
0644	0910	M–F
0745	1010	M–F
0848	1050	M–F
0950	1141	Su

M–F service continues at 50 minutes past each hour until 1450, then departs every 20–30 minutes until 2345; Sa service continues at half-hour intervals until 2100, then 2200 and 2250. Su service is at bi-hourly intervals from 0730 until 1330, then every 20–40 minutes until 1645, then departures at 10, 20, and 40 minutes past the hour until 2040.

DEPART NEW STREET STATION	ARRIVE EUSTON STATION

M–Sa service departs at half-hour intervals from 0536 to 1936; then 2036, 2136, and 2245 M–F; then 2049, 2155, and 2215 Sa.

Sunday service continues hourly 0800–1200; then hourly 1319–2019, with final departure at 2149.

One of the most striking landmarks marking the city center is the **Rotunda,** a 250-foot tower. Beneath the tower is the world's first under-one-roof shopping complex, which includes The Bullring, The Palisades, The Pavilions, and the City Plaza. The redevelopment of the forty-acre Bullring site has transformed Birmingham into a world-class retail capital with department stores for Debenhams and Selfridges and more than 140 shops, cafes, and restaurants. There's a five-ton bronze bull standing in front—you can't miss it. *Internet:* www.bullring.co.uk. *Hours:* 0930–2000 Monday–Saturday, 1100–1700 Sunday.

Birmingham's National Exhibition Centre is a modern exhibition-and-conference center on a 310-acre site readily accessible by rail through the New Street Station on any trains departing in the direction of London. The stop, Birmingham International, is a short, seventeen- to twenty-minute ride. Full details are available from the tourist centers. With 1.2 million square feet of air-conditioned exhibition space in twelve halls, it is by far the largest complex in Britain, and it's still growing.

Located in the Victoria Square vicinity and noteworthy for its classic elegance and Victorian style is the **Town Hall.** It was designed by Joseph Hansom, the inventor of the Hansom cab, and is the concert hall in which Mendelssohn conducted the first performance of *Elijah* in 1846. Many distinguished musicians have appeared there since it opened in 1834, including Sir Edward Elgar.

Sarehole Mill, on Cole Bank Road (served by Hall Green Station), is an eighteenth-century water mill restored to working order, and would become an exciting adventure for J.R.R. Tolkien fans. So inspired by this mill was Tolkien that he chose it as the setting for his *Middle-Earth*. The mill is open 1330 to 1730 Wednesday through Saturday between April and September. This particular area of Birmingham was where Tolkien, author of *The Hobbit* and the *Lord of the Rings* trilogy, spent his childhood. His family's home, Gracewell, is now privately owned, but you can visit Edgbaston, a house he often used for holiday lodging. For a beautiful view of the hills and trees where Tolkien may have seen his first hobbit, stop at **Lickey Hills** in Rednal, just outside Birmingham.

Blakesley Hall, Blakesley Road, Yardley (Stechford Station), is a delightful sixteenth-century timber-framed yeoman's house, furnished in period style, with an interesting garden, barn, and historical vehicles. *Hours:* Easter–October, 1130–1600 Tuesday–Sunday. Two and a half miles north of the city center on Trinity Road is a seventeenth-century gem, **Aston Hall** (Wilton Station). The magnificent Jacobean mansion was begun in 1618 and took seventeen years to complete. Admission is free for both museums.

For rail buffs, a visit to the **Birmingham Railway Museum** is a must. It houses the world's oldest steam engine, which was built in 1784, along with displays of early machinery, steam engines, and the Tyseley Locomotive Works. You can even learn to drive a main line express.

Birmingham's Civic Centre is a modern contribution to the city's skyline. It includes a repertory theater and one of the largest and best-stocked libraries in Europe, featuring a comprehensive Shakespeare collection. The city's **Central Museum and Art Gallery** houses works by Van Gogh, Botticelli, and Gainsborough. Its pre-Raphaelite painting collection is the best.

After all the sightseeing, you may develop a thirst. Well, you came to the right city. Birmingham has long been one of Britain's major brewing centers, and its beer is recommended highly by both locals and visitors. There are plenty of pubs in which to conduct your own taste tests.

Birmingham is justly proud of its restaurants, which cater to every palate and purse. The city has stylish theater-restaurants with entertainment by international cabaret stars, as well as a wide selection of eateries providing French, Italian, Spanish, Greek, "Balti" (from northern India), Chinese, and traditional English cuisine. There's no reason to leave Birmingham with an empty stomach or an unquenched thirst.

Having undergone many structural changes in recent years, Birmingham undoubtedly is becoming one of Europe's outstanding cities. Enjoy!

Day Excursion to

Brighton
Colorful Seaside City

Depart from Victoria Station
Distance by train: 51 miles (82 km)
Average train time: 49 minutes
Train information and InterCity services: (0845) 748 4950
Tourist information: Brighton and Hove Visitor Information Centre, 10 Bartholomew Square, Brighton, East Sussex BN1 1JS; *Tel:* (0906) 711 2255 (50p per minute); *Fax:* (01273) 292594
Internet: www.visitbrighton.com
E-mail: brighton-tourism@brighton-hove.gov.uk
Hours: Monday–Friday 0900–1700, Saturday 1000–1700, Sunday and bank holidays 1000–1600.
Notes: Brighton's visitor information center is located in Bartholomew Square next to the Town Hall, about a ten-minute walk from Brighton's rail station. Walk directly out of the rail station down Queens Road to the sea. Turn left at that point onto Kings Road. Where Kings Road becomes Grand Junction, turn left again and proceed to the Town Hall to the visitor information center.

Brighton is, and always has been, much more than a traditional seaside destination. Since the earliest days of travel, visitors have been attracted by the destination's unique sense of style and architectural splendor. Having merged with its neighbor, Hove, in 1997, the city's special qualities are as strong as ever. But they are only part of a continuing success story that secures Brighton's position as Britain's liveliest seaside city.

Perhaps Brighton would have remained a tiny, humble fishing village originally known as Brighthelmstone were it not for the efforts of Dr. Richard Russell and the Prince Regent who later became King George IV. In 1750 Dr. Russell, a Brighton resident, published a book extolling the magical effects of sea air and salt water. This started a fashionable trend that brought royalty and commoner alike to Brighton. The good doctor prescribed bathing in the sea and drinking a pint and a half of seawater daily as a cure for glandular diseases. Such a prescription, incredible as it seems, must have initiated a whole new series of maladies. Chronicles of that period, however, have failed to note them.

The gifted and wayward Prince Regent first visited Brighton in 1783. Enamored by it all (and well heeled with royal funds), he ordered his Royal Pavilion constructed there. Completed in 1822 from an architectural style taken somewhere east of the Suez, it has been termed one of the most bizarre and exotic palaces in all Europe. The **Royal Pavilion**'s ostentatious onion-domed exterior, looking very much like a series of hot-air balloons about to ascend, is only surpassed by its even more amazing interior. Fully furnished in its original style, it is open to the public daily 0930–1745 April–September 1000–1715 October–March. *Tel:* (01273) 290900. Guided tours are daily at 1130 and 1430 (£1.25 in addition to admission fee: £5.80 adult, £3.40 child). *Internet:* www.royal pavilion.org.uk.

Visit **The Lanes,** where you step backward into the old fishing-village days. The buildings in these narrow, twisting passages were fishermen's cottages in the seventeenth century. Today they house quaint and fascinating antiques, jewelry, high-fashion shops, pubs, and cafes.

Part of the changing scene in Brighton has been the introduction of English-language schools, which attract international students from a score of foreign lands. With the resident student population from Sussex and Brighton Universities, this youthful input has made it one of the most vibrant destinations in Britain.

In English-style directions, had you denied yourself the turning at Grand Junction, you would have come quickly upon the gates of the **Brighton Pier,** which extends out into the English Channel like a silent sentinel. Constructed in 1899, the pier has been restored, illuminated with 13,000 lightbulbs, and features free entrance, free deck chairs, and free entertainment. It opens daily at 0900.

For a guided walking tour of Brighton's "Old Town," obtain details from the visitor information center. From April through mid-September, the tours start at the tourist information center. Or you can pick up the *Brighton and Hove City Guide* at the information center. The town plan in the guide shows the best of where to go, what to see, and where to shop.

Attention, shoppers: The £90 million indoor shopping center, Churchill Square, is unique to southern England and only minutes from the seafront. Swank designer shops can be found in Brighton's east side and the adjoining **Regent Arcade.** For the more bizarre, shop the **Upper Gardner Street Junk Market** on Saturday mornings and the station car park's "carboot" (junk and antiques) sale on Sunday mornings. A visit to the North Lane's quirky shops is a must for a real mix of the ethnic, offbeat, and downright funky.

Because of the city's number and variety of shopping areas, Brighton is often referred to as "London by the Sea." New bars, cafes, and restaurants in the Victorian seafront arches offer an uninterrupted view of the

Services shown are from London Victoria Station; other service available from London Blackfriars and London Bridge Stations.

DEPART VICTORIA STATION	ARRIVE BRIGHTON STATION	NOTES
0632	0803	M–F
0706	0800	Sa
0732	0850	Su
0802 (0808 Sa)	0907	M–Sa
0836 (0832 Su)	0928 (0947 Sa, 0949 Su)	Daily
0906	0958	M–Sa
0936	1027	M–Sa

M–Sa service continues at half-hour intervals to 2308; Su service continues at hourly intervals until 2332.

DEPART BRIGHTON STATION	ARRIVE VICTORIA STATION	NOTES
1619	1711	M–Sa
1649	1743	Daily
1719	1812	M–Sa
1749	1841	Daily

M–Sa service is every half hour at 20 and 50 minutes past the hour, then hourly from 1950 to 2150, then 2200 and 2302. Su service is hourly to 2200, then 2302.

sea along the beachfront and boardwalk. While exploring, try not to miss the **Artists' Quarter** or the **Fishing Museum.** Farther along the revamped beachfront, you'll find beach volleyball and basketball courts, a redesigned children's play area, and lots of bold new works of art. The kids will love the **Sea Life Centre** and the new rides on Brighton Pier.

Young and old alike should take a ride along the seafront on the **Volks Railway,** Britain's first public electric railway. Open daily between Easter and Labor Day, the railway travels along the beach on Madeira Drive to Black Rock. Lacking the speed of the InterCity 125s, the Volks Railway makes up for it with its nostalgia.

Brighton's **Marina** is one of the largest in Europe. Whether you are a boating enthusiast or not, a visit there is well in order. A complete village is now the centerpiece of the marina, with an eight-screen movie theater, elegant shops, quayside restaurants, bowling complex, and, of course, traditional British pubs on the waterfront. The marina also stages many colorful events, such as boat shows and sailing regattas throughout July and August. Visit the £3 million casino complex and the Walk of Fame, a Hollywood-style route of Brighton's famous people, both past and present.

Time permitting, we suggest a stroll along the Hove promenade with its elegant Regency squares and crescents, or stop by the **Brunswick Town House** for a fascinating insight into Regency lifestyle. For steam enthusiasts, do *not* miss the **British Engineerium.**

Brighton has more than 400 restaurants, pre–West End theater, superb sports, and year-round event programs of fun and festivities. Annually in May, the Brighton Festival takes over the city with the biggest arts festival in England. So, if you're caught up in Brighton's buoyancy, check with the visitor information center for hotel accommodations and catch a morning train back to London. Hove also has its own train station, with regular service to London. For those flying into or out of Gatwick Airport, Brighton is only thirty fast-train minutes away—the perfect starting point or destination.

Day Excursion to

Bury St. Edmunds
Magna Carta

Depart from Liverpool Street Station
Distance by train: 95 miles (153 km)
Average train time: 2 hours
Train information and InterCity services: (0845) 748 4950
Tourist information: Tourist Information Centre, 6 Angel Hill, Bury St. Edmunds, Suffolk IP33 1UZ; *Tel:* (01284) 764667; *Fax:* (01284) 757084
Minicom: (01284) 757023
Internet: www.stedmundsbury.gov.uk
E-mail: tic@stedsbc.gov.uk
Hours: Easter–end of October: Monday–Saturday 0930–1730, Sunday and bank holidays 1000–1500; November–Easter: Monday–Friday 1000–1600, Saturday 1000–1300.
Notes: Follow the pedestrian signs to the Tourist Information Centre, located immediately opposite the Abbey Gate entrance to the ruins of the Abbey of St. Edmund, approximately 1 mile from the train station. A city map is displayed in the station (map dispensers available also), or station personnel will gladly provide directions. Taxi stand is located outside.

I n his *Pickwick Papers,* Charles Dickens described Bury St. Edmunds as "a handsome little town of thriving and cleanly appearance." So it remains today.

A Christian community was founded on the present site of Bury St. Edmunds in A.D. 633. In 903, thirty-four years after King Edmund of East Anglia was killed by the Danes at Hoxne, his body was brought to the town and consecrated around 905. Thus, the town became known as Bury St. Edmunds (the place of St. Edmund). The abbey church was built soon afterward to honor the memory of the king. It is said that in 1214, barons gathered at the high altar of the abbey to take a solemn oath to force King John to grant a charter of liberties, one of the events leading to the granting of the Magna Carta in 1215.

The town center is most notable for its pleasant Georgian atmosphere; the town is still a leading social center within East Anglia. The great **Abbey of St. Edmund** was one of the largest in Europe during medieval times. Sacked in 1327 by townspeople protesting monastic control, and again in 1381 during the Peasants' Revolt, the Abbey Gate was severely damaged and many monks were killed. In 1465 a severe fire damaged the church, and it had to be extensively repaired. A placard on the Abbey Gate indicates that the gate was destroyed and the abbey badly damaged by the townspeople in 1327 but was rebuilt on a spot adjacent to the old one in 1347. The dissolution of the monasteries in 1539 brought about the closure of the abbey. The stone and other material was then sold off to the locals and used in other buildings.

Across from the Abbey Gate is the **Angel Hotel,** more than 500 years old, known for its association with Charles Dickens. His room, No. 15, is preserved exactly as it was more than a century ago. The site has seen three East Anglian inns over the years. Unique attractions of the Angel Hotel include its tavern room, dating from 1433—fifty-nine years before Columbus discovered America—and the restaurant located in the medieval vaults of the structure.

During World War II, Bury St. Edmunds was ringed with American air bases. Today the U.S. Air Force European Command operates a base at Mildenhall and Lakenheath, west of Bury St. Edmunds. Visitors are welcome there if they have contacted the base information office or its community relations adviser before going. The information center can provide details.

The highlight in Bury St. Edmunds is the abbey ruins and gardens. **St. Mary's Church,** the southern boundary of the abbey precinct, is also popular. The **Borough Council's Museum of Local History** is housed in Moyse's Hall in the town center. It has been renovated and now includes the Suffolk Regiment Collection. Constructed in the latter part of the twelfth century, it is a fine example of Norman domestic architecture and houses eclectic collections from archaeology to crime and punishment. The **Manor House Museum** faces the great churchyard. This

London–Bury St. Edmunds–London

Service shown is from London Liverpool Street Station via Ipswich and requires a change of trains in Ipswich; other service is available via Cambridge, with a change of trains necessary in Cambridge, with service from both London King's Cross and Liverpool Street Stations.

DEPART LIVERPOOL STREET STATION	ARRIVE BURY ST. EDMUNDS STATION	NOTES
0830	1017 (1023 Su)	Daily (1)
1000	1141 (1158 Su)	Daily (1)
1100	1323	M–Sa (1)
1330	1527	Su (1)

Departures every half hour M–F beginning at 0602; 0730 Sa and 0800 Su.

DEPART BURY ST. EDMUNDS STATION	ARRIVE LIVERPOOL STREET STATION	NOTES
1452	1652	M–Sa (1)
1521	1720	M–Sa (1)
1622	1825	Su (1)
1658	1855	Daily
1721	1925 (1921 Sa)	M–Sa (1)
1746	1955	M–Sa (1)
1854	2055 (2053 Sa)	M–Sa (1)
1921	2157	M–Sa (1)
2106 (2057 Su)	2301	Daily (1)

(1) Change trains in Ipswich

restored Georgian mansion houses clocks, paintings, and costumes from the seventeenth to the twentieth centuries.

There are two distinct parts to the town. As was customary in most medieval towns with a monastic foundation, there was a division between the monastery and the townspeople—possibly the first example of separation of church and state. This division resulted in the business section and public buildings standing on a hill only 100 meters away to the west of the abbey ruins today.

The **Theatre Royal,** one of three surviving Georgian playhouses in Britain, was built in Bury St. Edmunds during 1819 by English architect William Wilkins. He also designed Downing College at Cambridge

University. Almost a miniature version of the West End London Theatre (seating only 352 people), the historical Theatre Royal's architecture displays, in elegant fashion, the style and form for which the Georgian architects were famous. The repertoire features a broad range of entertainment, plays, dance, opera, and every form of music from classical to jazz and rock. In 1892, the Theatre Royal made international headlines by presenting the world premiere of *Charlie's Aunt,* a comedy that is still performed in every major language throughout the world.

Bypassed by time, Bury St. Edmunds is essentially a country town that was spared the industrial expansion of the Victorian Age. But the town stands tall in history. The principles of the Magna Carta, which had their foundation in Bury St. Edmunds and were developed over the centuries into English common law, have become the heritage not only of the British Isles but also of countless millions throughout the world. As history records, the signing of the Magna Carta by King John is the basic source of the constitutional liberties of English-speaking peoples.

One of Bury St. Edmunds's local products is ale. Try Abbot Ale and St. Edmund Ale for great local flavor. We suggest that you sample a pint in the **Nutshell,** the smallest pub in England. Its single barroom measures only 12 feet by 7 feet.

Ask at the Tourist Information Centre about tours of Bury St. Edmunds. Modestly priced, all are guaranteed to be enjoyable and educational. Audiotapes may be picked up at the center, allowing you to be led through the sites by the historical voices of Brother Jocelin, Henry Lomax, and other town notables.

Day Excursion to

Cambridge
University City

Depart from King's Cross Station
Distance by train: 56 miles (90 km)
Average train time: 1 hour
Train information and InterCity services: (0845) 748 4950
Tourist information: Tourist Information Centre, The Old Library, Wheeler Street, Cambridge, CB2 3QB; *Tel:* (0906) 586 2526 (60p per minute); *Guided Tours:* (01223) 457574; *Fax:* (01223) 457588
Internet: www.visitcambridge.org
E-mail: tourism@cambridge.gov.uk
Hours: Easter weekend–August: Monday–Friday 1000–1800, Saturday 1000– 1700, Sunday 1030–1530; September–October: Monday–Friday 1000–1800, Saturday 1000–1700; November–Easter weekend: Monday–Friday 1000–1730, Saturday 1000–1700.

Notes: To reach the center, take the bus (No. 1) located immediately in front of the railway station to St. Andrew's Street. After getting off the bus at St. Andrew's Street, ask for directions to the tourist information center on Wheeler Street (behind the Guildhall), a few short blocks away.

Oxford graduates often refer to Cambridge as "the other place." Both universities hold one thing in common: Organized along the classic federal structure, they house a number of largely autonomous colleges. Comparisons stop here. Cambridge is Britain's "University City." It is said that if you visit only one other English city besides London, it should be Cambridge.

Cambridge is a complex blend of market town, regional center, tourist attraction, and university. It is situated on the River Cam around the original bridge over which all trade and communications passed between central England, East Anglia, and continental Europe 1,000 years ago. It was a natural spot for travelers to pause to exchange news and opinions, thereby preparing the area for a center of learning.

Several religious orders, including the Franciscans and Dominicans, established monasteries and affiliated schools in Cambridge early in the twelfth century. Students from the University of Oxford and the University of Paris left to study in Cambridge during the thirteenth century. The present-day colleges originated at that time, when students began residing in hostels and halls.

Daily walking tours with guides can tell you about the university and its colleges. Schedules may be obtained from the Tourist Information Centre. The main colleges are closed to visitors from mid-April until the end of June. A note of academic etiquette: College members are happy to welcome you to the grounds and their historic buildings, but they ask you to respect their need for quiet and privacy.

Ask at the tourist office for the *Cambridge Where to Go—What to See* pamphlet (nominal fee). It provides basic information about the colleges and museums and includes a street plan of the city.

King's College Chapel is regarded universally as one of Cambridge's finest architectural structures. It was constructed in stages over a period of nearly seventy years and was completed in 1536. The chapel (admission £4.00 adults; £3.00 children/students) displays the carved coats of arms of Henry VIII. His initials, along with those of Anne Boleyn, can be seen on the screen. The chapel's stained-glass windows depict stories from the Old Testament and the New Testament. Rubens's *Adoration of the Magi* is the altarpiece. *Internet:* www.kings.cam.ac.uk/chapel.

Trinity College's great court is one of the largest collegiate quadrangles in England. It's so large that much of its detail goes unnoticed. It is

Frequent service with departures from both King's Cross and Liverpool Street Stations. Trains that take 61 minutes or less depart from London King's Cross Station; trains from Liverpool Street Station take 75 to 90 minutes.

LONDON KING'S CROSS TO CAMBRIDGE

M–F   Depart at 0545, 0645, 0715, 0745, and every half hour until 2015, then at 15 and 51 minutes after the hour until 2315.

Sa   Depart at 0545, 0645, 0745, 0815, and every half hour until 1945, then at 6 and 51 minutes after the hour until 2206, then 2315 and 0001.

Su   Depart at 0651 and 0751, then at 15 and 51 minutes after the hour until 2315, then 0001.

CAMBRIDGE TO LONDON KING'S CROSS

M–F   Depart Cambridge at 0545, 0615, 0645, and every half hour until 1945, then three times hourly until 2054, then 2131, 2154, 2231, and 2322.

Sa   Depart Cambridge at 0631, 0645, 0731, 0745, and 0815, then every half hour or more until 2311.

Su   Depart Cambridge at 0631 and 0731, then 15 and 31 minutes after the hour until 2231, then 2301.

---

said that taking advantage of this situation, Byron bathed nude in the fountain and shared his room with a pet bear, which he claimed he kept for the purpose of taking examinations. Sir Isaac Newton first measured the speed of sound in the great court by stamping his foot in the cloister along the north side.

The admission qualifications to the University of Cambridge are exceptionally demanding. Each year, approximately 8,000 students apply for admission, but only about 20 percent are admitted.

The Cam River, the source of Cambridge's being and delightful in any season, deserves a portion of your visit. A tour of the city by boat along the "backs," as the placid stretch of the river is called, is an experience not to be missed. You can hire a punt, rowboat, or canoe to boat along the backs. If your selection is the punt—which is propelled with long wooden poles—be aware that these poles frequently stick in the mud and have been known to vault a punter into the river. A "chauffeured punt" service is also available.

Visitors have a large selection of museums covering a wide range of interests. The **Fitzwilliam Museum** on Trumpington Street features Greek and Roman artifacts and a famous collection of paintings. *Internet:*

www.fitzmuseum.cam.ac.uk. The **Folk Museum** on Castle Street contains a vast array of domestic articles. Another point of interest is **Kettles Yard Art Gallery** at Castle Street on Northampton, with its fine collection of modern paintings and sculpture.

Steeped in history, Cambridge has a reminder of a more recent historical event. **Duxford Airfield,** located 8 miles south of the city, houses a fabulous collection of aircraft owned by the Imperial War Museum (headquartered in London). Visitors can also walk through several hangars to view the aircraft being restored. Another very interesting part is the Imperial War Museum's Land Warfare Hall with displays of military vehicles and other wartime equipment. During World War II Allied aircraft flew raids from Duxford to continental Europe.

The **American Military Cemetery,** 4 miles from Cambridge, contains the graves of 3,811 American airmen who operated from bases in Britain. The cemetery and the museum may be reached by bus. For some preliminary knowledge, visit the Imperial War Museum's Web site at www.iwm.org.uk.

Day Excursion to

Canterbury
and the Cathedral

Depart from Victoria Station
Distance by train: 62 miles (99 km)
Average train time: 1 hour, 25 minutes
Train information and InterCity services: (0845) 748 4950
Tourist information: Canterbury Information Centre, 12–13 Sun Street, The Buttermarket, Canterbury, Kent CT1 2HX; *Tel:* (01227) 378100; *Fax:* (01227) 378101
Accommodations: (01227) 378188
Theater and concert bookings: (01227) 455600
Internet: www.canterbury.co.uk
E-mail: canterburyinformation@canterbury.gov.uk
Hours: Monday–Saturday 0930–1700, Sunday 1000–1600.
Notes: Canterbury has two railway stations: West Station and East Station. There's a taxi queue just outside the station entrances, or you may walk to the city center and the cathedral in about fifteen minutes.

Canterbury, the Metropolitan City of the Anglican Communion, has a history going back to prehistoric times. It was once a Roman settlement and the Saxon stronghold of the men of Kent. Here in A.D. 597 St. Augustine began the conversion of the English to Christianity, where Ethelbert, king of Kent, was baptized.

Only ruins remain of the Benedictine **St. Augustine's Abbey,** the burial place of the Jutish kings of Kent, but **St. Martin's Church,** on the eastern outskirts of the city, is still in use. This church is said to have been the place of worship of Queen Bertha, the Christian wife of King Ethelbert, before the arrival of St. Augustine.

In 1170 the rivalry of church and state culminated in the murder in Canterbury Cathedral, by Henry II's knights, of Archbishop Thomas à Becket. His shrine became a great center of pilgrimage, as described by Chaucer in his *Canterbury Tales.* After the Reformation the pilgrimage ceased, but the prosperity of the city was strengthened by an influx of Huguenot refugees from the Continent, who introduced weaving.

Trains departing London's Charing Cross and Waterloo Stations arrive at Canterbury West. Those departing London's Victoria Station arrive at Canterbury East. For simplicity, day-excursion schedules are given for Victoria and Canterbury East Stations only.

Arriving in Canterbury East Station, use the pedestrian bridge to reach the city walls. **The Cathedral,** with architecture ranging from the eleventh to the fifteenth century, is world famous. Modern pilgrims are attracted particularly to the **Martyrdom, the Black Prince's Tomb, the Warriors' Chapel,** and the many examples of medieval stained glass. The medieval city walls are built on Roman foundations, and the fourteenth-century **West Gate** is one of the finest buildings of its kind in the country.

From the station entrance, you'll see a sign across the street that says, CITY CENTRE–MARLOWE THEATRE–CATHEDRAL. A blue sign showing a person walking indicates where to cross the highway. Proceed along the city's old Roman walls, which enclose Dane John Gardens. Climb the mound in the gardens for a view of the town and the cathedral. Farther along you'll come to the city bus station. Descend from the wall at this point onto St. George's Street. Turn left and walk until the cathedral is in view on your right through the Christ Church Gate. Passing through the gate will bring you onto the cathedral grounds.

The poet and playwright Christopher Marlowe was born and reared in Canterbury, and there are also literary associations with Defoe, Dickens, Joseph Conrad, and Somerset Maugham. The *Mayflower* was provisioned in Canterbury before setting sail for Plymouth and its historic journey to America.

During World War II Canterbury suffered a severe bombing raid, and parts of the city center have been rebuilt. Modern-day Canterbury has a wide range of quality shops and comfortable hotels, many of these small, family-run businesses. The 1,000-seat **Marlowe Theatre** offers first-class plays, operas, musicals, and one-night shows. Each autumn, Canterbury celebrates the **International Arts Festival.**

Service shown is from London Victoria Station to Canterbury East Station; other services available are from London Charing Cross Station and Waterloo East Station to Canterbury West Station. Passengers should be aware that trains may be split at Faversham, some coaches going to Canterbury East and others going elsewhere; passengers should be sure they are in a coach going to Canterbury before the train reaches Faversham. Consult the conductor if you are unsure.

DEPART VICTORIA STATION	ARRIVE CANTERBURY EAST STATION	NOTES
0641	0832	M–Sa
0804	0931	Daily
0834	1003	M–Sa
0904	1028	M–Sa
0934	1011	Daily

M–Sa service continues at half-hour intervals until 2004, then 2104 and 2204; Su service 0805, then hourly, with last train at 2205.

DEPART CANTERBURY EAST STATION	ARRIVE VICTORIA STATION	NOTES
1519	1648	M–Sa
1549 (1553 Su)	1723 (1748 Su)	M–F, Su
1619	1758	Sa
1619	1757	M–F
1647	1817	M–Sa
1716	1848 (1847 Sa)	M–Sa
1749	1917	M–Sa

Service continues at half-hour intervals 22 and 49 minutes past the hour (Sa) until 1849, followed by hourly departures 18 minutes past the hour. Sunday departures (hourly) 52 minutes past, then hourly from 1948, then 2019 and 2121 (M–F), 2118 (Sa), 2148 (Su). M–F bi-hourly departures until 1919.

Not far from the Christ Church Gate is the Longmarket, a paved pedestrian area beginning at the intersection of Rose Lane and St. George's Street. Walking directly away from the Christ Church Gate on St. Margaret's Street will bring you to the Canterbury Information Centre. City tours depart from this point.

From High Street, where it intersects St. Margaret's Street, walk down until you pass over a narrow bridge on the River Stour. On the far right of the bridge you will see the **Old Weaver's House**, which was built in 1500 and now houses a restaurant and is a starting point for river tours. Canterbury was the background for Dickens's *David Copperfield,* so let your imagination take over for a few fleeting moments and transport you back into English history and literature.

Following World War II, Canterbury became a great educational center. In 1962 Christ Church College was opened adjacent to St. Augustine's College. More recently, the University of Kent was established on a hill overlooking the cathedral and city from the west. Its buildings are modern in design, emphasizing artistic and cultural development.

A Friday market takes place in addition to the traditional Wednesday Market in the city center. Beach bums will want to take the seafront trek to **Whitstable,** world famous for its oysters. The annual Oyster Festival takes place at the end of July. Or visit Herne Bay, especially around the first two weeks of August when the annual **Herne Bay Festival** is held—family events, fireworks, live music, and more. The annual two-week **Canterbury Festival** is held every October.

We suggest taking in the award-winning **Canterbury Tales Visitor Attraction** as well; or make a night of it and take the **Ghost Tour of Canterbury.** This street-theater spook shows Canterbury in a whole new light and runs every Friday and Saturday all year: £5.00 adult, £4.00 child, £4.50 senior.

Canterbury, proud of its historical past, is nonetheless eager to respond to the demands of present "pilgrims"—visitors who come to see the cathedral, the other historical landmarks, and new sites. The city of Canterbury has done an excellent job by exhibiting its history as a living part of a modern community.

Visitors who wish to extend their visit may inquire at the **Magnolia House,** a lovely bed-and-breakfast owned by friendly Brits Ann and John Davies. It's located at 36 St. Dunstans Terrace [*Tel/Fax:* (01227) 765121; *E-mail:* magnolia_house_canterbury@yahoo.com]. Phone, fax, or e-mail for nightly rates, which vary according to type of room and length of stay. All rooms include private bath/shower and toilet facilities, and all are nonsmoking. *Britain by BritRail* readers receive a 10 percent discount.

Day Excursion to

Chester
A Modern "Medieval" City

Depart from Euston Station
Distance by train: 178 miles (287 km)
Average train time: 2 hours, 30 minutes
Train information and InterCity services: (0845) 748 4950
Tourist information: Visitor and Craft Centre, Vicar's Lane, Chester, Cheshire CH1
    1QX; *Tel:* (01244) 351609; *Fax:* (01244) 403188. Town Hall tourist information:
    Tel: (01244) 402111; *Fax:* (01244) 400420
Internet: www.chestercc.gov.uk/tourism
E-mail: tis@chestercc.gov.uk
Hours: Monday–Saturday 0900–1730 and Sunday 1000–1600 all year.
Notes: The railway station in Chester is about a fifteen-minute walk from the city's
    center. City Road, at the front of the station, will get you started in the right direc-
    tion. Change at the pedestrian underpass onto Foregate Street, which turns into
    Eastgate Street and brings you to the center of the city's historic area. Or board a
    bus outside the station. The bus arrives at Town Hall in about ten minutes for a
    charge of 45 pence. Taxi meters click off around £3.00.

A ll's well" in Chester, but don't take our word for it. Check personally with Chester's Town Crier. He appears at noon (Tuesday
through Saturday, May through August) in the center of the city to
announce that fact. Chester is one of the few cities in England with its
encircling walls completely intact—a splendid example of a fortified
medieval town.

The center of Chester, known as The Cross, takes its name from the
stone "High Cross" standing in front of **St. Peter's Church.** From this
point you may view Chester's distinctive landmark, **the Rows**—two tiers
of shops (one at ground level, the other immediately above), each with
its own walkway.

Developed in the thirteenth century, the Rows are unique and justly
world famous. The upper levels are great for people-watchers who like to
linger undisturbed while observing the stream of passersby in the streets
below. The true origin of the Rows has never been satisfactorily explained, but they far exceed any modern-day shopping center in utility
and beauty. One opinion is that they served as a means of defense against
the incursions of the Welsh raiders, who came to plunder their richer
English neighbors.

The Romans gave Chester its street plan. Walk today along the four
main streets within the city's walls, and you will follow the lines laid
down by Roman engineers almost 2,000 years ago. Part of the Roman

wall survives and is incorporated in the massive tenth-century fortifications enclosing the city. You can find out more about the city's Roman heritage at the **Deva** (pronounced "Dewa") **Roman Experience,** just off Bridge Street (01244 343407). Admission: £3.95 adult, £2.25 child. A walk on the walls provides an opportunity to enjoy the vista of the surrounding countryside.

Restoration has thrived on a large scale in Chester. Entire blocks were renovated in massive programs. The city's famous "black and white" Tudor buildings survived the ravages of time but did not escape alterations to their facades by Victorian architects. In all, however, Chester has managed to preserve its pleasant medieval appearance.

Your first call should be at the tourist information center at the town hall on Northgate Street across from the entrance to Abbey Square. The center offers a wide range of facilities, including a national room-finder service and ticket agency.

Special guided walks are also available: **Pastfinder Tours** depart daily year-round at 1030; the **Ghosthunter Trail** departs at 1930 Thursday through Saturday from June through October; and the **Roman Soldier Wall Patrol** sets forth at 1400 on Wednesday, Friday, and Saturday from June through September. Other tours may be made by special arrangement. All depart from the Chester Visitor and Craft Centre. The Pastfinder and Roman Soldier tours are £3.00,while the Ghosthunter Trail is £3.50.

Opposite the town hall is **Abbey Square,** an island of quiet in the center of the city. By entering the square through its massive fourteenth-century gateway, you will find various buildings constructed from the sixteenth to the nineteenth century.

Chester Cathedral is within sight of the town hall. An abbey was founded on this site in the tenth century. It remained a monastery until its dissolution in 1540, when the building was made a cathedral. The bell tower of the cathedral is a concrete structure that was finished in 1974, the first freestanding bell tower for a cathedral built since the fifteenth century.

Chester's prestigious event—the **Chester Mystery Plays**—occurs in July once every five years and is next scheduled to take place in July 2005. This medieval tradition draws from biblical stories, and the plays are performed on carts as they originally were in the Middle Ages. Chester's Mystery Plays texts are the most complete, with the earliest surviving records dated 1546. For more information, contact the Visitor and Craft Centre at (01244) 402111 or www.chester.gov.uk/tourism.

An interesting observation point that provides a splendid view of the city, the **River Dee,** and the locks of the Chester canal is located at the north end of the city walls. A spur wall connects there with the water

DEPART EUSTON STATION	ARRIVE CHESTER STATION	NOTES
0620	0919	M–F (1)
0710 (0655 Sa)	0938	M–Sa (1)
0730	1041	Sa (1)
0750	1119	Sa (1)
0810	1011 (1100 Sa)	M–F (1), Sa
0830	1106 (1133 Sa)	M–Sa
0900	1224	Su (1)
1000 (1005 Su)	1309 (1250 Su)	Daily (1)
1100 (1035 Sa, 1055 Su)	1337 (1421 Su)	Daily (1)

DEPART CHESTER STATION	ARRIVE EUSTON STATION	NOTES
1428	1717 (1748 Sa)	M–Sa (1)
1448	1806	Sa (1)
1517	1747	M–F (1)
1528 (1521 Sa, Su)	1805 (1833 Sa, 1814 Su)	Daily
1529	1816 (1849 Sa)	M–Sa (1)
1634	1930 (1948 Sa)	M–Sa (1)
1727 (1701 Su)	2025 (2104 Sa, 1958 Su)	Daily (1)
1751	2050	Su (1)
1834 (1838 Su)	2118 (2135 Sa, 2143 Su)	Daily (1)
1930 (1920 Su)	2238 (2252 Sa, 2228 Su)	Daily (1)
1955 (1935 Sa)	0018 (2301 Su)	Daily

(1) Change trains in Crewe

Note: Some trains from Crewe to Chester have standard-class service only.

tower, which was built to protect the port of Chester. Another vantage point is from **Bonewaldesthorne's Tower,** about 100 feet from the water tower. If you participate in the Roman Soldier Wall Patrol tour, you will be able to enjoy this view.

Also in view at a bend in the River Dee is the **Roodee,** home of the Chester racecourse, the oldest in Britain. The main racing season is held in May and its richest prize, the Chester Cup, was first awarded in 1824. As a matter of interest to sportive North Americans, the Roodee was, before horse racing, a football field. But due to the violent nature of the football matches, the city assembly members voted to terminate the sport in 1540.

Day Excursion to

Coventry
Lady Godiva–Show & Tell

Depart from Euston Station
Distance by train: 96 miles (155 km)
Average train time: 1 hour, 10 minutes
Train information and InterCity services: (0845) 748 4950
Tourist information: Tourist Information Centre, Bayley Lane, Coventry, West Midlands CV1 5RN; *Tel:* (024) 7622 7264; *Fax:* (024) 7622 7255
Internet: www.visitcoventry.co.uk
E-mail: tic@cvone.co.uk
Hours: Monday–Friday 0930–1700 (until 1630 in winter), Saturday–Sunday 1000–1630. It remains open on bank holidays (except Christmas), 1000–1600.
Notes: Coventry's rail station lies outside its "ringway," a circular superhighway surrounding the city. At the bus stop, you'll find a city map and information regarding Coventry's information center. Buses marked "Pool Meadow" (No. 17 or 27) will take you to the center of town in five minutes along a route that requires about twenty minutes to walk. Dismount at the Broadgate stop near the shopping square by the Leofric Hotel. The Tourist Information Centre is located at Bayley Lane and may be found via well-placed direction signs.

This is a city of myth and magic, from St. George the Dragon Slayer to the legend of Lady Godiva. Did she actually put everything on a horse—or has this tale, retold through the ages, changed with the telling? Was there really a "Peeping Tom"? Was he late for the show? Coventry holds the answers.

Coventry is best described as a modern city with ancient roots. Among its office buildings, new streets, and attractive shops, there is a scattering of old homes and churches, Coventry's remnants of its far-reaching past. The **new cathedral**, consecrated in 1962, stands as visible proof that today's craftspeople can create memorable works of supreme beauty, as did their medieval counterparts. In the new cathedral you will see outstanding examples of some of the finest modern works of art, including the **Baptistery Window,** the largest piece of modern stained glass in the world. The tapestry **"Christ in Glory"** hangs behind the altar. Weighing nearly a ton, it is the largest tapestry in the world; ten men worked for three years to complete it. The cathedral, open from 0900 to 1930 in summer, closes at 1730 in winter.

Alongside the new stands the **old Cathedral of St. Michael,** reduced to ruins by one dreadful air raid in November 1940. An altar of broken stones surmounted by a charred cross stands at the eastern end of the ruins, backed by the words "Father, forgive." In the nineteenth century

London–Coventry–London

DEPART EUSTON STATION	ARRIVE COVENTRY STATION	NOTES
0644	0845	M–Sa
0744	0945	M–Sa
0848	1040	Sa
0848 (0855 Sa)	1017	M–Sa
0925	1051	Sa
0950	1117	M–F
1020	1149	M–F

M–F service continues at 20 and 50 (25 and 55 Sa) minutes past the hour until 1950 (1825 Sa), then hourly at 30 minutes past the hour until 2030.

Su service is hourly until 1939 by bus only.

Su trains available with change in Nuneaton.

DEPART COVENTRY STATION	ARRIVE EUSTON STATION	NOTES
1326	1451 (1508 Sa)	M–Sa
1406	1607 (1625 Sa)	M–Sa
1436	1653 (1608 Sa)	M–Sa
1526	1703 (1725 Sa)	M–Sa

M–Sa service continues at 6 and 36 minutes past the hour until 1906; then various departures until 2332.

Su service hourly until 2054, then 2235, all by bus only. Su trains available with change in Nuneaton.

John Ruskin wrote, "The sand of Coventry binds itself into stone which can be built halfway to the sky." Attesting to this, the tower and spire of the old cathedral survived intact after the bombing. Built in the fifteenth century, it is the third highest spire in England. A visit to both cathedrals should not be missed.

Lady Godiva was the wife of Leofric, the "grim" Lord of Coventry. Evidently, she bugged him about the heavy tax burdens he had levied on the townspeople. Legend says Leofric, weary of her nagging, agreed to decrease the tax rate if Her Ladyship would increase the town's morale by riding naked through its streets. Modern historians seriously doubt that Godiva made her gallop without benefit of even a riding crop. They believe her husband challenged her to ride stripped of her finery and her jewels and to ride humbly as one of his people and in full sight of them.

Stripped of her rank—or just plain stripped—Her Ladyship did make the ride and taxes were lowered, but she commanded the people to remain indoors with windows barred. Legend says that one town resident called "Tom" unbarred his window to peep as she rode by. Before he could satisfy his gaze, he was struck blind, poor man!

In modern-day reenactments, Lady Godiva now rides her horse through Coventry wearing a body stocking—a considerable improvement over when the event was reenacted in Victorian days and she was dressed in billowing petticoats.

Oddly enough, the Godiva story was told for some 500 years before the "Peeping Tom" version was added. In any case, a stunning bronze statue perpetuates Her Ladyship's memory in **Broadgate Park** as Tom peeps out at her on the hour from the Broadgate clock. We can't help but wonder what effect Lady Godiva's ride would have on our modern-day Internal Revenue Service.

Lady Godiva's statue stands under the **Cathedral Lanes Shopping Centre**'s canopy and immediately opposite the **Leofric Hotel** near the Tourist Information Centre. Be certain to read the inscriptions on the east and west sides of the statue's pedestal. They were written by Alfred, Lord Tennyson, England's poet laureate.

Be sure to acquire *Coventry's Historic Heart, A Walking Tour* booklet from the Tourist Information Centre, containing a plan of the city's central area, along with a brief description of places of interest. It will lead you from Broadgate to a number of interesting places, including the two cathedrals. It also provides a map and key to attractions.

When ready to head back to the hotel in your base city, board the bus at the shelter directly in front of the **Holy Trinity Church,** opposite the Leofric Hotel to return to the rail station.

Day Excursion to

Dover
On the White Cliffs

Depart from Charing Cross Station
Distance by train: 77 miles (124 km)
Average train time: 1 hour, 30 minutes
Train information and InterCity services: (0845) 748 4950
Tourist information: Dover Tourist Information Centre, Old Town Gaol, Biggin Street, Dover, Kent CT16 1DL; *Tel:* (01304) 205108; *Fax:* (01304) 245409
Internet: www.dover.gov.uk or www.whitecliffscountry.org.uk
E-mail: tic@doveruk.com

Hours: April, May, and September: 0900–1730 Monday–Friday, 1000–1600 Saturday–Sunday, June–August: 0900–1730 daily; October–March: 0900–1730 Monday–Friday, 1000–1600 Saturday; closed Sunday.

Notes: The tourist information center is next to the Town Hall, about a five-minute walk from the rail station. Head down Folkestone Road and, at the roundabout, turn left. You will see the Town Hall on your right.

For centuries Dover has been one of Britain's major channel ports. In theory, this is where England ends and the Continent begins, where countless Englishmen have been parted from, or united with, their homeland. Here stand the **White Cliffs of Dover.** Below, on the beaches, the legions of the Roman Empire stormed ashore in 55 B.C., only to be repelled and to land again, successfully, at Deal. Take the time to pause to enjoy; most people pass on through. There is no other point in all of Britain more majestic than Dover—it is the very cornerstone of Britain.

Atop the cliffs broods **Dover Castle.** Initially constructed in the 1180s by Henry II to repel invaders, it has been reinforced at every threat to England's shores, including Hitler's in 1940. From its ramparts, on a clear day you can look across the 21 miles of the English Channel and see France. Approaching from the sea, a dramatic panorama unfolds as the white cliffs slowly rise from the horizon.

You cannot deny it—Dover is dramatic. Brooding clouds hang over it on a rainy, windswept day; grandeur surrounds it on a clear one when Boulogne in distant France becomes discernible. Although the deafening ramjets of the World War II German "buzz bombs" were replaced by the humming vacuums of the hovercraft, the screams of the gulls and the relentless crashing of the sea continue on, unchanged by time. If you are one to "stand in history," Dover is a must visit during your stay in Great Britain. Few other places swell the imagination as do the White Cliffs of Dover.

Train service from London to Dover follows two routes. Departures from Victoria Station split destinations at Faversham. Part of the train goes to Dover, the other part to Margate and Ramsgate. As a precaution against "trainsplitting," our rail schedule is based on direct service to Dover from London's Charing Cross Station. Readers can, however, avail themselves of either route. As a suggestion, depart Charing Cross and return via Faversham to Victoria Station. This way, you will be "joined" by the Ramsgate train instead of being "split" by it.

The tourist information center is extensive, since Dover is a major debarkation point for visitors from the Continent. The center can provide information on all of Great Britain, as well as the local area. Pick up the *Days Out* brochure for White Cliffs Country for visitor vouchers to get either a free adult or child admission or a free or discounted gift from the many attractions of the area.

Ask for information on Dover Castle and how to reach it. No doubt you will also be interested in visiting the **Roman-Painted House,** Britain's buried Pompeii, discovered by an archaeological unit in 1971. Roman legions took over the structure about A.D. 300 for shore-defense purposes. The house gains its name from the brilliantly painted plaster of its walls, the oldest and best-preserved painted walls in Britain. Incredible as it seems, the Romans even installed an elaborate under-the-floor heating system. The house is a permanent museum, open April–

London–Dover–London

Schedules shown are for direct trains from and to London Charing Cross Station. Other services are available from London Victoria Station and may require a change of trains.

Readers who may be planning trips from England to France by train and sea are advised that these schedules are not valid for those services: Trains shown here terminate at Dover Priory Station, which is some distance from the Dover Docks used by ferries.

DEPART CHARING CROSS STATION	ARRIVE DOVER PRIORY STATION	NOTES
0700	0856	M–Sa
0755	0945	M–Sa
0855 (0900 Sa, Su)	1043	Daily
0953	1141	M–Sa
1055	1243	Daily

M–Sa service continues after 1053 at hourly intervals until 1553 and afterward at other intervals until 2330. Note: Some departures are from Canon Street Station. Su service continues after 1000 at hourly intervals until 2242.

DEPART DOVER PRIORY STATION	ARRIVE CHARING CROSS STATION	NOTES
1444 (1423 Su)	1637	Daily
1537 (1519 Sa)	1738 (1705 Sa)	M–Sa
1523	1706	Su
1637 (1651 Sa)	1835	M–Sa
1746	1937	M–Sa

M–Sa service continues with departures at 1844,1948, 2048, and 2203. Su service continues after 1523 at hourly intervals until 2023, then at 2108.

September: 1000–1700 Tuesday–Saturday, 1400–1700 Sunday. Admission: £2.00 adults; 80 pence children. Don't miss out on viewing the more than 2,000-year-old Bronze Age vessel (found in 1992) on display in the Dover Museum.

Legend has it that if Romans are left alone long enough, they will build something. Apparently this was the case in the second century, when the Roman legions constructed two lighthouse beacons on Dover's cliffs for the purpose of guiding their galleys into the sheltered anchorage below. A single lighthouse, reaching a height of more than 40 feet, is the tallest surviving Roman structure in Britain.

Dover can hardly be compared with the Continent's Riviera. Its beaches are small, tiny enclaves in the rugged face of the looming cliffs. And the height of the surf frequently becomes more than the average bather cares to contend with. Dover and its environs, however, lend themselves well to sunbathing, walking, and viewing.

During World War II, Dover was subjected to long-range artillery shelling from the Pas de Calais German gun emplacements. Dover's residents dug cellars deep into the cliffs as bomb shelters. The surviving structures, most of which are now small hotels, still maintain the shelters for use as wine cellars, bars, and boutiques. In addition, the secret underground tunnels of Dover, used by the British to mastermind the evacuation from Dunkirk, were declassified and opened to the public.

Have you ever been to France? If not, now's your chance! Day trips from Dover to Calais in France via catamaran or ferry are very popular. Stock up on wine and cheese, plus a yard or so of crusty French bread during your visit, and load up with duty-free tobacco and booze on the return journey. Plan ahead by asking any train information office for information on ferry, hovercraft, or catamaran services (see "Crossing the English Channel" or the Appendix for contact information).

Day Excursion to

Folkestone
Traditional Seaside Resort

Depart from Charing Cross Station
Distance by train: 70 miles (113 km)
Average train time: 1 hour, 20 minutes
Train information and InterCity services: (0845) 748 4950. Also departs Waterloo East Station 3 minutes after Charing Cross departure time.
Tourist information: Shepway District Council Tourist Information Centre, Harbour Street, Folkestone, Kent CT20 1QN; *Tel:* (0130) 325 8594; *Fax:* (0130) 325 9754

Internet: www.kents-garden-coast.co.uk

E-mail: tourism@folkestone.org.uk

Hours: Monday–Saturday 0900–1730, Sunday 1000–1600; closed 1300–1400 for lunch.

Notes: Walk from the Folkestone Central Station to the town center, along the pedestrian precinct and down to the Old High Street (which is paved with cobblestones and was a favorite haunt of Charles Dickens).

Folkestone is a "multiple treat" seaside resort—enjoy a delightful day of sightseeing, shopping, and seafood; take a memorable journey across Romney Marsh on the world's smallest public train, the Romney, Hythe and Dymchurch Railway; go antiques shopping in quaint English villages; or take a day trip to Boulogne, France, aboard Hoverspeed's SeaCat. Any of these options will take at least one full day. With so many possibilities, we suggest that you make your way to Folkestone's tourist information center immediately upon arrival, especially if you decide to look into accommodation information and stay over for a day or two.

The opening of the Channel Tunnel in 1994, with the terminal situated on the outskirts of Folkestone, has given car travelers to France another option. Cars are driven straight onto shuttle trains and arrive at Cocquelles in France, between Calais and Boulogne, in thirty-five minutes. Special arrangements for rental cars have been made with Hertz and Eurotunnel to exchange left- or right-hand-drive vehicles at the Hertz/Eurotunnel terminal in Calais. This information is also useful if you have purchased a BritRail Pass 'n Drive package. For Le Shuttle Information, call (0870) 535 3535.

Once down in the harbor area, take a stroll under the arches and imagine what life must have been like in the time of Napoleon when the smuggling of contraband was prevalent. From the harbor it is just a stone's throw to the Hoverspeed pier office, where tickets for the catamaran are available (or purchase them at the tourist information office). If you are tempted to set foot on French soil, the office will provide you with current fares and schedules to cross the Channel "topside" rather than go under it. Hoverspeed's SeaCat catamaran service takes just fifty-five minutes.

Folkestone has a dual distinction. As a cross-channel port, it is second only to Dover in total passenger traffic. For beauty of location, it probably stands second to none. The Bayle area was said to be the site of a fort built around A.D. 659 and also the site of a castle built around 1068. The pub in the square, the **British Lion,** claims to be one of the oldest in the country and asserts that it has served ale since the fifteenth

London–Folkestone–London

DEPART CHARING CROSS STATION	ARRIVE FOLKESTONE CENTRAL STATION	NOTES
0700	0845	M–Sa
0755	0934	M–Sa
0855 (0900 Sa, Su)	1031	Daily
0953	1129	Daily

M–Sa service continues at hourly intervals until 2300, with Su service hourly until 2200.

DEPART FOLKESTONE CENTRAL STATION	ARRIVE CHARING CROSS STATION	NOTES
1455	1637	M–Sa
1549 (1603 Sa)	1738 (1735 Sa)	M–Sa
1649 (1703 Sa)	1835	M–Sa

M–Sa service continues at approximately hourly intervals until 2249; Su service continues at approximately hourly intervals until 2034 and then at 2120.

century—it was certainly frequented by Charles Dickens, who resided just around the corner on The Leas.

The Leas, Folkestone's famous mile-long cliff-top promenade, served as an inspiration for some of H. G. Wells's finest works and surveys the town's beach from a vantage point of more than 200 feet above. From there, one can view the landscape from Dover to Dungeness. Stretching behind The Leas are the spacious, well-planned business and residential quarters.

The Leas is the most popular attraction for visitors to Folkestone. With its breathtaking views of the English Channel, colorful flowers, and intriguing pathways zigzagging down to the lower Coast Road, it truly is a tranquil reminder of Victorian and Edwardian elegance.

At the west end of The Leas are steps that lead down close to **Spade House,** H. G. Wells's home from 1900 to 1910. Midway along, **The Leas Cliff Hall** is one of Kent's leading entertainment centers, while a little farther down is the **Bandstand**—constructed in 1895 and still in regular use. Before leaving this delightful area you should experience a trip on the **Cliff Lift.** The second oldest of its kind in the country, this original water-balance lift operates from the top of The Leas down to the lower end.

Sandgate, on the western outskirts of Folkestone and on the Coast Road, is one of the major antiques centers in England. Numerous antiques and curio shops beckon from narrow High Street. Also competing for shoppers' attention are several old-world inns and the **Sandgate Castle,** which has retained its English village atmosphere with friendly residents, as well as affording visitors a brisk sea-air promenade before continuing the journey toward Hythe.

A bus service operates from Folkestone, along the Coast Road and into Hythe, approximately twelve minutes from Folkestone town center. There the young—and those not so young—may board the fascinating **Romney, Hythe and Dymchurch Light Railroad** for a delightful journey by steam traction to **New Romney,** with stops in Dymchurch and St. Mary's Bay. At New Romney there is a wonderful model railway museum. Service is generally every hour; you may pick up a timetable at the tourist information center beforehand.

Before leaving Hythe, visit the crypt of **St. Leonard's Church.** Warning: This is not for the faint of heart. It houses a fascinating, macabre collection of hundreds of skulls and thousands of other bones dating from before the Norman Conquest of 1066. St. Leonard's Church, built in A.D. 1080, is beautiful and has several architectural features similar to those found in Canterbury Cathedral, as well as its own very special and unique Saxon, Norman, and medieval historic features. Hythe has many small specialty shops and restaurants and is renowned for its **Royal Military Canal** and **Martello Towers.**

Stop en route at **Dymchurch,** England's "children's paradise," or at **St. Mary's Bay,** where boating and fishing are two highlights of that holiday center. The RH&D Railroad terminates its service at Dungeness, another 5½ miles down the RH&D "road," where you'll find great contrast between its fishermen's shacks and its atomic plant.

Those with the use of a car should explore the peaceful flatlands of **Romney Marsh.** Hundreds of years ago this area was part of the English Channel, and ships were moored to the castle walls at Lympne. Now drained by a series of dikes, the marsh is a haven for wildlife. Dotted around the waterways, fields of sheep, and crop pastures, nestle little villages. A surprising number of old churches are here, with their own mysterious pasts steeped in smuggling tales. Each of the thirteen medieval churches dotting this land has unique features and is well worth a visit. Notices inform visitors where the church keys can be obtained: Some are kept by local homeowners, some in the nearby pubs, and some require almost an expedition in themselves to locate the ancient artifacts.

Day Excursion to

Gloucester
On the River Severn

Depart from Paddington Station
Distance by train: 114 miles (184 km)
Average train time: 1 hour, 50 minutes
Train information and InterCity services: (0845) 748 4950
Tourist information: Gloucester Tourist Office, 28 Southgate Street, Gloucester GL1
    2DP; *Tel:* (01452) 396572; *Fax:* (01452) 309788
Internet: www.gloucester.gov.uk/tourism
E-mail: tourism@gloucester.gov.uk
Hours: Monday–Saturday 1000–1700.
Notes: Gloucester's Central Station is within walking distance of the city center, or
    you may hail a taxi or ride a city bus. To reach the tourist center on foot, walk
    toward the cathedral from the Central Station until you reach Northgate Street,
    then turn left to where it intersects Eastgate Street at The Cross. (Northgate and
    Eastgate Streets take their names from the ancient city routes through the Roman
    wall.) Continue past The Cross into Southgate Street.

Gloucester is steeped in history. First to arrive were the Romans, following their invasion of the British Isles. A legion fort was erected at the site of the present city center, and by A.D. 96–98, the Roman city of Glevum (now Gloucester) was established and flourishing. Little remains of the Roman presence in modern Gloucester. None of the Roman wall is now visible aboveground, but its line is still followed by the principal streets of the city.

Although Gloucester is situated some distance from the open sea, Queen Elizabeth I declared it a port in 1580. Oceangoing ships of up to 5,000-ton capacity are able to dock at Sharpness, the terminal dock of the city's port system. The entire dock complex has been given a new lease on life: An ambitious redevelopment program converted the site into a haven of recreation, education, and commerce.

The **National Waterways Museum** is the principal tourist attraction in the dock complex. Two hundred years of history, which shaped the fortunes of Britain, may be viewed there, housed in an imposing three-story building. The historic docks are also home to three other museums, shops, restaurants, pubs, and Gloucester Antique Centre (*Hours:* 1000–1700 daily), with more than one hundred dealers under one roof.

Gloucester's showplace is, of course, its **Cathedral**, the oldest building in the city. A Norman nucleus (1089–1260) incorporates additions in every known style of Gothic architecture. Topped by a towering

DEPART PADDINGTON STATION	ARRIVE GLOUCESTER STATION	NOTES
0703	0847	M–F
0803	0948	M–Sa (1)
0835	1028	Su (1)
1003	1155	Daily
1100	1249	M–F
1203	1355	M–F (1)
1137	1325	Su
1415	1611	M–F

DEPART GLOUCESTER STATION	ARRIVE PADDINGTON STATION	NOTES
1420	1623	M–F (1)
1547 (1543 Sa)	1746 (1815 Sa)	M–Sa (1)
1617	1827	M–F
1630	1820	Su (1)
1635	1908	Sa (1)
1743	1933	Sa (1)
1746	1940	M–F (1)
1830	2025	Su (1)
1921	2130	M–F (1)
2054	2308	Sa (1)
2030	2230	Su (1)
2205	0048	M–F (1)

(1) Change trains at Swindon

fifteenth-century pinnacle rising 225 feet above ground level, Gloucester's cathedral is judged to be one of the six most beautiful buildings in Europe. If you have a limited amount of time to spend sightseeing in Gloucester, make the best use of it by concentrating on the cathedral and its surroundings.

The cathedral's origins began in A.D. 679, when the Saxons founded the Monastery of St. Peter on the site. In 909 Alfred the Great's daughter gave relics to the priory, making it the Church of St. Oswald. It is a magnificent example of medieval architecture with its great Norman piers still in the cathedral nave. Although craftspeople have continued to work on the structure since the fifteenth century, gracing it with an elegant exterior of later architectural designs, it remains a Norman edifice.

Sightseeing in Gloucester has been made easy by the **Via Sacra**, a walkway around the city center that follows the lines of the original city wall. Follow the pattern of dark paving placed in the sidewalk to keep visitors from going too far astray. Leaflets of the walk are available in the tourist information center.

The walking tour begins with a considerable variety of early English architecture, ranging from fifteenth-century timber-frame structures to the Tudor facades of the present county offices. You will pass **Blackfriars,** the best-preserved medieval Dominican friary in Britain. A portion is open to the public. **Greyfriars** is also on the route, but unlike Blackfriars, most of it stands in ruins.

Stopping in the city museum and art gallery affords the opportunity to examine many archaeological items, including a part of the original **Roman city wall.** The museum is open Monday–Saturday 1000–1700. It is also open Sunday 1000–1600 from July through September.

Just beyond the city museum, you will see the **Eastgate Shopping Centre,** which provides traffic-free areas at ground level. The tour ends at the cathedral in **St. Lucy's Garden,** the approach to the college green.

Gloucester abounds with interesting eating establishments ranging from the popular McDonald's to such ancient eateries as the **New Inn** on Northgate Street. Don't let the name fool you. The New Inn was built by St. Peter's Abbey to accommodate pilgrims in 1450. The inn courtyard was used for staging plays during the time of Queen Elizabeth I, and in the eighteenth century the inn became renowned for its association with traveling menageries and exhibitions of "curiosities." Said to be the finest medieval open-gallery inn in England, the food served there today matches the excellence of its medieval decor.

Day Excursion to

Greenwich
It's Time to Make a Difference

Depart from Charing Cross Station
Distance by train: 7 miles (11 km)
Average train time: 15 minutes
Train information and InterCity services: (0845) 748 4950
Tourist information: Tourist Information Centre, Pepys House, 2 Cutty Sark Gardens, Greenwich SE10 9LW; *Tel:* (0870) 608 2000; *Fax:* (020) 8853 4607
Internet: www.greenwichengland.com
E-mail: tic@greenwich.gov.uk
Hours: 1000–1700 daily.
Notes: Upon arrival in the Greenwich railway station, use the pedestrian subway (underpass) to the main station and the street. Turn left and walk along the road into town. Follow the signs guiding you to the National Maritime Museum and the *Cutty Sark.* Where they split, continue to follow the *Cutty Sark* signs until the

ship's masts come into view. The local Greenwich Tourist Information Centre is at the entrance of the *Cutty Sark* Gardens. Or, if you prefer, take the Historic Greenwich Shuttle Bus from the pier gates to visit all the principal sites. Guided walking tours leave from the tourist center daily at 1215 and 1415. Admission: £4.00 adult, free for children younger than fourteen.

A visit to Greenwich reveals the town known as the cradle of Britain's maritime history. Queen Elizabeth II knighted Sir Frances Chichester for his solo circumnavigation of the world at a public ceremony at the **Royal Naval College,** which now stands on the site of the Royal Palace of Greenwich, where both Henry VIII and Elizabeth I were born.

The *Cutty Sark,* launched in 1869 as one of the fastest sailing ships, now lies in dry dock at Greenwich. The clipper served in the China tea trade as well as the Australian wool trade. Her curious name, which means "short chemise," originated in "Tam O' Shanter," a poem by Robert Burns in which the witch, Nanny, appeared in a cutty sark. The ship's figurehead represents Nanny. Admission to the *Cutty Sark* is £4.25 for adults and £2.95 for children. The ship is open 1000–1700 daily. *Internet:* www.cuttysark.org.uk.

A few yards beyond the *Cutty Sark's* stern is the entrance to the former Royal Naval College. Built during the seventeenth-century reign of William and Mary, the present buildings were used as a hospital for disabled and aged naval pensioners. In 1873 it became the Royal Naval College to provide for the higher education of naval officers. The Royal Navy left Greenwich in 1999, and the buildings are now occupied by the University of Greenwich and Trinity College of Music.

Visitors are admitted to the Royal Naval College's **Painted Hall and Chapel** 1000–1700 Monday–Saturday and 1300–1700 Sunday. Admission is free with guided tours costing £5.00. *Tel:* (01818) 582154.

After the Battle of Trafalgar, the body of Lord Nelson lay in state in the Upper Hall. The interior decorating, by Sir James Thornhill, took nineteen years to complete. (You'll find out why when you see it.) Benjamin West's painting of the shipwrecked *St. Paul* in the college chapel is one of the highlights of this beautiful structure.

Pay a visit to the world's largest maritime museum, the **National Maritime Museum of Greenwich.** *Internet:* www.nmm.ac.uk. It houses more than two million items relating to Britain's maritime history. To get there, walk along the east side of the Dreadnought Library (on the Old Royal Naval College grounds) and cross Romney Road. The museum entrance is ahead, slightly to the left. Sixteen galleries, opened in 1999, lie beneath a spectacular free-span glass roof. On a tour of the galleries, you will see historic vessels such as *Miss Britain III*, the first boat to travel at 100 mph on open water, and the elaborately carved royal barge made for Frederick, Prince of Wales, in 1732.

The museum has an amazing display of old ship models and a gallery devoted entirely to the life and loves of Admiral Lord Nelson. Its library and archives, which can be accessed by computer, hold historic ships' draughts, transportation documents, and a collection of some 4,000 paintings.

Linked by a colonnade to the National Maritime Museum, the **Queen's House** is the first example of a classical domestic house in England. Designed in the Palladian style in 1616 for Anne of Denmark, the Queen's House is an architectural delight. The rooms have changing themed displays.

The **Royal Observatory,** on the hill in Greenwich Park, south of the museum and the Queen's House, is an integral part of the complex. The world's prime meridian—longitude 0—passes across the courtyard, and it is from here that GMT (Greenwich Mean Time) was first calculated. The chronometers, which enabled John Harrison to resolve the problem of how to measure longitude, are on display in the house designed by Christopher Wren in 1675 for John Flamsteed, the first Astronomer Royal.

Admission to the National Maritime Museum, the Queen's House, and the Royal Observatory is free; however, an admission charge may apply to special exhibitions or events. *Hours:* 1000–1700 daily.

The Greenwich and Docklands International Festival is held annually at the beginning of July and presents the finest in music, dance, literature, theater, and visual arts from around the world. A full program of events is available from the tourist office, or check out the festival Web site, www.festival.org.

Greenwich has no shortage of eating establishments—choose from more than sixty restaurants offering a wide variety of cuisine ranging from traditional English cooking to French haute cuisine or exotic Asian. Try the historic riverside **Trafalgar Tavern.** Located in a beautiful setting beside the Old Royal Naval College, the Trafalgar has been providing traditional ales and fine foods since 1837. *Tel:* (020) 8858 2437. *Internet:* www.trafalgartavern.co.uk.

London–Greenwich–London

From Central London to Greenwich:

1. Via the Tube, take the Jubilee line to the underground station in North Greenwich. From Waterloo, journey time is about 12 minutes; from Charing Cross, about 14 minutes. There are 24 trains per hour in each direction.

2. City Cruises operate on the Thames River from Westminster to Greenwich; journey time, 45 minutes. All services shown below operate from London Charing Cross Station and also stop at London Waterloo East Station approximately 3 minutes from Charing Cross and London Bridge.

DEPART CHARING CROSS STATION	ARRIVE GREENWICH STATION	NOTES
0728	0742	M–F
0735	0749	Sa
0802	0816	Su
0805	0820 (0819 Sa)	M–Sa
0824	0840	M–F
0832	0846	Su
0844	0900	M–F
0853	0907	Sa
0923	0937	M–F

M–F service continues after 0923 at half-hour intervals until midafternoon, more frequently afterward; Sa service continues after 0853 at half-hour intervals until 1753, then 1912 and at half-hour intervals until 2342; Su service continues at least three to four times hourly until late evening.

DEPART GREENWICH STATION	ARRIVE CHARING CROSS STATION	NOTES
1410	1427	M–Sa
1413	1440	Su
1427	1443	Su
1440	1457	M–Sa

M–F service continues after 1440 at half-hour intervals until 1610; later trains depart at 1626, 1639, 1654, 1708, 1728, 1737, 1805, 1831, 1846, and 1901, and arrive at London Bridge Station, after which service resumes to Charing Cross with departures at 1927 and then every half hour until 2327. Sa service continues after 1440 at approximately half-hour intervals until 2357. Su service continues after 1427 at half-hour intervals until the last train at 2257.

Day Excursion to

Hastings
Famous Battle Site

Depart from Charing Cross Station
Distance by train: 60 miles (87 km)
Average train time: 1 hour, 30 minutes
Train information and InterCity services: (0845) 748 4950
Tourist information: Hastings Tourist Office, Queens Square, Priory Meadow, Hastings, East Sussex TN34 1TI.; *Tel:* (0142) 478 1111; *Fax:* (0142) 478 1186
Internet: www.visithastings.com
E-mail: hic@hastings.gov.uk
Hours: Monday–Friday 0830–1815, Saturday 0900–1700, and Sunday 1030–1630.
Notes: Exit the station through the car park, and go straight on Devonshire Road. The office is on the right side, across from Mr. Bean's Coffee. To get to the office at Queens Square from the rail station, proceed down Havalock Road. At the end, turn left onto Queens Road, then turn left at the Town Hall onto Queens Square, where you will find the information center.

Undoubtedly, 1066 is one of the most well-known dates in history. When dusk fell near Hastings on October 14, 1066, William the Conqueror, the duke of Normandy, had defeated the Saxon army of slain King Harold and had become the new king of England.

Contrary to popular belief, the actual battle was not fought in Hastings. After landing at Pevensey, the Norman troops marched to Hastings, then northward about 5 miles to Senlac Hill, where they engaged the Saxons in battle. The castle, formerly a timber form, was converted to stone in 1067, one year after the battle. Hastings holds the lore of the Battle of Hastings plus the lure of its ancient fishing village and Norman castle.

Harold's troops were not pushovers. Nineteen days prior to the Battle of Hastings, his men had put a Norse army to rout at Stamford Bridge near York. In the initial onslaught at Senlac, the Normans retreated with the Saxons in hot pursuit. In so doing, the Saxons had to break the tight formation of their Saxon wall of shields, and the Norman cavalry quickly took advantage of the hole opening up in the line and inflicted heavy losses upon the Saxons. This tactic was twice repeated, and the conflict ended. Today's Super Bowl tactics may have developed in Hastings. To go sightseeing at the battleground, board any "Battle Abbey" bus.

During the Roman occupation, Hastings was one of the famous Cinque (five) Ports where the Caesars moored their galleys. Later the harbor was silted up by a series of violent storms, culminating with the great tempest in 1287. As a result, Hastings was reduced to the status of a small fishing community during the following four centuries.

London–Hastings–London

DEPART CHARING CROSS STATION	ARRIVE HASTINGS STATION	NOTES
0743	0925	Sa
0810	0953	Su
0843	1016	M–F
0945	1116	M–Sa

M–Sa service continues after 0945 at half-hour intervals until midafternoon, then hourly until 2330. Su service after 0910 is hourly until 2210.

DEPART HASTINGS STATION	ARRIVE CHARING CROSS STATION	NOTES
1332	1503	M–Sa
1408	1553	Su
1430	1604	M–Sa (1)
1551	1719	Sa
1631	1822	M–Sa
1738	1921	M–Sa
1846	2034	M–Sa

Plus other frequent service until 2041 M–Sa; 11 minutes past the hour until 2111 Su.
(1) London Cannon Street (M–F)

The tourist information center has an excellent brochure titled *Discover Hastings*. With it in hand, you can easily visit the Norman Castle via the West Hill lift. After visiting the castle, venture a few more paces to St. Clement's Caves for the Smugglers' Adventure. Set in a labyrinth of caverns and secret passageways beneath West Hill, the smugglers are brought to life.

Hastings is home to Britain's largest fleet of beach-launched boats, which continue to operate in the traditional manner. In addition to its rich historical heritage and fishing industry, Hastings has been an attractive seaside resort since the mid-eighteenth century, when London physicians began prescribing sea air and salt water as a panacea for all their patients' ills. Three miles of promenades line its beaches, many of them two-tiered with sun-trapped shelters overlooking the English Channel. Sun is more sought after than surf in Hastings because the water is very cold. Examine any photo of an English seaside resort, and you'll see that the majority of bathers are on the beach, not in the sea.

After drinking in the panoramic sights from atop the hill, you can drift back toward the sea and Hastings's "Old Town." On Hill Street, observe the two cannonballs on either side of **St. Clement's Church** belfry. The right one was shot into the tower by the French; the one on the left was added by the locals to balance things off.

The French artillery attack in 1337 also leveled the **All Saints Church** in the Old Town. Undaunted by the shelling, the locals got busy and reerected the church in 1436. The interior contains a well-preserved fifteenth-century mural depicting the *Last Judgment,* with the devil casting souls into hell. The mural was intended to portray a lesson in morality for illiterate people of the Middle Ages.

You'll pass many interesting points on your walk. Stop for a closer examination of the **Old Town Hall** on High Street, which is now a museum. Drop by the **Stables Theatre** opposite the Old Town Hall. It originally served as the stables for the Old Hastings House, which was spared demolition by being converted into a cultural center.

Your next stop should be **Shovells,** circa 1450, reputedly the oldest house in town. If you're desperate for a libation, you might try the **Stag Inn** opposite Shovells, where remains of mummified cats and rats decorate the bar. Nearing the end of the Old Town walk, you will pass an unusual wedge-shaped house called the "piece of cheese," no doubt the funniest house in town. If time permits, head out on Rock-A-Nore Road to the **Hastings Sea Life Centre** and take an incredible 3-D voyage from outer space to the depths of the earth's seas.

Don't miss the 243-foot embroidery in **Sussex Hall, White Rock Theatre.** It depicts eighty-one of the greatest events of British history since 1066, including the Battle of Hastings, the Boston Tea Party, and the first television broadcast.

The city of Hastings celebrates the famous 1066 battle every year by staging a program of events and attractions over a full week, encompassing the famed fourteenth day of October.

Day Excursion to

Ipswich
Chartered in A.D. 1200

Depart from Liverpool Street Station
Distance by train: 69 miles (111 km)
Average train time: 1 hour, 10 minutes
Train information and InterCity services: (0845) 748 4950
Tourist information: Tourist Information Centre, St. Stephen's Church, St. Stephen's
    Lane, Ipswich, Suffolk IP1 1DP; *Tel:* (0147) 325 8070; *Fax:* (0147) 343 2017
Internet: www.visit-ipswich.com or www.ipswich.gov.uk

E-mail: tourist@ipswich.gov.uk

Hours: Monday–Saturday 0900–1700; closed Sunday.

Notes: The tourist information center is easy to reach. Departing the rail station, proceed straight ahead down Princes Street to Friars Street and turn right. Friars Street curves and turns into Falcon Street. St. Stephen's Church will be on your left. If the weather is inclement, catch the "City Centre" bus, or hail a taxi immediately in front of the station.

The architecture of Ipswich reflects its history. Bypassed by the Romans, this town does not display the former grandeur of Rome. A seafaring community long before King John granted the town's first charter in 1200, Ipswich has always been engaged in commerce and has risen or declined along with the fortunes of its citizens' enterprises. The lack of Georgian buildings in Ipswich is evidence of the town's decline during that period, caused by the loss of its famous Suffolk cloth trade. A revitalization of its harbor by the mid-nineteenth century brought new prosperity to Ipswich and accounts for the number of splendid public buildings erected then, as well as the Victorian architecture of its homes.

Ipswich has withstood the onslaughts of the Vikings and other seaborne raiders through the ages. Starting with World War I, the town's docks became the targets of a new type of raider coming from the sky rather than from the sea. From 1915 to the end of the conflict, there were a number of zeppelin attacks, but damage was light. During the years 1943–1945, Ipswich was rimmed by no fewer than sixty-five air bases of the U.S. Eighth Air Force, from which were launched a staggering 3,000-plus bomber assaults against the Third Reich.

Today, with a population of 120,000, Ipswich has a developing port and is an important industrial and commercial center with fine shopping, sports, and entertainment facilities. Ipswich considers its **Tudor Christchurch Mansion,** set on sixty-five acres of parkland only a five-minute walk from the center of town, to be its finest attraction. The information office will gladly point out the way to you. Obtain a map there before going off to explore the endless streets and enticing alleyways leading off Ipswich's **Cornhill.**

The town's Leisure Services Department has devised an excellent series of brochures (*Ipswich Historic Churches Trail, Wet Dock Maritime Trail,* and *Ipswich Street Map*) available for a nominal charge. The trails are marked with black-and-white signs that are numbered to correspond with the descriptions in the brochures. No doubt the trail was laid out for British walkers, for it is much too ambitious a course for the average Yank to complete within the prescribed period of one hour—at least it was for us! The route is circular, so you can join (or leave) at any point.

DEPART LIVERPOOL STREET STATION	ARRIVE IPSWICH STATION	NOTES
0730	0839	M–Sa
0800	0902 (0928 Su)	Daily
0830	0939	Daily
0900	1007	M–Sa
0915 (0910 Su)	1028 (1036 Su)	Daily
0930	1039	M–Sa
0945	1101	M–Sa
1000 (1030 Su)	1102 (1139 Su)	Daily

M–Sa service continues at half-hour intervals until 2330; Su service continues on the
hour as well as 20 and 30 minutes after the hour until 2030, then 2130, 2230,
2300, and 2330.

DEPART IPSWICH STATION	ARRIVE LIVERPOOL STREET STATION	NOTES
1714	1825	M–Sa
1741	1855	Daily
1800	1919	Su
1816	1925	M–Sa
1841 (1842 Sa)	1953	Daily
1900	2015 Sa (2033 Su)	Sa–Su
1941 (1942 Sa)	2055 (2053 Sa)	Daily
2000	2115 (2129 Sa, 2133 Su)	Daily

Daily service every 14 and 41 minutes past the hour (on the hour and 41 minutes
Su), followed by schedule above, then frequent service with last trains out at 2245
M–F, Su and 2153 Sa.

Places along the trails that may be of interest to you include the
junction of Butter Market, St. Stephens Lane, and Dial Lane. As you can
probably guess, the **Butter Market** was once a marketplace for many
products, including butter. The **Ancient House** in the Butter Market will
remind you of the market's age (more than 500 years old), for its
windows represent the known world during its time—and Australia
is missing because it had not yet been discovered by Europeans. A
seventeenth-century merchant, Robert Sparrow, added the exquisite,
ornate plasterwork to the exterior.

Dial Lane is a traffic-free pedestrian area that gets its name from a
clock that was once on the St. Lawrence Church. Although most of the

church dates from the fifteenth and early sixteenth centuries, its tower was rebuilt in 1882 to reflect its original design.

By passing the church and turning left onto St. Lawrence Street and then right onto Tavern Street, you'll come upon the **Great White Horse Hotel.** It is the only surviving inn that can be traced in the city records before 1571. Completed in 1818, its Georgian brick facade covers a basically timber-frame structure from the sixteenth century. A young London news reporter, sent to Ipswich to cover an election, stayed in the Great White Horse and later wrote his recollections in a comic novel that changed the course of his life. The reporter was Charles Dickens; the novel, *The Pickwick Papers.*

Near the end of your walking tour, take time to pause at the junction of Tavern Street and Dial Lane. The view down Dial Lane to the Ancient House is one of the most photographed areas in Ipswich. The Tudor-style buildings reflect the detail and attention of the city's craftsmen. From this point, a left turn will take you to the Cornhill, the end of your Tourist Town Trail walk.

As you stand at Cornhill, it is sobering to consider that only 400 years ago, nine people were burned at the stake on this hill for heresy. Before becoming too sober, however, visit one of the bars in the Great White Horse Hotel. Distinguished visitors of the past, besides Charles Dickens, include such notables as King George II, Louis XVIII, and Lord Nelson, who quaffed many a draft there. A toast to these gentlemen would seem only proper. So have a go at it, mate, if you can get there before they call "time."

Day Excursion to

Isle of Wight
The Holiday Island

Depart from Waterloo Station
Distance by train: 88 miles (142 km)
Average journey time to Ryde: Train approx. 1 hour, 30 minutes; catamaran ferry, 14 minutes
Train information and InterCity services: (0845) 748 4950
Tourist information: Isle of Wight Tourism, *Tel:* (0198) 381 3818; *Fax:* (01983) 863047
Internet: www.islandbreaks.co.uk
E-mail: info@islandbreaks.co.uk
Hours: 0900–1700 daily.
Notes: There are seven tourist information centers on the island: Ryde, Sandown, Shanklin, Cowes, Newport, Yarmouth, and Ventnor. All except the Ventnor office are open year-round. The one at Ryde is on the Western Esplanade opposite the pier.

B ritain's Miniature" is a term often employed to describe the Isle of Wight. Shaped like a diamond, the island is a veritable jewel, with every feature of the mainland condensed into a mere 147 square miles. It is dotted with historic spots, sandy beaches, thatched villages, rolling countryside—and discotheques, if that's your pleasure. There is fun for everyone, and getting there can be fun as well.

The majority of trains departing Waterloo Station in London for Portsmouth Harbour are InterCity trains. As they glide through the scenery of southern England bound for the coast, you'll be treated to a delightful kaleidoscope of England's landscape from the wide-vision train windows. Stay aboard when the train halts briefly in the Portsmouth and Southsea Station. Your destination is the Portsmouth Harbour Station, five minutes farther on.

Board the Portsmouth-Ryde catamaran at the end of the harbor station. *Internet:* www.wightlink.co.uk. Your BritRail Pass does not cover the passage. The fare is £11.20 round-trip, and the crossing takes only about fourteen minutes.

After the boat docks at the Ryde pier head, you have three options for sightseeing on the island by train. The trains, by the way, run right onto the pier and look every bit like those of the Bakerloo Underground line in London. The three options? They are Ryde, Sandown, and Shanklin. All three lie along the 9 miles of track extending from the Ryde pier head to the terminal in Shanklin.

Ryde is the Isle of Wight's gateway. Set picturesquely on a hillside, it becomes a wonderful grandstand from which to watch the great ships of the world sailing by. The pier at Ryde is more than 2,300 feet long, so board the train after disembarking from the passenger ferry and ride the train to its first stop, **Ryde Esplanade,** where you will find the Tourist Information Centre ready to assist. Ryde has 6 miles of sandy beach backed by pleasant, wooded gardens. The town is also noted for its Regency and Victorian buildings and for its **Royal Victoria Arcade** shopping center.

Sandown is the next railway stop after passing the Brading Station. It has all the facilities for a summer holiday, including a modern pier complex that offers licensed bars, cafes, and a restaurant, amusements, plus adventure golf, "superbowl," and Dodgems (bumper cars). The sheltered **Sandown Bay** has more than 5 miles of attractive sandy beaches, where you may find such diversions as miniature golf and a canoe lake. Visit Dinosaur Isle, the exciting Geological Exhibition Centre, and the Tiger and Big Cat Sanctuary. Check at the Tourist Information Centre on High Street for details of all local attractions.

Sandown and Shanklin are considered twin resorts on the Isle of Wight. The distance between the two stations is only 2 miles. Select one

London–Isle of Wight–London

Depart from Waterloo Station

All service to Isle of Wight is by frequent train service approximately every 20–30 minutes M–Sa and hourly on Sundays to Portsmouth Harbour Station, frequent fast-ferry service to Ryde Head Pier on the Isle of Wight, and train from Ryde Head Pier to Shanklin; the return route is the reverse.

Schedules shown here are for trains that depart from London Waterloo Station and travel via Woking, Guildford, and Portsmouth and Southsea Stations. Other services are possible from London Victoria Station via Gatwick Airport Station and/or Brighton; these may also require a change of trains at Portsmouth and Southsea Station to reach Portsmouth Harbour Station.

DEPART WATERLOO STATION	ARRIVE PORTSMOUTH HARBOUR	NOTES
0708	0837	Sa
0720 (0723 Sa)	0852 (0907 Sa)	M–Sa
0743	0916	M–F
0745	0930	Su
0808	0941	M–Sa
0815	0948	Su
0838	1010	M–Sa
0908	1041	M–Sa
0915	1048	Su

DEPART PORTSMOUTH HARBOUR	ARRIVE WATERLOO STATION	NOTES
1517	1655	Daily
1517 (1540 Su)	1726 (1727 Su)	Daily
1617	1754 (1753 Su)	Daily
1647 (1640 Su)	1826 (1823 Su)	Daily
1717	1859	Daily
1747 (1740 Su)	1924	Daily
1817 (1821 Sa)	1956 (2012 Sa, 1953 Su)	Daily

M–F service continues until 2220; Sa service continues until 2221; Su service continues until 2237.

---

or both for your day excursion. There is much to see and do in either resort.

Shanklin frequently holds the British annual sunshine record. Built on a cliff with a sheltered mile-long beach lying below, it is the end of the line for rail travel. It is easy, however, to transfer to the buses operated by the island's bus company, Southern Vectis, for farther points such as Ventnor, Newport, and Cowes. Check with the Southern Vectis Travel Office on Regent Street, 2 blocks from Shanklin's train station, or at the Tourist Information Centre in Shanklin on High Street. To reach it, as you leave the station, walk straight to Regent Street, then turn right onto High Street. The center is on the right just up the hill—about a ten-minute walk from Shanklin Station. Taxi service is available.

Our personal selection of the Isle's options would be Shanklin, as it certainly is one of the prettiest towns in Britain. Shanklin's Old Village on Ventnor Road is world-famous for its quiet beauty. From there, you may descend to Shanklin's beach esplanade via a walk through **Shanklin's Chine,** a cleft in the town's cliff with overhanging trees, plants, ferns, and a cascading stream. There is a small charge to walk through the Chine, which also has an exhibition of PLUTO memorabilia. PLUTO is the pipeline under the ocean, through which fuel was piped to France for the D-Day invasion and the weeks thereafter.

John Keats, one of the most gifted and appealing of England's nineteenth-century poets, found Shanklin's climate congenial to his health and the town's scenic beauty so inspiring that he resided there for a long period of time. **Keats Green,** a spacious promenade on the cliff top of Shanklin, commemorates his association with the town.

Queen Victoria spent her holidays on the Isle of Wight and died there in **Osborne House** in 1901. This house, built by order of the queen in 1845, is maintained in good order, with the queen's furniture still in place. In a shed on the property, you can see the gardening tools of the royal children from more than a century ago. Each tool and wheelbarrow is marked with the small owner's initials.

The queen and Prince Albert used Osborne as a country residence, and it is said that the prince had a considerable influence on the design of the residence. The main rooms and many of the private apartments are open to the public between Easter Monday and the end of October. Situated at East Cowes, in the north of the island on the east side of the Medina estuary (the island's central river), Osborne House can be reached by bus from Ryde Esplanade Station. On the opposite bank is Cowes, the world-famous home of yachting.

Day Excursion to

King's Lynn
Rich in Architecture

Depart from King's Cross Station
Distance by train: 97 miles (156 km)
Average train time: 2 hours, 5 minutes
Train information and InterCity services: (0845) 748 4950
Tourist information: Tourist Information Centre, The Custom House, Purfleet Quay, King's Lynn, Norfolk PE30 1HP; *Tel:* (0155) 376 3044; *Fax:* (0155) 381 9441

Internet: www.west-norfolk.gov.uk
E-mail: kings-lynn.tic@west-norfolk.gov.uk
Hours: Monday, Tuesday, Thursday–Saturday 1030–1600, Sunday 1200–1600.
Notes: To reach the Tourist Information Centre, walk directly away from the front of
the train station (which faces the west) down Waterloo Street. The street under-
goes a name change at every intersection—Market, Paradise, New Conduit, Purfleet. The Tourist Information Centre is straight ahead in the Custom House.

King's Lynn, once "Bishop's Lynn" and renamed when Henry VIII took over the bishop's manor, is one of the most historic towns in England. The old section still seems medieval, complete with narrow streets, guildhalls, and riverside quays, where the gulls reel and scream overhead. The town's former prosperity has left it with a rich heritage of architecture. Set along the east bank of the wide and muddy Ouse River, King's Lynn is the northern terminal of the London-Cambridge-Ely rail line.

King's Lynn came into being during the eleventh century and is situated on the middle of three islands, where four streams ran into the Ouse River. Water highways became vital to the commerce of the town. With waterway connections to the English Midlands, the town of Lynn became an important trading port, bustling with the romance of exotic cargoes, sailing ships, and foreign accents. By the thirteenth century, the town found prosperity in the wool trade between England and the Continent. This aura of a wealthy medieval town still prevails. Today, the town is a thriving, modern port, an essential link between Britain and the rest of the Common Market.

Streets and alleyways in King's Lynn twist and wind about on a grand scale, so a town map will be an invaluable aid. Immediately make your way from the train station to the tourist information center located in the Custom House, about a ten-minute walk. Nearby, the town boasts England's oldest surviving **Hanseatic Warehouse.** The surrounding river-side area was restored in 2000. Visit the Green Quay environmental exhibition located in Marriott's Warehouse, a refurbished sixteenth-century barn.

You will be tempted to wander about in **Queen Street** with its lovely merchants' houses, each with a character all its own. At the information center equip yourself with a copy of the *King's Lynn Town Walk* booklet. This is a masterpiece of simplicity and is packed with facts about the town and its buildings. The trail follows a circular route, so you may start and finish wherever it is most convenient for you. We suggest starting at the **Town Hall.** Rebuilt in 1421 after a fire, it houses the "Tales of the Old Gaol House" exhibition, as well as King Lynn's regalia, including the magnificent King John Cup and the *Red Register*, purported to be one of the oldest books in the world.

DEPART KING'S CROSS STATION	ARRIVE KING'S LYNN STATION	NOTES
0645	0819	M–Sa
0715	0854	M–Sa
0745	0928 (0919 Sa)	M–Sa
0815	0956	Su
0845	1020	M–Sa (1)
0945	1120	M–Sa
1015	1149	Su
1045	1220	M–Sa
1145	1320	M–Sa
1215	1349	Su
1415	1549	Su (2)

(1) Then hourly until 1445 M–F (1945 Sa)

(2) Then hourly until 2215

DEPART KING'S LYNN STATION	ARRIVE KING'S CROSS STATION	NOTES
1356	1533	M–Sa
1426	1604	Su (3)
1456	1633	M–Sa
1556	1733	M–Sa
1656	1835	M–Sa
1738	1930	M–Sa
1756	1933	Sa
1838 (1834 Sa)	2030	M–Sa
1942 (1934 Sa)	2130	M–Sa
2042 (2034 Sa)	2230	M–Sa
2142 (2134 Sa)	2330	M–Sa

(3) Then hourly until 2126.

A focal point in King's Lynn is the **Tuesday Market Place**, into which King Street leads. True to tradition, a country market is conducted there every Tuesday in the shadow of the **Duke's Head Hotel,** a most impressive seventeenth-century structure. The market is everything that one would expect it to be—stalls packed with the agricultural and manufacturing products of the area, augmented by absolutely free entertainment as the hucksters bid for attention. Another impressive structure in the Tuesday Market Place is the magnificently restored **Corn Exchange,** now a popular concert hall and entertainment center.

If you miss the Tuesday market, there's another one on Saturday at a location appropriately named the **Saturday Market Place,** just opposite the Town Hall. A newer shopping center in the center of town is on the site of the former cattle market.

Visit **St. George's Guildhall** at 27 King Street—the largest surviving medieval guildhall. When not in use as a theater, it is open 1000–1700 Monday through Friday and 1000–1230 Saturday. Built about 1410, it has been used as a theater, a courthouse, and an armory. It is now a cultural center housing a theater and an art gallery.

King John, who ruled England between 1199 and 1216, granted the town its charter in 1204. The king came to Lynn in October 1215 in pursuit of rebellious barons. One story relates that after he was wined and dined by the burghers of Lynn, the king and his entourage set off in hot pursuit of the baronial rebels. Heading west out of King's Lynn toward Newark, the king and his entourage crossed the Norfolk tidal flats, where the River Ouse empties into **The Wash,** a shallow bay known for the treachery of its tides. During the crossing, a high tide from The Wash wiped out the king's baggage train. King John reached the safety of higher shores, but he lost the crown jewels and everything else that went with such a collection in those days. King John contracted dysentery (a bad "burger," perhaps?) and died a few days later. No one questioned the burghers as to exactly what they fed the king before he left Lynn. We have our suspicions, however, because reportedly all of the burghers felt fine the following morning.

Somewhere near King's Lynn, buried under centuries of silt, lies King John's lost treasure. None of it has been recovered, and no one knows where to look for it.

Day Excursion to

Lincoln
Hilltop Cathedral

Depart from King's Cross Station
Distance by train: 135 miles (217 km)
Average train time: 2 hours, 10 minutes
Train information and InterCity services: (0845) 748 4950
Tourist information: Lincoln Tourist Information Centre, 9 Castle Hill, Lincoln, Lincolnshire LN1 3AA; *Tel:* (01522) 873213; *Fax:* (01522) 873214
Internet: www.lincoln.gov.uk
E-mail: tourism@lincoln.gov.uk
Hours: Monday–Thursday 0930–1730, Friday 0930–1700, Saturday–Sunday 1000–1700.
Notes: On arrival in Lincoln's Central Station, go to the city bus station, which is in

front and to the right of the main station entrance (use the designated pedestrian walkways, because the vehicular traffic can be heavy at times). From the bus station, take city bus 1, 7, or 8 up the hill to the cathedral, and ask the driver to let you off at the corner of Eastgate and Nettleham Road (next to Forte Posthouse Hotel). Walk along Eastgate until reaching the White Hart Hotel; turn left, and the center is at the top of the hill at No. 9 Castle Hill.

Lincoln Tourist Information Centre: 21 The Cornhill, LN5 3HB; *Tel:* (01522) 873256; *Fax:* (01522) 873257

Hours: Same as the center at 9 Castle Hill, except closed Sunday.

Notes: Turn left from the rail station and cross over at St. Mary La Wigford Church on High Street. The center is in The Cornhill opposite the British Homes store.

Lincoln's greatest landmark is its cathedral, which stands on a ridge, dominating the skyline. The cathedral appears to be half church, half stronghold. Actually, there are two Lincolns—one, the cathedral and castle standing politely on the hilltop; the other, the city below girding the River Witham and buzzing with commerce. We suggest you scale the heights first and later return to the lower level by a dizzy descent down Steep Hill.

On the other hand, if you're ambitious, bear to the left when leaving the station and walk a short distance on St. Mary Street to where it intersects with High Street. Turn right at this point and, keeping the cathedral in sight, start walking in its direction up High Street. Disregard the fact that the street changes names several times. When you reach an area where a ski lift or a cable car would be most welcome, you'll be on Steep Hill—and it's appropriately named. Now gain the high ground (and your breath), and you will find yourself in Castle Square. With a right turn at the Exchequer Gate, you may enter the cathedral grounds.

Walking up the Lincoln hill from the railway station to the cathedral can give you a sense of accomplishment. It can also be hazardous to your health. Use discretion—take the bus or a taxi if there's any doubt in your mind about the climb. This is to be enjoyed, not endured.

Walking up Steep Hill, you will pass the **Norman House,** said to be the home of "Aaron the Jew," a moneylender from the twelfth century who reportedly became the richest man in England at that time. Halfway up Steep Hill, and turning off at Danesgate, your visit will be well rewarded by an inspection of the **Usher Gallery.** You can view an assortment of personal property belonging to England's poet laureate, Alfred, Lord Tennyson, born in Somersby, a Lincolnshire village, in 1809. The gallery also houses an extensive collection of paintings by Peter de Wint (1784–1849). If you arrive at Castle Square in need of lunch or a libation, seek out the **Wig & Mitre,** a licensed restaurant with a Dickensian atmosphere.

DEPART KING'S CROSS STATION	ARRIVE LINCOLN CENTRAL STATION	NOTES
0615	0809	M–F (1)
0708 (0700 Sa)	0858 (0852 Sa)	M–Sa (1)
0725*	1025	M–Sa (3)
0830	1058 (1100 Sa)	M–Sa (2)
0910	1150 (1104 Sa)	M–Sa (1)
0930	1201	M–F (2)
0955*	1235	Sa (3)
1010	1210	Su (1)
1110	1310 (1308 Sa)	M–Sa (1)

with frequent service thereafter.

DEPART LINCOLN CENTRAL STATION	ARRIVE KING'S CROSS STATION	NOTES
1425 (1436 Sa)	1635 (1630 Sa)	M–Sa (1)
1455	1729 (1712 Su)	Sa–Su (2)
1534 (1546 Su)	1725 (1718 Su)	M–F, Su (1)
1617 (1621 Sa)	1832 (1828 Sa)	M–Sa (1)
1627	1930	M–F (4)
1807 (1811 Sa)	2016 (2010 Sa)	M–Sa (1)
1909 (1905 Sa)	2124 (2111 Sa)	M–Sa (1)
1925	2125	Sa (5)
1928	2136	Su (1)
2032	2246	M–Sa (1)

*London St. Pancras

(1) Change trains at Newark North Gate

(2) Change trains at Peterborough

(3) Change trains at Loughborough

(4) Change trains at Retford

(5) Change trains at Doncaster

The **cathedral** is the main point of interest in Lincoln. When you view its exterior and examine the spacious areas under its roof, it becomes rather difficult to comprehend that it was built by medieval craftsmen in only twenty years. The Normans began construction of the cathedral in 1072. In 1141 the roof was destroyed by a fire, and in 1185 the main structure crumbled into ruins as a result of an earthquake. But it survived.

Reconstruction, which began in 1186, returned the cathedral to its original conforms, and, through the ensuing centuries, it was altered frequently. The central tower was completed around 1311. In more modern times, Lincoln's greatest attraction has withstood Cromwell's artillery and Hitler's bombs. If you have but a short period of time to visit in Lincoln, the cathedral must take priority over all else. Summer hours: 0715–2000 daily. Winter hours: 0715–1800 daily. Admission is £4.00 adults; children younger than age fourteen free. *Internet:* www.lincolncathedral .com.

Lincoln Castle was built by William the Conqueror in 1068 and became the Normans' military stronghold in the area. Its construction is unusual in that it has two mounds: one crowned by the twelfth-century Tower of Lucy, the other with Norman structures on which, in the nineteenth century, an observatory tower was constructed. From either of these vantage points, there are beautiful views of the cathedral and the surrounding countryside.

Today the Lincoln Castle is a huge, walled enclosure of lawns and trees. The crown courts and the old county jail are located in the castle yard. On permanent exhibition is one of only four surviving originals of King John's *Magna Carta.* The castle is open Monday–Saturday 0930– 1730, Sunday 1100–1730; winter closing time is 1530. Admission is £3.50 for adults and £2.00 for seniors and children. *Internet:* www .lincolncastle.com.

If you wish to visit the "other Lincoln," start by descending (or plunging down) Steep Hill with its bow-fronted shops until you again reach High Street. You will find interest in the twelfth-century **High Bridge**, which crosses the River Witham. It is the oldest one in Britain to still carry a building on its structure, in this case, a sixteenth-century timber-framed house. The route leading from the cathedral down Steep Hill is studded with other interesting structures such as numerous public houses and restaurants. Modern Lincoln blends easily with its historical counterparts.

Day Excursion to

Liverpool
Four Lads Who Shook the World

Depart from Euston Station
Distance by train: 194 miles (312 km)
Average train time: 2 hours
Train information: (0845) 748 4950
Tourist Information: Merseyside Welcome Centre, Queen Square Centre, L1 1RG
    Liverpool; *Tel:* (0906) 680 6886 (25p per minute), or (011) 44 151 709 5111
    from the U.S.; *Fax:* (0151) 708 0204

Internet: www.visitliverpool.com or www.makeitmerseyside.org
E-mail: askme@visitliverpool.com
Hours: Monday–Saturday 0900–1730 (opens Tuesday at 1000), Sunday 1030–1630,
   bank holidays 1000–1700.
Notes: To get to the Merseyside Welcome Centre at Queen Square from Liverpool
   Lime Street Station, exit the central Lime Street exit, cross the street, and head
   toward the Marriott Hotel. Turn left at the Penny Farthing onto Queen Square.

Throughout its fascinating 800-year history, Liverpool has been a "place to remember." According to *The Official Guide to the City of Liverpool*, "It only takes a few hours to fall in love with Liverpool, and a lifetime to get to know it."

Situated at the neck of the Mersey River, Liverpool has a long association with the river and the sea. In the twelfth century, King John used it as a launching pad for his forays to Ireland. By 1551 the Mersey River was a prominent gateway for transport of goods to other ports in Britain. By the eighteenth century Liverpool became an international port, trading goods with North America, Africa, and Europe; by the nineteenth century it had become one of the principal ports of the world, second only to London. With all the international trade and cultural exchanges, it is not surprising that Liverpool has its own Chinatown, the oldest Chinese community in Europe.

The cosmopolitan city of Liverpool is one of majestic architectural heritage, with more listed buildings—some 2,500 of them—than any other British city except London, and more Georgian buildings than Bath. Just across from Lime Street Station, **St. George's Hall** is an example of one of the finest neoclassical buildings in all of Europe. The tall concrete towerlike structure with the circular top is known as St. John's Beacon and houses the UK's largest commercial radio station. For a dramatic panoramic view of Liverpool, take a guided tour (available on weekends) from the Queen Square Tourist Information Centre.

Dramatically dominating the city center skyline, Liverpool boasts not one, but two cathedrals—the **Anglican Cathedral** and the **Roman Catholic Metropolitan Cathedral** at opposite ends of appropriately named Hope Street. The Anglican Cathedral is the largest in the world and was completed in 1978, taking nearly seventy-five years to build. The conical-shaped Metropolitan, known as "the Cathedral of Color," uses natural light to create an astonishing atmosphere. It took only five years to build and was completed in 1967. Ironically, the architect of the Anglican Cathedral, twenty-one-year-old Giles Gilbert Scott, later Sir Giles, was Catholic, whereas Sir Frederick Gibbard, the architect of the Metropolitan Cathedral, was Protestant. Young Giles's design won the Anglican design competition. He had never designed anything of

Schedules shown below are for direct train service.

DEPART EUSTON STATION	ARRIVE LIVERPOOL LIME STREET STATION	NOTES
0710 (0640 Sa)	1002	M–Sa
0810 (0745 Sa)	1105	M–Sa
0910 (0845 Sa)	1205	M–Sa
1010 (0945 Sa)	1305 (1336 Sa)	Daily

Hourly departures M–Sa until 2110 M–F and 1835 Sa; then 2025. Eight more departures Su until 2055.

DEPART LIVERPOOL LIME STREET STATION	ARRIVE EUSTON STATION	NOTES
1435	1735 (1806 Sa)	M–Sa
1510	1819	Su
1535	1838 (1903 Sa)	M–Sa
1610	1928	Su
1635	1940 (2013 Sa)	M–Sa
1710	2025	Su
1735	2038 (2123 Sa)	M–Sa
1810	2126	Su
1835	2141 (2212 Sa)	M–Sa
1935	2310 (2340 Sa)	M–Sa
2010	2355	Su

great significance before—except the famed fire-engine-red British telephone booth.

The Anglican Cathedral has the highest and heaviest bells in the world, the highest gothic arches, and the largest organ, with almost 10,000 pipes. Each stone of the cathedral is unique—no two are exactly the same, either in size or weight. After John Lennon was killed in New York, his wife, Yoko Ono, went to Liverpool to the Anglican Cathedral, where a special service was allowed for the first time to play "pop music"—a medley of John Lennon and Paul McCartney's songs.

Liverpool is also famous as the birthplace of The Beatles—John, Paul, George Harrison, and Ringo Starr, "the four lads who shook the world." Their music first captivated young people throughout the world four decades ago—and it still does so today.

There are myriad city and Beatles-related tours available, but for those who are short on time, we recommend heading to the famous

Albert Dock (named after Prince Albert) and the historical waterfront area. You can check in at the Merseyside Welcome Centre at Queen Square for information and directions.

Albert Dock is a beautifully restored waterfront complex. Purchase the **Waterfront Pass** at the Albert Dock Tourist Information Centre in the Atlantic Pavilion. It's open 1000–1700 daily. For £7.95, you'll receive entrance to **The Beatles Story** exhibition in the Britannia Pavilion; the **Merseyside Maritime Museum** to learn about Liverpool's interesting development as a port; the Museum of Liverpool Life; plus a fifty-minute cruise with commentary "'cross the Mersey" River to take in the stunning sights of the waterfront.

You can view Liverpool's "Three Graces"—the Liver, Cunard, and Port of Liverpool buildings. Liverpudlians are quite proud of the fact that the clocks in the towers of the lovely Liver Building are 2½ feet larger than Big Ben in London. There are two gigantic birds atop the towers. We surmise that the one facing outward toward the sea must be the female watching for sailors coming into port; the other one must be male, as he faces inward, as if to see what time the pub opens.

There is free admission to the **Tate Gallery**, named after Liverpool businessman Henry Tate, to view its extraordinary modern art collection, and there are plenty of elegant shops and excellent restaurants in the waterfront area. *Hours:* Tuesday–Sunday 1000–1750. *Internet:* www.tate .org.uk/liverpool. Thirsty? Visit the Pump House Pub. Formerly, the Pump House pumped pressurized water to provide hydraulic power. Now it pumps pressurized lager instead—great progress for lager lovers. Hungry? One of the world's most famous fish 'n' chips restaurants, Harry Ramsden's [(0151) 709 4545; *Internet:* www.harryramsdens.co.uk], is nearby Albert Dock at Brunswick Way, off Sefton Street.

Beatles' fans and even those who aren't (yet) will enjoy reliving "the Fab Four's" most sensational success story in the pop music world at **The Beatles Story** museum and exhibition center. The exhibition is open daily 1000–1800 April–October, 1000–1700 November–March; *Tel:* (0151) 709 1963; *Fax:* (0151) 708 0039. The souvenir shop is an excellent place to pick up Beatles' memorabilia and music. *Internet:* www .beatlesstory.com

Avid Beatles' fans will most certainly want to "take a ticket to ride" on the **Beatles Magical Mystery Tour.** This two-hour bus tour departs from The Albert Dock Bus Stop (just opposite the Pump House Pub) at 1340; from the Merseyside Welcome Centre, Queen Square, and from The Beatles Story on The Albert Dock at 1400. It includes the Beatles' homes, schools, Penny Lane, Strawberry Field, and many more landmarks associated with the Beatles. Tour price is £12.50. Advance booking is highly recommended. Telephone Cavern City Tours at (0151) 236 9091 or

Mersey Tourism at (0151) 709 3285 for information and booking. The tour finishes at the world-famous **Cavern Club** on Mathew Street. *Internet:* www.cavern-liverpool.co.uk. The original Cavern Club was demolished during the construction of Liverpool's Underground transport system. Fortunately, city leaders readily recognized their gross error and reconstructed the Cavern Club, using much of its original brick, a few yards from where it initially stood.

If you have the time—and the energy—to extend your visit to Liverpool, there is no shortage of exciting nightlife. Nightlife aficionados come from all over Britain to the "cream of the crop of clubs"—Cream. Live-music fans will want to "drink in" the atmosphere at the Picket, L2, Lomax, the Jacaranda Club—with a bar on three floors—and, of course, the Cavern Club. Irish music and Guinness beer, dubbed by the Irish as their "water supply," can be found at Flanagan's Apple, also located on Mathew Street. Classical music fans can take in the Royal Liverpool Philharmonic Orchestra at the Philharmonic Hall [Box Office (0151) 709 3789]. Seemingly all of Liverpool is lively with all kinds of music—live bands play in pubs and clubs throughout the city. For overnight stays, check out the 120-bedroom Beatles-themed hotel, The Hard Day's Night Hotel, on Mathew Street.

Liverpool is a place you'll remember. As Prince Albert succinctly put it, "I have heard of the greatness of Liverpool, but the reality far surpasses the expectation."

Day Excursion to
Nottingham
Tales of Robin Hood

Depart from St. Pancras Station
Distance by train: 127 miles (204 km)
Average train time: 2 hours
Train information and InterCity services: (0845) 748 4950
Tourist information: Nottingham Information Centre, 1–4 Smithy Row, Nottingham, Nottinghamshire NG1 2BY; *Tel:* (0115) 915 5330; *Fax:* (0115) 915 5329
Internet: www.visitnottingham.com
E-mail: tourist.information@nottinghamcity.gov.uk
Hours: Monday–Friday 0900–1730, Saturday 0900–1700, and Sunday 1000–1500 in summer (April 1–first Sunday of October).
Notes: The main tourist information office is within walking distance of the train station. But if your time is limited, hail a cab at the station and save some time as well as your shoe leather. Otherwise, take Carrington Street on your right as you leave

the station. Cross Canal Street and pass Broad Marsh Bus Station. Continue straight through Broad Marsh Shopping Centre and exit onto Listergate–Albert Street–Exchange. Walk in the same direction toward Exchange Arcade Shopping Centre until you come to Smithy Row. The Old Market Square will be on your left. You can't miss it—but if you do, just inquire at one of the taxi queues in the area.

Nottingham is famous for many things, among them the legend of Robin Hood. Many tales of Robin and his band of merry men have been passed down through the ages by ballad and legend, though only scattered fragments remain of his origin. It appears that one Robert Fitzooth, reputed to be the Earl of Huntingdon, was born in 1160 during the reign of Henry II. Of noble birth, he squandered his inheritance at an early age; so either by necessity or by choice, he sought refuge in the forest. Here he was joined by men in similar circumstances, such as Little John, Will Scarlet, Friar Tuck, and—to add the love-interest angle to the legend—Maid Marian.

Robin Hood reigned in the forest, defying the powers of government, protecting the poor, and giving to the needy. The king's deer provided food, and the king's forest provided fuel. Other necessities were obtained through barter. Taking the king's property was, of course, illegal, and it drove the Sheriff of Nottingham "bananas," to the point where he offered a substantial reward for Robin's capture—dead or alive. Robin Hood eluded capture and supposedly lived to be eighty-seven years old. Records show his death occurred on November 18, 1247. This man, who lived in an age of feudal tyranny, endeared himself to countless generations and became the legendary hero of Nottingham. A fine statue to his memory stands in the courtyard of **Nottingham Castle.**

The castle was built as a fortress in 1068 by William the Conqueror. It was destroyed during the English civil war, rebuilt, and again destroyed by an angry mob in 1831. Following its second restoration, the castle was transformed into a museum and art gallery late in the nineteenth century. A series of underground passages run beneath the castle. Naturally, there are many tales of intrigue relating to their purpose. The castle is open to the public daily; the underground passages can be seen only on conducted tours. Don't miss the *Story of Nottingham* at the Castle Museum and Art Gallery.

For centuries, Nottingham has been famous for its lace. Visit the fascinating **Lace Market Centre** at 3–5 High Pavement for demonstrations of working lace machines and the history of lace making. *Hours:* daily 1000–1700. *Tel:* (0115) 9897365; *Fax:* (0115) 9897301.

If your time in Nottingham is limited, no doubt you should first see the historic castle area and return another day to see modern downtown Nottingham. To visit the castle, turn right as you exit the rail station onto

Carrington Street. Turn left onto Canal Street, and 3 blocks farther along in the same direction, you will come to Castle Road running up the hill to your right. Following it a short distance brings you to England's oldest inn, **Ye Olde Trip to Jerusalem,** where we suggest you rest before continuing up Castle Road to the Nottingham Castle entrance, just off Castle Place. Built in 1189, a portion of the inn was dug into the almost vertical rock formation supporting Nottingham Castle above. Legend has it that Robin Hood scaled this rock in his invasions of Nottingham Castle. The pub's "grub" isn't bad—in fact, it's downright good—so you might want to arrive there about lunchtime. Books about Nottingham and the lore of Robin Hood are on sale in the Ye Olde Trip to Jerusalem pub and in Nottingham Castle. *Internet:* www.triptojerusalem.com.

The train trip from London's St. Pancras Station passes through England's Midlands en route to Nottingham, passing St. Albans, where Britain's first Christian martyr was executed, and Bedford, where John Bunyan wrote *Pilgrim's Progress.* For variety, you might want to return to London via Peterborough, transferring there to a train for King's Cross Station. Consult the train information office in Nottingham's station. It is open Monday–Saturday 0800–1830, and Sunday 1000–1900.

Nottingham's main tourist information center lies astride the city's two huge shopping centers—the **Victoria** and the **Broad Marsh.** Both are somewhat mind-boggling in size, and they are linked by wide pedestrian avenues as well as a bus service (No. 90) running between the two establishments every fifteen minutes throughout the day, Monday through Saturday. The young modern shopper must not miss the **Hockley** area of shops to catch up on the latest craze, and antiques aficionados would enjoy the abundance of shops along **Derby Road.**

A site for crime and punishment fans is *"Condemned!"* at the **Galleries of Justice.** Be prepared as you visit the nineteenth-century Shire Hall to assume the identity of a criminal, experience a public trial, and be taken off to the hangman's gallows.

If your trip permits being in Nottingham on a Friday or Saturday evening, we suggest you "eat, drink, and be merry" by enjoying the five-course medieval meal at the **Sherriff's Lodge Medieval Banqueting Hall** or at the **Tales of Robin Hood.** Ale and entertainment are included. Book in advance by calling (0115) 948 3284; *Internet:* www.robin hood.uk.com

Meanwhile, back at the **Old Market Square,** the tourist information center has details of walking tours of Nottingham that take you, among other places, along one of the city's main thoroughfares, **Maid Marian Way.** Also inquire about the **Explorer Pass** that gives access to five top attractions at a great price.

London–Nottingham–London

DEPART ST. PANCRAS STATION	ARRIVE NOTTINGHAM STATION	NOTES
0755	0935 (0937 Sa)	M–Sa
0855	1037	M–Sa
0955	1134	M–Sa
1030	1241	Su
1055	1234	M–Sa
1155	1336	M–Sa

Then hourly following the same pattern until 2100 (M–Sa); then 2200, 2210, and 2340 (M–F).

DEPART NOTTINGHAM STATION	ARRIVE ST. PANCRAS STATION	NOTES
1430	1616 (1623 Su)	Daily
1530 (1531 Su)	1712 (1721 Su)	Daily
1630 (1634 Su)	1812 (1821 Su)	Daily
1730 (1729 Su)	1912 (1924 Su)	Daily
1830	2016	M–Sa

Then the same pattern until 2032; then 2035 and 2132; Su 1835, 1948, and 2115.

Day Excursion to

Oxford
Ancient City Campus

Depart from Paddington Station
Distance by train: 63 miles (102 km)
Average train time: 1 hour
Train information and InterCity services: (0845) 748 4950
Tourist information: Oxford Information Centre, 15–16 Broad Street, Oxford OX1 3AS; *Tel:* (0186) 572 6871; *Fax:* (0186) 524 0261
Internet: www.oxford.gov.uk/tourism or www.visitoxford.org
E-mail: tic@oxford.gov.uk
Hours: Monday–Saturday 0930–1700, Sunday (during summer) and bank holidays 1000–1530.
Notes: The Oxford Tourist Information Centre is located behind the bus bays on Gloucester Green, a short walk from the rail station. Just follow the black and gold pedestrian signs via either Hythe Bridge Street or Park End Street.

T he first glimpse of Oxford as you approach it by train from London confirms its title, "the city of dreaming spires." Towers, domes, and pinnacles soar on its skyline as an impressive preview of one of the great architectural centers of the world. For here in this small and compact city center are some 900 "listed" buildings, illustrating practically every style of architecture from the eleventh century to the present day.

Oxford is home to the oldest university in Great Britain, with its beginnings in the twelfth century. Apparently there is no single explanation as to exactly how and when the university actually began. One theory claims that it was founded by English students who were expelled from the University of Paris in 1167. Others claim it came about from a gathering of various groups of students from monastic institutions in and around the growing city. From whatever origins, by the end of the twelfth century, Oxford was the established home of the first center of learning in England.

Dating from between the thirteenth and fifteenth centuries, the university became an established national institution and now has a history of 800 years of continuous existence. The student body has doubled in the past thirty years to about 16,000 students, of which the majority are undergraduates. There is no separate campus; most of its buildings lie within the center of the city. The university is a federation of independent colleges. Visitors coming to Oxford during the summer may miss the sight of students passing between classes and student sporting activities, but the buildings alone are worth the trip.

Fewer than half the students come to Oxford University from such exclusive schools as Eton, which was founded by Henry VI in 1440. Students are required to meet their tutor only once or twice a week, either individually or with one other student. This seemingly free and easy system, which builds on individuality and confidence, is the hallmark of an Oxford education. All students live in the college for their first year and one other year prior to graduation. Students are usually housed in single rooms; the restrictions on coming and going or on having guests are few.

A renaissance of reconstruction and rebuilding in Oxford during the eighteenth century destroyed much of the old street system and the houses inhabited by many religious groups. From this, the city that emerged was more spacious than before. Notwithstanding this urban renewal program, Oxford still has a certain organized clutter about it that becomes readily discernible as you move from the rail station to the city center.

In addition to being a seat of learning, Oxford (unlike Cambridge) has a strong industrial background. It was here that William Morris

Very frequent service is available from London Paddington Station to Oxford, with journeys taking from 44 to 96 minutes. Departure times given here are for trips taking 73 minutes or less.

LONDON PADDINGTON TO OXFORD

M–F   Depart Paddington Station at 0600, 0718, 0748; then every 30 minutes until 2148, (also 0936, 1106, 1712, and 1827, with 2018 on Fri) and every 30 minutes until 2348.

Sa   Depart Paddington Station at 0618, 0748, 0818, and every 30 minutes; then 1805, 1827, 1848, 1918, and hourly until 2348 with extra trains at 0905, 0936, 1036.

Su   Depart Paddington Station at 0803, 0843, 0943, and then hourly until 2243; then 2348 (also 0903, 1206, 1827).

OXFORD TO LONDON PADDINGTON

M–F   Depart Oxford Station at 1345, 1415, and every 30 minutes until 2015; also at 1635, 1655; then 2030, 2115, 2126, 2215, 2229, 2315 (and 0022 T–F).

Sa   Depart Oxford Station at 1345, 1415, and every 30 minutes until 1915; then 2015, 2115, 2215, 2227, 2238, and 2315 (also 0900, 1000).

Su   Depart Oxford Station at 1345, and hourly until 1745; then 1815, 1835, 1933, 2019, 2032, 2115, 2206, 2228, and 2359.

founded his automobile empire, now Rover Group. The commercial and academic worlds have combined to create other flourishing industries such as publishing, research and development, and tourism. Oxford is also famous as the home of several distinguished hospitals.

Today the use of cars is discouraged in the city center, with visitors making the most instead of Oxford's excellent train services, supplemented by an extremely efficient Park-and-Ride system for motorists. The city leaders also urge everyone to return to the traditional Oxford method of propulsion, the bicycle. By the way, during your visit be on the lookout for bicycles propelled by students pedaling themselves to lectures or laboratories.

Guided walking tours leave the information center daily throughout the year at 1030, 1100, 1300, and 1400. Adult fare: £6.50; children (age six to sixteen): £3.00. The two-hour tours take you around the most interesting parts of the city and into those colleges open to the guides on that day.

Those with inquisitive minds may choose the **Inspector Morse Walking Tours** and follow in the footsteps of Oxford's most famous detective. Adult fare: £7:00; children (age six to sixteen): £3.50. These tours leave the information center on Saturdays at 1330 from March to October. Or, for ghouls and gore, try the **Ghost Tour,** which departs the center at 1945 on Friday and Saturday June–September and on October 31. Adults £5.00; children £3.00. *Tel:* (01865) 726871.

From this beginning, build your own plan of activities, perhaps to include the **Oxford Story Exhibition,** punting and cruising on the **Thames** or **Cherwell,** an open bus tour, or a visit to the ancient **Bodleian Library** or one of the university's five excellent museums, all of which are free.

Day Excursion to
Portsmouth
Britain's Naval Port

Depart from Waterloo Station
Distance by train: 74 miles (119 km)
Average train time: 1 hour, 30 minutes
Train information and InterCity services: (0845) 748 4950
Tourist information: Tourist Information Centre, The Hard, Portsmouth PO1 3QJ;
    Tel: (023) 9282 6722; *Fax:* (023) 9282 7519
Internet: www.visitportsmouth.co.uk
E-mail: vis@portsmouthcc.gov.uk
Hours: October–March: 0930–1715 daily; April–September: 0930–1745 daily.
Notes: Trains call first at the Portsmouth and Southsea Station, so stay aboard to the end of the line. Then, instead of moving straight ahead to the ferry dock, exit the station on the right-hand side of the platform to the main street. The Hard is right next to the Portsmouth Naval Base and the Harbour Rail Station. The Hard Information Centre, from where you will be able to see the gate of the naval base, is to your left.

Another center is located next to the Blue Reef Aquarium Portsmouth, Clarence Esplanade, Southsea.

A visit to Portsmouth requires prioritizing. The city abounds in vast quantities of history, architecture, amusements, and literature. Portsmouth has variety, contrasts, and veneration. Ask at the tourist center about the 2005 guided walks.

Old Portsmouth is for those who relish fine buildings. Lombard Street is flanked by natural harbors, east and west, and is the home of one of the world's greatest naval bases, **Portsmouth Naval Base.** The resort area, **Southsea,** offers the largest amusement complex on England's south coast plus 4 miles of beaches, promenades, and gardens that boast splendid seventeenth- and eighteenth-century houses, many with distinctive Dutch gables. On adjoining High Street, the primarily eighteenth-century motif gives way to the ultramodern "new" Portsmouth, with its traffic-free shopping precinct, **Cascades,** on Commercial Road.

New public promenades are at the heart of the Portsmouth Harbour **Millennium Project.** A waterbus network connects the sights and attractions in the harbor area, including the City Quay/Portsmouth Harbour Rail Station, Historic Dockyard, Submarine World, Gosport Esplanade, and Priddy's Hard. According to the tourist center, a visit to the **Explosion Museum of Naval Firepower** is "guaranteed to blow your socks off and leave you thinking. . . ." At **Gunwharf Quays,** you can enjoy shopping at more than eighty-five shops, eat and drink at twenty-plus restaurants and bars, or take in a movie.

The literary greats of Portsmouth—Charles Dickens, H. G. Wells, Arthur Conan Doyle, Rudyard Kipling, and Neville Shute, to name a few— have left their mark on the city in birthplaces, residences, and museums. Resting in the world's oldest dry dock in Portsmouth Dockyard is Lord Horatio Nelson's flagship, **H.M.S. *Victory.*** Alongside the ship stands the **Royal Naval Museum** (www.flagship.org.uk) with relics of England's naval hero, ship models, and an outstanding collection of marine paintings. *Hours:* April–October 1000–1730 daily, November–March 1000–1700. For priority, our first selection is H.M.S. *Victory,* described as the proudest sight in Britain, and well it is. Meticulously preserved, it stirs the imagination as you relive the events of the Battle of Trafalgar that "made all England weep."

Some vital statistics in history regarding H.M.S. *Victory* may be beneficial while you are waiting to go aboard. The ship was launched on May 7, 1765. (Lord Nelson was six years old on that date.) It weighs 3,500 tons with an overall length of 226½ feet. *Victory* carried 104 guns and a complement of 850 officers and men. In 1801, the ship was rebuilt extensively and given its present appearance. Recommissioned in April 1803, *Victory* became Nelson's flagship. On October 21, 1805, the English fleet under Nelson's command vanquished the combined fleets of France and Spain off Cape Trafalgar. Lord Nelson was killed aboard *Victory* in the final moments of what has been called the most decisive battle ever fought at sea.

Portsmouth also features the Victorian ironclad **H.M.S. *Warrior* 1860.** Launched in 1860, it was the largest, fastest, and best-armored warship of the time. The ship has been restored throughout to its appearance during its first commission of 1861–1864; when you step aboard, you catch a unique glimpse of life as it was experienced on a nineteenth-century British warship. The Royal Naval Museum supports these famous ships with displays that set them in their historic context and

London–Portsmouth–London

Schedules shown are for direct trains that operate from and to London Waterloo Station. There are two stations in Portsmouth: the Portsmouth and Southsea Station near the center of the city, and the Portsmouth Harbour Station, which serves the Portsmouth Royal Naval Base (H.M.S. Victory, the Mary Rose, and other historic ships) and ferries to the Isle of Wight and is the final destination and origination station.

DEPART WATERLOO STATION	ARRIVE PORTSMOUTH HARBOUR STATION	NOTES
0720 (0723 Sa)	0852 (0907 Sa)	M–Sa
0743	0916	Su
0808	0941	M–Sa
0815	0948	Su
0838 (0845 Su)	1010 (1029 Su)	Daily
0908 (1915 Su)	1041 (1047 Su)	Daily

M–Sa service continues after 0838 on the hour and at 40–50 minutes after the hour until 2250; then 2345. Su service continues after 0945 every half hour until midafternoon; then 15 and 45 minutes after the hour until 2315.

DEPART PORTSMOUTH HARBOUR STATION	ARRIVE WATERLOO STATION	NOTES
1447 (1440 Su)	1623 (1628 Su)	Daily
1517	1656 (1655 Su)	Daily
1540	1727	Su
1547	1726	M–Sa

M–Sa service continues after 1550 at 30-minute intervals until 1950; then 2050 and 2220. Su service continues after 1540; then at 20 and 40 minutes after the hour until 2140; then 2237.

---

continues the story of the British Navy into the twentieth century, up to the Falklands Campaign of 1982.

In the resort department, Portsmouth offers the **Pyramids Centre**, a giant leisure attraction built by the sea next to King Henry VIII's **Southsea Castle.** A true tropical paradise, where the temperature never drops below 84°F, the center features four areas of entertainment, ranging from swimming pools, top-name entertainment, and a patio bar to a supervised "Fun Factory" where Mom and Dad can park the kids. Another great place for the family is **The Blue Reef Aquarium**, featuring marine life found along the South Coast. The touchpools provide close-up encounters with many marine marvels.

Close by the Southsea Castle and the Pyramids Centre, Portsmouth's **D-Day Museum** and **Overlord Embroidery** tell the story of that historic event through pictures, plans, and the re-creation of wartime scenes, along with exhibits of various weapons and vehicles. A special audiovisual presentation relates the events leading to the recapture of Normandy. More history unfolds in the castle, where an audiovisual show reconstructs scenes of "Life in the Castle."

Day Excursion to

Ramsgate
Seaside Resort

Depart from Victoria Station
Distance by train: 79 miles (128 km)
Average train time: 1 hour, 50 minutes
Train information and InterCity services: (0845) 748 4950
Tourist information: Ramsgate Visitor Information Centre, 17 Albert Court, York
   Street, Ramsgate, Kent CT11 9DN; *Tel:* (01843) 583333; *Fax:* (01843) 585353
Internet: www.tourism.thanet.gov.uk
E-mail: tourism@thanet.gov.uk
Hours: All three visitor information centers (Ramsgate, Margate, and Broadstairs)
   operate on similar schedules: Monday–Saturday 1000–1600. During July and
   August, they also are open on Sunday 1000–1500. There are tourist information
   centers in all three Thanet towns touched by rail service—Margate, Broadstairs,
   and Ramsgate.
Notes: The Margate Visitor Information Centre is northeast of the railway station near
   the harbor at 12–13 The Parade; *Tel:* (01843) 583333; *Fax:* (01843) 230099.
   The Broadstairs Visitor Information Centre is near the railway station at the foot
   of the hill at 6B High Street; *Tel:* (01843) 583333; *Fax:* (01843) 868373; *Internet:* www.broadstairs.gov.uk. The Ramsgate Visitor Information Centre is some
   distance from the railway station in the town center on York Street. Buses from
   the station will take you near there, or hail a taxi.

Although the sea inlets have almost been drained, Thanet still bears the semblance of an island with clusters of seaside towns—Margate, Broadstairs, and Ramsgate, each with its own unique character. Londoners were attracted to Thanet early in the nineteenth century, and it has been a thriving resort area ever since. The attractive sandy beaches, miles of coastline for swimming under the watchful eyes of fully trained lifeguards, entertainment, and a diverse cultural heritage are among the assets the area has to offer.

Ramsgate has been selected as the primary point for the day excursion, for it is the terminal stop for trains departing London's Victoria Station on the North Kent line. En route stops at other Thanet towns are made on this rail line at Margate and Broadstairs. It should be noted that it is possible to return to Victoria Station via another rail route from Ramsgate through Ashford, or yet another route calling at Dover and Folkestone. With so many possibilities, you should consult the timetables posted in all three of the Thanet towns for possible variations of your own itinerary. The train schedule shown here gives details for the London Victoria Station–Chatham–Faversham–Margate–Ramsgate rail line only.

This frequent train service departs from the first bay (platforms 1–8) of London's Victoria Station. A word of caution: The first cars (usually four) closest to the ticket barrier will go to Dover. The balance of the cars (usually eight) at the head of the train will terminate in Ramsgate. The train "splits" at Faversham. You will be reminded of this by a train announcement when the train stops briefly in the Bromley South Station after leaving Victoria Station and crossing the Thames. Stay alert and board one of the proper cars.

Ramsgate, being strong on regency flavor, centers its activities around the **Royal Harbor and marina**. Annual events include the May Spring Festival, the July Ships Open Days Weekend, August Harbour Heritage Festival, and September Model Ship Rally. The harbor is a source of constant interest, as is the model village at **West Cliff,** a charming miniature of England's Tudor countryside.

Permanently moored on the cliff tops at **Pegwell Bay** in Ramsgate is a Viking ship commemorating the original Viking landing in A.D. 449. Ramsgate Harbour has seen Wellington's troops embark for the Continent, where they continued on to defeat Napoleon at Waterloo. The harbor also received thousands of battered British troops during the evacuation from Dunkirk in 1940.

Many recall memories of their travels through their senses of sight and sound. In the case of Ramsgate, we recall our visits there by our sense of taste. Most memorable was a dining experience at **Harvey's Crab & Oyster House,** located at 50 Harbour Parade. Walk down to the harbor area—you can't miss it. As the name indicates, seafood is the house specialty. Reservations are recommended; call (01843) 591110.

Margate is the Thanet town that has been conjuring up visions of holidays for years. Its biggest drawing card is the famous amusement park **Dreamland Fun Park,** set on a twenty-acre complex. The municipality of Margate owns 9 miles of seafront with sandy beaches and promenades running practically its full distance. The atmosphere of the area differs somewhat from that of England's south coast in that it is more

Note: Some trains on this route split at Faversham, part of the train continuing to Ramsgate and other cars going to Dover.

DEPART VICTORIA STATION	ARRIVE RAMSGATE STATION	NOTES
0734	0929	M–Sa (1)
0804	0952 (0947 Su)	Daily
0834 (0835 Sa)	1030	M–Sa (1)
0904	1051 (1046 Su)	Daily
0934	1128	M–Sa (1)

(1) M–Sa service continues after 0934 at 4 and 34 minutes after the hour until midafternoon, with frequent service until 2304. Su service is hourly at 4 minutes after the hour until 2305.

DEPART RAMSGATE STATION	ARRIVE VICTORIA STATION	NOTES
1420 (1427 Su)	1617 (1617 Su)	Daily
1457	1648	M–Sa
1520	1716 (1717 Su)	Daily
1552 (1600 Sa)	1758 (1747 Sa)	M–Sa
1620 (1622 Sa, 1627 Su)	1817 (1817 Su)	Daily
1648 (1700 Sa)	1848 (1847 Sa)	M–Sa
1722 (1722 Sa, 1733 Su)	1917 (1923 Su)	Daily
1750 (1800 Sa)	1947	M–Sa
1821 (1836 Su)	2017 (2023 Su)	Daily
1848 (1852 Sa)	2048	M–Sa
1923	2117	Su
1948 (1952 Sa)	2147	M–Sa
2023	2217	Su
2050 (2053 Sa)	2247	M–Sa
2123	2316	Su
2155	2347 (2349 Su)	Daily
2210	0018	M–F

sedate in mood and tempo. Perhaps the presence of the North Sea is one of the contributing factors.

When you arrive at Margate Station, the first sight to greet you is the golden sand of the beach. The **promenade** paralleling the beach is a length of souvenir shops, restaurants, confectioneries, and amusement halls. Beyond the Dreamland Fun Park lies Margate's main shopping center, where courteous Kentish clerks are most eager to assist you in your shopping. Extending from the promenade, Margate's **Old Town** of narrow streets and houses clusters around the town's harbor.

Broadstairs, known as "Kent's Best-Kept Secret," has a Victorian atmosphere about it and became a fashionable watering hole during the regency of King George IV. Victorians, one of the most eminent being Charles Dickens, favored holidays in Broadstairs. A leaflet from the information center will permit you to follow in his footsteps and see many interesting points within the town. Every June, townspeople remember Dickens by appearing in costume while attending a series of plays, readings, parades, and parties set against the backdrop of Victorian Broadstairs.

Day Excursion to

St. Albans
From Romans to Roses

Depart from King's Cross Thameslink
Distance by train: 20 miles (32 km)
Average train time: 25 minutes
Train information and InterCity services: (0845) 748 4950
Tourist information: St. Albans Tourist Information Centre, Town Hall, The Market Place, St. Albans, Hertfordshire AL3 5DJ; *Tel:* (0172) 786 4511; *Fax:* (0172) 786 3533
Internet: www.stalbans.gov.uk
E-mail: tic@stalbans.gov.uk
Hours: Easter–October: Monday–Saturday 0930–1730 and Sunday (mid-July to mid-September only) 1030–1630; November–Easter: Monday–Saturday 1000–1600.
Notes: Arriving in St. Albans, leave the train station and walk uphill toward the city center on Victoria Street. The uphill walk takes about fifteen minutes. At the junction of St. Peter and Chequer Streets, the tourist information center can be seen opposite, in the Town Hall. The alternative is city bus transportation, which departs from a bus shelter in the station area. The bus stop for returning to the station is at the top of Victoria Street.

St. Albans takes its name from Britain's first Christian martyr, a Romano-British citizen who was beheaded for his faith on a hilltop outside Verulamium, one of the most important towns at that time in the western Roman Empire. A magnificent fifteenth-century Norman cathedral now stands on the hilltop, and Verulamium has become a parkland on the western side of the city.

St. Albans has much to offer its visitors. Tucked away in various corners of the city are old coach inns, many with a fascinating history. The **White Hart Inn,** built in the fifteenth century, was restored in 1930. The **Fleur-de-Lys Inn** on French Row was erected between 1420 and 1440 on the site where King John of France was held prisoner after the Battle of Poitiers. Another inn, the **Fighting Cocks,** claims to be the oldest licensed house in England, deriving its name from the cockfights that were held there for many years. All three of these ancient "watering holes" are open to the public during licensed hours. St. Albans has always had an open mind concerning alcoholic beverages; Elizabeth I granted the city permission to issue wine licenses in 1560.

French Row in St. Albans, a narrow street of medieval appearance, is fronted by a clock tower built between 1402 and 1411 from the flint and rubble of Verulamium. Its original curfew bell was cast in 1335. Across from the bell tower stands the **Wax House Gate,** where candles and tapers were made and sold to pilgrims visiting the shrine of St. Albans. The path through the gate is still the shortest route for pedestrians en route to the cathedral, proving that the ancients had a sharp eye for customer traffic flow. **St. Albans Cathedral** contains traces of an eighth-century Saxon church and has one of the largest Gothic naves in Europe. The tower was built largely of stone from Verulamium. *Internet:* www.stalbanscathedral.org.

Many of the points of interest in St. Albans must be reached on foot. The information center has a pamphlet describing a walking tour, **St. Albans's Town Trail,** which includes the cathedral and the abbey. The tour (2½ miles) may prove a bit too ambitious for the less-experienced, less-conditioned walker, but paths lead past one or more of the previously described inns, where a libation will probably instill a desire to press on—or stay at the inn until closing. Check your rail schedules if doing so or book a room at one of the old coach inns.

Helpful publications to take on the trails are *A Historical Map of St. Albans* and *Mini Guide.* The center has them available for a small fee. The information center is close to the marketplace. Markets are held in St. Albans every Wednesday and Saturday. If you are in town on these days, be sure to "go to market" and enjoy watching the locals barter back and forth with the vendors. Everything from apples to zinnias, including the weather and current prices, will become subjects of discussion.

The Roman city of **Verulamium** is engrossing. You can spend an entire day at the site visiting its 200-acre grounds, which include a temple, forum, museum, hypocaust, and theater. The museum houses an impressive collection of Roman antiquities. From the center of St. Albans, you can reach Verulamium in about twenty minutes on foot, or you can opt for a local bus. The tourist information office will give you the directions.

London–St. Albans–London

This is a very heavily traveled route, often crammed with commuters. Typically, on M–Sa there are 3 or 4 or more trains each hour in either direction, and on Su usually 2 trains per hour. The best advice is that you make your way to the appropriate station, where you can be assured you won't have to wait more than 15 minutes for a train.

Note: King's Cross Thameslink Station is not the same as King's Cross Station. King's Cross Thameslink Station can be reached from the King's Cross underground station and from the King's Cross train station by following the appropriate signs. King's Cross Thameslink Station is approximately 300 meters from King's Cross train station. The Thameslink trains also operate from London Bridge Station, Blackfriars Station, and other stations in Central London. Information and a complete timetable may be obtained at most London train station information offices.

DEPART KING'S CROSS THAMESLINK	ARRIVE ST. ALBANS STATION	NOTES
0801	0820 (0832 Su)	Daily
0804	0825	M–Sa
0811	0836	M–Sa
0816	0827	M–Sa
0831	0850 (0902 Su)	Sa, Su
0845	0904	M–Sa
0901	0920 (0932 Su)	Daily
0916	0935	M–Sa
0931	0950 (1002 Su)	Daily
0946	1005	M–Sa

Pattern continues with frequent service throughout the day.

DEPART ST. ALBANS STATION	ARRIVE KING'S CROSS THAMESLINK	NOTES
1434	1454	Daily
1449	1509	Daily
1504	1524	Daily
1519	1539	Daily
1534	1554	Daily
1549	1609	Daily
1604	1626	Daily
1619	1639	Daily
1634	1654	Daily
1649	1710	Daily

Pattern continues with frequent service through 2354 M–Sa, 2324 Su (additional trains on Su).

At the **Verulamium Museum,** artifacts taken from the ruins are displayed in an environment of natural surroundings. The small items from the houses and shops range from iron hinges, latches, and locks to personal ornaments worn by the inhabitants. A full range of pottery and glassware, for both table and kitchen use, is on exhibit.

Exploratory excavations of the site have taken place from time to time, but experts estimate that only one-third of the area within the Roman town walls has been uncovered. Modern techniques such as aerial photography continue to reveal additional features.

The gardens of the **Royal National Rose Society** are in St. Albans. The society made its first award for a new rose in 1883 and subsequently established its own trial grounds, where you can see the future "greats" of the rose world. New varieties from all over the world are sent to St. Albans to undergo a comprehensive three-year assessment. The twelve acres of gardens, a spectacle for the casual visitor, are a total fascination to rose enthusiasts. Now open in spring from mid-April through early June and in summer from mid-June to late September; the gardens are accessible to the public during varying hours daily; group discounts are offered. Call (01727) 850461 for details.

The range of history in St. Albans extends from A.D. 43, with the first evidences of the Roman enclosure at Verulamium, to the moment you arrive to enjoy the vitality of this timeless city. To step over St. Albans's threshold is to step into a land of enchantment and history.

Day Excursion to

Salisbury
Magna Carta Archive

Depart from Waterloo Station
Distance by train: 84 miles (135 km)
Average train time: 1 hour, 25 minutes
Train information and InterCity services: (0845) 748 4950
Tourist information: Salisbury Tourist Information Centre, Fish Row, Salisbury, Wiltshire SP1 1EJ; *Tel:* (01722) 334956; *Fax:* (01722) 422059
Internet: www.visitsalisbury.com
E-mail: visitorinfo@salisbury.gov.uk
Hours: October–April: Monday–Saturday 0930–1700; May: Monday–Saturday 0930–1700, Sunday 1030–1630; June–September: Monday–Saturday 0930–1800, Sunday 1030–1630. The center operates a booking service for local accommodations as well as the popular Book-a-Bed-Ahead program.
Notes: Salisbury's Tourist Information Centre is situated at the rear of the Town Guildhall where Market Square meets Fish Row. Proceed on foot down Fisher-

ton Street, which you will find to your far left as you exit the station. After crossing the River Avon, the street will narrow and change names several times until it becomes Fish Row. The tourist information center at the rail station (platform 4) is open from Easter–September, Monday–Saturday 0930–1630.

Salisbury holds the distinction of being one of the few English cities not originally founded by the Romans. The old town, Old Sarum, had been in existence since the Iron Age. The Romans fortified it, and the Saxons later developed it into an industrial town. All went well in Old Sarum until arguments between the occupants of the church and the castle caused a new church to be built in the valley below the original town site. This new location proved to be more popular than the old. Consequently, although known as Salisbury, the town's official name is New Sarum.

The center of Salisbury has traditionally been divided into two distinct areas: the cathedral and the marketplace. This tradition still exists, and the gates leading to the cathedral and the buildings in the "close" surrounding it are locked every night. Beautiful houses of medieval and Georgian architecture overlook the green.

The **marketplace** has a history all its own. In the original Charter of 1227, the town was authorized to hold a Tuesday market. This got out of hand and grew into almost a daily market until protests from nearby towns resulted in a reduction of market days in Salisbury to Tuesdays and Saturdays only. Today Salisbury maintains those traditional market days.

Salisbury boasts a number of historic inns that have given rest and refreshment to travelers down through the centuries. The fireplaces in the **King's Arms Inn** have the same stone as that used in the construction of the cathedral. The **Haunch of Venison,** an old English chophouse, was built about 1320. The **Red Lion Hotel,** dating from the same era, was the starting point for the Salisbury Flying Machine, the nightly horse-drawn coach to London.

In Salisbury, you will find many impressive examples of architectural styles, ranging from the town's thirteenth-century cathedral to a modern pedestrian shopping district known as the Old George Mall. The most unexpected structure is the foyer of the movie theater on New Canal Street. Once the banqueting hall of the merchant John Halle, four-time mayor of Salisbury, it is now a splendid example of fifteenth-century black-and-white timbering.

From April through September you may join a daily guided **walking tour** of Salisbury at 1100 and 1800 (none at 1800 on Sundays) from in front of the information center on Fish Row. The tour lasts approximately one and a half hours. On Friday night the 1800 walking tour becomes a special ghost walk at 2000.

London–Salisbury–London

DEPART WATERLOO STATION	ARRIVE SALISBURY STATION	NOTES
0710	0836	M–Sa
0833	0954	M–Sa
0903	1026	Su
0933	1054	M–Sa
1003	1136	Su
1033	1154	M–Sa
1103	1229	Su
1133	1254	M–Sa

Then hourly until 2135 M–Sa, 2103 Su.

DEPART SALISBURY STATION	ARRIVE WATERLOO STATION	NOTES
1425	1547	M–Sa
1523 (1526 Sa, Su)	1646 (1648 Sa, 1651 Su)	Daily
1625 (1618 Su)	1748	Daily
1647	1815	M–F
1726	1850	Daily
1750	1915	Su
1815 (1818 Su)	1945 (1951 Su)	Daily
1910 (1904 Su)	2040 (2036 Su)	Sa, Su
1954 (2000 Sa, 1957 Su)	2119 (2125 Sa, 2131 Su)	Daily
2020 (2045 Sa)	2153 (2225 Sa)	M–Sa
2105 (2113 Su)	2235 (2243 Su)	M–F, Su

The cathedral has a unity of design that no doubt is attributable to the fact that, unlike most other cathedrals, which took centuries to complete, the **Salisbury Cathedral** was constructed in only thirty-eight years. In other words, it wasn't affected by several different periods of architecture. Foundation stones were laid in 1220, during the heyday of Gothic design. One of its greatest treasures is its ancient clock mechanism, which originally stood in a detached belfry and dates from 1386 as one of the oldest pieces of operating machinery in the world.

The cathedral contains a library founded at Old Sarum in 1078; seventy of the books installed in the library at that time are still there. The great treasure of the cathedral, housed in **Chapter House,** is the *Magna Carta,* written at Runnymede on June 15, 1215. Brought to Salisbury by William, Earl of Salisbury, he placed it in the cathedral for safekeeping and there it remained until World War II.

Among its many historical achievements, Salisbury made its mark in the annals of medical care. Of the four hospitals currently in or near the city, the **Trinity Hospital,** on Trinity Street, has an interesting story concerning its founding in 1379 by Agnes Bottenham. Chronicles relate that Ms. Agnes ran a "house of ill repute" on the site, and when it prospered, she built a hospital and almshouse there as an act of penitence.

Visitors interested in seeing **Old Sarum,** 1½ miles north of the new town, can do so by city bus or taxi. Excavations and reconstruction have been under way for some time. Oddly enough, even after the old city was abandoned, two representatives of Parliament continued to be sent, despite the fact that the city had no inhabitants—a case of representation without taxation.

Day Excursion to
Sheffield
Trademark of Quality

Depart from St. Pancras Station
Distance by train: 165 miles (265 km)
Average train time: 2 hours, 20 minutes
Train information and InterCity services: (0845) 748 4950
Tourist information: Sheffield Visitor Information Centre, 1 Tudor Square, Sheffield, South Yorkshire S1 2LA; *Tel:* (0114) 221 1900; *Fax:* (0114) 201 1020
Internet: www.sheffield.gov.uk
E-mail: visitor@sheffieldcity.gov.uk
Hours: Monday–Thursday 0930–1715; Friday 1030–1750; Saturday 0930–1615.
Notes: The Visitor Information Centre is about a ten-minute walk from the rail station. Cross the road by the traffic light–controlled pedestrian crossing. Pass to the left of the Sheffield Hallam University Nelson Mandela Building and walk straight up steep Howard Street, passing the university's main entrance on your right. Cross the road straight ahead; at the other side turn right, then go up the slope on your left, on to Surrey Street. Walk past the city library and Graves Art Gallery on your right until you come to Tudor Square and the Crucible and Lyceum Theatres. The information center is on the corner of Tudor Square and Surrey Street. Taxi service is also available from the rail station.

Sheffield, England's fourth largest city, is world-famous for steelmaking, toolmaking, engineering, and cutlery. Surviving records show that cutlery was being made in Sheffield in 1297, and Chaucer referred to a Sheffield thwitel (knife) in his *Canterbury Tales*. By the late nineteenth century, the area was regarded as the steel capital of the world, and in 1913 Harry Brearley made one of the great discoveries of our century, stainless steel, at Sheffield's Firth Brown Laboratories.

Forget images of smoke-belching chimneys. Present-day Sheffield is still England's greenest city. Built on seven hills and five river valleys (fast-flowing streams drove the waterwheels that powered the cutlery industry before the steam age), Sheffield has more than fifty parks and green spaces—and four trees to every person! Surrounded by open countryside, more than a third of the city lies within the beautiful Peak National Park.

The unique Heart of the City development has provided Sheffield with three new public squares and the **Millennium Galleries,** which house national exhibitions from the Victoria and Albert Museum in London, Sheffield's impressive metalware gallery, and the Ruskin Collection of the Guild of Saint George, left to the city by Victorian sage, artist, and critic John Ruskin. *Internet:* www.sheffieldgalleries.org.uk. Under construction is a Winter Garden, the first temperate plant house to be built in Europe and possibly the most important one built in Britain in the last one hundred years. The project includes offices, shops, cafes, and pubs.

Sheffield has won a reputation for sporting excellence and in 1995 was the first city to be awarded the official title "National City of Sport." The country's top teams in ice hockey (Sheffield Steelers) and basketball (Sheffield Sharks) are based here, as is the national diving squad. The city has hosted more than 200 national and international sports events over the past several years.

With the **Peak National Park** nearby, outdoor sports are particularly popular. A completely unexpected attraction, set in the heart of the city, is Europe's largest artificial ski slope complex, **Sheffield Ski Village.** Just bring your gloves; you can rent everything else.

Another well-known export is music. Joe Cocker, Def Leppard, Pulp, and many other bands started here. This heritage is recognized at the **National Centre for Popular Music,** currently undergoing an exciting redevelopment. The National Centre hosts a lively program of events, including club nights and live bands most evenings.

Two traditional museums, commemorating Sheffield's industrial heritage, are **Kelham Island** and **Abbeydale Industrial Hamlet.** At the former, the largest working steam engine in Europe can be seen in action. The latter museum displays scythe-producing, water-driven machinery, some of which dates from the seventeenth century. The **City Museum,** Weston Park, has excellent collections of Sheffield cutlery and Sheffield plates. **Cutler's Hall,** on Church Street, is the headquarters of the Cutler's Company, which was formed in 1642. The present Cutler's Hall dates from 1832 and houses the company's silver and cutlery collections, which can be viewed by appointment only (inquire at the Visitor Information Centre).

A heritage site is **Victoria Quays,** Sheffield's canal basin. The canal

London–Sheffield–London

DEPART ST. PANCRAS STATION	ARRIVE SHEFFIELD STATION	NOTES
0605 (0620 Sa)	0858 (0912 Sa)	M–Sa
0725	0947	M–Sa
0825	1042	M–Sa
0925 (0930 Su)	1142 (1236 Su)	Daily
1025 (1030 Su)	1242 (1324 Su)	Daily
1030	1322	Su
1125 (1130 Su)	1343 (1412 Su)	Daily

Hourly departures, then 1630, 1715, 1740, and 1800, then hourly again from 1925 to 2225 M–Sa; continue Su hourly departures half past the hour until 2130 (also 1800 and 1900).

DEPART SHEFFIELD STATION	ARRIVE ST. PANCRAS STATION	NOTES
1428 (1424 Su)	1642 (1700 Su)	Daily
1451	1804	M–Sa
1528 (1524 Su)	1750 (1755 Su)	Daily
1628 (1622 Su)	1846 (1852 Su)	Daily
1725 (1720 Su)	1943 (2006 Su)	Daily
1825	2043 (2057 Su)	Daily
1906	2147	Sa
1922	2138	M–F
1858	2056	Su
2025	2306	M–F

was built to ship in iron ore from Sweden and ship out steel products to England's east coast ports; now Victoria Quays is a waterside oasis in the heart of the city center, with its beautiful warehouse buildings, a cobbled waterfront, and the Waterways Cafe.

Another historic building in the city center is the **Lyceum** in Tudor Square, a magnificently restored Victorian theater that together with the modern **Crucible Theatre** forms the country's largest theatrical complex outside London.

A fifteen-minute journey from the city center on the Supertram, Britain's largest and most advanced urban light-rail transport system, will take you to one of Britain's most successful shopping malls, **Meadowhall**, with 270 shops, a food court, and cinemas.

The Visitor Information Centre offers an excellent city map. The center also offers accommodation information and advance booking services. Helpful brochures, including *A City in My Pocket,* the *Mini Guide, It's Happening in Sheffield Visitor Guide,* and a number of other visitor publications, are available at no cost. With one of the largest student populations in the country (more than 40,000), Sheffield has a wide variety of nightlife choices for fun-loving tourists.

Shops highlighting the local steel-crafting trade include Osbournes Silversmiths Ltd., Rivelin Cutlery Works, United Cutlers of Sheffield, George Butler Ltd., Hiram Wild Factory Shops, Mortons of Sheffield, and Don Alexander. The Visitor Information Centre can supply addresses and hours.

Day Excursion to

Southampton
An Imposing Heritage

Depart from Waterloo Station
Distance by train: 79 miles (127 km)
Average train time: 1 hour, 10 minutes
Train information and InterCity services: (0845) 748 4950
Tourist information: Southampton City Information Office, 9 Civic Centre Road, Southampton SO14 7FJ; *Tel:* (023) 8083 3333; *Fax:* (023) 8083 3381
Internet: www.southampton.gov.uk
E-mail: touristinformation@southampton.gov.uk
Hours: Monday, Tuesday, Thursday, and Friday 0830–1730, Wednesday 1000–1730, Saturday 0900–1200 and 1300–1600.
Notes: From the railway station, you can board any "City Centre"–bound bus and ask the driver to "deposit" you at the Civic Centre, next to which you will find the City Information Office. There is a map outside the Southampton railway station showing the route to the center.

I n the minds of many, Southampton conjures visions of the great transatlantic ocean liners, for it is Britain's prime ocean-passenger port and home of many of the world's greatest passenger ships, including Britain's flagship, the *Queen Elizabeth II (QE2)*. Many visitors, however, know little about Southampton's span of centuries, which has given it a rich heritage of England and of Europe. Southampton's museums, classic old-town area, and beautifully preserved medieval town walls help reveal this rich and interesting history.

Southampton is best seen on foot, with the assistance of a bus now and then. Pick up the free *Southampton's Visitors Guide* at Southampton

City Information Office—it contains suggestions for sightseeing. Visitors from the United States will take special interest in the sailing of the *Mayflower* from Southampton in 1620. Persons proving descent from the original *Mayflower* passengers can have their names entered on the memorial. The center also can make hotel and bed-and-breakfast reservations in Southampton and its surroundings.

As mentioned in the official handbook, there are many places of interest within easy walking distance of the city information center. A visit to them will gradually unfold a picture of Southampton's past. To catch Southampton's seagoing flavor, a visit to the Ocean Village or the Town Quay Marina would be in order.

Similar to the harbor renovation of Baltimore, Maryland, Southampton's **Ocean Village** has transformed some of its old docks into a cosmopolitan playground with a bevy of specialty shops, eateries, and attractions overlooking a yacht basin. Quayside at Southampton's port, you stand in history. Four hundred years before the Pilgrim fathers departed on their journey to the New World, Richard the Lion-Hearted embarked on the Third Crusade. The **Town Quay Marina** plays host to the cream of the yacht-racing world. Both areas are close to the terminal used by the *QE2*. Check with the information center concerning walking directions and the possibility of the *QE2* being in the harbor.

Next in line is the **Tudor House Museum,** where the costumes, paintings, and furniture of centuries past are displayed against the oak beams and stone carvings of Tudor House itself. One of the few surviving examples in Southampton of a large town house from the early Tudor period, it contains a banquet hall and is surrounded by an authentic Elizabethan herb garden. Don't miss the tunnel entrance to the remains of a twelfth-century merchant's home. The kids will love it.

Next on the agenda is the **Southampton Maritime Museum,** also known as the Wool House. Once a medieval warehouse, it is now a showplace for the city's involvement with the sea. Since early times, Southampton has been an important port of call. Docks were piled high with luxuries from the Mediterranean and the East, brought there by Genoan and Venetian fleets.

With all of the rekindled global interest in the sinking of the *Titanic* on her maiden voyage, one cannot miss visiting the **"Story of the White Star Line" Exhibition.** The *Titanic*'s story is told through the voices of some of the actual survivors and the people of Southampton whose lives were affected by the tragedy. A free **Titanic Trail** brochure is available in the visitor center of the museum, which illustrates the various monuments and memorials dedicated to the victims of the tragedy. The walking tour begins at the Docks, the departure point of the *Titanic*, April 10, 1912.

London–Southampton–London

DEPART WATERLOO STATION	ARRIVE SOUTHAMPTON STATION	NOTES
0730	0851	M–F
0745 (0750 Su)	0914 (0910 Sa, 0931 Su)	Daily
0755	0919	M–Sa
0830	0944	M–Sa
0845 (0850 Su)	1015 (1010 Sa, 1031 Su)	Daily
0855	1019 (1015 Sa)	M–Sa
0930	1044	M–Sa

M–Sa service continues after 0915 at 15-minute intervals until midafternoon with several departures following until 2355; Su service continues after 0930 at 30 and 50 minutes after the hour until 2130; then 2155 and 2255.

DEPART SOUTHAMPTON STATION	ARRIVE WATERLOO STATION	NOTES
1515	1631 (1638 Su)	Daily
1545	1701 (1703 Sa, 1723 Su)	Daily
1615	1803 (1736 Su)	Daily
1645	1808	M–Sa
1700	1827	M–Sa
1715	1834 (1828 Sa, 1838 Su)	Daily
1730	1900	M–Sa
1745	1907 (1902 Sa, 1923 Su)	Daily

Daily service continues at 15-minute intervals until 1945; then other frequent service until 2250 (2245 Su).

Southampton is the place to shop in south England, with a wide choice of shopping areas and stores catering to all tastes. **West Quay** is the region's premier shopping destination, with a delightful combination of fashion and lifestyle retailers and a wide variety of restaurants and coffee shops. The Marlands Shopping Centre has an exciting mix of stores, and the Bargate Centre is an ideal shopping and leisure experience for the younger set.

Also in Southampton's repertoire is the **Hall of Aviation** on Albert Road. The museum is a memorial to R. J. Mitchell, Southampton's famous aircraft designer of the Spitfire, the fighter that valiantly defended the country during the Battle of Britain. The exhibits include a Spitfire Mark 24, possibly one of the last of 24,500 Spitfires produced by the Supermarine Aircraft Company in nearby Woolston, a quarter mile from the museum. The museum's collection also includes a Sandringham Flying Boat as well as hundreds of photographs, plans, and models connected with R. J. Mitchell and the Supermarine factory.

The route between the museums, by the way, is dotted with historic buildings, such as the **Duke of Wellington Pub** and the **Red Lion Pub.** Pausing for a pint may provide a pleasant period for pondering Southampton's past and present.

Free guided walks through medieval Southampton depart from the Bargate at varying times throughout the year. Ask for complete details at the Leisure and Visitor Centre.

Day Excursion to

Stonehenge
Mysterious Pagan Shrine

Depart from Waterloo Station
Distance by train: 84 miles (135 km)
Average train time: 1 hour, 45 minutes
Train information and InterCity services: (0845) 748 4950
Tourist Information: Stonehenge, English Heritage, First Floor Abbey Buildings, Abbey Square, Amesbury, Wiltshire SP4 7ES; *Tel:* (01980) 625368; *Fax:* (01980) 623465; *Information Line:* (01980) 624715
Internet: www.english-heritage.org.uk
Hours: Stonehenge is open daily March 16–May 31 0930–1800, June 1–August 31 0900–1900, September 1–October 15 0930–1800, October 16–March 15 0930–1600. Closed December 24–26 and January 1.
Notes: There are several ways to get to Stonehenge from the Salisbury railway station (see below). A gift shop, refreshments, and public toilets are available at the site, and all facilities provide access for the disabled.

The poet Sir John Squire wrote about Stonehenge: "Observatory, altar, temple, tomb, erected none knows when by none knows whom, to serve strange gods or watch familiar stars . . ." Stonehenge is unmatched—truly one of the wonders of the world. There are many opinions regarding the use and purpose of the monument. Whatever the reason for its existence, however, Stonehenge remains an awe-inspiring reminder of the past.

The landscape for a few miles around the Stonehenge monument reportedly contains more prehistoric remains than any other area of the same size in Britain. There are earthworks, burial sites, erected stones, and hill carvings. Because they belong to the prehistoric period, long before any written records were made, there are many questions about them that we shall never be able to answer. Through technology, we have been able to tell *how* they were made and, in some cases, *when* and by *whom.* The unanswered question is *"Why?"*

Stonehenge sits on the Salisbury plain, an almost treeless, windswept plateau. With its origins dating from about 2950 to 1600 B.C., Stonehenge comprises a circular group of stones roughly 110 feet in diameter that stand in an area surrounded by a low earthen rampart and ditch approximately 330 feet in diameter. The largest stones, some weighing as much as 50 tons, were brought to the site from quarries some 20 miles distant. The stones are placed in such a manner as to reflect the position of the sun on the four main dates of the seasons, the solstices and equinoxes, possibly as an agricultural almanac or for spiritual purposes.

The monument stands on approximately 300 feet of solid chalk. Unfortunately, Stonehenge has been robbed constantly of its stone throughout the centuries. In Victorian times, it was common practice for visitors to bring hammers and chisels to carve their names and other graffiti and to chip off souvenir sections of the temple stones.

Diodorus Siculus, historian to Julius Caesar, described Stonehenge as a temple to the sun god Apollo. Modern Britons have marked the area with small clumps of trees to commemorate the Battle of Trafalgar in 1805.

If time is of the essence to get to Stonehenge, a taxi can get you there in about twenty minutes. Buses, operated by Wilts & Dorset, depart from the station for Stonehenge via Salisbury and Amesbury daily, Sundays and public holidays included, *Tel:* (01980) 624715. The adult round-trip fare is £4.80; admission to the Stonehenge site is £5.20. The Wilts & Dorset bus schedule is arranged so as to connect with all express trains to and from the Waterloo Station in London. If you plan to linger at the site, this will provide you with ample time to do so.

In conjunction with Wilts & Dorset, City Sightseeing, one of Britain's leading operators of town and city tours, offers a tour of Stonehenge departing from Salisbury train station for an adult fare of £15.00 (senior citizens and students, £12.00; children younger than age twelve, £7.50). *Internet:* www.city-sightseeing.com; *E-mail:* info@city-sightseeing.com. Fares include entrance to Stonehenge, and you are accompanied by a guide throughout the tour. Tour time is just under two hours. For complete details and bus schedules, we suggest calling ahead to the Wilts & Dorset travel office in Salisbury, (01722) 336855.

Two tour companies, AS Tours and Days Out Tours, also offer excellent one-day tours from the rail station to Stonehenge. Check with the tourist information center for details.

Time permitting, upon arriving back in Salisbury, you may want to explore the city prior to boarding your London-bound train. If so, stay

London–Stonehenge

No train service to Stonehenge; take a bus from Salisbury. Consult the London–Salisbury timetables for train service to Salisbury.

153

aboard the bus returning from Stonehenge until it arrives at the Salisbury bus terminal approximately five minutes after its arrival at the rail station. See the day excursion to Salisbury for ideas and sites.

Do use one of the special excursion buses. If you use the regular public bus system between Salisbury and Amesbury, you will have to walk or take a taxi for the 2 miles between Amesbury and the Stonehenge site.

A sad note: Because of damage to the monument, visitors are not permitted to enter the actual stone circle, but can view it only from a distance. Visitors are required to remain behind a fence built around the Stonehenge temple to protect it. "TIME," as the announcement observes, "IS TAKING ITS TOLL."

Day Excursion to

Stratford-upon-Avon
Shakespeare Country

Depart from Paddington Station
Distance by train: 121 miles (195 km)
Average train time: 2 hours, 12 minutes
Train information and InterCity services: (0845) 748 4950 or (0121) 643 2711
Tourist information: Stratford-upon-Avon Centre, Bridgefoot Street, Stratford-upon-Avon, Warwickshire CV37 6GW; *Tel:* (01789) 293127; *Fax:* (01789) 295262
Internet: www.shakespeare-country.co.uk, also www.heritagecities.co.uk
E-mail: stratfordtic@shakespeare-country.co.uk
Hours: Summer: Monday–Saturday 0930–1730, Sunday 1030–1630; Winter: Monday–Saturday 0930–1700, Sunday 1000–1500.
Notes: The tourist center is about a 15-minute walk or £2.00 taxi ride from the railroad station. If you decide to walk, turn left onto Alcester Street and follow to Greenhill Street. Turn left. Follow Greenhill to Wood Street, and continue to Bridge Street, which is a main road at the bottom of the town. Cross over the canal bridge; you will see the center on the left side.
Guide Friday Tourism Centre: Civic Hall, 14 Rother Street, Stratford-upon-Avon, Warwickshire CV37 6LU; *Tel:* (01789) 294466; *Fax:* (01789) 414681
Notes: The Guide Friday center is a short walk from the rail station. Turn left out of the station and go toward the town center. Pass the crossroad. At the second traffic light, turn right. Civic Hall is the large white building on the right.

William Shakespeare, the English poet and playwright recognized universally as the greatest of all dramatists, was born in Stratford-upon-Avon in 1564. His mother was the daughter of a local farmer; his father was a glove maker and a wool merchant who entered politics to become mayor of Stratford. Although Shakespeare lived throughout his professional career in London, he kept his home ties with Stratford. In 1597 he purchased New Place, one of Stratford's largest houses. He died there in 1616 and was buried in Stratford's parish church.

Rail travelers can go from London's Paddington Station to Stratford-upon-Avon via Thames Trains. Trains depart from Paddington beginning at 0918 and at regular intervals throughout the day, Monday through Friday. There are four direct return services from Stratford-upon-Avon to London, including a late train especially for theatergoers. For more detailed information on these services, call (0845) 330 7182, fax (0118) 957 9006, or visit the Web site at www.thamestrains.co.uk. Saturday and Sunday departures on this route are limited. InterCity services also are available to Leamington Spa or Birmingham, with connecting services to Stratford; call (01788) 560116 or (0121) 643 2711.

When visiting Shakespeare Country from London, you can take advantage of the one- or three-day Shakespeare Country Explorer tickets. They provide for travel to Stratford-upon-Avon, Leamington Spa, Warwick, and Warwick Parkway from London Marylebone or Paddington Stations, plus unlimited train travel between these stations and others within the Stratford-upon-Avon zone. One-day fare: £25.00 adults, £12.50 children. Three-day fare: £30.00 adults, £15.00 children.

Advance booking is not necessary. Simply purchase your ticket on departure from London Marylebone or Paddington. If you do wish to purchase in advance, call (0870) 516 5165.

Our advice is to take a guided tour of Stratford-upon-Avon. The popular "Stratford and Shakespeare Story Tour" is operated by City Sightseeing Tours. The open-top bus tours stop at each of the Shakespearean properties: the newly refurbished **Shakespeare's Birthplace** on Henley Street; **Anne Hathaway's Cottage; Mary Arden's House,** where Shakespeare's mother grew up; **New Place/Nash's House,** in which Shakespeare spent his retirement years before his death in 1616; and **Hall's Croft,** home of Shakespeare's daughter, Susanna. Visitors may get on and off the bus as frequently as they wish since the ticket is valid all day.

From May to September, tours depart every fifteen minutes; March to mid-May and October to November, every half hour; December and Jan-

London–Stratford-upon-Avon–London

LONDON Stratford-upon-Avon

Schedules shown are for direct trains from and to London Paddington Station. Other service is possible by changing trains in Reading or in Leamington Spa.

DEPART PADDINGTON	ARRIVE STRATFORD-UPON-AVON	NOTES
0918	1127	M–Sa
0948	1203	Su
1118	1327	M–Sa
1148	1403	Su
1348	1556	M–Sa
1448	1658	Su
1648	1908	M–Sa
1848	2108	M–Sa

DEPART STRATFORD-UPON-AVON	ARRIVE PADDINGTON	NOTES
1355 (1350 Sa)	1614 (1556 Sa)	M–Sa
1435	1650	Su
1737 (1737 Sa)	1945 (1953 Sa)	M–Sa
1755	2020	Su
2000	2216 (2218 Sa)	M–Sa
2315	0130 +1	M–F

+1=Arrives next day

uary, every hour. You can join the tours at any of the Shakespearean properties, as well as outside the tourist center at Bridgefoot, Evesham Place, or on Windsor or Meer Streets. City Sightseeing Bus Tour tickets are £8.00 adults, £3.50 children, £19.50 family, and £6.00 senior citizens and students.

Other tour highlights include the **Royal Shakespeare Theatre**, the **Swan** and **Other Place Theatres;** the **Holy Trinity Church**, where Shakespeare is buried and protected by a purportedly cursed tombstone; the **Old Fifteenth-Century Grammar School**, which he attended; and **Harvard House**, home of Katherine Rogers, whose son founded the library in the United States that became Harvard University.

A visit to see a performance by the Royal Shakespeare Company at one of its three theaters in Stratford is a must. Reserve theater seats as far in advance as possible. Telephone (01789) 403404 for twenty-four-hour information on program and seat availability. To book seats, telephone the theater box office: *Tel:* (0870) 609 1110; *Fax:* (01789) 403 413.

Advance tickets may also be purchased in the United States through Global Tickets in New York at (800) 223–6108. For backstage tours, telephone (01789) 403405. The theater has several restaurant/bar facilities. Telephone (01789) 403415 for more information and reservations for special restaurant/theater packages.

The **Box Tree,** a luxuriously appointed restaurant overlooking the Avon River, serves classic cuisine (closed on Sunday). The **River Terrace** is a modern restaurant/coffee shop/wine bar serving light international dishes. You can even "Pick-up-a-Picnic" here by placing your order with the cashier two hours in advance.

Day Excursion to

Windsor
The Royal Castle

Depart from Waterloo Station
Distance by train: 25 miles (41 km)
Average train time: 50 minutes
Train information and InterCity services: (0845) 748 4950
Tourist information: Royal Windsor Information Centre, 24 High Street, Windsor SL4 1LH; *Tel:* (01753) 743 900; *Fax:* (01753) 743 904; *Accommodations:* (01753) 743 907
Internet: www.windsor.gov.uk
E-mail: windsor.tic@rbwm.gov.uk
Hours: July and August: Monday–Saturday 1000–1730, Sunday 1000–1700; October–March: Monday–Friday 1000–1600, Saturday 1000–1700, Sunday 1000–1600; April–June: daily 1000–1700; September: Monday–Saturday 1000–1700, Sunday 1000–1600.
Notes: The traditional "**i**" will lead the way to the tourist information center from either arrival point, Windsor Riverside Station or Windsor Central Station. The grounds of Windsor Castle are immediately across the street from the information center.

You have a choice of two rail routes from London to Windsor. For the schedule here, we have selected the route from Waterloo Station in London to Windsor Riverside Station. This line does not require changing trains en route. The alternate route, which departs Paddington Station in London, requires a change at Slough to a shuttle train before arriving at Windsor Central Station. If you take the Paddington–Slough route, the shuttle train arrives and departs in Slough from track 1. Either route gives you a magnificent view approaching Windsor Castle. On either train, sit on the left-hand side (outbound) to take full advantage of the scenery. Be sure to purchase an illustrated guidebook on Windsor Castle—it will become a fond reminder of your visit.

Historic **Windsor Castle** is the official home of English royalty, and it is the largest inhabited castle in the world. *Tel:* (0207) 776 7304; *Fax:* (0207) 930 9625; *Internet:* www.the-royal-collection.org.uk; *E-mail:* windsorcastle@royalcollection.org.uk. William the Conqueror built the first structure on this site, a wooden fort that doubled as a royal hunting lodge. Other English kings added to the castle during their reigns, but despite the multiplicity of royalty and architects, the castle has managed to retain a unity of style all its own.

Queen Elizabeth II uses the castle far more than any of her predecessors, usually on weekends. When she is in residence, her Royal Standard will be flying atop the Round Tower's flagpole. Chances of seeing Her Majesty, should she be in residence, are very slim, since she has her own private rooms. Nevertheless, during that time you may find Prince Philip watching his son Charles, the Prince of Wales, and his polo team bashing about in **Windsor Great Park.**

The £50 million restoration effort after the devastating fire in the castle on November 20, 1992, was completed in 1998. Refurbishment of the Queen's Private Chapel, St. George's Hall, and the State Dining Room were painstakingly replicated and updated.

While in **St. George's Chapel,** dedicated to Britain's highest order of chivalry, The Most Noble Order of the Garter, ask the guards about the knights' shields. Some of the shields are totally covered up and the reason is . . . well, you'll find out. Perhaps they had forgotten their royal oath! The chapel is home of the ***King's Champion,*** a full-armored statue commemorating the throwing down of the gauntlet in defense of the sovereign. Directly to the right of the *King's Champion* begins the wood paneling engraved with the names of the original members of the Order. The next three walls contain a chronological listing of all those who have been knighted—including the women who have been added in recent decades.

Rare state occasions such as the Investiture of the Garter, when the queen proceeds down the walks of Windsor Castle accompanied by a full entourage of castle guards and Knights of the Garter, are difficult for the general public to view. The **changing of the castle guard,** however, is an event conducted in a manner in which the general public can participate. The new guard leaves the Victoria Barracks precisely at 1055, then marches along High Street to the castle. The guard changing takes place at 1100 and the old guard returns by the same route at 1130. By positioning yourself along High Street or Castle Hill, you will have a good view of the pageantry as it unfolds. Note that the changing of the guard does not take place during wet weather or on Sundays.

From the battlements of Windsor Castle, you may look down and across the stately River Thames onto the playing fields of **Eton College,** where "how the game is played" has always been more important than the final score. The importance of Eton lies less in what it is than in what it stands for. The schoolyard and cloisters are open 1400–1630 except during school holidays, when they are open 1030–1630. Guided tours are at 1415 and 1515 daily.

Your initial entry into the single-street town of Eton may be a bit frightening at first. You will probably find yourself surrounded by a group of young gentlemen uniformed in pin-striped trousers, white bow ties, and formal black coats with tails. These are the students of Eton College. This school for kings is one of Britain's most exclusive educational institutions and a strong reminder that the British on occasion can cling fiercely to their traditions.

Cruising on the River Thames offers a respite from pageantry and tradition during your visit. At the bottom of High Street, at its intersection with Barry Avenue, the Windsor Boat Pier offers two cruises. The first is a thirty-five-minute trip upstream, and the other is a full two-hour trip with light refreshments and a licensed bar aboard.

Kids of all ages will enjoy a visit to **Legoland Windsor,** located a mere 2 miles from the Windsor town center (www.lego.com/legoland /windsor). Take the Legoland shuttle bus from either of the Windsor rail stations. The theme park opens at 1000 daily from March to November. Closing times vary from 1700 to 1900. Learn to drive your own Lego car on a real road system with traffic lights and roundabouts. At the Waterworks, fire water cannons and make water flow uphill or squirt from fountains. Cruise down Fairy Tale Brook in a boat or whirl around on the Whirly Birds Helicopter. In My Town, you don't just watch the circus— you're part of the show. You can even watch airplanes being built at Legoland Airport. Tickets may be purchased at the Royal Windsor Information Centre. Admission fees are £23 adults, £20 for children age three to fifteen and for seniors (older than sixty). You can save by purchasing tickets online or by phone at (0870) 504 0404.

Windsor Guildhall, on High Street opposite the information center, was designed by Sir Christopher Wren. Legend has it that the Council Chamber insisted Wren add four internal columns to the design for safety reasons. Somewhat insulted, he did add the four internal columns, defiantly leaving them about 1 inch short of the ceiling to prove that his original design was sound. The guildhall is open to visitors on Mondays 1000–1400 (on Tuesdays during bank holiday weeks).

If you have not yet been introduced to the British public house (pub), there is no better time than now. **The Royal Oak,** directly across the street from Windsor Riverside Station, is highly recommended for a

London–Windsor–London

There are two train stations in Windsor–Eton: the Windsor & Eton Riverside Station and the Windsor & Eton Central Station. Direct service to Windsor & Eton Riverside Station is available from and to London Waterloo Station; service from and to Windsor & Eton Central Station requires a change of trains at Slough. Schedules shown here are direct trains from and to Windsor & Eton Riverside Station.

DEPART WATERLOO STATION	ARRIVE WINDSOR & ETON RIVERSIDE STATION	NOTES
0712	0803	M–F
0742 (0728 Sa)	0833 (0819 Sa)	M–Sa
0758 (0747 Su)	0847 (0845 Su)	Sa, Su
0812	0904	M–F
0828	0919	Sa
0843	0936	M–F
0858 (0847 Su)	0947 (0945 Su)	Daily
0909	0950	Su

M–Sa service continues after 0858 at 30-minute intervals until late afternoon; Su service continues after 0847 at hourly intervals until late afternoon.

DEPART WINDSOR & ETON RIVERSIDE STATION	ARRIVE WATERLOO STATION	NOTES
1355 (1402 Su)	1447 (1459 Su)	Daily
1427 (1419 Su)	1517 (1501 Su)	Daily
1455 (1502 Su)	1547 (1559 Su)	Daily
1527 (1519 Su)	1617 (1601 Su)	Daily
1555 (1602 Su)	1647 (1659 Su)	Daily

and continuing very frequent service with a similar pattern until 2245 M–Sa, 2302 Su.

relaxing break prior to trekking uphill to the castle entrance, and as a resting spot to royally reminisce before boarding the train back to London Town. No more prim a pub can you find in all of England. Its impeccable oaken interior matches the high quality of its food and service. The inn was constructed as an alehouse in 1736 and restored in 1937. Should we meet you there, we'll buy the first round!

Day Excursion to

York

Fine Medieval City

Depart from King's Cross Station

Distance by train: 188 miles (302 km)

Average train time: 1 hour, 57 minutes

Train information and InterCity services: (0845) 748 4950

Tourist information: Tourist Information Centre, De Grey Rooms, Exhibition Square, York, North Yorkshire YO1 2HB; *Tel:* (01904) 621756; *Fax:* (01904) 551888

Internet: www.york-tourism.co.uk

E-mail: tic@york-tourism.co.uk

Hours: De Grey Rooms: Open 0900–1700 Monday–Saturday (until 1800 in summer), 1000–1600 Sunday (until 1700 in summer). York Station: 0900–1700 Monday–Saturday (1800 in summer), 1000–1600 Sunday (0930–1630 in summer).

Notes: Check in with the Tourist Information Centre in the rail station and request the *First Stop York* free booklet that offers half-price vouchers to many attractions in the town. Then turn left leaving the train station and proceed along the city wall toward the tower of the York Minster. After crossing the River Ouse, at the intersection of Duncombe Place and St. Leonard's Place, you will see the Minster straight ahead. York's main tourist office is nearby in Exhibition Square, just beyond Theatre Royal.

The history of York," according to King George VI, "is the history of England." The Romans took York from a Celtic tribe, the Brigantes, in A.D. 71. According to legend, King Arthur captured the city sometime after the Roman legions retreated in A.D. 406. The Saxons took charge in the seventh century, and the Danes ran the Saxons off in 867, only to get their comeuppance from the Anglo-Saxons in 944. In 1066, York saw the fastest turnaround ever when King Harold of England defeated the King of Norway at Stamford Bridge, 6 miles from York. Nineteen days later, York (and all of England, in fact) passed to the Normans when Harold was killed in the Battle of Hastings.

William the Conqueror, following his victory at Hastings, came north to quell a rebellion, which he accomplished through his version of urban renewal—the "scorched earth" policy. The ruins and rubble of the Romans, the Saxons, the Vikings, and the Anglo-Saxons, however, remain today.

Charles I, fleeing the fermenting civil war, left London in 1639 to take residence in York. Cromwell's troops finally took York in July 1644. A condition of surrender was that there would be no pillaging; thus, the fine medieval stained glass of York Minster was saved. It is estimated that the Minster contains more than half of all the medieval stained glass in England.

York, similar to Chester, has retained most of its fourteenth-century city walls. You will see part of them as you exit from York's railway station. The city of York is best explored on foot. Once armed with a map from the tourist information center, proceed on foot into the city. Although it's a ten- to fifteen-minute walk, you'll see a lot of history en route. While at the tourist office, ask for the York City Council's parents' folder for those traveling with youngsters. York is considered to be "the child-friendly city." And if during your journey you start to think, "I wish I could spend more time in York," as is often heard by the tourist officials, inquire about overnight accommodations.

The York Association of Voluntary Guides provides excellent **free tours** that depart daily from Exhibition Square at 1015 throughout the year, with an additional tour at 1415 from April to the end of October, and an evening tour at 1900 in June, July, and August. The tour lasts about two hours. To request special theme tours or private tours, write to The Hon. Secretary, Tourist Information Centre, DeGrey Rooms, Exhibition Square, York YO1 7HB, or telephone (01904) 640780 between 0930 and 1130 Monday to Friday.

We highly recommend **The Complete York Tour**—an extensive four-hour tour that includes a stop for a beverage and offers a discount for *Britain by BritRail* readers. Just book your tour in advance by telephoning (01904) 706643. The tour covers the York Minster and direct admission (no queuing) to the Jorvik Viking Centre. It also includes discount vouchers for several other attractions and free maps. The normal price is £12.00 for adults, £11.50 for students/senior citizens, and £6.00 for children. Meet your guide by the tree in front of the West End of the Minster or make arrangements to be met at the rail station (no extra charge) when you book the tour.

Too tired or unable to walk? A horse-and-carriage service operates outside York Minster during good weather. Hour-long, open-top bus tours depart from the rail station and travel different routes as well.

Among its points of interest, **York Minster** draws first choice. Built between 1220 and 1472, the Minster is England's largest Gothic cathedral. As the mother church of the Church of England's northern province, it is outranked in religious importance only by Canterbury Cathedral. A superb view can be had from the tower top . . . 275 steps above! Those who make it to the top can ask for a certificate (£1.00 donation). No sightseeing is allowed on Sundays or other times of religious services.

Also be certain to visit the **National Railway Museum** on Leeman Road, a ten-minute walk from the York railway station. The Great Railway Show at the museum commemorates the Railway Age from the 1820s to the present day. Visitors walk down station platforms and, in imagination, become passengers on an Edwardian Express or on a boat

London–York–London

DEPART KING'S CROSS STATION	ARRIVE YORK STATION	NOTES
0615	0832 (0830 Sa)	M–Sa
0700	0856 (0904 Sa)	M–Sa
0730	0940	M–F
0800	0951 (1000 Sa, 1021 Su)	Daily
0830	1030 (1039 Sa)	M–Sa
0900	1058 (1057 Sa, 1106 Su)	Daily
0930	1135 (1134 Sa, 1128 Su)	Daily
0940	1125	Sa
1000	1151 (1157 Sa, 1201 Su)	Daily

and continuing every half hour until mid- or late afternoon; then hourly 1900–2200 M–F and Su; last train Sa 2030.

YORK TO KING'S CROSS STATION

M–F Depart York Station 1429, 1452, 1505, 1530, 1555, 1630, 1656, 1727, 1750, 1828, 1855, 1939, 2001, 2137, and 2344; journey time approximately 2 hours.

Sa Depart York Station 1432, 1449, 1527, 1554, 1632, 1727, 1826, 1938, 2001, and 2105; journey time approximately 2 hours.

Su Depart York Station at 1458, 1516, 1550, 1631, 1657, 1708, 1754, 1841, 1901, 1910, 1931, 1958, 2045, and 2124; journey time approximately 2 hours, 20 minutes.

train to Paris. The museum's National Railway Collection ranges from a lock of Robert Stephenson's hair to the splendor of the *Royal Train.*

York's **Castle Museum** is one of the most interesting folk museums in the world. Famous streets of York have been reconstructed to depict the daily life and occupations of various periods from Tudor to Edwardian times. The museum also contains an eighteenth-century water mill that operates throughout the summer. Other sections are devoted to Yorkshire crafts, costumes, and military history; the Tea Room has 1960s decor and style of music. Whoa, flashback!

In 1992, York's impressive medieval gatehouse, Monk Bar, was converted into the **Richard III Museum.** Since many feel that historians gave King Richard a "bum rap," the exhibition puts Richard on trial for you to decide his guilt or innocence. Based on the evidence presented, *you* hand down the verdict. Did Richard murder his own nephews, The Princes in the Tower?

You'll find the narrow, winding streets of York the most fascinating of all the city's attractions. The streets developed from the original Roman street plans. In turn, each century added a bit more color—and perhaps confusion. The Vikings left their mark in the use of street names ending in "gate," such as Petergate and Castlegate. But Stonegate existed *before* the Vikings' arrival.

For purchasing fine china and crystal, pay a visit to one of the world's leading fine-china and crystal specialists, **Mulberry Hall,** on Stonegate. *Tel:* (01904) 620736; *Fax:* (01904) 620251; *Internet:* www.mulberry hall.co.uk; *E-mail:* mailorder@mulberryhall.co.uk. It's only about 200 yards from York Minster. A fifteenth-century private house, Mulberry Hall has been a shop since the eighteenth century. Here, you will find an incomparable stock of fine china, including Wedgwood, Spode, and Royal Doulton, as well as crystal by Waterford, Stuart, and Baccarat, which can be shipped anywhere in the world.

The medieval citizens following the Vikings gave York its winding streets. One of these streets, **The Shambles,** is reputed to be one of the best-preserved medieval streets in Europe. Originally the street was crammed with butcher shops in half-timbered overhanging buildings. The east-west line of the street kept the meat in cool shade for most of the day and now houses an interesting assortment of stores and bookshops, where the meat hooks still hang.

Scotland

"The pipes, the pipes are calling. . . . " They are calling you to Scotland, a country where there is much more than first meets the eye. Come to Scotland with an open mind, a keen eye, and a sense of adventure. A land of contrasts—friendly, bustling towns and cities but with easy escape to solitude—Scotland has some of the least-populated parts of Europe and yet one of the largest arts festivals.

Scotland forms the northern part of the island of Great Britain and is divided into three main regions: the Southern Uplands, the Midland Valley, and the Highlands. Filled with patriotic pride, many Scots consider themselves to be the "true Brits." With more than 5,000 years of history, they predate their Anglo-Saxon cousins by several centuries. You may visit ancient towns built even before the pyramids of Egypt.

Although Scotland has been part of the United Kingdom since the formal Act of Union in 1707, it still issues its own banknotes and maintains its own legal and educational systems as well as its own culture and traditions. From bagpipes and kilts to fine Scotch whisky and that mysterious food known as haggis, Scotland is unique.

Scotland has produced some of the world's most talented people. Alexander Graham Bell, inventor of the telephone, was originally from Scotland, as is the famous actor Sean Connery; Robert Burns, from Ayr, wrote "Auld Lang Syne;" and John Paul Jones, who established the U.S. Navy, was born in Dumfriesshire. Other famous Scots include Robert Louis Stevenson, author of *Kidnapped* and *Treasure Island;* Sir Arthur Conan Doyle, creator of the detective Sherlock Holmes; the 1970s band the Bay City Rollers; and the pop band Garbage.

Rail Travel in Scotland

What better way to visit a country famous for its hospitality, scenery, and history than by train? ScotRail provides a variety of ways to discover Scotland. It operates 2,000 daily departures to 354 stations in Scotland and provides a connecting sleeper service to London. Any BritRail Pass is valid, of course, in Scotland. ScotRail, however, also has rail passes available for travel only in Scotland.

The **Freedom of Scotland Travelpass** is valid for travel any four days within an eight-day period, or any eight days within a fifteen-day period. See the Appendix for prices, or, in North America, call toll-free (877) RAILPASS (877–724–5727) or visit www.railpass.com to order or for more information.

The Travelpass includes unlimited standard-class rail travel on all ScotRail and Strathclyde Passenger Transport services and all scheduled Great North Eastern Railway and Virgin Trains operating wholly within Scotland, including Carlisle and Berwick-upon-Tweed. The pass also includes all Caledonian MacBryne and Strathclyde ferry services to the islands, a discount on some P&O ferry routes, and a free packet of timetables upon validation of your pass in Scotland. The discounts are available on reclining-seat fares only and do not apply to cabins. Some bus services between cities and all Glasgow Underground services are also included.

ScotRail Short Breaks will help you discover Scotland's breathtaking beauty, hospitality, and some of the world's most romantic rail journeys on its famous railway lines, including the West Highland line (Glasgow–Oban, Fort William, and Mallaig), the Kyle line (Inverness–Kyle of Lochalsh), and the North line (Inverness–Thurso and Wick).

We have selected the two base cities of Edinburgh, Scotland's capital, and Glasgow, Scotland's largest city. The day excursions listed can be visited from either base city, and our rail schedules include departures from both Edinburgh and Glasgow. So sit back, relax, and enjoy the ride.

ScotRail Railways Limited, Caledonian Chambers, 87 Union Street, Glasgow G1 3TA. Fares and train times, telephone in the United Kingdom: (0845) 748 4950; *Internet:* www.scotrail.co.uk; *E-mail:* enquiries@scot rail.co.uk.

Base City:

Edinburgh

Internet: www.edinburgh.org
E-mail: info@visitscotland.com

"This profusion of eccentricities, this dream in masonry and living rock is not
a drop-scene in a theater, but a city in a world of everyday reality!"
—Robert Louis Stevenson

There is an understandable feeling of rocklike perpetuity envelop-
ing Edinburgh. Formed by volcanic heat and scoured and shaped
by Ice-Age glaciers in a valley punctuating its skyline with upward-
thrusting crags, the setting of Scotland's capital city of Edinburgh is nothing short of dramatic.

Edinburgh's exact origins are lost in antiquity. Although dissenting
opinions exist, it seems that a primitive fortress was established around
A.D. 452 by the Picts on the sloping ground leading from the great Castle
Rock on which Edinburgh Castle stands today. There have been fortresses
on Castle Rock since that time, each in turn razed by a challenger and then
rebuilt only to be razed again. By the eleventh century, however, events
around Edinburgh began to calm down and the town got on with the task
of becoming civilized and prosperous. From its earliest days, Edinburgh
offered a stern, almost aloof countenance to the world and inspired great
individuals to great achievements.

Edinburgh is actually two cities. The Old Town, built on a rocky
ledge running from Edinburgh Castle to the Royal Palace of Holyroodhouse, is steeped in ancient history. Huddled on high ground in typical
medieval fear of attack, it is full of winding and cobbled off-streets, so be
sure to wear comfortable walking shoes. The New Town, formed on the
lower side of Nor' Loch, a lake created from a swamp and eventually
drained in 1816, spreads serenely in a succession of streets and avenues,
reflecting the optimism of later centuries. Conceived in 1767 when the

Scottish Parliament approved an extension of the city, the Town Council lost no time in proceeding with the work. The city planning that followed made possible Edinburgh's present wide streets and spacious squares.

The two cities within a city further reflect two great attributes: on the one hand, Edinburgh's reserved exterior, and on the other, its ability to express great warmth and even, on occasion, a high degree of gaiety. Edinburgh has been called one of the most attractive capital cities in the world. As Oliver Wendell Holmes aptly put it, "Edinburgh is a city of incomparable loveliness."

From the beauty of its setting, enhanced by its architecture, to the turbulence of its history and the stalwart qualities of its citizens, Edinburgh is a city of inexhaustible delight. Edinburgh Castle, the Palace of Holyroodhouse, the Royal Mile, and Princes Street await you. Welcome to Scotland's capital.

Arriving by Air

Although Edinburgh has its own international airport, direct service to or from North America is not available. International air service is provided to Edinburgh from most European cities. Travelers arriving in Britain via London (Gatwick or Heathrow), Birmingham, or Manchester Airport may take either a connecting flight to Edinburgh or the train. From London's King's Cross Station, the Great North Eastern Railway line will get you to Edinburgh's Waverly Station in only four hours. Or sleep through your journey to Edinburgh aboard a comfortable Caledonian Sleeper train departing from London's Euston Station just before midnight.

Glasgow is a convenient port of entry for visitors arriving in Scotland from overseas. **Glasgow's International Airport** is located 10 miles west. Express train service from Glasgow's Queen Street Station to Edinburgh takes only fifty minutes; one hour, forty-five minutes by bus. The airport is situated in an area that is relatively fog-free during most of the year, for the wind moving across the Irish Sea has few natural obstructions to interrupt its flow. See the "Arriving by Air" section of the Glasgow chapter for further information. **Prestwick Airport** (29 miles southwest of Glasgow), which for years served as the international airport for the area, is the most fog-free airport on the British Isles.

Arriving by Train

Waverley Station is the main train station in Edinburgh. Some Inter-City trains from London go on to Aberdeen after a brief station stop in Edinburgh. If you are aboard one of these trains, be prepared to "set down" in the Waverley Station as quickly as possible following your arrival. Edinburgh's other station, Haymarket, is where all trains halt en route to Glasgow or Aberdeen. Trains arriving from England via Newcastle and York, however, bypass Haymarket Station.

Waverley Station appears to be completely immersed in an open ravine. The area was once a swamp that was converted into a lake as a northern defense for Edinburgh Castle during the reign of King James II (1437–1460). The lake was drained in 1816 to become the site of the Princes Street Gardens, which separate the Old Town and New Town in Edinburgh.

Today's Waverley Station complex is the second largest in Britain and has twenty-one tracks strewn about in a labyrinth of steps and passageways. But there are plenty of signs, and station map/guide leaflets are available.

Basically there are three accesses to Waverley Station. The first is a set of rather steep steps, the Waverley Steps, connecting the north side of the station (the trackage runs east and west) with Princes Street, the city's main artery. The second and third approaches are ramps leading from the main floor of the station to the Waverley Bridge, which runs between the Old Town and New Town. Both ramps have pedestrian walkways. The northern ramp serves incoming vehicles; the one to the south is for outgoing vehicles.

Tracks 12 to 18 form the backbone, or center, of the Waverley Station. At the entrance to these tracks is a digital-display board for train arrivals, departures, and special announcements. If your train is departing from tracks other than 12 to 18, ask the railroad personnel at the ticket barriers for directions.

Pay special attention to multiple train departures from the same track. A line of coaches on a single train track can actually be two trains departing for two separate destinations. They are announced with red-bannered front train or rear train signs. It pays to ask questions.

The Rail Travel Centre (train information center) is located in the waiting-room area of the station and is open 0700–2300 daily. Covered by a huge glass dome, the waiting area contains digital arrival/departure information and a series of facilities, including restrooms, a magazine kiosk, and eateries. The principal entrance to this area is located across the main-station concourse from the stub ends of tracks 16 and 17. Train reservations may be made at any of the counters.

Money exchange (Bureau de Change) is available from the Edinburgh & Scotland Information Centre.

Hotel accommodations, including bed-and-breakfast reservations, are provided by the Edinburgh and Scotland Information Centre. For advance reservations from *outside* Britain, dial country code 44 + (131) 473 3800.

The Balmoral Hotel at Waverley Station is a five-star hotel that has been a landmark for Waverley Station, and the city of Edinburgh, since 1902 when it was known as the North British Hotel. The Balmoral is located between the station and Princes Street. Topped by a mammoth 200-foot Gothic clock tower, the hotel serves as a transition between the hustle of commerce on Princes Street and the bustle of the passengers arriving at and departing from the station.

The Victorian-style hotel has undergone a £23 million restoration and is exquisite throughout. We enjoyed the pampering we received during our stay. Undoubtedly, the hotel is one of Edinburgh's most familiar and elegant landmarks, commanding an important position at the east end of Princes Street. *Tel:* (0131) 556 2414; *Fax:* (0131) 557 3747; *Internet:* www.thebalmoral hotel.com; *E-mail:* thebalmoralhotel@rfhotels.com.

Edinburgh and Scotland Information Centre, 3 Princes Street EH2 2QP; *Tel:* (0131) 473 3800; *Fax:* (0131) 473 3881. *Hours:* 0900–1900 Monday–Saturday, 1000–1900 Sunday.

The center is located on the rooftop of Waverley Station beyond the north end of Waverley Bridge at the corner of Waverley and Princes Streets. Use the pedestrian ramp on the north side of the station, turning right as you reach the Waverley Bridge level. There are several tourist information signs to help guide the way.

Many of the facilities sought by incoming passengers—such as money exchange, city information, and hotel accommodations (reservation fee, £3.00)—may be found in the Edinburgh and Scotland Information Centre. The first section has information on Edinburgh and all of Scotland. Go straight ahead as you enter for self-service; go to the right for counter service. For entertainment information, proceed through the shopping section, where Scottish books, maps, and posters are available at the ticket desk; *Tel:* (0131) 558 1072.

Getting around in Edinburgh

Two bus departure points serve the area surrounding the Waverley Street rail station. The first, at Waverley Bridge, is located immediately up the ramps leading out of the rail station. This departure point serves the city bus system and the sightseeing buses. Coach service for the Glasgow Airport and other main destinations utilizes the bus terminal on St. Andrew Square. To reach it, cross Princes Street where it intersects with Waverley Bridge. Then walk north 1 block to St. Andrew Square.

City Sightseeing Edinburgh, Platform 1, Waverley Railway Station; *Tel:* (0131) 556 2244; *Fax:* (0131) 557 4083; *Internet:* www.city-sight seeing.com and www.edinburghtour.com.

For bus tours of Edinburgh, go to the tourist information office and its selection of bus-tour brochures. You can readily recognize the City Sightseeing open-top double-decker buses. You can get on and off at your leisure. Tours depart a minimum of every fifteen minutes and include Edinburgh Castle, Palace of Holyroodhouse, Princes Street, the Royal Mile, and New Town. Purchase your tickets from the bus driver, the City Sightseeing office at platform 1 in Waverley Station, or from the tourist information center. Fares: £8.50 adults, £7.50 students/seniors, £2.50 children. Save up to £2.50 per tour by prebooking online or by telephone.

Follow in the footsteps of royalty—visit the **Royal Yacht** *Britannia,* which has traveled more than 1 million miles and served the Royal Family and their guests for more than forty years. This is one tour you won't want to miss. To be guaranteed admission, however, purchase tickets in advance. *Tel:* (0131) 5555566; *Internet:* www.royalyachtbritannia.co.uk; *E-mail:* enquiries@royalyachtbritannia.co.uk. In person, visit the **Edinburgh Tattoo Office,** 33–34 Market Street. Admission fees: £8.50 adults, £6.50 seniors, £4.50 children; family ticket (two adults and up to three children) £23.00. The Royal Yacht is berthed at the Port of Leith, about 2 miles from the city center. *Britannia* tour buses depart from Waverley Bridge.

Guided walking tours (Robin's Walking Tours) depart daily from outside the tourist information center. There are several to choose from: The Grand Tour of the City departs at 1000; then explore the Royal Mile at 1100, and at 1900 see Ghosts and Witches.

Or try the ones offered by **Mercat Tours,** Mercat House, Niddry Street South EH1 1NS. *Tel* and *Fax:* (0131) 5576464; *Internet:* www .mercattours.co.uk; *E-mail:* info@mercattours.com.

Explore where the history of the old underground city meets the supernatural in the Ghosts and Ghouls Tour, presented by Mercat Tours and the city of Edinburgh. Dramatic guides, who are graduate historians, will lead you from the Mercat Cross, where the "entertainment" of the ages occurred (criminals hanged, flogged, tortured, and dismembered), down through the deserted, dark, and ghostly places of Old Town Edinburgh. Paranormal activity is logged on record, so don't be surprised if you happen to see or feel something from beyond. Tours depart nightly at 1900, 2000, and 2100 (April–September); 1900 and 2000 October–March. The ninety-minute tour costs £7.50; group discounts are offered. Buffet, refreshment, and specialty combination tours are also available. We heard of one brave group actually spending the night among the spirits in one of the bridge caverns. Be sure to ask the guide about the most haunted pub in Edinburgh; you may need a stiff one after this tour. Other tours include the Secrets of the Royal Mile, Ghost Hunter Trail, the Vaults Tour, Haunted Underground Experience, and Ghosts and Witches.

A guided tour of the **Real Mary King's Close,** 2 Warriston's Close, Writers' Court (off the Royal Mile) takes visitors beneath Edinburgh's city chambers for a fascinating step back into the seventeenth, eighteenth, and nineteenth centuries. *Hours:* April–October 1000–2200 (last tour at 2100);

November–March 1000–1600 (last tour at 1500). *Tel:* (0870) 243 0160. According to the tourist board, "access may prove difficult to people with certain disabilities," and no children younger than age five are permitted. Cost: £7.00 adults, £6.00 seniors/students, and £5.00 children.

The Murder & Mystery Tour is usually scheduled at 2100 and 2200 throughout the year, although the tour departure times may vary. Duration of the tour is ninety minutes. Cost: £7.00 per person. Both tours include a copy of the *Witchery Tales* book. If you're up to braving the ghosts and goblins, murders and mysteries, book your tickets in advance and meet your guide outside the Witchery Restaurant, Castlehill, Royal Mile (by Edinburgh Castle). We hope you return.

Enticing Edinburgh

Magnificent **Edinburgh Castle** is the national symbol of Scotland and one of its top attractions. The castle radiantly crowns an ancient volcanic mount above Edinburgh proper. Guided tours of Edinburgh Castle are available, or you may pick up a free headset and tour at your own pace. As you follow numbered plaques throughout the castle, your headset will provide you with its fascinating story.

Stand in the oldest building in Edinburgh, **St. Margaret's Chapel,** just as the Queen of Scotland did more than 900 years ago. A beautiful stained-glass memorial to Sir William Wallace faces the altar. You may also see the Crown Jewels of Scotland, the Scottish National War Memorial, and the Stone of Destiny.

The castle is still garrisoned and every day (except Sunday) a cannon is fired at 1300. It makes a rather dramatic time check for unsuspecting visitors who end up doing the "One o'Clock Jump."

During the annual **Edinburgh Military Tattoo,** the castle provides a most provocative backdrop for this dazzling celebration of music, theater, dance, and traditional Scottish pipes and pipers, drums and drummers marching on the castle esplanade. Undoubtedly one of the world's greatest shows, each tattoo has overseas contingents as well as traditional Scottish, but it always closes with the moving appearance of the lone piper on the castle battlements, a very touching moment.

Originated in the seventeenth and eighteenth centuries in the Low Countries, "tattoo" was derived from the cry of the innkeepers at closing time. Local regiments would then march through the street playing fife and drums to signal a return to quarters, and the shout would go up *"Doe den tap toe"* (turn off the taps). This became the basis for many marvelous massed military bands' performances given around the globe, with the Edinburgh Military Tattoo being the leader.

The Edinburgh Tattoo occurs annually in August. Contact the Edinburgh Military Tattoo Box Office, 33–34 Market Street, Edinburgh EH1 1QB; *Tel:* +44 8707 555 1188 (from outside the United Kingdom); *Fax:*

(0131) 225 8627 (open 1000–1630 Monday–Friday); *Internet:* www
.edintattoo.co.uk. Tickets range from £9.50 to £30.00. Please order well
in advance as this is an extremely popular event.

Amid the contrasting charms of its Old Town and New Town, Edinburgh takes its place among an elite group of European cities conspicuous for their romance and physical attributes. As more enclosures were
built during the post-medieval period, the term *close* came into existence
in old Edinburgh to describe the narrow passageways giving access, or
right-of-way, to the buildings in the rear of others. There are well over
one hundred closes in Old Town, many of which have brass tablets at
their entrances to explain their historical significance.

There are many aspects of Edinburgh to see on conducted tours, but
the city's real beauty is best seen by exploring it on foot at your own pace.
Walk the **Royal Mile** in Old Town from Edinburgh Castle to the Palace of
Holyroodhouse. For some background before traveling, visit www
.royalmile.com. En route, you'll pass a fantastic assembly of picturesque
old buildings, such as Brodie's Close, the John Knox House, the Cannonball House, Anchor Close, and the Canongate Tolbooth.

Brodie's Close housed Deacon Brodie, a respectable town councillor
by day and a burglar by night. Brodie's lifestyle supposedly provided the
basis for Robert Louis Stevenson's *Dr. Jekyll and Mr. Hyde.* The **John Knox
House** dates from the sixteenth century and is traditionally connected
with both John Mossman, Keeper of the Royal Mint to Mary, Queen of
Scots, and John Knox, Scotland's religious reformer. A brief video presentation amid original timber-framed galleries and oak paneling will
take you back to the sixteenth century. The John Knox House is located
at the halfway mark of the Royal Mile in the Netherbow Arts Centre.

The Cannonball House, dating from 1630, got its name from a cannonball lodged in its gable, ostensibly fired from the castle by an errant
cannoneer during the blockade of 1745. **Anchor Close** is the site where
the first edition of the *Encyclopaedia Britannica* was printed as well as the
Edinburgh edition of Robert Burns's poems. Reportedly, Burns himself
read the proofs on the premises. Last renovated in 1591, the **Canongate
Tolbooth** has been used as the Town Council House and a prison for the
ancient village of Canongate, now incorporated into the city of Edinburgh. The Canongate Tolbooth houses the People's Story Museum,
which relates the life and work of ordinary folk in Edinburgh from the
late eighteenth century to the present.

Although the **Palace of Holyroodhouse** originated as a guesthouse
for the Abbey of Holyrood, most of the palace we see today was built for
Charles II in 1671. The most famous figure associated with the palace,
however, was Mary, Queen of Scots, who spent six years of her tragic
reign there. On the palace grounds, you may view Queen Mary's Bath
House where, according to today's Scottish tour guides, she bathed daily.

The guides also explain that her cousin Queen Elizabeth I bathed once a month—whether she needed it or not.

The Royal Mile was for many centuries the center of Edinburgh life. Its citizens lived and conducted their affairs on this busy, crowded street. At the entrance to the Palace of Holyroodhouse, you will find a line of the letter S embedded in the pavement. Until 1880 it marked the limits of sanctuary extended by Holyrood Abbey. It is said that debtors were often seen running toward the line with creditors in hot pursuit and bystanders wagering on the outcome.

At the end of the Royal Mile, next to the Palace of Holyroodhouse, visit **Our Dynamic Earth** exhibition. It uses special effects and technology to dramatically tell the story of how our planet developed.

Greyfriars Bobby. On Candlemaker Row, a short distance from Edinburgh's Royal Mile, stands a statue in tribute to a small dog's affection and fidelity to his master. In 1858 a wee Skye terrier named Bobby followed the remains of his master, Auld Jock, to Greyfriars churchyard, where the dog lingered and slept on his master's grave for fourteen years until his death in 1872.

People tried to take Bobby away. They even found a home for him in the country. Still, Bobby returned to the churchyard, where friends began bringing food to sustain him during his vigil. The story of Greyfriars Bobby spread throughout Edinburgh, and soon Bobby's tale of devotion reached Queen Victoria in London. She sent a special envoy, Lady Burdett-Coutts, to investigate this unusual story.

Bobby, in the meantime, had made friends with children in a nearby orphanage. The terrier brought joy and love to the children, particularly to Tammy, a crippled boy with whom Bobby would play by the hour. Bobby lived his own life, however, and returned nightly to his master's grave—at first secretly, for the presence of a dog in a churchyard was unthinkable in those times. But as Bobby won hearts, he gained privileges too. He even won the heart of the Lord Provost of Edinburgh, who had a collar made for the dog in 1867 and paid Bobby's licensing fee. (The collar can be seen today in the Canongate on the Royal Mile.)

Bobby never went to London to see the queen, but royal annals reflect that the queen actually was planning to pay him a visit at Greyfriars. Bobby died, however, before that honor became a reality.

The dog's body was buried alongside that of his master. Although Bobby is no longer visible, his presence is felt so strongly by the residents of the area that they frankly admit to opening their doors briefly before retiring at night, just in case. Perhaps when the door to heaven is opened for them, they will see Bobby again, running on the green pastures at the heels of his master, beside the still waters.

Bobby's statue stands close to the iron gates of Greyfriars churchyard, where Auld Jock and his faithful dog are interred. The story of Greyfriars

Bobby was filmed by Walt Disney. We think it's worth your while to visit Greyfriars, just as we do each time we return to Edinburgh.

Shopping in Edinburgh. The city of Edinburgh is well known for its fine boutiques, shops, and department stores, where you may still find bargains in the famous Harris tweeds, Fair Isle sweaters, and tartan plaids. Princes Street is lined with shops displaying a variety of Scottish wares, from argyles and bagpipes to whiskey. And when you run out of stores and shops to visit on Princes Street, turn north 2 blocks to George Street and continue your shopping there. (You may need to stop by the bank on the way.)

Shoppers' havens on Princes Street include Jenners, the largest and oldest independently owned department store in the world, and C&A, both opposite the Scott Monument in the Waverley Street Station area. If you've never been in a store more than 195 years old, try Romanes & Paterson, Ltd., at 62 Princes Street. You will find traditional Scottish tweed, exquisite Edinburgh crystal, Caithness glass, knitwear from the borders, and, of course, tartans. They are everywhere, as is the whiskey.

Still not tired of shopping? The Scotch House nearby contains more than 300 tartans available by the meter, along with Shetland knitwear and original gifts. If you know a wee one, check out Hop Scotch, The Scotch House's special department for children.

Food, foam, and fun. With all that shopping, you may be ready for a snack and a libation. You don't have far to go—between and parallel to Princes Street and George Street is Rose Street, which probably has more convivial pubs to the meter than any other street in the world. In fact, Edinburgh was voted Britain's "Best City for Pubs." You'll have no problem finding food, foaming pints, and fun at more than 700 pubs ranging from traditional neighborhood pubs to chic wine bars.

For historical atmosphere, fine wines, and an innovative style of Scottish cuisine, visit The Witchery by the Castle, Castlehill, Royal Mile EH1 2NF; *Tel:* (0131) 255 5613; *Internet:* www.thewitchery.com; *E-mail:* reservations@thewitchery.com. A two-course lunch is £9.95; a three-course meal (without wine) averages about £27.00. The Witchery is open daily 1200–1600 and 1700–2330.

Day Excursions

A baker's dozen—thirteen exciting day excursions—have been selected for our readers. All were chosen so those who prefer staying in Glasgow rather than in Edinburgh may enjoy them as well.

Scotland is known as "the land that likes to be visited." To ensure your opportunity to visit this marvelous country by rail includes seeing as many of its features as possible, we have divided the selected day excursions into Scotland's four geographic areas: the east coast, central region, west coast, and Highlands.

Day Excursion to

Aberdeen
The Granite City

Depart from Waverley Station
Distance by train: 131 miles (211 km)
Average train time: 2 hours, 30 minutes
Train information and InterCity services: (0845) 748 4950
Tourist information: Aberdeen Visitor Information Centre, 23 Union Street, Aberdeen AB11 5BP; *Tel:* (01224) 288828; *Fax:* (01224) 252219
Internet: www.agtb.org
E-mail: info@agtb.org
Hours: October–May: Monday–Friday 0900–1700, Saturday 1000–1400; June and September: Monday–Saturday 0900–1700, Sunday 1000–1600. July and August: Monday–Friday 0900–1900, Saturday 0900–1700, Sunday 1000–1400. On public and local holidays, with the exception of Christmas and New Year's Day, the center is normally open 0900–1700.
Notes: Walk across the carpark at the station, cross over to the Criterion Bar, and turn right. Walk along to Market Street and turn left up the hill. Then turn right onto Union Street, and the Visitor Information Centre is at No. 23 Union Street.

Since the discovery of oil in the North Sea, Aberdeen has earned the title of "Europe's offshore oil capital." The city, however, has not been spoiled by its industry. Oil does not come ashore in Aberdeen; only occasionally can an oil rig be seen on the horizon, under tow to a new location or at anchor awaiting a new contract.

The development of North Sea oil plus the gathering strength of northeast Scotland's agriculture, fishing, and manufacturing industries have combined to give Aberdeen one of the highest growth rates of any city in Great Britain. Therefore, you will find Aberdeen a city of many moods and steeped in history. An ancient university town and thriving seaport, Aberdeen has grown very cosmopolitan, yet it remains old in grace. Above all else, the Aberdonians always have time—time to help, time to be interested, and time to talk.

Today, with more than two million roses, eleven million daffodils, and three million crocuses, Aberdeen is the "Flower of Scotland." Parks, gardens, and floral displays please every visitor, with the most popular being the **Winter Gardens** at the Duthie Park.

Aberdeen lies between the rivers Dee and Don with 2 miles of golden sand connecting them. But don't think of Aberdeen merely as a large city with a beach. Union Street bisects the city and provides a mile-long shopping center lined with excellent stores sure to satisfy every shopper.

Edinburgh–Aberdeen–Edinburgh

DEPART WAVERLEY STATION	ARRIVE ABERDEEN STATION	NOTES
0555	0827	M–Sa
0710	0937	M–Sa
0810	1037	M–Sa
0855	1126	Su
0910	1133	M–Sa
1010	1233	M–Sa
1025	1300	M–Sa
1055	1325	Su
1110	1335	M–Sa

DEPART ABERDEEN STATION	ARRIVE WAVERLEY STATION	NOTES
1425	1648	M–Sa
1455	1722	M–Sa
1510	1736	Su
1520	1749	M–Sa
1622	1848	M–Sa
1710	1930	Su
1722	1948	M–Sa
1825	2050	M–Sa
1910	2133	Su
1925	2148	M–Sa
2010	2238	Su
2022	2300	M–Sa
2122 (2120 Su)	2359 (2345 Su)	Daily

Standing like a tall sentinel, the gleaming white **Girdleness Lighthouse** guarding Aberdeen's harbor will be the first welcoming sign you'll see. As you approach Scotland's third-largest city, the lighthouse becomes visible on the right as the train curves away to the left from Nigg Bay to cross the River Dee, then glides to a halt in Aberdeen's rail station.

The port of Aberdeen is the jumping-off place for adventurers bound for the Orkney Islands and Shetland Islands to the north. Don't be surprised if you see a cruise ship or two in Aberdeen's harbor. Aberdeen has attracted the cruise ships by constructing a passenger landing stage in its Victoria Dock area. By all appearances you'd believe everyone wants to visit Europe's offshore oil capital.

Aberdeen maintains tourist information in the form of a well-stocked literature stand alongside the travel center information counter in the rail station. There's also a twenty-four-hour "View Data" service—a very user-friendly computerized inquiry unit.

The information center has a wide variety of booklets, leaflets, and posters of Aberdeen and the surrounding area. Also available are the publications of the Scottish Tourist Board covering the entire country. The center is divided into three operating sections: inquiries, accommodations, and tickets. Walking-tour and bus-tour information is also available here.

Clustered around the tourist information center on Broad Street, only a short walk away, are many of Aberdeen's places of interest. In the restored **Provost Skene's House** on Broad Street, the oldest domestic dwelling in Aberdeen, dating from 1545, you will find rooms furnished in styles covering different periods in Aberdeen's history. After exploring the grandeur of the rooms, traverse upward to the top floor, where displays of Scottish social and archaeological history are to be found. The **Costume Gallery** has a marvelous collection of fascinating costumes from over the ages. Admission is free.

Aberdeen's **Maritime Museum** is housed in Provost Ross's House overlooking one of Britain's busiest harbors. Here, attractive displays not only depict the area's maritime heritage of fishing, shipbuilding, and trade, but also showcase its offshore oil industry. Visitors can experience life on board a working scale model of an oil rig, or see the nineteenth-century lens assembly from the Rattray Head Lighthouse, plus much more. Admission is free.

Provost Ross's House, a restored sixteenth-century dwelling, also houses a visitor center featuring audiovisual displays of National Trust for Scotland properties, a fascinating collection of more than one hundred properties representing a rich variety of castles, gardens, scenic areas, islands, and historic sights.

The **Tolbooth Museum,** housed in the seventeenth-century prison at Castlegate, explores the history of crime, punishment, and incarceration of witches, debtors, and other lawbreakers (plus some of their ingenious escapes). Originally the city seat of government, it also shows the evolution of local power, from the sixteenth century to the present day. Admission is free.

Winston Churchill called the British Army's Gordon Highlanders "the finest regiment in the world." Therefore, an absolute must-see is the **Gordon Highlanders Museum** on Viewfield Road, which contains treasures spanning more than two centuries. *Hours:* April–October: 1030–1630 Tuesday–Saturday, 1330–1630 Sunday; November–March: by appointment only. *Internet:* www.gordonhighlanders.com.

Aberdeen is not only a cultural center, but a family-friendly town as well. Those traveling with the wee ones may find the award-winning **Satrosphere** to be phenomenally fascinating. This hands-on discovery place is located at 179 Constitution Street and is the only one like it in Scotland. Exhibits allow kids to explore science and technology first-hand. Admission helps fund a registered charity and is £5.25 for adults and £3.75 for children. The Satrosphere is open Monday–Saturday 1000–1700 and Sunday 1130–1700. For more information, call (01224) 640340 or visit www.satrosphere.net.

The **Baxters Visitors Centre** is popular with any age. The Baxters have been making quality jams, marmalades, soups, and sauces from the finest ingredients for the upper crust for nearly 130 years. Take a factory tour, then stop by the **Spey Restaurant** for a famous Fochabers Pancake. Before leaving be sure to shop in the "Best of Scotland" to find wonderful gifts or visit the Cellar to take home some of the famous goodies for which the Baxters are so well-known.

Just north of the city center is **Old Aberdeen,** where you will find one of the oldest universities in Britain. **Aberdeen University** comprises Marischal College and King's College. Both are architecturally attractive yet totally different. Marischal College, one of the largest granite build-ings in the world, was founded in 1593 and united with King's College in 1860 to form the University of Aberdeen. King's College, in Old Aberdeen, was founded in 1495. The ivy-covered building with its dis-tinctive crown tower has stood for centuries as a symbol of Aberdeen. The **Zoology Museum** offers a diverse look at the animal kingdom, with a special collection of Scottish birds. For quiet and peaceful walks, visit the eleven-acre **Cruickshank Botanic Garden** on campus and the 400-year-old roses. Or take one of the many guided walks offered, such as the one that leads from Seaton Park to the Brig O'Balgownie across the River Don.

Day Excursion to

Ayr
Burns's Tam o' Shanter Inn

Depart from Edinburgh Waverley Station
Distance by train: 88 miles (142 km)
Average train time: 1 hour, 50 minutes
Train information and InterCity services: (0845) 748 4950
Tourist information: Ayr Tourist Information Centre, 22 Sandgate, Ayr KA7 1BW; *Tel:* (01292) 290300; *Fax:* (01292) 288686
Internet: www.ayrshire-arran.com
E-mail: info@ayrshire-arran.com
Hours: April–June and September: Monday–Saturday 0915–1700, Sunday 1000–1600 (Sunday hours apply over Easter weekend); July–August: Monday–

Saturday 0915–1800, Sunday 1000–1700; October–March: Monday–Saturday 0915–1700, closed Sunday.

Notes: Upon leaving the station, cross the road and walk down past Burns Statue Square, following the road round to the right into Alloway Street. Continue straight down into the partly pedestrianized High Street. On the left-hand side, about two-thirds of the way down the street, you will come to a large building with the pavement continuing behind it. Take this route, then turn immediately left into Newmarket Street. Go straight up Newmarket Street, and when you are at the top, the Tourist Information Centre is facing you across the street. There is a pedestrian crossing here. Total walking time is approximately ten minutes.

What William Shakespeare is to England, Robert Burns is to Scotland. Ayr is the acknowledged center of "Burns Country." The town is rich in the history of Scotland's bard. Many famous landmarks remain in Ayr today to tell the Burnsian stories.

The Tam o' Shanter Inn on High Street is where Tam began his celebrated ride. The Auld Brig (old bridge), which was the only bridge in town for 500 years, still offers a delightful passage across the River Ayr. In a conspicuous location outside the Ayr train station, a statue of Robert Burns waits to greet travelers.

In Alloway, a pleasant southern suburb of Ayr, you will find the **Burns National Heritage Park,** where visual displays introduce you to the life of Robert Burns and acquaint you with locations in and around Ayr that you may later want to visit. A brief walk from the exhibit will bring you to **Burns' Cottage,** where the poet was born on January 25, 1759. More than 300,000 visitors pass through the park annually. *Internet:* www.burnsheritagepark.com. The ruins of the **Alloway Auld Kirk** (old church) where Tam spied on dancing witches, also close to the center, were the inspiration for Burns's narrative poem "Tam o' Shanter." Visitors may watch an audiovisual reenactment of the epic tale.

It was from the ruins of the Auld Kirk that witches pursued Tam, but he escaped over the Auld Brig O' Doon—the bridge over the River Doon—and eluded his pursuers, because, according to legend, witches were unable to cross running water. Maggie, the mare that Tam rode, was less fortunate: "Ae spring brought off her master hale, / But left behind her ain gray tail / The carlin caught her by the rump, / And left poor Maggie scarce a stump."

Ayr was a seaside resort long before the term was invented. Well-heeled Glasgow merchants came to Ayr for short vacations, liked what they saw, and built houses there. In addition to providing Scottish gentry with suburban abodes, Ayr also is a market center, for good measure. With all these assets, Ayr is assured of retaining its prosperous, bustling atmosphere even after the summer visitors have gone.

Edinburgh–Ayr–Edinburgh

All schedules require a change of station in Glasgow, either from Queen Street to Central or the reverse. It's only a five- to ten-minute walk; such changes can also be accomplished by taxi, underground rail, or bus.

DEPART WAVERLEY STATION	ARRIVE AYR STATION	NOTES
0700	0928	M–Sa
0730	0952	M–Sa
0800	1026	M–Sa
0830	1052	M–Sa
0900	1126	M–Sa
0930	1152	M–Sa

M–Sa service continues after 0930 every half hour until 2200; Su service continues after 0930 at hourly intervals until 1730, then 1900, 2000, 2100, 2130, and 2330.

DEPART AYR STATION	ARRIVE WAVERLEY STATION	NOTES
1413	1618	Daily
1443	1633 (1650 Su)	Daily
1513	1718 (1720 Su)	Daily
1543	1733 (1802 Su)	Daily
1601	1750	Su
1613	1824 (1820 Su)	Daily

M–Sa service continues after 1613 at half-hour intervals until 2213; Su service continues after 1613 at half-hour intervals until 2143.

Literature on Ayr, the district surrounding it, and Scotland's famous poet, Robert Burns (who traveled extensively around Ayrshire), abounds by the pound in the information center. You can visit many places that have been developed to tell the story of Burns and his lifetime. If interested in exploring on your own or taking a bus around "Burns Country," you should gather all the details associated with the poet from the information center.

With more than 2 miles of golden, sandy beach, Ayr gets more than its fair share of the summer sun. Golf, bowling, and tennis are among the many sports activities that can be enjoyed there. The town has three golf courses, forming part of the famous 15-mile stretch of "golfing coast" you'll see from the train approaching Ayr. All the traditional seaside amusements may be enjoyed in Ayr, as well as horse racing, held at Scotland's premier **Ayr Racecourse** throughout the year.

Away from the beaches, there are many beautiful parks and gardens, notably **Belleisle, Craigie,** and **Rozelle.** Rozelle is also the home of Ayr's **Maclaurin Art Gallery** and displays one of the very few Henry Moore sculptures to be seen in Scotland. Ayr's beauty has frequently brought it the coveted titles "Britain's Floral Town" and "Scotland's Floral Town." Enjoy the Ayr Flower Show and Gardening Festival, second only to Chelsea's, if visiting the area in late August. If you delight in old houses, Ayr has many, including one that was built in 1470—twenty-two years before Columbus sailed to America!

Day Excursion to

Dunbar
"Fort on the Point"

Depart from Edinburgh Waverley Station
Distance by train: 29 miles (46 km)
Average train time: 30 minutes
Train information and InterCity services: (0845) 748 4950
Tourist information: Dunbar Tourist Office Centre, 143 High Street, Dunbar EH4 21ES; *Tel:* (01368) 863353; *Fax:* (01368) 864999
Internet: www.dunbar.org.uk
E-mail: esic@eltb.org
Hours: Summer: Monday–Saturday 0900–2000, Sunday 1100–1800. The rest of the year: Monday–Saturday 0900–1700, closed Sunday.
Notes: The tourist information center is a short walk from the railway station. Station Road runs from the front of the station to where it crosses Countess Road and becomes Abbey Road. When you reach the general post office on your right, the thoroughfare has another name change to High Street and remains so until you reach the information center, about 50 yards beyond the Town House on the same side of the street. Part of the Town House, incidentally, is a tollgate dating from the seventeenth century, when a toll road between Edinburgh and Newcastle ran through Dunbar.

Put on your walking shoes—we're going to Dunbar. The town offers two wonderful walking opportunities: one through the historic center of Old Dunbar to appreciate the great and varied wealth of its traditional Scottish buildings, the other along the cliffs brooding over the

North Sea in the John Muir Country Park. Those who like a slower pace may take in Dunbar's harbor area and watch colorful fishing boats bob about on the tide. Further assurance of a pleasant outing for all is the presence of several public houses in the harbor area. Among them is the **Volunteer Arms,** which houses the Volunteer Bar and the Haven Lounge.

Dunbar is situated amid some of the most beautiful countryside and coastline in Scotland. There are few other places where it is possible to witness the full range of history of a Scottish east-coast fishing port and market center. Dunbar has always played an important part in Scotland's history. Due to its strategic location, the town has been a stronghold down through the centuries. Dunbar, Gaelic for "the fort on the point," had a castle fortress at least as early as A.D. 856. The remains of the castle stand on the promontory overlooking Dunbar's Victoria Harbour.

The **Dunbar Castle** was where Bothwell brought Mary, Queen of Scots, when he abducted her in 1567. That same year the Scottish Parliament ordered that Dunbar Castle be demolished. When Victoria Harbour was constructed in the nineteenth century, the channel leading into the harbor was cut through the rocky palisade where the ruins of the castle lay. The remains that you may inspect during your visit to Dunbar are only a fragment of the original great castle.

There are two harbors: the **Old Harbour,** extended by Oliver Cromwell, and **Victoria Harbour.** Construction on the Old Harbour began in 1655, and it was improved and extended in the eighteenth century. This harbor, now nearly deserted, still retains the old paving stones as well as a fisherman's barometer that was erected in 1856. As part of the redevelopment, the harbor areas have had cottage-type houses built since 1951 to the special design of Sir Basil Spence, the architect of the new Coventry Cathedral. Perhaps the best evidence of Dunbar's beauty is the large number of visitors walking about simply admiring the scenery.

An interesting part of Victoria Harbour is the **Lifeboat Museum,** which is well worth a visit. Lifeboats out of Dunbar have saved more than 200 lives since beginning operation in 1808.

For the town trail tour, the book *John Muir's Dunbar* details a new guided walk, available May through September. The cliff-top trail is prominently marked on the local town map. The map is available at the tourist information office, as is other information on the town, including the two harbors. John Muir, regarded as the father of U.S. national parks, was born (1838) in Dunbar and emigrated to Wisconsin in the United States when he was a youth. Later, when he moved to California, he founded the Sierra Club and played a fundamental role in lobbying efforts to create Yosemite National Park.

Edinburgh–Dunbar–Edinburgh

DEPART WAVERLEY STATION	ARRIVE DUNBAR STATION	NOTES
0700	0720	M–Sa
0900	0922	M–F
0930	0950	Sa
1200	1220	Su
1400	1420	M–Sa

Also 7 more departures until 2300 M–F; 3 more trains until 1900 Sa, and 4 more trains until 2100 Su.

DEPART DUNBAR STATION	ARRIVE WAVERLEY STATION	NOTES
1303	1330	M–F
1449	1513	Su
1701	1729	M–F
1716	1742	Sa
1753	1818	Su
2106	2131	Sa
2146	2214	M–F
2220	2246	Su

Begin your tour at the **John Muir House** at 128 High Street, and follow the trail outlined in his book.

If you brought your walking shoes, the place to use them is the **John Muir Country Park,** which begins at Dunbar Harbour and extends to the Ravensheugh sands to the west, and on the south it approaches the Firth of Forth. The cliff-top trail has controlled public beaches below. Throughout the summer, a park ranger is normally on duty and available to answer your questions and provide directions. You may join the ranger on a ramble along the trail, but times and routes may vary; check with the tourist office. There are several horse-riding routes within the park as well.

If you are a golf nut and have not been able to obtain a tee time for the Old Course at St. Andrews, try the par-64 **Winterfield Golf Course** maintained by the town of Dunbar.

Prefer a game of lawn bowling? There is a bowling green on the right-hand side of the Station Road as you proceed toward town. We asked an old Scot, "How can such a green be so smooth and flat?" "It's easy," he explained. "You just plant the best of grass seed and then roll it for a few hundred years."

Day Excursion to

Dundee
City of Discovery

Depart from Edinburgh Waverley Station
Distance by train: 60 miles (96 km)
Average train time: 1 hour, 30 minutes
Train information and InterCity services: (0845) 748 4950
Tourist information: Angus & Dundee Tourist Board, 21 Castle Street, Dundee DD1
    3AA; *Tel:* (01382) 527527; *Fax:* (01382) 527551
Internet: www.angusanddundee.co.uk
E-mail: enquiries@angusanddundee.co.uk
Hours: June–September: Monday–Saturday 0900–1800, Sunday 1200–1600;
    October–May: Monday–Saturday 0900–1700.
Notes: From the rail station proceed across the pedestrian bridge, then follow White-
    hall Street to the right until you come to Crichton Street. Turn left up this street
    until you reach the top. Turn right again, and you have reached the City Square.
    The next street down to the right is Castle Street.

As your train approaches the city of Dundee, you will be able to witness a scene of railroading history—one of disaster and one of triumph. Following the station stop at Leuchars, watch as the train passes through the local station of Wormit and on to the railway bridge crossing the Firth of Tay inbound to Dundee. The bridge, a double-track structure 11,653 feet long, was opened in 1887 and was considered to be a triumph of railroad engineering. Alongside the present bridge, you will see a series of old bridge piers. These once supported a single-track bridge that was swept away during a violent storm in 1879, along with a train and seventy-five of its passengers. The River Tay and its rail and vehicular bridges are a vital part of Dundee's existence.

Dundee, the capital of Tayside, is Scotland's fourth-largest city and lies in the heart of Scotland in a magnificent setting between the Sidlaw Hills and the banks of Britain's finest salmon river, the Tay. Dundee is where the game of golf originated. The latest count reveals forty golf courses within one hour's drive of the city. Three actually lie within the city's district. In Dundee, the name of the game is golf, and its citizens have proven to the world that they can construct courses that can confound and confuse but always entertain.

The cultural aspects of Dundee are enhanced by its **McManus Galleries** and the **University Botanical Gardens. Camperdown Park** and the **Wildlife Centre** are also stellar attractions for those who prefer outside activities.

Edinburgh–Dundee–Edinburgh

EDINBURGH *Dundee*

DEPART EDINBURGH WAVERLEY STATION	ARRIVE DUNDEE STATION	NOTES
0710	0824	M–Sa
0810	0924	M–Sa
0855	1011	Su
0910 (0915 Su)	1022 (1048 Su)	Daily
1010	1124	M–Sa
1025	1144	M–Sa
1055	1208	Su
1110	1224	M–Sa
1115	1251	Su

Then minimum hourly service through 2310 M–Sa; twice per hour until 1915, 2100, and 2225 Su.

DEPART DUNDEE STATION	ARRIVE EDINBURGH WAVERLEY STATION	NOTES
1431	1548	M–Sa
1501	1620	Su
1532 (1525 Su)	1648 (1629 Su)	Daily
1606	1722	M–Sa
1629 (1625 Su)	1749 (1736 Su)	Daily
1732 (1725 Su)	1848 (1859 Su)	Daily
1832 (1819 Su)	1948 (1930 Su)	Daily
1936 (1925 Su)	2050 (2059 Su)	Daily
2032 (2020 Su)	2148 (2133 Su)	Daily
2107	2225	M–F
2128 (2121 Su)	2300 (2259 Sa, 2238 Su)	Daily
2228 (2226 Su)	0001+1 (2345 Su)	Daily

+1= Arrives next day

Discovery Point is a state-of-the-art visitor center portraying the history of Captain Scott's Royal Research Ship *Discovery* and its Antarctic voyages. Built in Dundee, Britain's first scientific research vessel set sail on a voyage to the Antarctic in 1901. You may visit *Discovery* berthed adjacent to the visitor center. *Internet:* www. rrs-discovery.co.uk.

Verdant Works is a mill dating from 1833 that celebrates Dundee's jute industry. The Scottish industrial heritage center offers a range of audiovisual displays, computer activities, and sound and light effects along with a cafe and gift shop.

Dundee's other attractions include its four castles—Dudhope, Mains, Claypotts, and Broughty—its old steeple, and the **Mercat Cross,** which is moved about as the population center changes. The old steeple, standing at a height of 156 feet above the ground, dates from the fourteenth century. Climb to the top for a spectacular view. A replica of the old structure that was demolished in 1877, the Mercat Cross is currently located at the end of High Street.

Attention shoppers: Visit Tayside's regional shopping center, **Overgate.** From the rail station, proceed across the pedestrian bridge. Head up Union Street and at the top, turn left onto Nethergate. Cross the street to the Overgate Centre. Constructed in a curve around St. Mary's Church, its curved glass wall has the effect of bringing the outside inside. A series of balcony cafes provide respite and refreshment to weary shoppers.

The **Dundee Contemporary Arts Center,** at 152 Nethergate, contains works by artists from Scotland and from around the world. From the rail station, walk across the car parking area (or use the overpass) until you arrive at the main road called Marketgait. Turn left and walk about 200 yards up Marketgait. Turn left onto Greenmarket and follow the signs SCIENCE CENTER/SEABRAES CAR PARK. *Hours:* 1030–1730 Tuesday–Sunday; admission is free. Adjacent to the arts center is the £5 million-plus **Dundee Science Centre "Sensation."** Award-winning Scottish architects Merrylees and Robertson effectively utilize natural light to convey the cathedral-like effect in Dundee's most recent attraction, touted as "a cathedral of science." *Internet:* www.sensation.org.uk.

Day Excursion to
Dunfermline
Andrew Carnegie's Birthplace

Depart from Edinburgh Waverley Station
Distance by train: 17 miles (27 km)
Average train time: 32 minutes
Train information and InterCity services: (0845) 748 4950
Tourist information: Tourist Information Centre, 1 High Street, Dunfermline, Fife, Scotland KY12 7DL; *Tel:* (01383) 720999; *Fax:* (01383) 625807
Internet: www.dunfermlineonline.net
E-mail: info@dunfermlineonline.net
Hours: March–September: Monday–Saturday 0930–1700; July 1–September 15: Sunday 1100–1600.
Notes: Cross St. Margaret's Drive in front of the station and follow the signposts to the tourist information center. Taxis queue at the front of the station. About £3.50 will see you to the city center. The bus stop is close to the station at an underpass on the left.

D unfermline was once the capital of Scotland and holds an important position in Scottish history. The main points of interest are the Dunfermline Abbey, Abbot House, Pittencrieff Park, and Andrew Carnegie's birthplace. We suggest visiting the tourist information center first.

The walk is not too distant to the tourist information center and the main attractions in town. On foot, allow about fifteen minutes to cover the ground between the train station and the center of the city.

The majestic spires of the **Dunfermline Abbey** dominate the town's skyline. Within the abbey are the graves of seven Scottish kings, including the **Tomb of Robert the Bruce.** The abbey was founded by Scotland's King David in the twelfth century as a Benedictine monastery. In the course of time, through royal gifts and other extensive endowments, it became one of the most magnificent establishments in Scotland. In its time, the monastery has played host to a wide range of people, from Edward I of England to Oliver Cromwell.

The site of the Dunfermline Abbey has had continual Christian worship for about 1,500 years. In the fifth or sixth century, the first building on the site was the Culdee Church. Later it was rebuilt on a larger scale by Malcolm III, father of King David I, and was dedicated in 1072. Traces of both buildings are visible beneath gratings in the floor of the abbey's Old Nave.

From April through October the abbey church is open 1000–1630 Monday–Saturday and 1400–1630 on Sunday. Between November and March the abbey is closed, except for services. The abbey shop is open during the same hours as the church between April and October.

The **Abbot House** is the oldest domestic building in Dunfermline and now houses the award-winning Heritage Centre, unfolding the history of Dunfermline. *Hours:* daily 1000–1700 year-round.

Another attraction is **Pittencrieff Park,** a lovely area with its flower gardens, music pavilion, aviary, and museum. Andrew Carnegie, the Scottish-American philanthropist who was born in a humble weaver's cottage in Dunfermline in 1835, generously donated Pittencrieff Park and gave funds for its upkeep. The park has become a popular place for visitors to pause and reflect on his donations of a library, public baths, and a theater in addition to the park. During your stroll through the park, swing aboard *Old Pug* and marvel at the advances that have been made in railroading since its engine's fires were banked for the last time.

Andrew Carnegie's birthplace is open to the public daily from April through October from 1100 to 1700 (Sunday opening, 1400) and attracts thousands of visitors every year. From his humble beginnings,

Edinburgh–Dunfermline–Edinburgh

DEPART WAVERLEY STATION	ARRIVE DUNFERMLINE TOWN STATION	NOTES
0720	0750	M–Sa
0813	0843	M–Sa
0850	0920	M–Sa
0950 (0955 Su)	1020 (1028 Su)	Daily
1020 (1015 Su)	1050 (1139 Su)	Daily
1050	1120	M–Sa
1150 (1155 Su)	1220 (1228 Su)	Daily

with frequent service continuing at 20 and 50 minutes past the hour M–Sa, and alternating 15 and 55 minutes past the hour Su.

DEPART DUNFERMLINE TOWN STATION	ARRIVE WAVERLEY STATION	NOTES
1405	1437	M–Sa
1435 (1432 Su)	1507 (1559 Su)	Daily
1505	1537	M–Sa
1535 (1539 Su)	1608 (1614 Su)	Daily
1605	1637	M–Sa
1635 (1625 Su)	1707 (1757 Su)	Daily
1705	1737	M–Sa
1733 (1739 Su)	1805 (1812 Su)	Daily
1805	1837	M–Sa

with frequent service until 2322 M–Sa.

Carnegie found his fortunes in the New World. Nevertheless, with his philanthropist attitude, he never forgot his hometown. At age thirty-three, with an annual income of $50,000, Carnegie said, "Beyond this never earn, make no effort to increase fortune, but spend the surplus each year for benevolent purposes." This he certainly did. His generosity in Dunfermline is administered today by a trust fund. A statue of the steel millionaire, erected by the citizens of Dunfermline in grateful appreciation of his many gifts to his native city, stands in the center of Pittencrieff.

When you visit Dunfermline, you will be following in the footsteps of British royalty. Both Queen Victoria and Queen Mary visited here, and in 1972 Queen Elizabeth and Prince Philip were present to dedicate a Royal Pew in celebration of the abbey's 900th anniversary. You'll find, however, that Dunfermline extends a royal welcome to all of its visitors.

An *"Out-and-Back" Excursion to*

Inverness

Highland Gateway

Depart from Edinburgh Waverley Station
Distance by train: 176 miles (283 km)
Average train time: 3 hours, 40 minutes
Train information and InterCity services: (0845) 748 4950; ScotRail services: (0845) 7550 0339
Tourist information: The Highlands of Scotland Tourist Board, Castle Wynd, Inverness IV2 3BJ; *Tel:* (01463) 234353; *Fax:* (01463) 710609.
Internet: www.visithighlands.com
E-mail: inverness@host.co.uk
Hours: Mid-July and August: Monday–Saturday 0900–2030, Sunday 0930–1800. During the off-season, we suggest calling the center for information and hours of operation.
Notes: For the shortest route, turn left when leaving the train station and continue until you see Marks & Spencer. Cross the street and continue up Inglis Street, then turn right onto High Street, walking until you come to McDonald's. Cross the pedestrian walk, past the Town House and across Castle Wynd, where the tourist information center is located at the top of a short flight of stairs.

The position of Inverness at the eastern head of Loch Ness, Scotland's famous inland sea loch, earns the city its title, "Capital of the Highlands." From Inverness, you may get to more places in the Highlands than from any other location in Scotland. For this reason, we have termed the excursion to Inverness an "out-and-back" excursion, for you may want to use Inverness as your base for exploring the Highlands.

There is so much to do in and around Inverness that not even a series of action-packed days could absorb all of the possible activities. Here are but a few of the sightseeing possibilities in and around Inverness: Visit the castle grounds and walk along the garden paths at the River Ness. Cruise on Loch Ness, as far away as Urquhart Castle if you like, where most of the sightings of the Loch Ness "monster" (or "beastie," as the locals call it) have occurred. Journey on the renowned railway line between Inverness and Kyle of Lochalsh along 82 miles of railroad right-of-way that involved beauty, romance, history, and endurance in its building. Forge northward to Thurso, Scotland's most northerly town, on a dramatic rail route along 162 miles of Scotland's better scenery. If you prefer the solitude of surf breaking on a shore, take a train east to Nairn, 15 miles from Inverness. Or train south a mere 30 miles to Scotland's St. Moritz, where the ski boom has transformed the town of Aviemore into a continental sports village.

Edinburgh–Inverness–Edinburgh

DEPART WAVERLEY STATION	ARRIVE INVERNESS STATION	NOTES
0640	1025	M–Sa (1)
0840	1157	M–Sa
0935	1310	Su
0940	1335	M–Sa (1)
1140	1517	M–Sa
1340 (1355 Su)	1707 (1747 Su)	Daily

DEPART INVERNESS STATION	ARRIVE WAVERLEY STATION	NOTES
1245	1559	M–Sa
1300	1630	Su
1440	1814	M–Sa
1610	2007	Su (2)
1650	2030	M–Sa (1)
1830	2209 (2202 Su)	Daily
2013	0001+1	M–Sa (1)

(1) change trains in Perth
(2) change trains in Stirling
+1=Arrives next day

EDINBURGH *Inverness*

Eons ago, **Loch Ness** was carved out along a geological fault between two land masses in northern Scotland. The earth's forces formed a long, narrow lake of approximately 24 miles with depths of up to 750 feet, possibly 1,000 feet in some parts. To go to Inverness and not have a look at Loch Ness would be like eating one potato chip and throwing the rest of the bag away. We urge you to dip into the mystery, history, and beauty of Loch Ness.

Loch Ness is reportedly the home of "Nessie," the Loch Ness monster, which has often been described as one of the world's greatest mysteries. The first recorded sighting of Nessie was made by an unimpeachable witness (St. Columba, no less) in A.D. 565. According to the report, the monster attacked one of the members of his group. Since then, there have been too many visual and photographic sightings of the monster for it to be easily explained.

Fact or fiction, there is a continuing similarity in the descriptions of Nessie given by most of those who claim to have seen the monster over the years. Photographs also support a common description, that of a small head at the end of a long, thin neck, with an overall body length between 20 and 30 feet. Underwater evidence gathered by every means from space-age technology to yellow submarines suggests it may have four flippers. Zoologists recognize this description as a plesiosaur, a type of marine dinosaur that existed more than seventy million years ago and should be extinct.

Scientific data notwithstanding, the fact that malt whiskeys have been produced in large volumes throughout the area since the beginning of recorded time may account for many or all of the sightings!

Inverness also offers the town attractions of the **James Pringle Weavers and Clan Tartan Centre**, the **Scottish Kiltmaker Visitor Centre, Floral Hall, St. Andrew's Cathedral**, and the **Inverness Museum and Art Gallery.** Enjoy the **Castle Garrison Encounter** and the **Aquadome and Sports Centre.** Dolphin fans should not miss the **dolphin-watching** boat trips.

If your visit to Inverness is limited, you may want to try the excellent Caledonian Sleeper services. For example, you can board a sleeper one night in London and awaken the following morning in Inverness. Spend an entire day sightseeing, then board another sleeper back to London.

Going in and out of Inverness by sleeper could permit you to board the 1048 train from there to the Kyle of Lochalsh, where you arrive at 1318, then ferry to the Isle of Skye, soak in the sights, and leave Lochalsh on the 1718 to be back in Inverness by 1950 with some time to spare before boarding the sleeper again.

Departing from the Inverness Station, the journey to Kyle of Lochalsh takes about two and a half hours. The railway between Inverness and Kyle of Lochalsh has been accorded the distinction of being the premier scenic rail line in Great Britain. It offers a lovely ride through the Highland towns of Dingwall, Garve, Achnasheen, and Stromeferry before terminating on the western shores of Scotland overlooking the Isle of Skye. The rail line passes through a region of superlative natural beauty loaded with Scottish folklore. This 82-mile journey, which appears rather uninspiring in the cold prosaic type of the timetable, is in reality a rare mixture of beauty, romance, history, and endurance.

An "Out-and-Back" Excursion to

Kyle of Lochalsh
Scenic Journey

Tourist Information: The Highlands of Scotland Tourist Board, Tourist Information Centre, Kyle of Lochalsh: Car Park IV40 8AQ; *Tel:* (01599) 534276; *Fax:* (01599) 534808.
Internet: www.visithighlands.com
E-mail: kyle@host.co.uk

Notes: The tourist information center is conveniently located midway between the train station and the ferry dock. To reach it, use the stairs to the overpass and then walk downhill.

When the railroad opened in 1870, the western terminal was the town of Stromeferry on the saltwater Loch Carron. Although the original intention was to build right through to Kyle of Lochalsh, construction money ran out and Stromeferry remained the terminus for twenty-seven years. Completing the remaining 26 miles of right-of-way proved to be a formidable task of engineering, forging through solid rock and requiring cuts up to 88 feet deep. Even the area of the train terminal at Kyle required blasting and removing rock. When you reach Kyle of Lochalsh, pause to appreciate the backbreaking toil that created the train station and the right-of-way leading to it.

A bridge was built between Kyle of Lochalsh and Kyleakin on the Isle of Skye. The ruins of **Castle Moil** stand on a promontory close to the Kyleakin ferry dock. During the time of the Vikings, the castle was the home of a Norwegian princess. History relates that the princess made quite a bundle during her stay in the castle by exacting a toll from ships passing through the narrow straits. To ensure prompt payment, she had a heavy chain attached between the castle and the Kyle of Lochalsh, which was drawn taut when a ship approached. The chain was probably depreciated and charged off as a business expense, for there's no evidence of its existence today.

Scottish legends leap out at you as the train plies between Inverness and Kyle. **The Castle at Dingwall** was said to have been ruled by Finlaec, the father of Macbeth. In a graveyard opposite the castle ruins, the ghost of a young girl wanders nightly in search of her faithless lover. Approaching Garve, you'll pass **Loch Garve**, where even in the dead of winter there is a small part that never freezes—attributed to the waterhorse monsters who carry off local girls. The inn at Garve purveys Athole Brose, a libation of Scottish whiskey, oats, and honey, several drafts of which could produce a whole herd of water horses.

The right-of-way passes areas that stir the imagination. Departing Achnasheen en route to Stromeferry, passengers may get a fleeting glance at the **Torridon Mountains,** the oldest mountains on Earth. They are so old that geologists have been unable to find any trace of fossils, indicating the mountains were formed long before life of any description began. The range, consisting of peaks such as Liathach (3,456 feet), Beinn Eighe (3,300 feet), and Beinn Alligin (3,021 feet), has sparkling quartzite peaks, often mistaken for snow.

Note: A day trip from Edinburgh to Kyle of Lochalsh and return to Edinburgh is not possible on Sundays because the only Sunday trip from Inverness to Kyle of Lochalsh arrives in Kyle at 2030; there is no return trip from Kyle on Sundays later than 1515. A two-day weekend excursion is possible, however, by departing Edinburgh on Saturday at 0640 or 0840 and returning on Sunday by departing Kyle at 1006 (change trains in Inverness) and arriving Edinburgh at 1637 or departing Kyle on Sunday at 1515 (change in Inverness) and arriving Edinburgh at 2202.

DEPART WAVERLEY STATION	ARRIVE KYLE STATION	NOTES
0640	1318	M–Sa (1)
0840	1503	M–Sa (2)

DEPART KYLE STATION	ARRIVE WAVERLEY STATION	NOTES
1504	2209	M–Sa (2)
1515	2202	Su (3)
1718	0001+1	M–Sa (1)

(1) change trains in Perth
(2) change trains in Inverness
(3) July 1 to September 23
+1=Arrives next day

In the seventeenth century, Brahan Seer, the Highlands' prophet extraordinaire, said, "The day will come when every stream will have its bridge, balls of fire will pass rapidly up and down the Strath of Peffery and carriages without horses will cross the country from sea to sea." And so it came to pass: On August 10, 1870, the railroad steam engines began operating from sea to sea.

Day Excursion to

Linlithgow
Birthplace of Mary, Queen of Scots

Depart from Edinburgh Waverley Station or Glasgow Queen Street Station
Distance by train: 18 miles (29 km)
Average train time: 21 minutes
Train information and InterCity services: (0845) 748 4950

Tourist information: Edinburgh & Lothians Tourist Board, Burgh Halls, The Cross, Linlithgow, West Lothian EH49 7EJ; *Tel:* (01506) 844600; *Fax:* (01506) 671373
Internet: www.linlithgow.com
Hours: March–September: 1000–1700 daily; October–February: closed except for bank holidays 0930–1700.
Notes: Exit the train station main exit onto Station Road. Turn left onto High Street. Walk until you see the traffic lights and pedestrian crossing. Cross over High Street, then turn left toward The Cross. The tourist center is at The Cross, recognizable by the cross-shaped well in the center.

L inlithgow lies between Edinburgh and Glasgow and stands in the midst of Scotland's history. The town offers so many attractions that we advise going there early and planning to stay late, very late.

Linlithgow Palace, the birthplace of Mary, Queen of Scots, is the town's main attraction. It lies in what historians would describe as a splendid ruin. Nevertheless, it tells a poignant tale of Scotland's royal history in an intriguing manner. The palace was the successor to a wooden fortress that burned down in 1424. King James V, father of Mary, Queen of Scots, was born in Linlithgow Palace in 1512. Defeated by the English at the Battle of Solway Moss in November 1542, the king died on December 14 of that year, only six days after the birth of his daughter. The infant child became Mary, Queen of Scots, at six days of age.

In the years to follow, Bonnie Prince Charlie and Oliver Cromwell took brief residence in the palace. At the beginning of 1746, troops belonging to the Duke of Cumberland's army were billeted there. As they marched out on February 1, fires were left burning that soon spread throughout the building. Since then, the palace has remained unroofed and uninhabited. There has been talk about restoring Linlithgow Palace, but as it stands now, just let your imagination "restore" it. *Tel:* (01506) 842896. *Hours:* April–September: 0930–1830 daily; October–March: Monday–Saturday 0930–1630 and Sunday 1400–1630. *Admission:* Adults £3.00, children £1.00, senior citizens £2.30.

A short walk westward from the palace along High Street you'll discover **"The Linlithgow Story,"** a fascinating museum telling of life in one of Scotland's most important royal burghs.

A mere 100 yards from the rail station, the Union Canal runs through the center of Linlithgow. Some 31 miles in length, it was once a major thoroughfare for taking coal from the mines in Falkirk to Edinburgh. From the Canal Basin at Manse Road, you can board the *St. Magdalene,* a diesel-powered replica of a Victorian steam packet boat, for a cruise to the Avon Aqueduct (two-and-a-half-hour cruise: £6.00 adults, £3.00 children, £15.00 family). For shorter trips (about twenty minutes), board a steam packet boat replica, the *Victoria.* Departures are every half hour on Saturday and Sunday afternoons from Easter until

Edinburgh–Linlithgow–Edinburgh

DEPART WAVERLEY STATION	ARRIVE LINLITHGOW STATION	NOTES
0745 (0750 Su)	0802 (0835 Su)	Daily
0803	0824	M–Sa
0815	0832	M–Sa
0833	0854	M–Sa
0845 (0850 Su)	0902 (0935 Su)	Daily
0903 (0900 Su)	0924 (0945 Su)	Daily
0915	0932	M–Sa
0933 (0950 Su)	0954 (1035 Su)	Daily

M–Sa service continues at 3, 15, 33, and 45 minutes past the hour; Su service continues hourly on the hour and 50 minutes past the hour.

DEPART LINLITHGOW STATION	ARRIVE WAVERLEY STATION	NOTES
1435 (1440 Su)	1459 (1525 Su)	Daily
1444 (1450 Su)	1504 (1535 Su)	Daily
1505 (1510 Su)	1528 (1555 Su)	Daily
1514	1535	M–Sa
1535 (1540 Su)	1558 (1625 Su)	Daily
1544 (1550 Su)	1604 (1635 Su)	Daily

Plus other very frequent service until 2335 with departures at 5, 14, 35, and 44 minutes past the hour M–Sa, and 10, 40, and 50 minutes past the hour Su.

the end of September; the last departure is at 1630 (£2.50 adults, £1.50 children/senior citizens).

A short distance from the town, visit **The Binns,** one of the most "lived in" mansions in Scotland. It has been occupied by the Dalyell family for more than 350 years. The house dates from the sixteenth century. General Tam Dalyell (1599–1685) had some hair-raising adventures in his lifetime, including an escape from the Tower of London and military service in Russia. The house reflects the early-seventeenth-century transition from a fortified castle to a gracious, more comfortable house. Open daily from May through September, 1400–1700, except Friday (£5.00 adults, £3.75 children/senior citizens, £13.50 family). *Internet:* www.nts.org.uk.

A short bus ride will take you to the seaport town of **Bo'ness** with its own attractions ranging in historical significance from Roman ruins to the Industrial Revolution. *Internet:* www.bo-ness.org.uk. Bo'ness also has a reconstructed Victorian railway station, where you may board the **Bo'ness & Kinneil Railway** steam train for a delightfully romantic 7-mile round-trip, including a stop at the **Birkhill clay mine,** where fireclay was mined. Without fireclay, many say there could never have been an Industrial Revolution.

The Bo'ness & Kinneil Railway operates April–December on Saturday and Sunday at 1100, 1215, 1345, 1500, and 1615; July–August departures are at the same times Tuesday through Sunday. Train fare: £4.50 adults, £2.00 children, £3.50 senior citizens, £11.00 family. Train and clay mine: £7.50 adults, £4.00 children, £6.00 senior citizens, £19.00 family. The Scottish Railway Exhibition is free. *Internet:* www.srps.org .uk/railway.

Back in Linlithgow, be sure to stop at the **Four Marys' Public House** on High Street for great atmosphere, excellent libations, and superb food. Don't miss it!

Day Excursion to
Montrose
Seaside Resort

Depart from Edinburgh Waverley Station
Distance by train: 90 miles (145 km)
Average train time: 2 hours, 8 minutes
Train information and InterCity services: (0845) 748 4950
Tourist information: Montrose Tourist Information Centre, Bridge Street, Montrose DD10 8AB; *Tel:* (01674) 672000
Internet: www.angusanddundee.co.uk
E-mail: enquiries@angusanddundee.co.uk
Hours: April–June and September: Monday–Saturday 1000–1700; July and August: 0930–1730.
Notes: From the station, turn right onto Western Road until it reaches Hume Street, where a quick left followed by a right turn 1 block away onto High Street puts you in view of the Town House and its grand piazza. Stay on the right-hand side of High Street and walk a short distance south. Just after reaching the town's public library, you will come to the tourist information center on Bridge Street.

Travelers who have visited many villages, towns, and cities throughout continental Europe and the British Isles learn to "read" the history of a place through its architecture and street names. Montrose is an outstanding example of this point.

Even at first glance, Montrose does not look like a typical Scottish town. High Street is wide and has many elegant houses with gabled ends on the street side. There was a time in the city's history when only Edinburgh surpassed it in prosperity and elegance. The **Town House of Montrose**—Americans would consider it the city hall—is fronted by a broad piazza. From its facade, Montrose looks more like a page out of a Flemish picture book rather than a Scottish one. Great houses are surrounded by garden walls—not ordinary ones, but remarkably high garden walls. It has oddly named streets, such as "America" and "California"—another hint that the history of Montrose is different.

When Glasgow was still a village, Montrose was one of Scotland's principal ports. For centuries, the merchants of Montrose traded with the Low Countries. It was only natural that they would bring back some of the things they admired on the Continent: for example, houses with gabled ends to the street side as they are constructed in the Netherlands. The wide streets? From the promenades of Europe, no doubt. And what about the street names? Almost within living memory, ships sailed from Montrose to North America carrying emigrants and returned laden with lumber.

For the last thirty years, North Sea oil has virtually pumped life back into the city's harbor, where, until the recent past, an air of sleepiness prevailed as trade with North America subsided. The first part of the civic motto of Montrose—*Mare ditat* (the sea enriches)—is again true.

Baffled by the high garden walls? More than 300 years ago, the streets of Montrose ran red with blood when a band of Highlanders raided the town. The inhabitants were defenseless as they slept without the protection of a city wall and with only low garden walls about their residences. The carnage was swift and horrible. Within months, the majority of the walls within the town were built up to their present height to prevent attacks from intruders.

When you arrive in Montrose from Edinburgh, take a moment at the train station to look west, away from the town. You will see the **Montrose Basin Wildlife Centre,** where thousands of wildfowl forage for food, including the pink-footed Arctic goose during the winter. It is well worth a visit. *Internet:* www.montrosebasin.org.uk.

The tourist office has a wealth of information available regarding both Montrose and the area surrounding it. The *Town Guide* leaflet (free) provides information on Montrose. There is also a street map for sale that lists many points of interest. Note for shoppers: Many stores have "half-day closing" on Wednesday afternoons.

Montrose is one of Scotland's leading seaside resorts, and it can become crowded during the peak summer season. Four miles of magnificent sandy beaches attract many an inlander to the sea. Beaches also have a way of indicating their latitudes, just as places reflect their history

Edinburgh–Montrose–Edinburgh

DEPART WAVERLEY STATION	ARRIVE MONTROSE STATION	NOTES
0710	0855	M–Sa
0855	1044	Su
0910	1052	M–Sa
1025	1217	M–Sa
1055	1242	Su
1110	1255	M–Sa
1240	1424	Su

DEPART MONTROSE STATION	ARRIVE WAVERLEY STATION	NOTES
1401	1548	M–Sa
1429	1620	Su
1534 (1538 Sa)	1722	M–Sa
1550	1736	Su
1558	1749	M–Sa
1749	1930	Su
1802	1948	M–Sa
1904	2050	M–Sa
1948	2133	Su
2050	2238	Su
2058	2230	M–Sa
2216 (2157 Su)	2329 (2345 Su)	Daily

in their names and facades. Beaches in Britain, for example, attract huge crowds in summertime, but note the distribution of the people on the beach. Except for a hardy few, the majority of holiday makers are on the sands and not in the water.

The city's large indoor swimming pool and two eighteen-hole golf courses, plus numerous other sports facilities, make up for the other-than-tepid temperature of the North Sea waters off Montrose. The seaside also offers something rather unusual—on the beaches beside Elephant Rock, you can search for semiprecious stones such as agates, amethysts, carnelian, and onyx.

Cultural life is not lacking in Montrose. The name of William Lamb immediately relates to the world of art in fine sculptures and etchings. This well-known artist's studio is maintained at 24 Market Street. On Panmure Place, the **Montrose Museum** houses an excellent collection of art relating to the natural and maritime history of the area.

If you've been waiting for us to drop the other shoe, the second part of the Montrose civic motto is *rosa decorat* (the rose adorns). If you walk in the **Mid-Links Park** on a summer day, the air is scented with the perfume of roses. Although the city's name has nothing to do with roses—it was originally called "Monros" (the mossy promontory)—there are few towns in Scotland where roses grow more abundantly.

Day Excursion to

Perth
First Capital of Scotland

Depart from Edinburgh Waverley Station
Distance by train: 58 miles (93 km)
Average train time: 1 hour, 30 minutes
Train information and InterCity services: (0845) 748 4950
Tourist information: Tourist Information Centre, Lower City Mills, West Mill Street, Perth PH3 1LQ; *Tel:* (01738) 450600; *Fax:* (01738) 444863; *Activity Line:* (01738) 444144
Internet: www.perthshire.co.uk
E-mail: perthtic@perthshire.co.uk
Hours: April–June: Monday–Saturday 0930–1730, Sunday 1100–1600; July–August: Monday–Saturday 0900–1900, Sunday 1000–1800; September–October: Monday–Saturday 0930–1730, Sunday 1100–1600; November–March: Monday–Friday 0930–1700, Saturday 1100–1400.
Notes: The tourist information center is located in the Mill buildings. From the rail station, turn left onto Leonard Street. Follow until you reach the modern A.K. Bell Library; then cross onto York Place and go straight ahead to a small street called New Row. Follow to the end and take a right onto West Mill Street. The Mill buildings lie ahead.

Behold a river more mighty than the Tiber!" History relates that these words were uttered by a Roman commander as, approaching what is now the city of Perth, he caught his first glimpse of the River Tay. Beginning as a mountain stream at Ben Laoigh, the Tay trickles down the hillsides, gaining tributaries as it flows on its 120-mile journey to the sea. Perth stands astride the Tay, their history inextricably linked.

Two vehicular bridges, plus a rail bridge (all with pedestrian footpaths), cross the River Tay today, but "Old Man River" Tay kept the locals quite busy in earlier years, when floods swept away the first bridge in 1210 and its successor in 1621, leaving travelers no alternative but ferries for the 150 years to follow.

Edinburgh–Perth–Edinburgh

DEPART WAVERLEY STATION	ARRIVE PERTH STATION	NOTES
0640	0758	M–Sa
0840	0955	M–Sa
0940 (0935 Su)	1056 (1154 Su)	Daily
1140	1256	M–Sa
1340 (1355 Su)	1455 (1523 Su)	Daily

5 more trains until 2233; final departures at 1716 and 2233 Su.

DEPART PERTH STATION	ARRIVE WAVERLEY STATION	NOTES
1447	1559	M–Sa
1525	1638	Su
1655	1814	M–Sa
1910	2030	M–Sa
2054 (2044 Su)	2209 (2202 Su)	Daily
2308	0001+1	M–Sa

+1=Arrives next day

Perth is often referred to as "the gateway to the Highlands." This is not its only attraction, for its prominent position in the history of Scotland has left a legacy of distinctive buildings in an area compact enough to be easily examined on foot. Perth's architecture mixes the modern with the ancient. City fathers are justly proud of Perth's sports centers, with an ice rink, swimming pools, tennis courts, and indoor bowling stadium.

Tay Street fronts the river on the city side. Without straying too far from the river, it is possible to enjoy the riverside and visit places of interest such as St. John's Kirk, the Perth Art Gallery and Museum, the Fergusson Gallery, the Lower City Mills, and the Fair Maid's House, as described in Sir Walter Scott's novel *The Fair Maid of Perth*. Turn left off Tay Street at Queen's Bridge and proceed 2 blocks to sight St. John's to your right. One of Perth's most famous landmarks, **St. John's Kirk** is where the Protestant reformer John Knox, following his return from exile in Geneva, preached his famous sermon against idolatry in 1559. The congregation was so taken with his sermon that they wrecked the church and then went on to create similar outrages on the monastic houses of the friars. Originally founded in 1126 and revamped over the centuries, St. John's Kirk now is a fine example of Gothic-style architecture from the mid-sixteenth century.

Returning to Tay Street, continue to walk to the Perth Bridge, where you will find the **Perth Art Gallery and Museum** on George Street close to the bridge approach. In quest of the **Fair Maid's House,** ask directions when leaving the museum to its location at North Port, a short distance away; there are several ways to reach it.

Close by the Fair Maid's House is the **North Inch,** a beautifully situated park bordered by Georgian terraces and the River Tay and overlooked by Balhousie Castle, the historic home of the **Black Watch Regimental Museum.** Across the river lies the colorful Branklyn Garden, owned by the National Trust for Scotland and said to be "the finest two acres of private garden in the country." It sits on the wooded slopes of Kinnoull Hill and offers an excellent view over the town.

For centuries Perth has been a prosperous market town, serving a rich agricultural hinterland and profiting from its geographical position in the heart of Scotland. The town's livestock markets flourish, with the famous Perth Bull Sales in February and October attracting buyers from all over the world. Perth's reputation as a trading center, however, rests principally with its excellent shops. Much of Perth's center is traffic-free and bedecked with floral displays.

An excellent addition to Perth's city center attractions is the **Fergusson Gallery** in the Round House (Perth's old waterworks) at Marshall Place. Here you can view the largest and most important collection of the works of the famous Scottish colorist John Duncan Fergusson. Three specially designed galleries display rotating exhibits taken from a total collection of 6,000 items.

Scone Palace, a mile north of Perth, stands close to the historic spot where Scottish kings were crowned through 1651. The Moot Hill, which stands in front of the palace, is an artificial mound that was constructed in the Dark Ages. Traditionally, Scottish chiefs and lairds came to Scone to pledge their allegiance to the king. This they did, filling their boots before they left home with the earth of their own districts. Thus, with the earth still in their boots, they were standing on their own land when they swore allegiance to their king. Afterward they ceremoniously emptied their boots on the Moot Hill (or Boot Hill, as it is appropriately known today).

The palace is open to the public, and there is an admission charge. Take bus No. 58 from the Leonard Street bus station, and check with the information center for details if you plan to go. By the way, don't plan to heist the Stone of Scone—it is resting safely back in Edinburgh Castle.

Day Excursion to

St. Andrews
World's Golf Capital

Depart from Edinburgh Waverley Station
Distance by train: 57 miles (92 km)
Average train time: 1 hour
Train information and InterCity services: (0845) 748 4950
Tourist information: St. Andrews Tourist Information Centre, No. 70 Market Street, Fife KY16 9NU; *Tel:* (01334) 472021; *Fax:* (01334) 478422
Internet: www.standrews.com, www.standrews.co.uk
E-mail: standrewstic@kftb.ossian.net
Hours: July and August: Monday–Saturday 0930–1900 and Sunday 1000–1800; May, June, and September: Monday–Saturday 0930–1800 and Sunday 1100–1700; October–March: Monday–Saturday 0930–1700; April: Monday–Saturday 0930–1700 and Sunday 1100–1700.
Notes: Leuchars is the rail station serving St. Andrews. From outside Leuchars Station, take the No. 95 bus (check latest bus numbers by calling 01334 474238). The trip to the town of St. Andrews is about fifteen minutes by bus. Buses run regularly from Monday to Saturday, usually every thirty minutes. Limited Sunday bus service is available. Disembark at St. Andrews Bus Station, then turn right onto City Road. Cross the street here and take the next street on your left to Market Street. Walk down Market Street for about five minutes, and you will see an old fountain in the middle of the street. Walk another 500 yards, then cross the street to the tourist information center. Watch for the blue thistle sign. Or, if you're in a hurry, a taxi into St. Andrews costs about £9.00.

N o town in the world is so completely identified with one game as St. Andrews is with golf. No matter where in the world they have played the game, there is nothing as exhilarating to devoted golfers as a round on the **Old Course** at St. Andrews. *Internet:* www .standrews.org.uk. Anyone may play the Old Course, provided he or she can produce a current, official handicap certificate, or a letter of introduction from a bona fide golf club, together with proof of identity. This rule applies only to play on the Old Course. Play on the other six courses at St. Andrews is not affected. The links belong to the townspeople and, as such, are open to all.

In summer and autumn, most available tee times on the Old Course are reserved, in many instances a year in advance. Tiger Woods has increased St. Andrews' popularity even more. To be certain of obtaining a starting time for the Old Course, it is essential to apply well in advance of the date of play. Latecomers still have a chance because some starting times are retained each day for issue by a random ballot procedure. To

EDINBURGH *St. Andrews*

Edinburgh–St. Andrews—Edinburgh

There is no train service to St. Andrews; the nearest station is Leuchars, 10 km from St. Andrews. A number of local bus services provide direct travel from Leuchars to St. Andrews. Consult the bus timetable in the station bus stop shelter.

DEPART WAVERLEY STATION	ARRIVE LEUCHARS STATION	NOTES
0555	0656	M–Sa
0710	0811	M–Sa
0810	0910	M–Sa
0855	0955	Su
0910 (0915 Su)	1009 (1037 Su)	Daily
1010	1111	M–Sa
1025	1127	M–Sa
1055	1155	Su

DEPART LEUCHARS STATION	ARRIVE WAVERLEY STATION	NOTES
1544	1648	M–Sa
1619	1722	M–Sa
1641 (1637 Su)	1745 (1736 Su)	Daily
1744 (1737 Su)	1848 (1859 Su)	Daily
1844 (1831 Su)	1948 (1930 Su)	Daily
1937	2059	Su
1949	2050 (2048 Sa)	M–Sa

M–Sa departures continue at 2044, 2119 (M–F), 2140, 2240, and 2326 (M–F). Su departures continue at 2032, 2133, 2240, and 2326.

enter your ballot, it is necessary to apply to the starter by 1400 on the previous day. (The Old Course is closed on Sunday.)

To obtain full details and reservations for golf in St. Andrews, telephone the St. Andrews Links Trust at (01334) 466666 at least one day in advance of your intended visit. In total, St. Andrews and its surrounding area list sixteen courses from which to choose. For information on courses throughout the St. Andrews area, call the St. Andrews Links Trust or the St. Andrews Tourist Information Centre.

How old is the game of golf? Apparently, no one knows. Seemingly it originated on the stretches of grassland along Scotland's east coast next to the sandy beaches—the ground known in Scotland for centuries as "links." The sand dunes interspersed throughout the grasslands became the original traps or bunkers. A round of golf consisted of whatever number of holes were possible in the terrain of a particular link. For more on the history of golf, ask the tourist information center about the British Golf Museum.

At first the pastime of golf was indulged in predominantly by the Scottish aristocracy. With the advent of the inexpensive golf ball, however, golfing in Scotland soon became a mass sport. Aristocracy again moved to the fore by establishing clubhouses for the leisured gentlemen, where they could attend dinners to observe the end of matches between players.

Such was the case at St. Andrews in 1754 when twenty-two "noblemen and gentlemen, being admirers of the ancient and healthful exercise of the golf," founded the Society of St. Andrews Golfers, which is now known throughout the world as the Royal and Ancient Golf Club.

St. Andrews and history go together hand in hand. Such stellar sights as the St. Andrews Castle, with its bottle dungeon and secret passage, vie for your attention along with the ruins of **St. Andrews Cathedral** (*Internet:* www.historic-scotland.gov.uk), once the largest in Scotland. Mary, Queen of Scots, had a house in St. Andrews that you can still see. The town is the home of Scotland's oldest university, founded in 1410–11. Long before Columbus arrived in America or Cooke disembarked in Australia, students were attending classes at **St. Andrews University.** Another attraction is **St. Mary's College** and its unique quadrangle. Founded in 1537, St. Mary's is a part of the university complex. To visit St. Andrews and to roam its streets and scenes is to establish a tangible link with the past.

Of all the places and views, we give our nod to **St. Andrews Castle** [*Tel:* (01334) 477196] overlooking St. Andrews Bay. Initially constructed in 1200, the castle was destroyed and rebuilt during a war between Scotland and England, only to be demolished again during the Reformation. The savagery of those times can be noted on a stone outside the castle gate where George Wishart was burned at the stake. The castle has been in ruins since the seventeenth century, when much of its stone was removed for repairing the harbor. Admission: £3.00 adult, £1.00 child.

St. Andrews Castle may be reached by proceeding along North Street until reaching Castle Street, where you turn left and then proceed 1 block to the castle. Continuing 1 block farther on North Street will put you in front of the ruins of **St. Andrews Cathedral.**

Golfer or not, you must see the **Royal and Ancient Clubhouse of St. Andrews** during your stay. Though founded in 1754, the present clubhouse was built in 1854. The Royal and Ancient Golf Club is now the ruling authority of the game, and its clubhouse is recognized as the world headquarters for the game of golf. From the castle ruins, walk along The Scores until you come to Gillespie Terrace. From this point, the clubhouse and the eighteenth hole of the Old Course come into view.

Day Excursion to

Stirling
Stirling Castle

Depart from Edinburgh Waverley Station
Distance by train: 37 miles (59 km)
Average train time: 50 minutes
Train information and InterCity services: (0845) 748 4950
Tourist information: Stirling Tourist Information Centre, 41 Dumbarton Road, Stirling FK8 2QQ; *Tel:* (0807) 200620; *Fax:* (01786) 450039
Internet: www.scottish.heartlands.org
E-mail: stirlingtic@aillst.ossian.net
Hours: July and August: Monday–Saturday 0900–1830, Sunday 0930–1830. The center operates on more restricted hours during winter.
Notes: To get there from the train station, cross the road directly in front of the station and follow Station Road; then make a left turn onto Murray Place, a short distance. Walk to the first traffic light to the pedestrian section of Port Street and turn right onto Dumbarton Road, immediately opposite the city wall. Total walking time is no more than ten minutes.

All the information you might need for an enjoyable day excursion in Stirling is available at the Royal Burgh of Stirling Visitor Centre, Castle Esplanade; *Tel:* (01786) 462517. Several publications describing walks around Stirling are available. One of particular interest is *Stirling Heritage Trail*, published by the Stirling District Council. It covers a course starting and ending at Stirling Castle and includes photographs and drawings as well as colorful text on the history of Stirling Old Town.

Stirling Castle cannot be ignored. Standing on a 250-foot rock overlooking the River Forth Valley, it offers one of the finest panoramic views in Scotland. The area surrounding the crag on which the castle sits has given up relics of early human's presence from the Stone Age down through the Bronze Age. There is no evidence that the Romans occupied the area, but it seems implausible that they didn't "take the high ground."

Stirling Castle has witnessed endless struggles for power. Kings and queens have been crowned in its halls and great battles fought on the plain below it. Originally named Striveling, which may be translated as "a place of streams," Stirling has been the scene of strife within the Scottish nation since before the time of recorded history. The town of Stirling and its castle truly stand at the crossroads of Scotland. Its position overlooking the Forth Valley and the crossing of the River Forth at its tidal limits has contributed to its past and present importance.

Edinburgh–Stirling–Edinburgh

DEPART WAVERLEY STATION	ARRIVE STIRLING STATION	NOTES
0703	0752	M–Sa
0733	0822	M–Sa
M–Sa service continues every 30 minutes until 1500.		
0933	1025	Su
1033	1125	Su
Su service continues hourly until midafternoon.		

DEPART STIRLING STATION	ARRIVE WAVERLEY STATION	NOTES
1405	1458	M–Sa
1435	1528	M–Sa
M–Sa service continues every 30 minutes until 2105, then 2205 and 2308.		
1405	1458	Su
1505	1558	Su
1605	1700	Su
Su service continues hourly until 2205.		

The castle as seen today began to develop around 1370 with the accession of the Stuart kings, serving as a royal residence from then until the son of Mary, Queen of Scots, James VI of Scotland, departed for London in 1603 to become James I of England. Scotland's tragic queen spent the first five years of her life in and around Stirling Castle. The castle is perhaps the finest example of Renaissance architecture in Scotland, most of its buildings dating from the fifteenth and sixteenth centuries. As it was the royal Stuart residence, Scotland's kings and queens held court there, and parliaments met on its premises.

The Royal Burgh of Stirling Visitor and Tourist Information Centre just below the castle combines a multilanguage audiovisual presentation and photographic exhibition of Stirling Castle through seven centuries. A bookstore and souvenir shop are included. According to its innovators, it is the first building in Europe to be designed specifically to bring alive the history of a town.

All is bustle and noise as ships from France and the Netherlands unload their cargoes and farmers drive their cattle to market. Stirling's market, now the city's Broad Street, is lined with shops selling everything from swords to spices. Meanwhile, back at the castle a roistering banquet is being held in the great hall, packed with honored guests.

Throughout Stirling during the summer months, the presence of flowers is always evident. You will notice this first in the railway station, and it continues all around town. Possibly Stirling developed its love for flowers from the King's Knot, an octagonal, stepped mound laid out as the royal gardens in 1627–1628 beneath the walls of Stirling Castle by an Englishman, William Watts, who was brought from London to supervise the project. The raised central portion of the Knot is thought to have originated as a Bronze Age burial mound and was probably used as an outdoor royal court for tournaments before being incorporated into the formal gardens by Mr. Watts.

There are many historic buildings in Stirling. Below the castle stands the imposing **Church of the Holy Rood.** It has witnessed great moments in history. Here, at its altar, James VI of Scotland, and subsequently James I of England, was crowned at the age of eighteen months to succeed his exiled mother. The tower of the church still bears the marks of the 1745 rebellion, when Bonnie Prince Charlie's troops attempted to capture Stirling Castle. In the overture to the Reformation, the strident voice of John Knox boomed from the church pulpit.

Stirling is indeed a historic center that has played a vital role in the making of Scotland—an atmosphere that is hard to match. Over the centuries of its involvement in historical events, Stirling has preserved its heritage.

Day Excursion to

Stranraer
Gateway to Northern Ireland

Depart from Edinburgh Waverley Station
Distance by train: 147 miles (237 km)
Average train time: 4 hours, 45 minutes
Train information and InterCity services: (0845) 748 4950
Tourist information: Tourist Information Centre, Burns House, Harbour Street, Stranraer DG9 7RA; *Tel:* (01776) 702595; *Fax:* (01776) 889156
Internet: www.stranraer.org
E-mail: stranraer@dgtb.ossian.net
Hours: November–June: Monday–Saturday 1000–1700; July–October: Monday–Saturday 0930–1730, Sunday 1000–1630.
Notes: The tourist information center is located on Harbour Street to the right of the Stena Line Terminal.

Stranraer is primarily the terminal for passenger and car ferry service to Belfast in Northern Ireland. At press time, however, the BritRail Pass was not accepted for travel on trains operated by the Northern Ireland Railways. Travelers crossing from Stranraer to Belfast must purchase regular rail tickets or a BritRail Pass + Ireland option, which includes the sea crossing on Stena Line plus rail travel in England, Scotland, Wales, Northern Ireland, and the Republic of Ireland.

Arrangements for visiting Northern Ireland should be completed before departure rather than en route. One important requirement is a control ticket each passenger must have prior to boarding the Stranraer–Belfast ferry. These tickets are issued free of charge. Ticketing and reservations are available in the Stena Line ferry terminal, along with a comfortable passenger lounge with restrooms and refreshments.

The crossing between Stranraer and Belfast usually takes three hours by conventional ferry, but Stena Line's HSS Fast Craft takes only one hour and forty-five minutes. Trains are waiting at the terminals to take travelers to their final destinations. In Stranraer, the train terminal is directly alongside the ferry dock. Porter service is available. The BritRail Pass + Ireland option is valid on the Stena Line.

Stranraer has direct, daytime express-train connections to London For sleeper services to London, go to Glasgow for departures from Glasgow Central. The last train leaves Stranraer for Glasgow at 2110. Frequent train service connecting with ferries to and from Belfast is also available from Glasgow. Edinburgh passengers should use the Edinburgh–Glasgow service for the fastest connections to Stranraer.

The old section of Stranraer clusters around its port area and is entwined with interesting streets and alleyways. The Stranraer Castle, which houses a visitor center, is a relic of the sixteenth century and adds a certain attraction to the area. The information center can provide you with a map of the town and suggest various sights to see on a walking tour. The area is renowned for its golf and fishing, and there are a number of beautiful gardens, which flourish in the mild climate.

The Stranraer Castle, with the formal title of **Castle of St. John,** is known locally as the "Old Castle." Built in what is now the heart of Stranraer around 1510, it was erected on a site that gave the settlement its original name, Chapel. The name was later changed to Chapel of Stranrawer and finally shortened to Stranraer. Stranrawer was believed to have referred to a row of original houses on the strand, or beach, now buried beneath the town's streets.

An interesting hotel in Stranraer, one that you might mistake as the town's castle when you first see it, is the **North West Castle Hotel.** Its

Edinburgh–Stranraer–Edinburgh

DEPART WAVERLEY STATION	ARRIVE STRANRAER STATION	NOTES
0715	1111	M–Sa
1030	1356 (1351 Sa)	Daily

DEPART STRANRAER STATION	ARRIVE WAVERLEY STATION	NOTES
1437	1748	M–Sa
1440	1750	Su
1940	2320 (2323 Su)	Daily

All schedules shown require a change in Glasgow from Queen Street to Paisley Gilmour Street or the reverse. Schedules shown allow 15–25 minutes for this change.

castle tower cleverly conceals two well-stocked bars. If you are anticipating a long train trip, you may want to bolster your spirits here in the quaint tower. In the lower bar, there are some fossiliferous wooden beams (no, they are not former patrons), while topside in the Explorers Lounge you are treated to a fine view of the harbor.

The hotel was originally the home of Sir John Ross, the famous Arctic explorer. He gave it the name North West Castle as a reminder of his journeys to the northern and western reaches of the Arctic. Although the "castle" has been transformed into the largest hotel in southwest Scotland, its origins with Sir John have been carefully preserved. An indoor ice rink caters to curling fans, and the hotel proprietor added a swimming pool, sauna baths, and several restaurants. A brochure at the hotel desk gives the full history of this most interesting hostelry.

Stranraer lies at the southern end of Loch Ryan, known since Roman times as a safe harbor. At the point where Loch Ryan meets the Irish Sea, the granite bulk of **Ailsa Craig** stands as a sentinel guarding the enclosed waters of the loch from the ravages of the storms that sweep into the area from the Atlantic.

Base City:

Glasgow

Internet: www.seeglasgow.com
E-mail: enquiries@seeglasgow.com

Glasgow has undergone a sweeping renaissance, shaking off its former image of a grim, depressed industrial city to dawn as one of Europe's foremost culture hubs. Emerging from a century or so of accumulated grime, the cleaning-up process has highlighted some of Europe's finest Victorian architecture in gleaming gold and red sandstone. Bustling city streets lined with imposing hand-carved facades pay homage to the optimism of the Victorian city fathers, as do the stunning marble staircases of the opulent City Chambers in central George Square. Glaswegians have reason to be proud of their city and cordially invite you to enjoy it.

Glasgow is Scotland's largest metropolis. As the gateway to bonnie Loch Lomond and the western Highlands, Glasgow's River Clyde flows into the Firth of Clyde, thus opening its western waterways to myriad islands and the Irish Sea. At the height of its shipbuilding boom, Glasgow was launching more than one-third of the world's shipping tonnage. The *Queen Mary,* the *Queen Elizabeth I,* and the *Queen Elizabeth II (QE2)* were built there. With the industry now only a shadow of its former self, the River Clyde has become a scenic waterway where you can cruise aboard luxury riverboats or the paddle-wheel steamer *Waverley.*

Glasgow abounds with sights to see, ranging from its great twelfth-century cathedral to a variety of museums and universities. It is said that Glasgow has more parks than any other European city of its size. George Square, opposite the Queen Street railway station, projects a panorama of Scottish and British history in its statues of individuals who forged the British Commonwealth through their scientific, leadership, and literary endeavors.

213

Direct transatlantic flights into the Glasgow Airport, only fifteen minutes from the city center, as well as regular train services from London and the south, make Glasgow an ideal "base city" for Scotland. The same day excursions from Edinburgh may just as easily be made from Glasgow. With the excellent train service between the two base cities and to all of the day excursions from either city, which one you choose as a base is your personal decision.

Arriving by Air

Along with its excellent weather, Glasgow offers travelers the opportunity of "open jaw" airline ticketing: arriving or departing on one leg of their transatlantic flight in Scotland rather than flying both in and out of the London complex of Gatwick, Stansted, or Heathrow. Glasgow Airport is the busiest of Scotland's three main international airports.

The Glasgow Tourist Information Desk, located in the international arrivals concourse, provides information to incoming passengers. The office is open from 0715 to 2230 daily. Currency exchange services are available daily in summer between 0700 and 2300; in winter (November to April), the office is open Monday–Saturday 0800–2000, Sunday 0800–1800.

Frequent airport bus service (No. 905) is offered between the airport and Glasgow city center 0600–2400 Monday–Saturday, 0700–2400 Sunday. Contact Scottish Citylink. *Tel:* (08705) 505050; *Internet:* www .citylink.co.uk. Journey time is approximately twenty-five minutes; the fare is £3.30. Taxi fare from the airport to Glasgow city center is about £16.50. Taxi and frequent bus service also can transport travelers to the nearest rail station, Paisley Gilmour Street Station, just 2 miles from the airport. Direct rail service connects Paisley Gilmour Street with Glasgow Central station, Ayr, and Clyde Coast destinations.

Arriving by Train

Glasgow has two main railway stations. Trains arriving from southwestern Scotland and England terminate in the Glasgow Central Station. For train travel north and east out of Glasgow to Edinburgh, Perth, and Inverness or west to Oban and Fort William, the Glasgow Queen Street Station becomes the departure point. A convenient city bus service links the two rail stations. The twenty-minute walk between them, however, runs through some of the city's finer shopping areas, thereby offering the opportunity to walk off a few British "pounds." If you choose to walk from the Queen Street Station to the Central Station, walk past George Square and the tourist information center to St. Vincent Street. Turn right and walk 1 block farther to Buchanan Street, a pedestrian shopping precinct. Turn left onto Buchanan Street and walk until your path intersects with Gordon Street. The intersection is easy to locate because this section of Gordon Street is reserved for pedestrians (and shops). Turning right at this point and continuing along Gordon Street for 2 blocks will bring you to the Glasgow Central Station, on your left.

From the Central Station to the Queen Street Station, merely reverse your line of march. Those who wish to avoid running the shopper's gauntlet on Buchanan Street may proceed between the two stations by traversing Queen and Argyle Streets. A map of central Glasgow is available at the tourist information center at 11 George Square.

The Interstation Bus Link provides passenger transfer service between the Central and Queen Street Stations with no stops en route. Departures are approximately every fifteen minutes.

Don't look for a kiosk or a newsstand where you can purchase tickets; you pay your fare when you get on the bus. BritRail Passes are not accepted for the bus transfer between rail stations. The time en route varies between five and ten minutes, depending on traffic conditions. For those in a hurry or heavily loaded with luggage, taxis are standing by in queues at both stations.

If you are arriving in one of Glasgow's rail stations to transfer to the Glasgow Airport at Abbotsinch, frequent bus service departs from Buchanan Bus Station. Paisley Gilmour Street Station is the closest rail terminal to the airport. Transport via taxi or local bus is located here as well to make the 2-mile journey to the airport.

Glasgow Central Station

Glasgow Central Station, transformed radically in recent years, caters to the needs of the train traveler, ranging from restrooms with bathing facilities to a grand Victorian hostelry, the Central Hotel. The station's old ticket office was transformed into a delightful array of quality shops, bars, and restaurants. Pick up a copy of *The Station Guide* leaflet for a detailed guide to station facilities.

The Glasgow Central Station provides InterCity electric services for English destinations, including Liverpool, Manchester, Birmingham, and London (Euston Station). Also provided are connections for Wales, the west of England, and destinations in south and west Scotland, which include Ayr and Stranraer (for connections to Larne and Belfast in Northern Ireland). Commuter-train service to Gourock and Wemyss Bay for connections with steamer services on the River Clyde also operate from Central Station.

Money exchange is available at Thomas Cook by the Gordon Street entrance. ATMs are located near the Upper Crust at the entrance to platform 5.

Hotel reservations may be arranged at the **tourist information center** at 11 George Street [*Tel:* (0141) 204 4400; *Fax:* (0141) 221 3524].

Train information is displayed in the Central Station by means of a digital departures-and-arrivals board located between tracks 2 and 5. For expanded train information, visit the Inquiries and Reservations Office (travel center) on the right side of the main hall at the end of platforms 1, 2, and 3.

Train reservations may be arranged in the travel center. For sleeping-car reservations, you will be directed to the InterCity Sleeper Centre at the entrance to platform 1.

Queen Street Station

Queen Street Station is the terminal for trains operating on the scenic West Highland Line to Oban, Fort William, and Mallaig, where steamer connections may be made to the Scottish islands. From the Queen Street Station, InterCity express trains depart for Edinburgh and connect with destinations in England including York, Doncaster, and London (King's Cross Station).

Services for north and east Scotland, including Stirling, Perth, Dundee, Aberdeen, Inverness, and the Kyle of Lochalsh, depart from the Queen Street Station. Electric trains to Dumbarton and Balloch (for Loch Lomond cruises) also operate from this station.

Money exchange services are not available within the Queen Street Station. There are several banks in the general area, including an office of the Royal Bank of Scotland adjacent to the main entrance of the Central Station.

Hotel reservations for Glasgow and for all of Scotland may be arranged through the "Book-a-Bed-Ahead" service with the Greater Glasgow & Clyde Valley Tourist Board located at 11 George Square; *Tel:* (0141) 204 4480.

Tourist information in Glasgow is also available at the **Greater Glasgow and Clyde Valley Tourist Board**. *Hours:* June–September: Monday–Saturday 0900–1900 (2000 in July–August), Sunday 1000–1800; October–May: Monday–Saturday 0900–1800, closed on Sunday until Easter, open 1000–1800 Sunday after Easter.

The center has a wealth of Glasgow tourist information on hand. Call to request a copy of the *Greater Glasgow Quick Guide* booklet. In addition to a listing of city attractions, the booklet contains information on restaurants, pubs, events, and shopping that will be very helpful for getting to know Glasgow. There is a Bureau de Change in the center as well as an office for theater and sporting-events tickets.

Train information is available in the British Rail Travel Centre located on the left-hand side of the station as you face the train platforms. Train reservations can be made in the travel center. For sleeper reservations, however, use the InterCity Sleeper Centre in Central Station.

Glasgow Gazette

Glasgow's modern subway system is a circular line with trains running in both directions beneath the center of the city. A three-minute service from each of its fifteen stations is provided, achieving a circular journey in about twenty-two minutes. A separate subway, the Argyle Line, links the suburban networks. The main link with British rail services, however, is the subway station at Buchanan Street, connecting with the Queen Street Station by a moving pedestrian platform similar to those found in airports. The Scotland TravelPass allows passholders to travel the Glasgow Underground at no charge.

For travelers going to Loch Lomond, the rail route departing Glasgow is an electric-train service that departs from subterranean platform 8 in the Queen Street Station. To reach it, after entering the main hall of the station, turn left and exit the station by the side entrance, where you turn right to follow the well-marked platform 8 signs.

In the Queen Street Station's Travel Centre, you may obtain information and tickets for cruising on the Clyde River aboard the paddle steamer *Waverley*. Connecting rail services to the ship's pier originate in the Queen Street Station. The vessel offers a number of interesting cruises on the Clyde River and the Firth of Clyde, including a special upriver cruise on Saturdays during the summer. Advance bookings are recommended. *Tel:* (0845) 130 4647; *Internet:* www.waverleyexcursions .co.uk.

Throughout the summer a two-hour bus tour of Glasgow aboard specially converted double-decker buses will take you around some of the best-known places—and some of the more-out-of-the-way places—in the city. For bus tour schedules and rates, check with the Greater Glasgow Tourist Information Centre.

Every visitor to Glasgow, and model railroad buffs in particular, will not want to miss Glasgow's **Museum of Transport** in Kelvin Hall on Argyle Street. The museum is located in the west end of Glasgow only ten minutes from the city center by bus or subway. Open Monday through Saturday from 1000 to 1700 and Sunday between 1100 and 1700. Displays include ship models, Glasgow trams and buses, locomotives of Scottish origin, Scottish-built motorcars, fire engines, and a reconstructed subway station. There is also a section in the museum known as "The Clyde Room," where meticulously detailed models illustrate the story of shipbuilding and shipping on the River Clyde. An operating model railroad is one of the museum's highlights. Admission is free.

St. Mungo Museum of Religious Life and Art, at 2 Castle Street (in front of Glasgow Cathedral), provides an exploration of the different faiths of the world through paintings and religious artifacts. Included in the collection is Salvador Dali's *Christ of St. John of the Cross*. The museum is open Monday through Saturday 1000–1700 and Sunday 1100–1700. Admission is free.

Glasgow's Art Gallery and Museum is directly opposite Kelvin Hall. Home of Britain's finest civic collection of British and European paintings, the museum also features displays of natural history, archaeology, and collections of silver, pottery, arms, and armor. In the performing-arts sector, **Glasgow's Mayfest** (which, of course, occurs in the merry month of May) is a key international festival for theater, dance, music, and related performing arts in Europe.

Among the many superb galleries and museums throughout Glasgow is the renowned Burrell Collection in the Pollok Country Park, a unique collection of more than 8,000 *objets d'art* donated to the city by one man, Sir William Burrell.

Previously, we identified the area of the city between the two rail stations as an ideal place to "walk off a few British 'pounds.'" It is. Glasgow is a shopper's paradise. Department stores line the great pedestrian shopping districts of Argyle and Buchanan Streets. Adjacent to them, Princes Square provides some of Europe's top specialty shops blended with an exciting array of restaurants and bars. Slightly farther than a stone's throw from the square, St. Enochs indoor shopping mall offers a wide variety of stores beneath the same roof, and Argyll Victorian Arcade is the place to look for jewelry and fine gifts. Farther out, but well worth it if you are visiting Glasgow over a weekend, is the city's famous **"Barras Street Market,"** a bargain collector's delight with goods ranging from Victorian bric-a-brac to high fashion, all flavored by the antics of the stall holders.

Glasgow Connections to Day Excursions

All-day excursions described departing from Edinburgh also may be taken from Glasgow. Refer to the "Train Connections to Other Base Cities" schedules. In fact, two of the day excursions (to Ayr and Stranraer) require passing through Glasgow. For these excursions, readers residing in Glasgow need only refer to the appropriate day-excursion schedule.

Two of the day excursions—Dunbar and Dunfermline—may be reached conveniently only through Edinburgh. Consequently, readers need refer only to the Glasgow–Edinburgh shuttle-service schedule for these day excursions.

Five day excursions—Aberdeen, Dundee, Montrose, St. Andrews, and Stirling—are so situated on Scotland's rail lines that they may be reached either by direct connection from the Queen Street Station in Glasgow or through Edinburgh.

GLASGOW

Two other day excursions—Inverness and Perth—are reached more conveniently from Glasgow by direct train service from the Queen Street Station rather than through Edinburgh.

All services shown are subject to change. Readers are advised to consult with the schedules posted in the train stations or with a British Rail Travel Centre for train information before commencing each journey.

Regardless of which city you select as your base, don't forget that the frequent train service between Glasgow and Edinburgh enables you to make a day excursion to the one you didn't select as your base. For what to see and do in Edinburgh, consult the chapter on Scotland's capital.

There are times throughout the year when one of the two cities, either Glasgow or Edinburgh, may be fully booked. This can take place in Glasgow during May when the city hosts a Mayfest, a festival focusing attention on Glasgow's many activities within its cultural sphere. On the other hand, Edinburgh can be filled to overflowing when visitors attend its world-famous Military Tattoo. When this happens, and your reservationist gives up on the city of your choice, try the other. Your chances of finding accommodations there are very good, and the ease of rail travel between Glasgow and Edinburgh will make it an "easy commute," far better than anything that the Long Island Railroad could come up with!

GLASGOW

Glasgow Connections to Day Excursions

EXCURSION DESTINATION	DEPART QUEEN ST. STATION	ARRIVE DESTINATION	DEPART DESTINATION	ARRIVE QUEEN ST. STATION	NOTES
Aberdeen	0555	0839	1342	1615	M–Sa
	0742	1013	1442	1715	M–Sa
	0842	1117	1538	1815	M–Sa
	0942	1213	1641	1915	M–Sa
	1042	1313	1753	2032	M–Sa
			1841	2115	M–Sa
	0940	1227	1530	1815	Su
	1140	1423	1750	2027	Su
			1935	2215	Su
Dundee	0742	0902	1451	1615	M–Sa
	0842	1001	1551	1715	M–Sa
	0942	1101	1646	1815	M–Sa
	1042	1201	1751	1915	M–Sa
			1909	2032	M–Sa
			1951	2115	M–Sa
			2051	2215	M–Sa
	0940	1109	1443	1615	Su
	1140	1310	1643	1815	Su
			1902	2027	Su
			2046	2215	Su
Inverness	0708	1025	1650	2015	M–Sa
	1008	1335	2013	2335	M–Sa
	Su schedule not conducive to day excursions.				
Montrose	0742	0933	1716	1915	M–Sa
	0842	1033	1833 (1828 Su)	2032 (2027 Su)`	Daily
	0942 (0940 Su)	1133 (1144 Su)	1916	2115	Daily
Perth	0708	0809	1513	1615	M–Sa
	0742	0840	1613	1715	M–Sa
	0842	0939	1710	1815	M–Sa
	0942 (0940) Su	1039 (1044 Su)	1930 (1924 Su)	2032 (2027 Su)	Daily
St. Andrews	Train from Glasgow Queen Street Station to Dundee, first train out 0555. Transfer to St. Andrews bus, departing every hour on the half hour.				
Stirling	At 18, 42, and 48 minutes past each hour.				M–Sa
	At 0940 and every 2 hours thereafter.				Su
	Depart Stirling at 19, 43, and 49 minutes past each hour				M–Sa
	Depart Stirling at 1557, 1738, 1902, 1953, or 2141				Su
	Journey time: 26 minutes				

Train Connections to Other Base Cities from Glasgow

Glasgow–Cardiff

DEPART GLASGOW CENTRAL	ARRIVE CARDIFF CENTRAL	NOTES
0610	1348 (1334 Sa)	M–Sa (1)
0750	1448 (1445 Sa)	M–Sa (2)
0948	1632 (1635 Sa)	M–Sa (1)
1037	1732	Su (3)
1037	1748	Sa (1)
1145	1917	Su (4)
1146	1807 (1810 Sa)	M–Sa (1)
1205	1848	M–F (2)
1245	2018	Su (3)
1351 (1347 Su)	2012 (2007 Su)	Daily (5)
1410	2029	Su (1)
1457	2219	Su (1)
1606	2331	Sa (3)
1612	2257	Su (1)
1649	2329	M–Sa (1)

(1) Change trains in Crewe

(2) Change trains in Wilmslow

(3) Change trains at Gloucester

(4) Change trains at Birmingham New Street

(5) Change trains at Cheltenham Spa

Glasgow–Edinburgh

There are two services between Glasgow and Edinburgh. Frequent commuter trains depart from Glasgow Queen Street Station to Edinburgh Waverley Station. There is a less frequent service on the mainline between Glasgow Central Station and Waverley—service provided on mainline trains that arrive in Glasgow Central from stations in England such as Carlisle, London, and York. Average train time to Edinburgh: 48–50 minutes.

COMMUTER SERVICE: DEPART GLASGOW QUEEN STREET STATION

M–Sa   Departs every 15 minutes from 0700 to 1900; then every 30 minutes until 2330.

Su   Departs hourly from 0830 to 1230; then every 30 minutes until 2330.

MAINLINE SERVICE: DEPART GLASGOW CENTRAL STATION

M–F   Departs at 0700, 0800, 1000, 1200; then every 2 hours until 2000.

Sa   Departs hourly from 0700 until 1000; then at 1200, 1400, 1500, 1600, 1730, and 1800.

Su   Departs at 1055, 1255; then hourly from 1455 to 1955.

Glasgow–London

GLASGOW

Direct trains from Glasgow arrive in London at King's Cross or Euston Station, King's Cross arrivals are labeled "KC"; Euston arrivals, "ES."

DEPART GLASGOW CENTRAL	ARRIVE LONDON KC OR ES	NOTES
0610	1221 ES	M-F
0720 (0718 Sa)	1318 (1345 Sa) ES	M-Sa
0700	1241 (1243 Sa) KC	M-Sa
0800	1343 (1346 Sa) KC	M-Sa
0935	1502 (1545 Sa) ES	M-Sa
0954	1633 ES	Su
1000	1545 (1542 Sa) KC	M-Sa
1146	1720 (1745 Sa) ES	M-Sa
1200	1742 (1740 Sa) KC	M-Sa
1255	1835 KC	Su
1339	1852 ES	M-F
1400	1920 (1938 Sa) KC	M-Sa
1451	2104 ES	Su
1500	2036 KC	Sa
1535	2117 ES	M-F
1555	2200 KC	Su
1600	2145 (2148 Sa) KC	M-Sa
1649	2217 (2254 Sa) ES	M-Sa
1714	2337 ES	Su
2315*	0700+1 ES	Su
2340*	0702+1 (0711+1 Fri) ES	M-F

*Sleeper service; reservations required.

+1=Arrives next day

Reservations recommended for above-listed trains.

Wales

Internet: www.visitwales.com
E-mail: info@tourism.wales.gov.uk

Welcome to Wales, the passionate area of Britain. You will readily notice the distinctly romantic spirit of the Welsh through their lilting language and their crooning, mellifluous voices. According to the Wales Tourist Board's brochure, "Something as simple as travel directions can become a lyrical journey, taking in history, folklore and a fair amount of local gossip." You may be dumbfounded by the language, but don't let it frighten you. Although Welsh is considered the oldest living language in Europe—it has been around for more than fourteen centuries—everyone in Wales speaks English.

The Welsh are well known for their extraordinary vocal talent, and in the towns and villages you can hear some of the finest male choirs in the world. With their gift for oratory, it is no wonder the Welsh have figured so prominently in British politics.

Wales is about 170 miles (256 kilometers) long and 60 miles (96 kilometers) wide, about the size of Massachusetts. This compact little country has an abundance of scenic natural beauty, including three national parks and beautiful rivers, streams, lakes, and mountains. Add the myth and magic of a king named Arthur, a magician named Merlin, a knight named Lancelot, and a queen named Guinevere, stir in a castle called Caerleon, and you've got Camelot. If you like castles, you can choose from more than 400 castles and monuments to visit in Wales—more castles than any other country in Europe. Take a peek at www.castlewales.com or www.cadw.wales.gov.uk (Welsh Historic Monuments).

Wales is the home and inspiration of many performers and poets, including actress Catherine Zeta Jones, the great brooding actors Sir Anthony Hopkins and the late Richard Burton; popular singers Tom Jones, Shirley Bassey, and Charlotte Church; great bass baritone opera singer

Bryn Terfel; and one of the twentieth century's greatest English-language poets, Dylan Thomas.

South and West Wales contain the majority of the country's people as well as Cardiff, the capital of Wales and a base city for five day excursions. This region also has some of Britain's most outstanding natural beauty: the Gower Peninsula, the sandy beaches of Pembrokeshire Coast National Park, and the resort town of Tenby.

In North Wales, visit a special little village with the title of longest name in Britain and the second longest name in the world—Llanfairpwllgwyngyllgogerychwyrndrobwllllantysiliogogogoch—whew! (Raymond Mathias, Wales Marketing Director, USA, can actually pronounce it. Visit www.visitwales.com to hear the pronunciation.) It means "Saint Mary's Church in the hollow of the white hazel near a rapid whirlpool and the Church of Saint Tysilio of the red cave." Found on the island of Anglesey, it is the next stop after Bangor on the North Wales Coast Line.

Or travel to "the roof of Wales" and view England, Wales, and Ireland from the summit of Snowdon, the highest peak, at 3,560 feet (1,085 meters). As Hilaire Belloc wrote: "There is no corner of Europe that I know which so moves me with awe and majesty of great things as does this mass of northern Welsh mountains."

Snowdonia National Park extends southward through Mid Wales, which also contains the smallest town in Britain—Llanwrtyd Wells—the mountainous Brecon Beacons National Park, and the spectacular showcaves of Dan-yr-Ogof, Europe's largest showcaves complex.

Wales Tourist Board, Brunel House, 2 Fitzalan Road, Cardiff CF24 OUY; *Tel:* (029) 2049 9909; *Fax:* (029) 2048 5031; *Internet:* www .visitwales.com. For brochures and travel information, call (800) 462–2748 (U.S. only).

Rail Travel in Wales

National Rail Enquiries: (0845) 748 4950

The Great Little Trains of Wales LLR, Dept GLTW, Gilfach Ddu, Llanberis, Gwynedd LL55 4TY, is the joint markting group for the narrow-gauge steam trains (some of which are more than one hundred years old) that provide a special way of seeing some of the best scenery in Britain. The Rover Ticket is vaid for nine consecutive days on any of the eight-member narrow-gauge railways listed below: £55 adults; £15 children. Tickets may be purchased online at www.gltw.co.uk; or *Tel/Fax:* (01286) 870549.

Bala Lake Railway, Yr Orsaf, Llanuwchllyn, Bala, Gwynedd, Wales LL23 7DD; *Tel:* (01678) 540666; *Internet:* www.bala-lake-railway.co.uk.

Brecon Mountain Railway, Pant Station, Merthyr Tydfil, Wales CF48 2UP; *Tel:* (01685) 722988; *Fax:* (01685) 384854; *Internet:* www.brecon mountainrailway.co.uk.

WALES

Ffestiniog Railway, Harbour Station, Porthmadog, Gwynedd, Wales LL49 9NF; *Tel:* (01766) 516024; *Fax:* (01766) 516006; *Internet:* www.festrail.co.uk; *E-mail:* info@festrail.co.uk.

The Ffestiniog Railway and the country house Hotel Maes-y-Neuadd have joined forces to create "Steam and Cuisine," a unique "dining by rail" experience. The narrow-gauge steam train travels some 13½ miles through delightful scenery from the coast at Porthmadog to the former slate mining town of Blaenau Ffestiniog. Imagine sipping a glass of champagne while enjoying the haute cuisine of talented Chef Peter Jackson. The complete package includes a stay at the Hotel Maes-y-Neuadd set in eight acres of beautifully landscaped gardens with stunning views across Snowdonia National Park.

Llanberis Lake Railway, Llanberis, Caernarfon, Gwynedd, Wales LL55 4TY; *Tel:* (01286) 870549; *Internet:* www.lake-railway.co.uk.

Talyllyn Railway, Wharf Station, Tywyn, Gwynedd, Wales LL36 9EY; *Tel:* (01654) 710472; *Fax:* (01654) 711755; *Internet:* www.talyllyn.co.uk; *E-mail:* enquiries@talyllyn.co.uk.

Vale of Rheidol Railway, Park Avenue, Aberystwyth, Cardiganshire, Wales SY23 1PG; *Tel:* (01970) 625819; *Fax:* (01970) 623769; *Internet:* www.rheidolrailway.co.uk.

Welsh Highland Railway, Gelerts Farm Works, Madoc Street West, Porthmadog, Gwynedd, Wales LL49 9DY; *Tel:* (01766) 513402; *Internet:* www.whr.co.uk; *E-mail:* enquiries@whr.co.uk.

Welshpool & Llanfair Light Railway, The Station, Llanfair Caereinion, Powys, Wales SY21 0SF; *Tel:* (01938) 810441; *Fax:* (01938) 810861; *Internet:* www.wllr.org.uk; *E-mail:* info@wllr.org.uk.

Base City:
Cardiff

Internet: www.visitcardiff.info
E-mail: visitor@thecardiffinitiative.co.uk

Want to go from the first to the twenty-first century in short order? By all means go to Cardiff. The spectacular 2,000-year-old Cardiff Castle dominates the historic city center, while the futuristic Cardiff Bay waterfront development encompasses Techniquest, the United Kingdom's leading hands-on science discovery center.

Since 1991, when the Cardiff marketing campaign was launched by the late Diana, Princess of Wales, and the then eight-year-old Prince William, Cardiff has been recognized as a world-renowned international center for business, tourism, and leisure. Undoubtedly, Cardiff is one of the friendliest capital cities in the world and is rapidly becoming the United Kingdom's fastest-growing visitor destination.

Cardiff was first developed by the Romans and then by the Normans. Both left their marks in the form of formidable fortifications. The Romans found their way into South Wales and reached the area that is now Cardiff about A.D. 76. At first they erected a wooden fort, but as Cardiff grew in importance as a Roman naval base, a stone fortress was erected. Following the conquest of England in 1066, the Normans arrived in Cardiff in 1091 and established a stronghold on the site of the old Roman fort. By the sixteenth century Cardiff had established itself as an important port and trading center, complete with pirates and cutthroats who were primarily responsible for Cardiff's decline over the next couple hundred years. With the arrival of the Industrial Revolution, however, Cardiff was to become the world's premier coal-exporting port, thanks to the second Marquess of Bute, who was known as the "Creator of Modern Cardiff."

Today's city is largely a creation of the nineteenth century. Cardiff cast off its grim mantle of industrialism to reveal a sparkling paradise of shopping arcades, a glistening white array of impressive neoclassical civic buildings, a cast iron and glass indoor market, a memorable museum, a transformed harbor area, and the restored (or "reinvented") Cardiff Castle.

Arriving by Air

Visitors to Wales from North America most likely will use either Heathrow or Gatwick Airport. Refer to the London chapter for information regarding these airports. Travelers wishing to avoid a trip into central London and head directly to Cardiff from Heathrow Airport can take a bus from any terminal to Reading rail station and then a train into Cardiff. All trains for Cardiff stop at Reading. Transatlantic flights also are available into Birmingham and Manchester Airports.

Cardiff International Airport, 19 kilometers from the city center, is one of the fastest-growing airports in the United Kingdom and provides direct flights to and from Amsterdam, Belfast, Brussels, Dublin, Guernsey, Isle of Man, Jersey, and Paris. A multimillion-pound expansion has provided an international departure lounge, shopping, and catering facilities. The airport's telephone number is (01446) 711111; *Internet:* www.cial.co.uk.

Arriving by Train

Hourly trains depart from London's Paddington Station and arrive in Cardiff Central Station in only about two hours. All facilities, including ATMs, train information, and lockers, are located in the main concourse.

National Rail Enquiries: (0845) 748 4950

Cardiff Visitor Information Centre, St. David's House, 16 Wood Street, Cardiff CF10 1ES; *Tel:* (029) 2022 7281; *Fax:* (029) 2023 9162; *Internet:* www.visitcardiff.info; *E-mail:* visitor@thecardiffinitiative.co.uk; *Hours:* 1000–1800 Monday–Saturday, 1000–1600 Sunday.

Exit the main concourse of Central Station onto Central Square. You will see the bus station ahead and Burger King on your right (on the corner). Head toward Burger King, then toward the two tall buildings and the main road—Wood Street. At the pedestrian crossing, cross to the other side of the road and turn left toward the Cardiff Bus Ticket Office (on the corner). Continue along Wood Street to the visitor center, a few doors away. A sign on the corner of Wood Street will direct you.

Hotel and bed-and-breakfast (B&B) accommodations may be made at the visitor information office on Wood Street. The Townhouse Hotel [*Tel:* (029) 2023 9399; *Fax:* (029) 2022 3214; *Internet:* thetownhouse cardiff.co.uk; *E-mail:* thetownhouse@msn.com] is a beautifully restored Victorian-style B&B located at 70 Cathedral Road, within walking distance of the city center, including Cardiff Castle. The rate for single occupancy starts at £42.50; twin/doubles from £52.50 (all rooms en suite; price includes full breakfast and VAT). The Townhouse is richly appointed with antiques and paintings. Breakfast is always good too. By taking a left at Sophia Close, you can walk through Bute Park and end up on Castle Street. Readers of *Britain by BritRail* are entitled to a discount. Just show them this book.

If The Townhouse Hotel is fully booked, try the Lincoln House Hotel [*Tel:* (029) 2039 5558; *Fax:* (029) 2023 0537; *Internet:* www.lincolnhotel .co.uk], only about 1 block farther at 118 Cathedral Road. The Lincoln House is another charming B&B. Single room rates: £50–£55; double room rates: £75–£95. All rooms have private shower and toilet facilities, and stays include breakfast and VAT.

If you prefer to fork out the extra pounds for superior first class, you'll want to stay at the Angel Hotel on Castle Street, superbly located between the Millennium Stadium and Cardiff Castle. Many a beautiful bride has descended the grand staircase to her "knight in shining armor." But the prices are steep too. Room rates begin at £46 *per person* per night, based on double occupancy; single en suite, £92. *Internet:* www.the angelhotel-cardiff.activehotels.com/THE.

Getting around in Cardiff

An easy, economical way to get around in Cardiff is by bus. Cardiff's regular bus service covers the entire city and beyond—even to attractions such as Llanerch Vineyard and Castell Coch. The Central Bus Station is immediately in front of the rail station: Cardiff Bus, St. David's House, Wood Street, Cardiff CF1 1ER; *Tel:* (029) 2039 6521. In the outlying areas, the train service can take you to attractions such as **Rhondda Heritage Park** (near Pontypridd) and **Methyr Tydfil**, location of **Cyfarthfa Castle**, the most impressive monument of the Industrial Iron Age in South Wales.

You can get a great introduction to Cardiff by booking a City Sightseeing tour. You can get on and off the double-decker sightseeing bus as you wish. The tours operate daily from April through October, and the bus departs from in front of Cardiff Castle every thirty minutes. Tickets cost £7.00 for adults, £5.50 for students and senior citizens, and £3.00 for children. To see an overview of the tour, go to www.city-sightseeing.com.

Capitalize on Cardiff

Begin your tour at **Cardiff Castle.** From Cardiff Central Station, proceed past the bus station in front, turn right onto Wood Street, then left onto St. Mary Street, which becomes High Street. As High Street intersects with Castle Street, you will see the mighty castle right in front of you.

Cardiff Castle is a lavishly restored medieval fortress with 2,000-year-old Roman foundations, parts of which still exist today. The castle's extensive Roman walls, which were 10 feet thick, were well preserved by earthen banks until their excavation in the nineteenth century. Visit the Roman Wall exhibition area immediately behind the ticket kiosk just inside the main castle entrance.

The medieval stronghold built by invading Normans fell into ruin after the Civil War in the seventeenth century and was saved by the first Marquess of Bute in the late 1700s. The third Marquess of Bute and his pal, the eccentric architect William Burges, lavishly reconstructed Cardiff Castle to the nineteenth-century splendor we see today. The extravagant, opulent rooms are laden with an eclectic mix of decor and architectural features inspired by medieval England, Arabia, the Old Testament, Islam, even the fairy tales of Hans Christian Andersen. Each room has a different theme.

Today the castle interior provides the setting for medieval "Welsh Nights" and private or public receptions. The castle and its grounds provide a dramatic backdrop for a series of spectacular events throughout the summer, ranging from a hot-air balloon festival to massed military bands and, in case you have the urge to say "I do" in a castle, even enchanted weddings.

The castle is open daily all year except Christmas Day, Boxing Day, and New Year's Day. *Hours:* March–October 0930–1800 (last tour/entry at 1700); November–February 0930–1700 (last tour at 1600). Admission is £6.00 for adults, £3.70 for children age five to sixteen and seniors, £4.85 students. *Tel:* (029) 2087 8100; *Internet:* www.cardiffcastle.com; *E-mail:* cardiffcastle@cardiff.gov.uk.

Cardiff Civic Centre lies beyond the castle, as does the National Museum & Gallery. The **Civic Centre** is one of the most impressive buildings in Europe. Separated by wide avenues and parks, the presence in the spring of cherry blossoms and tulip beds creates a perfect setting for the white stone buildings.

The **National Museum & Gallery** in Cathays Park is unusual in that it contains a variety of exhibits, from priceless works of art to dinosaurs. *Hours:* 1000–1700 Tuesday–Sunday and bank holidays. For more information telephone (029) 2039 7951, or visit the National Museums & Galleries of Wales' Web site: www.nmgw.ac.uk. Admission is free.

Ready for shopping? Cardiff is a shopaholic's paradise. According to Cardiff Marketing Limited, Cardiff "offers the best shopping in Britain outside London," with more big-name retailers than any comparable British city. Seven Victorian shopping arcades blend well with three modern shopping areas. Cardiff claims to have had pedestrian shopping areas long before the phrase was invented. The two main shopping streets, Queen Street and Mary Street, form an L-shape that partially encloses Cardiff's largest shopping mall, **St. David's Centre.** For those with the "shop till you drop" philosophy, this is the place.

A visit to **Castle Welsh Crafts** is a must: 1 Castle Street, Cardiff CF1 2BS, South Glamorgan; *Tel:* (029) 2034 3038; *Internet:* www.castlewelsh crafts.co.uk. Located across the street from Cardiff Castle, this shop has traditional Welsh crafts, including intricately hand-carved lovespoons. The tradition of the Welsh peasantry to give their loved ones a carved wooden spoon as a token of affection goes back many centuries. In fact, the English term *spooning* is almost certainly derived from this old Welsh custom.

Some people believe that the presentation and the acceptance of the lovespoon was confirmation that a courtship was about to start; others believe the lovespoon represented an early form of engagement ring. Certain designs have specific meanings. For instance, the giving of a spoon shaped as leaves or trees represents growing love, a horseshoe represents good luck and happiness, and bells indicate marriage. The lovespoon makes a perfect Welsh souvenir or gift.

To sample some traditional Welsh dishes served by waitresses in heritage costume, try the **Blas ar Gymru (A Taste of Wales) Restaurant** at 48 Crwys Road, about a twenty-minute walk from Cardiff Castle. Proceed north through the Civic Centre to Corbett Road, turn right and cross the bridge into Cathays Terrace, right onto Woodville Road, and left onto Crwys Road. Reservations are advised; *Tel:* (029) 2038 2132.

We enjoyed lunch at **The Hogshead Owain Glyndwr,** St. Johns Street [*Tel:* (029) 2022 1980 or (029) 2039 9303], near St. John's Church in the pedestrian shopping area. Their menu says it all: "There's ne'er a moment so sweet when the best of friends choose to meet when conversation fills the air with a jug o' ale and hearty fayre. Eat with gusto, drink with cheer good ale, good food, and good atmosphere." Hours for eating are 1200 to 1800; pub-only hours are 1800 to 2300.

Techniquest, Britain's leading science discovery center, is located in Cardiff Bay. *Tel:* (029) 2047 5475; *Internet:* www.techniquest.org. Admission to Techniquest is £6.75 adult, £4.65 children younger than age seventeen. The area is also home to the Butte Street Maritime Museum, the Norwegian Church Arts Centre, Lightship 2000, the Point, and, last but not least, the world's most famous fish 'n' chips restaurant, **Harry Ramsden's.** *Tel:* (029) 2046 3334; *Fax:* (029) 2046 0693; *Internet:* www .harryramsdens.co.uk.

Since improving the harbor area is an ongoing process, new venues are rapidly being established. The **Cardiff Bay** area is definitely one of the "hot spots" of Britain. You can telephone the Cardiff Bay Visitor Centre at (029) 2022 7281 or visit www.cardiffbay.co.uk on the Internet. To get to Cardiff Bay Inner Harbour area, take Bus 7, 7A, 7E, 8, or CB1. Shuttle trains operate from Queen Street Station.

The **Museum of Welsh Life** at St. Fagan's is one of Europe's largest open-air folk museums. *Tel:* (029) 2057 3500; *Internet:* www.nmgw .ac.uk; *Hours:* 1000–1700 daily. Here you can travel through time from the Celtic village of 2,000 years ago to a miner's cottage of the 1980s. "Living" buildings depicting daily Welsh life were reconstructed stone by stone. You'll see an ornate timber-framed barn originally built around 1550, a working blacksmith and bakery shop, an Elizabethan manor (St. Fagan's Castle), a medieval farmhouse, and much, much more. To get there, take Bus No. 32 from Central Bus Station, Stand B1. Admission is free.

Waverley and *Balmoral* steamer cruises depart from Penarth Pier, 4 miles from Cardiff. Take the Valley Line train to Penarth or Bus L1, L2, P10, or P20 to Penarth Pier from the Central Bus Station. Cost varies.

The *Waverley* is the last seagoing paddle steamer in the world. Both the *Waverley* and the *Balmoral* are beautifully restored and each can carry up to 925 passengers. An afternoon cruise affords the spectacular scenery of Bristol Channel; romantics should opt for an evening cruise. The cruises are conducted by Waverly Excursions Ltd., *Tel:* (0845) 130 4647 or check with the tourist office; *Internet:* www.waverleyexcursions.co.uk.

Tredegar House is a magnificent country house set in ninety acres of parkland and gardens and was the home of one of the great Welsh families, the Morgans, for more than five centuries. See the vastly different lifestyles of those of "the manor born" and their servants. Located in Newport, it is a twenty-minute bus ride (No. 30) from Central Bus Station, Stand E2. *Hours:* Easter–September, Wednesday–Sunday 1130–1600; August, open daily; October, weekends only. Entrance fees: £5.40 adults; £3.95 seniors/students; children admitted free. After the tour, opt for a carriage ride, go boating on the lake, or visit the craft workshops.

Llanerch Vineyard is an international award-winning winery in the Vale of Glamorgan. Producing estate bottle white, rosé, and sparkling wines, it is the largest vineyard in Wales. Of course, you may sample a bit o' the juice during your tour. Take Bus 32 from Central Bus Station, Stand B1. Entrance fees: £3.00 adults. *Internet:* www.llanerch-vineyard .co.uk.

Second in size only to Windsor Castle, **Caerphilly Castle** is one of the largest fortresses in Europe and is a mere fifteen-minute train ride from Cardiff's Queen Street Station. This Norman castle covers thirty acres, is

Train Connections to Other Base Cities from Cardiff

Cardiff–Edinburgh

DEPART CARDIFF CENTRAL	ARRIVE EDINBURGH WAVERLY	NOTES
0610	1345	M–F (2)
0720	1442	M–F (2)
0815	1556	Su (2)
0850	1521	M–Sa (5)
0925	1642 (1639 Sa)	M–Sa (2)
1025	1738	Daily (2)
1125	1831	Su (2)
1150	1839	M–Sa (4)
1225	1956	Sa, Su (2)
1244	1930	M–F (1)
1344	2058	M–Sa (3)
1425	2146	Daily (2)
1525	2243	Daily (2)

(1) Change trains at Crewe

(2) Change trains at Bristol Parkway

(3) Change trains at Wilmslow

(4) Change trains at Derby

(5) Change trains at Gloucester

remarkably well preserved, plus it's crammed with interesting things, including a tower that even Oliver Cromwell's gunpowder could not topple—at least not completely. Trains depart Queen Street Station thrice hourly, or take Bus 26 at Stand B3 from the Central Bus Station. *Hours:* April–May 0930–1700 daily; June–September 28: 0930–1800 daily; September 29–October 26: 0930–1700 daily; October 27–March: 0930–1630 Monday–Saturday and 1100–1600 Sunday. Entrance fees are £3.00 for adults; £2.00 for children age five to sixteen. *Tel:* (029) 2088 3143; *Internet:* www.castlewales.com/caerphil.html or www.caerphillycastle.org; *E-mail:* tic@caerphilly.gov.uk. The visitor center has a wealth of information and a fabulous gift shop.

Not satisfied being a one-castle owner, John Marquess of Bute commissioned William Burges to design a little country retreat, **Castell Coch,** which is perched on a wooded hillside just a few miles north of Cardiff at Tongwynlais. Known as the "fairy-tale castle in the woods," Castell Coch appears to have been magically removed from the pages of *Sleeping Beauty*. Unfortunately, Billy Burges died suddenly in 1881 before completing his Victorian dream of the Middle Ages. Castell Coch was

Cardiff–Glasgow

DEPART CARDIFF CENTRAL	ARRIVE GLASGOW CENTRAL	NOTES
0620	1318 (1210 Sa)	M–Sa (1)
0715	1406	M–F (2)
0805	1452	M–F (3)
0925	1637	Su (1)
1044	1718 (1654 Sa)	M–Sa (1)
1144	1849	M–Sa (4)
1230	2029	Su (2)
1244	1926	Sa (2)
1425	2200	Su (1)
1444	2119	M–Sa (2)
1544	2213	Sa (2)
1625	2345	Su (1)
1644	2317	M–F (2)

(1) Change trains at Bristol Parkway

(2) Change trains at Crewe

(3) Change trains at Stockport

(4) Change trains at Wilmslow

Cardiff–London

DEPART CARDIFF CENTRAL	ARRIVE LONDON PADDINGTON	NOTES
0550 (0600 Su)	0800 (0820 Su)	Daily
0620	0825 (0823 Sa)	M–Sa
0650	0852	M–Sa
0720	0915	M–F
0755	1000 (1003 Sa)	M–Sa
0815	1039	Su
0825	1027 (1029 Sa)	M–Sa
0925	1130 (1125 Sa, 1145 Su)	Daily
Continuing service at 25 and 55 min past each hour until 1925		Daily
2127 (2125 Su)	2338 (2335 Su)	M–F, Su

completed by colleagues who remained faithful to the rich, detailed decor, grandeur, and allusion of medieval architecture. To reach Castell Coch [*Tel:* (029) 2081 0101], take Bus 26 from Cardiff Central Bus Station, Stand B3. Entrance fees are £3.00 for adults, £2.00 for children age five to sixteen.

If you would rather sit and reflect on your day or daydream of days of yore, we suggest visiting one of the oldest restaurants in the area, **The Courthouse,** *Tel:* (029) 2088 8120. The view of Caerphilly Castle is spectacular; the back patio overlooks the moat, the walkway encircles the castle grounds, and the antique decor is almost as enticing as the ale. The Courthouse is on your left as you wind down the hill from the rail station toward the castle or on your right if you are ascending the incline.

Day Excursions

After you've seen Cardiff and its nearby attractions, you may want to venture farther afield. Visit Bath to learn more about Roman England, opt for visiting the most western point of England, the pirates' Penzance, or Plymouth, whose historical heritage is closely related to America. Or see the ideal Swansea and the Mumbles in South Wales. And there is always Tenby for the resort lover.

Day Excursion

Bath
Roman England—The Original Hot Tub

From Cardiff: Depart from Cardiff Central Station
Distance by train: 53 miles (62 km)
Average train time: 1 hour, 15 minutes
From London: Depart from London's Paddington Station
Distance by train: 107 miles (172 km)
Average train time: 1 hour, 30 minutes
Train information and InterCity services: (0845) 748 4950
Tourist information: Bath Tourism Bureau, Abbey Chambers, Abbey Church Yard, Bath BA1 1LY; *Tel:* (0906) 711 2000 (50 pence per minute); outside U.K., 011 44 (870) 444 6442; *Fax:* (01225) 477787
Internet: www.visitbath.co.uk or www.heritagecities.co.uk
E-mail: tourism@bathnes.gov.uk
Hours: October 1–April 30: Monday–Saturday 0930–1700; May 1–September 30: 0930–1800 Monday–Saturday; all year Sunday 1000–1600.
Notes: To reach the information center on foot, proceed up Manvers Street directly in front of the Bath Spa rail station until you cross North Parade Road at the traf-

fic light. At this point, you will see the Bath Abbey tower to your left. Looking to your left, enter York Street and proceed until reaching an open square on the right. The tourist information center will be in the building on the right of the square on the ground floor.

The **Roman Baths** (*Internet:* www.romanbaths.co.uk) are one of Britain's major tourist attractions and draw visitors from all points of the globe to their waters. The baths rank a close second to England's number one attraction, the Tower of London, and are well worth the short train ride from either Cardiff or London to see them and the "glory that was Rome," transposed to England.

Bath has been in the limelight as the social center "to see and be seen" during two eras of recorded history—once during the Roman occupation of Britain and again in the eighteenth century when Bath became the "gathering place" for royalty and other well-to-do folk. Development of the only hot springs in Britain is attributed to the Romans soon after Emperor Claudius invaded the land in A.D. 43.

To the Romans, the city's name was Aquae Sulis—literally translated, it means "the waters of Sulis." By the end of the first century, the Romans had established a great bathing facility. The magnificent hot baths were said to have curative powers. There is no doubt that the only hot mineral springs in Britain played a major role in establishing Bath as the "hot spot" for socializing.

The baths made *Aquae Sulis* famous throughout the empire. Its fame lasted 400 years until the rising sea level and the fall of the Roman Empire brought the city's prosperity to an end. By the end of the seventh century, the city was described as "a ghostly ruin with crumbled masonry fallen into dark pools, overgrown and bird haunted, but still a wondrous sight."

The second revitalization of the city, a cultural one, began in 1705 with the arrival of thirty-one-year-old Richard Nash. Like the Romans, he too conquered, but not by force. Nash was Bath's first public-relations expert. It was during his "reign" that Queen Anne visited Bath, and it again became an elegant and stylish resort for the wealthy. By the time Nash died at the age of eighty-seven, he had created a kingdom of taste and etiquette over which he reigned as Beau Nash, King of Bath.

Although the hot springs were used again from the Middle Ages, the Roman ruins remained buried during most of Beau Nash's time. Finally, the gilded bronze head of Minerva was uncovered by workmen digging a sewer in 1727. The statues and columns of present-day Roman baths were added by Victorian restorers, but the original bath area still has the lead floor and limestone paving installed by the Romans.

Cardiff–Bath–Cardiff

DEPART CENTRAL STATION	ARRIVE BATH SPA STATION	NOTES
0730	0835	M–Sa
0800	0918	Su
0830	0935 (0941 Su)	Daily
0905	1014	Sa
0930	1035 (1043 Su)	Daily
1009	1116	Sa
1030	1135 (1147 Su)	Daily
1100	1218	Sa
1130 (1135 Su)	1235 (1243 Su)	Daily
1230	1335	Daily

DEPART BATH SPA STATION	ARRIVE CENTRAL STATION	NOTES
1531	1630 (1644 Sa)	Daily
1624 (1625 Su)	1742 (1737 Sa, 1735 Su)	Daily
1637	1754	Su
1657	1828	M–Sa
1721	1848	Su
1729	1836	M–Sa
1800	1918	Su
1816	1929	Su
1822	1936	Su
1828	1944	M–Sa
1859	2018	Su
1929 (1916 Su)	2038 (2036 Su)	Daily
1955	2115	Su

Frequent service until 2237 M–F, 2149 Sa, and 2226 Su.

The real restoration and melding of Bath's Roman past and of the city's two eras of fame began in 1878 when the city engineer, while investigating a water leak, came upon the Roman reservoir and the huge complex of baths that it fed. Someone finally called a plumber.

Visitors to Bath can once again bathe in the city's natural thermal waters. The Bath Spa project combined the old with the new to produce a most remarkable health and leisure complex. The Sacred Cross Bath has been restored as a working spa, and a new state-of-the-art glass and stone building houses thermal pools, saunas, whirlpools, massage and treatment room, and a cafe.

Bath abounds in sightseeing opportunities. Bath Parade Guides, composed of thirty experienced, well-informed Blue Badge guides, specialize

London–Bath–London

Direct trains from London Paddington Station only; other service is available from London Waterloo Station and may require a change of trains.

DEPART PADDINGTON STATION	ARRIVE BATH SPA STATION	NOTES
0715	0845 (0844 Sa)	M–Sa
0745	0905	M–Sa
0800	0936	Su
0815	0945	M–Sa
0845	1010 (1009 Sa)	M–Sa
0915	1045	M–Sa
0930	1103	Su
0945	1112	M–F
1015	1140	M–Sa
1030	1158	Su

Plus other frequent service until 2345 (2330 Su) daily.

DEPART BATH SPA STATION	ARRIVE PADDINGTON STATION	NOTES
1422 (1442 Sa, 1441 Su)	1555 (1610 Sa, 1658 Su)	Daily
1452 (1503 Sa)	1623 (1718 Sa)	M–Sa
1522	1655	Daily
1541 (1542 Sa)	1755 (1710 Sa)	M–Sa (1)
1552	1725	M–F
1612	1740 (1750 Su)	Sa, Su
1652	1827 (1815 Sa, 1820 Su)	Daily
1712	1840	Sa
1722	1858 (1856 Sa)	M–Sa
1752 (1742 Sa, Su)	1924 (1908 Sa, 1915 Su)	Daily
1822 (1812 Sa, 1815 Su)	1955 (1940 Sa, 1950 Su)	Daily

Plus other frequent service until 2252 (2200 Su) daily.
(1) Arrives London Waterloo Station

in walking tours and Jane Austen tours. *Tel:* (01225) 426621; *Fax:* (01225) 337111; *Internet:* www.bathparadeguides.co.uk; *Hours:* Monday–Sunday 1100–1630 year-round.

Jane Austen fans will want to visit the **Jane Austen Centre** at 40 Gay Street to discover more about the importance of Bath in the great novelist's life and works. *Hours:* 1000–1730 daily year-round (1030–1730 Sunday). Admission: £4.45 adults, £2.45 children age six to fifteen,

£3.65 student/senior. *Tel:* (01225) 443000; *Internet:* www.janeausten.co.uk; *E-mail:* curator@jane austen.co.uk.

Those interested in fashion over the last 400 years will want to visit the **Museum of Costume and Assembly Rooms** (No. 25 on the pamphlet map), located on Bennett Street. Then, turn left onto Bennett Street and proceed to nearby **No. 1 Royal Crescent** (No. 29 on the pamphlet map) to tour the beautifully restored eighteenth-century town house designed by John Wood. *Internet:* www.museumofcostume.co.uk or www.bath-preservation-trust.org.uk.

Bath has won many awards for its floral displays, and its natural beauty makes a walking tour through the city a real pleasure. The tourist information center has a wealth of information about the city and its surroundings. The Tourist Information Centre sells a wide range of publications to help you get the most out of your stay. We recommend pamphlet 35, *Leisure Attractions in and around Bath*. This informative piece contains a city map and lists places of interest.

If you are on a tight schedule, the best sights in the city are clustered about the Roman Baths. The baths and the abbey practically adjoin each other. Upstairs from the baths, you may visit the Pump Room, which also contains a restaurant for lunch and light refreshments. Take time to touch the worn paving, and in that moment you can recall the glory that was the empire of Rome.

Day Excursion to

Penzance
Western End of the Line

From Cardiff: Depart from Cardiff Central Station
Distance by train: 245 miles (394 km)
Average train time: 5 hours, 30 minutes
From London: Depart from Paddington Station
Distance by train: 305 miles (491 km)
Average train time: 5 hours
Train information and InterCity services: (0845) 748 4950
Tourist information: Tourist Information Centre, Station Road, Penzance, Cornwall TR18 2NF; *Tel:* (01736) 362207; *Fax:* (01736) 363600
Internet: www.penzance.co.uk
Hours: Please call for hours.
Notes: The tourist information center is located immediately outside the rail station. The first item of information you should collect at the center is a Penzance & District map. This graphic presentation of the peninsula will help you put the area into the proper perspective for your visit. Publications that are available in the information center will be extremely helpful.

W hen you arrive in Penzance, you are literally at "the end of the line" insofar as rail travel is concerned. Geographically speaking, you are also at the western end of England. A mere 10 miles more would bring you to Land's End, where a road sign pointing to the west cryptically states, AMERICA 4,000 MILES. It is difficult to find a grander coastline. This is Land's End Peninsula—the sightseeing opportunities are endless.

Once you are fully armed with the publications needed to explore this most interesting area, we are certain that you will be immediately attracted to the harbor area lying to the left just beyond the rail terminal. We suggest making it your first "port of call," since it can readily put you in the proper adventurous mood to see the rest of the area.

At harborside inspect the old warehouse and granary overlooking Battery Rocks, which has been converted to a craft center and art gallery. Next door is the **Dolphin Inn,** formerly a smugglers' hideaway and said to be haunted by an old sea captain's ghost. From there, a walk up Chapel Street away from the harbor brings you to a part of Old Penzance filled with Georgian town houses, fishermen's cottages, and the **Museum of Nautical Art.** This unusual museum, in the form of an eighteenth-century battleship with gun decks and life-size figures manning muzzleloading guns, is filled with displays of actual navigational gear from former times. The museum is well worth a visit and is a delight to young and old alike.

For a unique treat, visit the **Trinity House National Lighthouse Centre,** which holds probably the largest and finest collection of lighthouse equipment in the world. Located on Wharf Road [*Tel:* (01736) 360077], it is open daily 1030–1630 Easter to October. Within the center, you can relax in the audiovisual theater and enjoy your trip back in time to the first lighthouses, those lonely citadels that guarded the treacherous waters around England's shores. Admission: £3.00 adult, £1.00 children, £2.00 senior/student.

Termed the "Capital of the Cornish Riviera," Penzance occupies an unusually well-sheltered position on England's western coast. Because the town faces due south and is protected from all other points of the compass by a ring of hills, its climate is ideal year-round. Winter is mild and virtually without frost, followed by an early spring and a temperate summer. Botanically, Penzance is noted for its early flowers and produce.

You need not confine yourself to the limits of Penzance, although you'll find it almost impossible to get away from its magnetic attractions. Local bus service can take you to **Land's End,** and rail connections (inquire at the rail station) can be made to other equally interesting points on the peninsula such as Falmouth, Newquay, and St. Ives. The tourist

Cardiff–Penzance–Cardiff

DEPART CENTRAL STATION	ARRIVE PENZANCE STATION	NOTES
0600	1208	M–F (2) or (3)
0715	1400	Su (2)
0800	1413	M–F (1), (2), or (3)
0915	1427	Sa (1) or (2)
1000	1607	M–F (2) or (3)
1100	1707	M–Sa
1200	1723	Sa (2)
1330	1849	Su (2)

DEPART PENZANCE STATION	ARRIVE CENTRAL STATION	NOTES
0615, 0721, 0848, 1100	1701	Sa (1)
0652, 0719, 0846, 0922	1610	M–F (1), (2), or (3)
0830	1947 or 2050	Su (1), (2), or (3)
0953	1947 or 2050	Su (1), (2), or (3)
1012	1610	M–F
1119	1947 or 2050	Su (1), (2), or (3)
1140	1654	M–F
1205	1947 or 2050	Su (1), (2), or (3)
1226	1956	M–F (2)
1332	1947 or 2050	Su
1450	1956	M–F (1) or (2)

(1) Change trains at Taunton

(2) Change trains at Bristol Temple Meads

(3) Change trains at Exeter St. Davids

information center can give you the background on these interesting places, and you can ask the Rail Travel Centre in the train station to work out the needed schedules.

From Cardiff or London, Penzance lends itself more to an "out-and-back" excursion than to a day excursion, although it is possible to visit England's westernmost town in the course of a day and still be back in Cardiff or London that evening.

An excellent way to visit Penzance is to board the sleeper that departs from London's Paddington Station just before midnight. You can board about an hour before departure time, have the attendant make a night-cap for you, and be well into dreamland by the time the train rolls out of London's suburbs. At 0820 you arrive in Penzance Station after being awakened by the attendant bringing your morning tea or coffee and biscuits. After a full day's sightseeing in Penzance, you can board either the sleeper departing at 2200 to return to London or the InterCity 125 at

London–Penzance

Schedules shown are for direct service that departs from London Paddington Station. Other services are possible by changing trains in Plymouth or by departing from London Waterloo and changing at Exeter St. Davids Station.

DEPART PADDINGTON STATION	ARRIVE PENZANCE STATION	NOTES
0745 (0735 Sa)	1315 (1254 Sa)	M–Sa
0800	1400	Su
0845	1427	Sa
0915	1452	Su
0933	1448	Sa
1030	1535	Sa
1035	1534	M–F
1115	1656	Su
1130	1635	Sa
1135	1653	M–F
1235	1810	Sa
1315	1842	Su
1335	1854	M–Sa
1433	2015	Su
1515	2045	Su
1535	2050	M–Sa
1615	2152	Su
1635	2217	M–F
1804	2304	M–F
1830	2355	Sa, Su
1903	0018	M–F
2350	0828	M–Th, Su

Last train shown conveys first- and standard-class sleepers and standard-class chair cars. Arrival time shown is next day. Reservations required for all overnight sleeper trains.

1630 (change in Plymouth) to return to London by 2222 or depart at 1730 and arrive in London at 2315 the same evening.

Penzance also offers a diversion. When you feel it's time to move on from London to the north toward Edinburgh, check out of your London accommodations and take the sleeper to Penzance. Go sightseeing in Penzance, then arrive back in London as previously described at 2222 and transfer leisurely to London's Euston Station to board a Caledonian Sleeper at 2340. You'll arrive in Edinburgh the next morning at 0717.

Sleeper reservations should be made well in advance. Don't wait until the last minute or you may be disappointed, especially during holidays and peak summer travel periods. Reservations may be made in the rail station

Penzance–London

DEPART PENZANCE STATION	ARRIVE PADDINGTON STATION	NOTES
0634	1156	M–F
0642	1159	Sa
0834	1400	Sa
0838	1417	M–F
0840	1425	Su
0939	1440	Sa
0944	1500	Su
0947	1447	M–F
1038	1550	Sa
1041	1611	Su
1142	1700	Sa, Su
1244	1815	Su
1335	1855	Sa
1346	1852	M–F
1350	1922	Su
1442	2008	Su
1541	2053	Sa, Su
1600	2117	M–F
1646	2236	Su
1730	2243	Sa
1730	2314	F Only
1730	2329	Su
2200	0511	M–F

The last train shown conveys first- and standard-class sleepers and standard-class chair cars. Arrival time shown is the next day. Reservations are required for all overnight sleeper trains.

once you are in Britain. Don't forget to check the standard-class sleeper availability if first class is filled. Sometimes if you show up on the departure platform about half an hour before the train leaves, you can pick up a berth cancellation, but don't count on it.

Day Excursion to

Plymouth
Pilgrim's Progress Port

From Cardiff: Depart from Cardiff Central Station
Distance by train: 166 miles (267 km)
Average train time: 3 hours, 15 minutes
From London: Depart from Paddington Station

Distance by train: 226 miles (363 km)

Average train time: 3 hours

Train information and InterCity services: (0845) 748 4950

Tourist information: Plymouth Tourist Information, Island House, 9 The Barbican
   Plymouth, Devon PL1 2LS; *Tel:* (01752) 304849; *Fax:* (01752) 257955

Internet: www.plymouthcity.co.uk

Hours: Monday–Saturday 0900–1700, Sundays and bank holidays 1000–1600.

Notes: You can reach the tourist information center, located in Plymouth's Elizabethan quarter, on foot from the train station in about twenty minutes through
   short underground passages and a pedestrian area. Look for the streams, fountains, and gardens, which form part of an outstanding display. If you don't feel
   like walking, then take Bus No. 25 (the "hop-on-hop-off" service), or board any
   bus stopping at the shelter to the right of the station entrance. Pay your fare and
   ask to be "deposited" at the Barbican. Folks who are in a real hurry can hail a taxi.
   There is also a taxi queue just outside of the rail station; the bus stop is a few
   steps beyond.

Plymouth has one of the finest natural harbors in Europe. From
Plymouth Hoe (a Saxon word meaning "high place above the sea"),
there are magnificent views over Plymouth Sound and the harbor. Stand
on this huge brow of a hill, one of the world's finest natural promenades,
and you stand in the midst of history. Sir Francis Drake continued his
game of bowls here before setting out to deal with the Spanish Armada in
1588. Earlier, in 1577, he set sail from the same harbor in the *Golden Hind*
on a three-year voyage around the world. Here, too, in 1620 the Pilgrims
embarked on the *Mayflower* for the New World. Too few remember that
the first airplane to cross the Atlantic Ocean, the U.S. Navy seaplane *NC4*,
touched down in Plymouth Sound. This spot is indeed steeped in historical heritage, much of it related to America. Stand here proudly!

While at the tourist information office, ask for a copy of the pamphlet
Plymouth in Your Pocket; it contains an easy-to-read map of things to see
and do within and near Plymouth. For an introduction to Plymouth, visit
the **National Marine Aquarium** or see the **Plymouth Dome**. Situated
on Plymouth's famous Hoe, the Dome is one of the most up-to-date centers of its kind in Britain. Here you can take a journey through time, use
high-resolution cameras to zoom the shoreline, and enjoy many other
exciting activities. We guarantee you won't run out of things to do while
in Plymouth.

The Plymouth of today is a city of two distinct parts: the original Elizabethan harbor area called the "Barbican" and the modern city center
that rose from the devastation and debris of World War II. If your time in
Plymouth is limited, concentrate on visiting the Barbican area of the city.

The Barbican section, where the old town of Plymouth is nestled,
derived its name from the fact that at the entrance to the harbor stood an

Cardiff–Plymouth–Cardiff

CARDIFF *Plymouth*

DEPART CENTRAL STATION	ARRIVE PLYMOUTH STATION	NOTES
0610	0918	M–F
0715	1400	Su (1), (2)
0800	1159	M–F
0900	1224	M–F
1000	1334	M–F
1110	1347	M–F (2)

DEPART PLYMOUTH STATION	ARRIVE CENTRAL STATION	NOTES
1300	1701	Sa (1)
1325	1717	M–F
1439	1956 or 2023	M–F (1), (2)
1453	1947 or 2050	Su (1)
1550	1956	M–F, Su (1), (2)
1614	2023	M–F
1558	1947	Su (1)
1608	1946	Su (2)
1652	1956	M–F
1710	2035 (2007 Sa, 2050 Su)	Daily (1)
1825 (1828 Su)	2130 (2237 Su)	Sa, Su (1)
1900	2158	Sa (1)
1930	2233	M–F (1)
1925	2338	Su

(1) Change trains at Bristol Parkway or Temple Meads
(2) Change trains at Exeter St. Davids

London—Plymouth—London

DEPART LONDON PADDINGTON STATION	ARRIVE PLYMOUTH STATION	NOTES
0735	1059	Sa
0745	1120	M–F
0800	1203	Su
0845	1229	Sa

DEPART PLYMOUTH STATION	ARRIVE LONDON PADDINGTON STATION	NOTES
1540	1855	M–Sa
1640	2000	Su
1800	2117 (2135 Su)	M–F, Su
1840	2220	Sa

outpost of the ancient Plymouth Castle. According to castle phraseology, such outer fortifications were called barbicans. The Barbican was spared much of the damage that Plymouth suffered during the bombardments of World War II. Consequently, there are still many old buildings and narrow streets in this area that recapture the Elizabethan atmosphere.

One Barbican landmark of particular interest to U.S. citizens is a **memorial stone** marking the place on the harbor pier from which the *Mayflower* sailed. Historic Elizabethan buildings include the **Black Friars Distillery,** home of Plymouth Gin since 1793. The distillery is still operating in buildings formerly used as a monastery and dating from 1425. Visitors are welcome. The **Merchants House** on St. Andrews Street is the largest and finest structure remaining from the sixteenth and seventeenth centuries. Restored, it is open daily, except Mondays (April–September), displaying Plymouth's history with the theme, "Tinker, Tailor, Soldier, Sailor . . ."

The **Plymouth Mayflower Centre** is Plymouth's newest attraction. Through films, models, and interactive games and historical artifacts, you can enjoy all the stories of emigration from Plymouth in the nineteenth century and learn about the fascinating Barbican history. It's located on Barbican Quay near the Barbican Glassworks. For more details, contact the Tourist Information Centre.

Towering over the Barbican, the **Royal Citadel,** built in the 1660s by Charles II, was erected as a warning to the citizens of Plymouth. Many of the fortress cannons still point toward the town and not out to sea, as one would normally expect them to do. They are open to the public daily between May 1 and September 30 for guided tours.

If you have ever sung a chorus or two of "The Eddystone Light," you are a likely customer for the engrossing book *The Four Eddystone Lighthouses,* by Robert Sanderson. Additional information on the lighthouses may also be found in the booklet *Smeaton's Tower and the Plymouth Breakwater.* The first Eddystone lighthouse was blown down in a storm. The second lighthouse withstood the elements but was destroyed by fire. **Smeaton's Tower** stood on the Eddystone Reef from 1759 to 1884 and subsequently was re-erected on Plymouth Hoe

If your urge "to go down to the sea in ships" overwhelms you, take a boat trip on **Plymouth Sound.** The information center has the details, including how to view the nearby **Royal Naval Base** at Devonport. If your call to the sea is more limited, browsing in the Barbican area will suffice if you throw an occasional glance seaward

Day Excursion to

Swansea
The "Ugly, Lovely Town"

Depart from Cardiff Central Station
Distance by train: 46 miles (74 km)
Average train time: 50 minutes
Train information and InterCity services: (0845) 748 4950
Tourist information: Tourist Board, Singleton Street, Swansea SA1 3QG; *Tel:* (01792) 468321; *Fax:* (01792) 464602
Internet: www.swansea.gov.uk
E-mail: tourism@swansea.gov.uk
Hours: Monday–Saturday 0930–1730.
Notes: Take any bus from the rail station to the bus station. The tourist center is just opposite the bus station. On foot, it's a ten- to fifteen-minute walk.

Birthplace of poet and playwright Dylan Thomas (1914–1953), who once referred to Swansea as the "ugly, lovely town," Swansea is the gateway to West Wales. Now Wales' second-largest city, it boasts one of Europe's most striking and successful waterfront developments. During the eighteenth and nineteenth centuries, Swansea became an important industrial center when the port was developed to export coal and its rapidly growing copper products.

Thanks to heavy destruction in World War II, Swansea's city center was rebuilt to include pedestrianized shopping areas. In 1974 it was expanded to include the scenic sandy beaches and resort area, the Gower Peninsula, which was designated Britain's first area of "Outstanding Natural Beauty."

Enjoy a panoramic view of Swansea Bay from the **Observatory Tower** in the magnificent Maritime Quarter. There's a footpath that runs from the Maritime Quarter for about 5 miles along the seafront to the Mumbles, a charming little resort. The 900-foot Victorian **Mumbles Pier** is one of Swansea's most famous landmarks and affords an excellent view of Swansea Bay. Hungry? Along Mumbles Mile, you'll find no shortage of excellent restaurants and pubs.

The world's first **Lovespoon Gallery** opened in the Mumbles in 1987 and features more than 300 designs of the traditional hand-carved Welsh gift of love. Visit daily from 1000 to 1730. Since the seventeenth century, Welshmen have given hand-carved wooden spoons, known as "lovespoons," to their lady friends as a prelude to courtship and an indication of their serious intentions. Over the years the carved designs on the spoons became more intricate, and certain symbols took on definitive meanings. For example, intricately carved boxes with balls inside came

Cardiff–Swansea–Cardiff

DEPART CENTRAL STATION	ARRIVE SWANSEA STATION	NOTES
0753	0849	M–Sa
0835	0929	Sa
0846	0957	M–F
0901	0956	M–F
1000	1055	M–Sa
1040	1200	Su
1100 (1105 Sa)	1155 (1158 Sa)	M–Sa
1139 (1135 Sa)	1243 (1218 Sa)	M–Sa
1200	1255	M–F

Then two or three departures hourly until 2300 M–F, until 1957 Sa; then five more trains until 2320. Hourly trains Su, then two per hour until 2150, then 2210 and 2310.

DEPART SWANSEA STATION	ARRIVE CENTRAL STATION	NOTES
1430	1525	M–Sa
1458	1615	Su
1530	1625	Daily
1530	1655	M–Sa
1600	1653	Su
1630	1725	Daily
1700	1754	Su
1730	1825	Daily
1735	1843	M–Sa
1830	1925	Daily
1900	2008	Su
1935	2037	Sa
2027	2128 (2155 Sa)	Daily
2100	2155	Su

to mean the number of children desired. Then, carved chains added to the spoon indicated the number of years together. Perhaps over the years, the original "prelude to courtship" lovespoon matured into the "ball and chain" anniversary spoon.

The heart of Swansea is a square bounded by four streets: Princess Way on the east side, Westway on the west, The Kingsway along the north, and Oystermouth Road on the south side. Within the square, you'll find the tourist information center, the Grand Theatre, St. David's Square, the Quadrant Centre, two shopping districts, and Swansea's famous **Covered Market,** featuring everything from antiques and books to

Schedules shown are for direct trains. Additional service is available by changing trains in Cardiff.

DEPART PADDINGTON STATION	ARRIVE SWANSEA STATION	NOTES
0700	0956	M–F
0700	0957	Sa
0800	1055 (1053 Sa)	M–Sa
0830	1200	Su
0900	1155 (1158 Sa)	M–Sa
0927	1218	Sa
1000	1255 (1328 Su)	Daily
1030	1342	M–F

Daily hourly service continues after 1100 until 1600 (2100 Sa, 2200 Su), then every half hour until 1900, then 2000, 2100, and 2210 M–F.

DEPART SWANSEA STATION	ARRIVE PADDINGTON STATION	NOTES
1430	1730 (1728 Sa)	M–Sa
1530	1829 (1829 Sa, Su)	Daily
1600	1900	Su
1630	1930 (1929 Sa, 1930 Su)	Daily
1730	2028 (2035 Su)	Daily
1830	2130 (2140 Su)	Daily

Seat reservations are available for above-listed trains.

pottery and fresh produce. Try the local delicacy, a spicy meat dish called hot faggots and peas.

Unfortunately, **Swansea's Maritime and Industrial Museum** is closed for expansion and reconstruction. However, at press time, the all new **National Waterfront Museum** is scheduled to open late fall 2004. *Tel:* (01792) 653763 for more information.

The **Abbey Woollen Mill** at the museum features the stages of manufacturing woolen products, and you can take home finished traditional Welsh woolen goods. Admission is free and the finished products are sold at bargain factory prices, so bring your credit card. The Maritime Quarter also is home to a leisure center, theater, arts workshops, and, of course, marinas dotted with colorful boats and yachts.

Follow the Dylan Thomas Trail around the Maritime Quarter to Dylan Thomas Square, where you will find the Dylan Thomas Theatre and a statue of Swansea's most famous son. Check out the Dylan Thomas Web site, www.dylanthomas.com, and visit Swansea's unique **Dylan Thomas Centre**, open 1000–1630 Tuesday–Sunday.

Excursion to

Tenby
Scenic Seaside Resort

Depart from Cardiff Central Station
Distance by train: 168 km (104 miles)
Average train time: 3 hours, 9 minutes
Train information and InterCity services: (0845) 748 4950
Tourist information: Tourist Information Centre, The Croft, Tenby SA70 8AP; *Tel:* (01834) 842402; *Fax:* (01834) 845439
Internet: www.virtualtenby.co.uk/
Hours: Open daily 1000–1730, with extended hours July–August 1000–2100.
Notes: To get to the tourist office, walk straight ahead from the rail station along Warren Street. At the crossroads, continue onward onto White Lion Street for 100 yards, then turn left onto The Norton. Continue for another 150 yards until you see the sea railings across the street from the Pelican crosswalk. Turn left onto The Croft. The center is on the left side overlooking the sea.

History buffs, as well as seaside-and-sun-soakers, will enjoy this picturesque walled town and lively resort. Evidence of coins indicates that Tenby probably existed in some form during Roman times, but it was not until about 875 when it was first mentioned in a poem, referred to as Dynbych-y-Pysgod (Fortlet of the Fishes).

Take Bridge Street down to the harbor, dotted with small, colorful boats and redolent with the scents of the sea. Take a boat trip to **Caldey Island,** where excavations revealed human remains from the Stone Age. Just 2 miles south of Tenby, Caldey measures about 2 miles wide and less than a mile long. The main attraction on the island is the **Caldey Abbey,** built in 1910 by Anglican Benedictine monks who first came to the island in 1906. The abbey was sold in 1926 to the austere Cistercian monks who occupy it today.

The tower on top of Castle Hill was first documented in 1153. Although the castle fell into ruins by 1386, Tenby continued to prosper as a port by importing wines and salt and exporting coal, culm, and cloth until the seventeenth century, when the town again suffered decline. During the Victorian era Tenby was rescued by the opening of the railway and by Sir William Paxton, among others, who developed Tenby as a resort for well-heeled tourists. Paxton's grand bathhouse promoted seawater as a cure for several ailments.

The **Tenby Museum & Art Gallery** is open daily 1000–1700; call (01834) 842809 for more information. The Tenby Lifeboat is exhibited year-round, and the museum features rotating art exhibitions, such as the watercolors of Augustus John.

Cardiff–Tenby–Cardiff

DEPART CENTRAL STATION	ARRIVE TENBY STATION	NOTES
0540	0829 (0839 Sa)	M–Sa
0950	1255	Su
1101	1354	M–Sa
1310	1542	Sa
1425	1751	Su
1639	1942	M–F
1839	2140	Daily

DEPART TENBY STATION	ARRIVE CENTRAL STATION	NOTES
1545 (1541 Sa)	1822	M–Sa
1653	2008	Su
1845	2121 (2155 Sa)	M–Sa
1916	2155	Su
2045	2353	M–F

+1=Arrives next day

London–Tenby

All service requires a change of trains in Cardiff; for schedules from London to Tenby, see the separate tables for London to Cardiff and Cardiff to Tenby, or visit the schedule pages on www.railpass.com.

The town's surviving sections of its thirteenth-century walls are about 20 feet high and stretch along the base of the promontory. Armed with a map from the tourist office, you can conduct your own walking tour of this charming little town. From the famous five-arched St. George's Gate, turn right onto St. George's Street and proceed to St. Mary's Church on the left-hand side. Most of what we see today was extensively modified in the fifteenth and nineteenth centuries.

On Quay Hill, just east of St. Mary's Church, is a rare example of a successful merchant's home during the late fifteenth century. This is the three-story **Tudor Merchant's House,** open April–October, Monday–Saturday 1000–1700 (closed Wednesday), Sunday 1300–1700; *Tel:* (01834) 842279.

Appendix

CALLING THE UNITED KINGDOM

To telephone or send a fax to the United Kingdom from the United States, you must first use the international dialing code 011. Then dial the United Kingdom country code 44. All of the area codes within Britain start with a 0, but you do not use it when you are dialing from the United States. For example, to telephone the tourist information office in Bath from the United States, dial 011 44 (870) 444 6442.

BRITISH TOURIST INFORMATION CENTERS

Below is a listing of British tourist information centers applicable to cities appearing in this edition.

Key to Listing:

✖ Train/railway
✭ National Express Coach
● Wheelchair/ramps
(B) Book-a-Bed-Ahead accommodations for personal callers (for same or next night) in any town with a tourist information center offering this service.
† Accommodation services available to personal callers (for same or next night)
(E) Bureau de Change currency exchange

BRITAIN
BTA British Visitor Centre ✖ ✬ ● (B)
✝ (E)
1 Regent Street
Piccadilly Circus
London SW1Y 4XT
Tel: (020) 7846 9000
Fax: (020) 7563 0302
Internet: www.visitbritain.com

ENGLAND
English Tourist Board
Thames Tower
Blacks Road
Hammersmith, London W6 9EL
Tel: (020) 8563 3362
Internet: www.travelengland.org.uk

Bath
Bath Tourism Bureau ✖ ✬ ● (B) ✝ (E)
Abbey Chambers
Abbey Church Yard
Bath, Somerset BA1 1LY
Tel: (0906) 711 2000
Accommodations: (0870) 420 1278
Fax: (01225) 477787
Internet: www.visitbath.co.uk or
    www.heritagecities.co.uk
E-mail: tourism@bathnes.gov.uk

Birmingham
Tourism Centre & Ticket Shop ✖ ✬ ●
    (B) ✝
The Rotunda
150 New Street
Birmingham B2 4PA
Tel: (0121) 202 5099
Fax: (0121) 616 1038
Internet: www.beinbirmingham.com
E-mail: callcentre@marketing
    birmingham.com

Birmingham Convention and Visitor
    Bureau ✖ ✬ ● (B) ✝
National Exhibition Centre
Birmingham, West Midlands B40 1NT
Tel: (0121) 202 5099

Brighton
Brighton & Hove Visitor Information
    Centre ✖ ✬ ● (B) ✝
10 Bartholomew Square
Brighton, East Sussex BN1 1JS
Tel: (0906) 711 2255
Accommodations: (0345) 573512
Fax: (01273) 292594
Internet: www.visitbrighton.com
E-mail: brighton-tourism@brighton
    -hove.gov.uk

Bury St. Edmunds
The Tourist Information Centre (B) ✝
6 Angel Hill
Bury St. Edmunds, Suffolk IP33 1UZ
Tel: (01284) 764667
Fax: (01284) 757084
Internet: www.stedmundsbury.gov.uk
E-mail: tic@stedsbc.gov.uk

Cambridge
Tourist Information Centre ✖ ✬ ●
    (B) ✝
The Old Library
Wheeler Street
Cambridge CB2 3QB
Tel: (0906) 586 2526
Fax: (01223) 457588
Internet: www.visitcambridge.org
E-mail: tourism@cambridge.gov.uk

Canterbury
Canterbury Information Centre (B) ✝
12–13 Sun Street, The Buttermarket
Canterbury, Kent CT1 2HX
Tel: (01227) 378100
Fax: (01227) 378101
Internet: www.canterbury.co.uk
E-mail: canterburyinformation@
    canterbury.co.uk

Chester
Visitor and Craft Centre ✖ ✬ ● (B)
    ✝ (E)
Vicar's Lane
Chester, Cheshire CH1 1QX

Tel: (01244) 351609
Fax: (01244) 403188
Internet: www.chestercc.gov.uk or
www.heritagecities.co.uk
E-mail: tis@chestercc.gov.uk

Chester Centre ✖ ✯ ● (B) †
Town Hall
Northgate Street
Chester, Cheshire CH1 2HJ
Tel: (01244) 402111
Fax: (01244) 400420

Coventry
City of Coventry Leisure Services ✖ ✯
● (B) †
Tourist Information Centre
Bayley Lane
Coventry, West Midlands CV1 5RN
Tel: (024) 7622 7264
Fax: (024) 7622 7255
Internet: www.visitcoventry.co.uk
E-mail: tic@cvone.co.uk

Dover
Dover Tourist Information Centre ✖ ✯
● (B) †
Old Town Gaol
Biggin Street
Dover, Kent CT16 1DL
Tel: (01304) 205108
Fax: (01304) 245409
Internet: www.dover.gov.uk or
www.whitecliffscountry.org
E-mail: tic@dover.uk.com

Folkestone
Shepway District Council Tourist
Information Centre ✖ ✯ ● (B)
† (E)
Harbour Street
Folkestone, Kent CT20 1QN
Tel: (01303) 258594
Fax: (01303) 259754
Internet: www.kents-garden-coast
.co.uk
E-mail: tourism@folkestone.org.uk

Gloucester
Gloucester Tourist Office ✖ ✯ ● (B) †
28 Southgate Street
Gloucester GL1 2DP
Tel: (01452) 396572
Fax: (01452) 309788
Internet: www.gloucester.gov.uk/tourism
E-mail: tourism@gloucestr.gov.uk

Greenwich
Tourist Information Centre ✖ ● (B) †
Pepys House
2 Cutty Sark Gardens
Greenwich SE10 9LW
Tel: (0870) 608 2000
Fax: (020) 8853 4607
Internet: www.greenwichengland.com
E-mail: tic@greenwich.gov.uk

Hastings
Hastings Tourist Office ✖ ✯ ● (B) †
Queens Square
Priory Meadow
Hastings, East Sussex TN34 1TL
Tel: (01424) 781111
Fax: (01424) 781186
Internet: www.visithastings.com
E-mail: hic@hastings.gov.uk

Ipswich
Tourist Information Centre ✖ ✯ ●
(B) †
St. Stephen's Church
St. Stephen's Lane
Ipswich, Suffolk IP1 1DP
Tel: (01473) 258070
Accommodations: (01473) 262018
Fax: (01473) 432017
Internet: www.visit-ipswich.com or
www.ipswich.gov.uk
E-mail: tourist@ipswich.gov.uk

Isle of Wight
Isle of Wight Tourist Office (B) †
67 High Street
Shanklin, Isle of Wight PO37 6JJ
Tel: (01983) 862942

Fax: (01983) 863047
Hotline: (01983) 813800
Internet: www.islandbreaks.co.uk
E-mail: info@islandbreaks.co.uk

King's Lynn
Tourist Information Centre
The Custom House ✖ ✰ ● (B) †
Purfleet Quay
King's Lynn, Norfolk PE30 1HP
Tel: (01553) 763044
Fax: (01553) 819441
Internet: www.west-norfolk.gov.uk
E-mail: kings-lynn.tic@west-norfolk
    .gov.uk

Lincoln
The Lincoln Tourist Information Centre
    ✰ (B) †
9 Castle Hill
Lincoln, Lincolnshire LN1 3AA
Tel: (01522) 873213
Fax: (01522) 873214
Internet: www.lincoln.gov.uk
E-mail: tourism@lincoln.gov.uk

The Lincoln Tourist Information Centre
    ✰ (B) †
21 The Cornhill
Lincoln, Lincolnshire LN1 3AA
Tel: (01522) 873256
Fax: (01522) 873257

Liverpool
Merseyside Welcome Centre ✖ ● † (E)
Queen Square Building, Roe Street
Liverpool, Merseyside L1 1RG
Tel: (0906) 680 6886 (25p/min.)
Fax: (0151) 708 0204
Internet: www.visitliverpool.com
E-mail: askme@visitliverpool.com
Tourist Information Centre ✖ ● † (E)
Atlantic Pavilion
Albert Dock, Liverpool, Merseyside
    L3 4AE
Tel: (0906) 680 6886 (25p/min.)

London
Britain Visitor Centre (B) † (E)
1 Regent Street
Piccadilly Circus, London SW1Y 4XT
Tel: (020) 7846 9000
Fax: (020) 7563 0302
Internet: www.visitbritain.com

London Tourist Board & Convention
    Bureau (B) †
Glen House
Stag Place
Victoria, London SW1 E5LT
Tel: (020) 7932 2000
Fax: (020) 7932 0222
Internet: www.visitlondon.com

Tourist Information Centre (Heathrow)
    ✰ ● (B) †
Heathrow Airport
Terminals 1, 2, 3
Underground Station Concourse
London Heathrow Airport
Middlesex TW6 2JA
Tel: (0839) 123 456
Fax: (020) 7824 8844

Tourist Information Centre
(Camden)
Town Hall
Argyle Street, London WC1H 8NN
Tel: (020) 7974 5974
Fax: (020) 7974 3210

Tourist Information Centre (Lewisham)
    ✖ ✰ ●
Lewisham Library Building
199–201 Lewisham High Street
London SE13 6LG
Tel: (020) 8297 8317
Fax: (020) 8297 9241

Tourist Information Centre
    (Southwark) ✖ ✰ † (E)
London Bridge
6 Tooley Street
Tel: (020) 7403 8299
Fax: (020) 7357 6321

Tourist Information Centre (Victoria)
✘ ✻ ● (B) †
Victoria Station Forecourt
London SW1V 1JU
Tel: (0839) 123 456
Accommodations: (020) 7824 8844
Fax: (020) 7931 7768

Nottingham
Nottingham City Information Centre
✘ ● †
1–4 Smithy Row
Nottingham
Nottinghamshire NG1 2BY
Tel: (0115) 915 5330
Internet: www.visitnottingham.com
E-mail: tourist.information@
    nottinghamcity.gov.uk

Oxford
Oxford Information Centre **✘ ● † (E)**
15–16 Broad Street
Oxford, Oxfordshire OX1 3AS
Tel: (01865) 726871
Fax: (01865) 240261
Internet: www.visitoxford.org or
    www.oxford.gov.uk/tourism
E-mail: tic@oxford.gov.uk

Penzance
Tourist Information Centre **✘ ● †**
Station Road
Penzance, Cornwall TR18 2NF
Tel: (01736) 362207
Fax: (01736) 363600
Internet: www.penzance.co.uk

Plymouth
Plymouth Tourist Information **✘ ● †**
    Island House
9 The Barbican
Plymouth, Devon PL1 2LS
Tel: (01752) 304849
Fax: (01752) 257955
Internet: www.plymouthcity.co.uk

Plymouth Discovery Centre **✘ ● †**
Crabtree

Plymouth, Devon PL3 6RN
Tel: (01752) 266030
Fax: (01752) 266033

Portsmouth
Tourist Information Centre (B) **†**
The Hard
Portsmouth PO1 3QJ
Tel: (023) 9282 6722
Fax: (023) 9282 7519
Internet: www.visitportsmouth.co.uk
E-mail: tic@portsmouthcc.gov.uk

Ramsgate
Visitor Information Centre (B) **†**
17 Albert Court, York Street
Ramsgate, Kent CT11 9DN
Tel: (01843) 583333
Fax: (01843) 585353
Internet: www.tourism.thanet.gov.uk
E-mail: tourism@thanet.gov.uk

St. Albans
St. Albans Tourist Information Centre
✘ ● †
Town Hall
The Market Place
St. Albans, Hertfordshire AL3 5DJ
Tel: (01727) 864511
Fax: (01727) 863533
Internet: www.stalbans.gov.uk
E-mail: tic@stalbans.gov.uk

Salisbury
Salisbury Tourist Information Centre **✘**
    ● † (E)
Fish Row
Salisbury, Wiltshire SP1 1EJ
Tel: (01722) 334956
Fax: (01722) 422059
Internet: www.visitsalisbury.com
E-mail: visitorinfo@salisbury.gov.uk

Sheffield
Sheffield Visitor Information Centre
✘ ● †
1 Tudor Square
Sheffield, South Yorkshire S1 2LA

Tel: (0114) 221 1900
Fax: (0114) 201 1020
Internet: www.sheffieldcity.co.uk
E-mail: visitor@sheffield.gov.uk

Southampton
Southampton Leisure and Visitor
 Center ✖ ● †
9 Civic Centre Road
Southampton SO14 7FJ
Tel: (023) 8083 3333
Fax: (023) 8083 3381
Internet: www.southampton.gov.uk
E-mail: tourist.information
 @southampton.gov.uk

Stonehenge
Stonehenge, English Heritage
First Floor Abbey Buildings
Abbey Square
Amesbury, Wiltshire SP4 7ES
Tel: (01980) 625368
Info Line: (01980) 624715
Fax: (01980) 623465
Internet: www.english-heritage.org.uk
See also Salisbury Tourist Information
 Centre

Stratford-upon-Avon
Stratford-upon-Avon Centre ✖ ● † (E)
Bridgefoot Street
Stratford-upon-Avon
Warwickshire CV37 6GW
Tel: (01789) 293127
Fax: (01789) 295262
Internet: www.shakespeare-country
 .co.uk or www.heritagecities.co.uk
E-mail: stratfordtic@shakespeare-
 country.co.uk

Windsor
Windsor Information Centre ✖ ● †
24 High Street
Windsor SL4 1LH
Tel: (01753) 743 900
Accommodations: (01753) 743 900

Fax: (01753) 374 904
Internet: www.windsor.gov.uk
E-mail: windsor.tic@rbwm.gov.uk

York
Tourist Information Centre ✖ † (E)
DeGrey Rooms
Exhibition Square
York, North Yorkshire YO1 2HB
Tel: (01904) 621756
Fax: (01904) 551888
Internet: www.york-tourism.co.uk
E-mail: tic@york-tourism.co.uk

Tourist Information Centre ✖ ● † (E)
Outer Concourse
York Railway Station
York, North Yorkshire YO1 7HB
Tel: (01904) 621756
Fax: (01904) 672753

SCOTLAND
Although the Scottish Tourist Offices do
not have a code system listing specific
services offered, the majority of offices
are able to assist in planning where to
go and what to see and in securing
hotel and advance reservations for most
events.

Scottish Booking & Info Centre ✖ ✭ ●
 (B) † (E)
P.O. Box 121
Livingston EH54 8AF
Tel: (01506) 832121 (outside U.K.);
 (0845) 2255 121 (U.K.)
Internet: www.visitscotland.com
E-mail: info@visitscotland.com

Aberdeen
Aberdeen Visitor Information Centre
23 Union Street
Aberdeen AB11 5BP
Tel: (01224) 288828
Fax: (01224) 252219
Internet: www.agtb.org
E-mail: info@agtb.org

Appendix

Ayr

Ayrshire & Arran Tourist Board
15 Skye Road
Prestwick KA9 2TA
Ayr Tourist Information Centre
22 Sandgate
Ayr KA7 1BW
Tel: (01292) 290300
Fax: (01292) 288686
Internet: www.ayrshire-arran.com
E-mail: info@ayrshire-arran.com

Dunbar

Dunbar Tourist Office Centre
143 High Street
Dunbar EH4 21ES
Tel: (01368) 863353
Fax: (01368) 864999
Internet: www.dunbar.org.uk
E-mail: esic@eltb.org

Dundee

Angus & Dundee Tourist Board
21 Castle Street
Dundee DD1 3AA
Tel: (01382) 527527
Fax: (01382) 527551
Internet: www.angusanddundee.
co.uk
E-mail: enquiries@angusanddundee
.co.uk

Dunfermline

Tourist Information Centre
1 High Street
Dunfermline KY12 7DL
Tel: (01383) 720999
Fax: (01383) 625807
Internet: www.dunfermlineonline.net
E-mail: info@dunfermlineonline.net

Edinburgh

Edinburgh & Lothians Tourist Board
3 Princes Street
Edinburgh EH2 2QP

Tel: (0131) 473 3800
Fax: (0131) 473 3881
Internet: www.edinburgh.org
E-mail: esic@eltb.org

Glasgow

Greater Glasgow & Clyde Valley Tourist
Board
11 George Street
Glasgow G2 1DY
Tel: (0141) 204 4480
Fax: (0141) 566 4073
Internet: www.seeglasgow.com
E-mail: enquiries@seeglasgow.com

Glasgow Tourist Information Centre
11 George Square
Glasgow G2 1DY
Tel: (0141) 204 4400
Fax: (0141) 221 3524

Inverness

The Highlands of Scotland Tourist
Board
Castle Wynd
Inverness IV2 3BJ
Tel: (01463) 234353
Fax: (01463) 710609
Internet: www.visithighlands.com
E-mail: inverness@host.co.uk

Kyle of Lochalsh

Tourist Board
Car Park
Kyle of Lochalsh IV40 8QA
Tel: (01599) 534276
Fax: (01599) 534808
Internet: www.visithighlands.com
E-mail: kyle@host.co.uk

Linlithgow

Edinburgh & Lothians Tourist Board
(Linlithgow)
Burgh Halls
The Cross

Appendix

Linlithgow, West Lothian EH49 7EJ
Tel: (01506) 844600
Fax: (01506) 671373
Internet: www.linlithgow.com

Montrose (April–September)
Montrose Tourist Information Centre
Bridge Street
Montrose DD10 8AB
Tel: (01674) 672000
Internet: www.angusanddundee.co.uk
E-mail: enquiries@angusanddundee
.co.uk

Perth
Tourist Information Centre
Lower City Mills
West Mill Street
Perth PH3 1LQ
Tel: (01738) 450600
Fax: (01738) 444863
Internet: www.perthshire.co.uk
E-mail: perthtic@perthshire.co.uk

St. Andrews
St. Andrews Tourist Information Centre
70 Market Street
Fife KY10 9NU
Tel: (01334) 472021
Fax: (01334) 478422
Internet: www.standrews.com
E-mail: standrewstic@kftb.ossian.net

Stirling
Stirling Tourist Information Centre
41 Dumbarton Road
Stirling FK8 2QQ
Tel: (0807) 200620
Fax: (01786) 450039
Internet: www.scottish.heartlands.org
E-mail: stirlingtic@aillst.ossian.net

Royal Burgh of Stirling Visitor Centre
Castle Esplanade
Stirling FK8 1EA

Tel: (01786) 479901
Fax: (01786) 461881

Stranraer
Tourist Information Centre
Burns House
Harbour Street
Stranraer DG9 7RA
Tel: (01776) 702595
Fax: (01776) 889156
Internet: www.stranraer.org
E-mail: stranraer@dgtb.ossian.net

WALES
Welsh Tourist Board ✖ ✰ ● (B) † (E)
Brunel House
2 Fitzalan Road
Cardiff CF2 1UY
Tel: (029) 2049 4473
Internet: www.visitwales.com
E-mail: info@tourism.wales.gov.uk

Caerphilly
Caerphilly Visitor Centre ✖ (B) †
Lower Twyn Square
Caerphilly, Mid Glamorgan CF83 1XX
Tel: (029) 2088 0011
Fax: (029) 2086 0811
Internet: ww.caerphilly.gov.uk
/tourism.html

Cardiff
Visitor Information Centre ✖ (B) †
St. David's House, 16 Wood Street
Cardiff CF10 1ES
Tel: (029) 2022 7281
Fax: (029) 2023 9162
Internet: www.cardiffmarketing.co.uk
E-mail: enquiries@cardifftic.co.uk

Swansea
Tourist Board ✖ (B) †
Singleton Street
Swansea SA1 3QG
Tel: (01792) 468321
Fax: (01792) 464602

Internet: www.swansea.gov.uk
E-mail: swantrsm@cableol.co.uk

Tenby
Tourist Information Centre ✖ (B) †
The Croft

Tenby SA70 8AP
Tel: (01834) 842402
Fax: (01834) 845439
Internet: www.virtualtenby.co.uk

RECOMMENDED INFORMATION SOURCES

Appendix

British Tourist Authority Offices in North America
www.visitbritain.com
New York: 551 Fifth Avenue, 7th Floor, Suite 701, New York, NY 10176-0799. *Tel:* (212) 986–2266 or (800) GO–2–BRIT; *Fax:* (212) 986–1188; *E-mail:* travelinfo@bta.org.uk
Chicago: 625 North Michigan Avenue, Suite 1001, Chicago, IL 60611-4977. *Tel:* (312) 787–0464; *Fax:* (312) 787–9641

National Rail Inquiries
www.railtrack.co.uk
Rail schedules and fare information within Great Britain.
Tel: (0845) 748 4950

RailPass.com
www.railpass.com
2737 Sawbury Boulevard, Columbus, Ohio 43235-4583.
Toll-free: 1 (877) RAILPASS (877–724–5727); *Fax:* (614) 764–0711
Rail passes, point-to-point and Eurostar tickets, seat and sleeper reservations, tours, and group rates.

Scottish Tourist Board
www.visitscotland.com
Contact information same as British Tourist Authority listed above.

Wales Tourist Board
www.visitwales.com
Contact information same as British Tourist Authority listed above.

USEFUL PHONE NUMBERS—LONDON

When dialing from the United States, use the codes 011 + 44 and omit the 0 from the beginning of the phone numbers listed below.

Accommodations	Telephone No.
British Hotel Reservation Centre,	
24-hour booking line	(020) 7340 1616
15 Monck Street	U.S. toll-free: 1 (866) 279–2925
London SW1P 2BJ	
(www.bhronline.com)	Fax: (020) 7828 6439
E-mail: hotels@bhronline.com	
Expotel Hotel Reservations	
Kingsgate House, Kingsgate Place,	
London NW6 4HG	(020) 7328 9841
(www.expotel.com)	Fax: (020) 7328 8021
Victoria Station, by Platform 9	(020) 7888 4646
Gatwick Station	(01293) 529372
King's Cross Station, adjacent to Platform 8	
Hotel Booking Service, Ltd.	(020) 7223 7226
(www.hotelbooking.co.uk)	Fax: (020) 7924 4371
Hotel Finders	(020) 8202 7000
20a Bell Lane, London NW4 2AD	Fax: (020) 8202 3871
The London Bed & Breakfast Agency	(020) 7586 2768
(www.londonbb.com)	Fax: (020) 7586 6567
71 Fellows Road, London NW3 3JY	
The London Tourist Board	(020) 7604 2890
(www.visitlondon.com)	

Airport Information (www.baa.co.uk)

Heathrow, general inquiries	(0870) 000 0123
London City Airport (www.londoncityairport.com)	(020) 7646 0088
Gatwick	(0870) 000 2468
Stansted	(0870) 000 0303

American Express

6 Haymarket, Piccadilly Circus	(020) 7484 9610

Bike/Scooter Rentals

Bikepark, 63 New Kings Road	(020) 7731 7012
London Bicycle Co., 1a Gabriel's Wharf	(020) 7928 6838
(www.londonbicycle.com)	
On Your Bike, 52–54 Tooley Street	(020) 7378 6669
Scootabout, 1–3 Leeke Street	(020) 7833 4607

British Tourist Authority, British Visitor Centre,

1 Regent Street, Piccadilly Circus SW1	(020) 8846 1000
www.visitbritain.com	

Canadian Embassy

Canada Centre 62–65 Trafalgar Square	(020) 7258 6356

Emergency
Police or Ambulance   999
Eurostar
www.eurostar.com   (0870) 160 6600
Express Bus Information
National Express   (08705) 808080
www.nationalexpress.co.uk
Hoverspeed Reservations   (0870) 240 8070
www.hoverspeed.co.uk   *Fax:* (0870) 460 7102
London Tourist Board (main office)
www.londontown.com   (020) 7932 2000
London Travel Transport Information   (020) 7222 1234
Post Office
Paddington Main Post Office   (020) 7239 2792
Rail Information
National Rail Inquiries   (0845) 748 4950 (U.K. only)
(1332) 387601 (international callers)
River Trips and Canal Cruises
Bateaux London/Catamaran Cruises   (020) 7925 2215
www.bateauxlondon.com
Capital Pleasure Boats   (020) 8297 5000
www.cpbs.co.uk
George Wheeler Launches   (020) 7930 4097
King Cruises   (020) 8303 0774
Thames Clippers   (020) 7977 6892
Thames Cruises   (020) 7740 0400
www.citycruises.com
Thames Leisure   (020) 7623 1805
www.thamesleisure.co.uk
Sleeper Reservations
Use rail inquiries no.:
in the U.K.   (0845) 748 4950
outside the U.K.   +44 (1332) 387601
Sports Events
Sports World   (01235) 555844
U.S. Embassy
55 Upper Brook Street, London W1A 1AE   (020) 7499 9000
www.usembassy.org.uk
Victoria Student Travel Service
Need student I.D. to book accommodations   (0870) 2401 010

Appendix

USEFUL PHONE NUMBERS—EDINBURGH

Airport Information	(0870) 040 0007
American Express	
139 Princes Street	(0131) 225 7881
Emergency	
Fire, Police, Ambulance	999
City Sightseeing Tours	(0131) 556 2244
Student Travel Centre	(0131) 668 2221
Edinburgh Military Tattoo Ticket Office	(0131) 225 1188
www.edinburgh-tattoo.co.uk	
Tourist Information	
City of Edinburgh Tourist Information and	
Accommodations, Waverley Market, Princes Street	(0131) 473 3800

USEFUL PHONE NUMBERS—GLASGOW

Airport	(0870) 040 0008
American Express	
115 Hope Street	(0141) 221 4366
Emergency	
Ambulance, Police, Fire, and Coast Guard	999
Glasgow Travel Centre	(0141) 226 4826
ScotRail	(0141) 332 9811
Tourist Information	
Tourist Information, 35 St. Vincent Place	(0141) 204 4400

USEFUL PHONE NUMBERS—CARDIFF

Cardiff Bay Visitor Centre	
Harbour Drive, Waterfront Park	(029) 2046 3833
Cardiff International Airport Information	
Rhoose, Wales	(01446) 711111
Cardiff Tourist Information Centre	(029) 2022 7281
Cardiff Central Station, Central Square	*Fax:* (029) 2023 9162
Emergency	
Ambulance, Police, Fire, and Coast Guard	999

TRAIN-OPERATING COMPANIES
www.nationalrail.co.uk

For general inquiries and timetable information, telephone the National Rail Inquiries number: within the U.K. (0845) 748 4950; outside the U.K., dial your country's international access code, plus 44–1332–387601. Web links to the individual train-operating companies are provided on www.national rail.co.uk.

Arriva Trains Northern, Customer Services   (0870) 602 3322
Arriva Trains, Wales   (0845) 606 1660

c2c, Customer Services   *Tel:* (0845) 601 4873
    www.c2c-online.co.uk

Central Trains, Ltd., Customer Services   *Tel:* (0121) 654 1200
    P.O. Box 4323, Birmingham B2 4JB   *Fax:* (0121) 654 1234
    www.centraltrains.co.uk

Chiltern Railway Co.   *Tel:* (01296) 332114
    Western House, 14 Rickfords Hill   *Fax:* (01296) 332126
    Aylesbury HP20 2RX
    www.chilternrailways.co.uk

Docklands Light Rail   *Tel:* (020) 7363 9700
    www.dlr.co.uk   *Fax:* (020) 7363 9532

Eurostar (UK) Customer Service   *Tel:* (01777) 77 78 79
    Eurostar House, Waterloo Station, London SE1 8SE
    Bookings in the U.S.   *Tel:* 877–RAILPASS
    www.eurostar.com   (724–5727)

First Great Western, Customer Care   *Tel:* (0845) 600 5604
    Milford House, 1 Milford Street
    Swindon SN1 1HL

First Great Western Link   *Tel:* (0845) 330 7182
Venture House, 37 Blagrave Street
Reading RG1 1PZ

First North Western, Customer Relations   *Tel:* (0845) 600 1159
    1st Floor, Bridgewater House, Whitworth Street
    Manchester M1 GLS

Gatwick Express   *Tel:* (0845) 850 1530
    52 Grosvenor Gardens   *Fax:* (020) 7973 5038
    London SW1W OAU
    www.gatwickexpress.com

Appendix

Great North Eastern Railway
   Main Headquarters Building, Room M93
   Station Road, York YO1 6HT
   www.gner.co.uk

Tel: (0845) 722 5333

Heathrow Express
   Freepost SEA 4589
   Hounslow, Middlesex TW6 2BR
   www.heathrowexpress.co.uk

Tel: (0845) 600 1515
Fax: (020) 8750 6615

Hull Trains
   Premier House, Ferensway
   Hull HU1 3UF

Tel: (0190) 452 5221
Fax: (0190) 452 5208

Island Line
   Ryde St. Johns Road Station
   Ryde, Isle of Wight PO33 2BA
   www.island-line.co.uk

Tel: (01983) 812591
Fax: (01983) 817879

Midland Mainline
   Midland House, Nelson Street
   Derby, East Midlands DE1 2SA
   www.midlandmainline.com

Tel: (0845) 722 1125

One
   St. Clare House, Princes Street
   Ipswich IP1 1LY
   www.onerailway.com

Tel: (0870) 040 9090

ScotRail Railways, Customer Services
   Caledonian Chambers, 87 Union Street
   Glasgow G1 3TA
   www.scotrail.co.uk

Tel: (0845) 601 5929
Fax: (01413) 354592

Silverlink Train Services, Customer Services
   Main Office, Hertford House
   1 Cranwood Street, London EC1V 9QA
   www.silverlink-trains.com

Tel: (0845) 601 4867
Fax: (01923) 207023

South Central Trains, Customer Services
   Go Ahead House
   26–28 Addiscombe Road
   Croydon CR9 5GA
   www.southcentraltrains.co.uk

Tel: (0870) 830 6000
Fax: (0870) 830 6001

Appendix

South Eastern Trains
    P.O. Box 125, Tonbridge TN9 2ZA
    www.setrains.co.uk
Tel: (0870) 603 0405

South West Trains
    Friars Bridge Court, 41–45 Blackfriars Road
    London SE1 8NZ
    www.southwesttrains.co.uk
Tel: (0845) 600 0650
Fax: (020) 7620 5460

Thameslink
    Friars Bridge Court, 41–45 Blackfriars Road
    London SE1 8NZ
    www.thameslink.co.uk
Tel: (0845) 330 6333
Fax: (020) 7620 5099

TransPennine Express
    Bridgewater House, 60 Whitworth Street
    Manchester M1 6LT
    www.firstgroup.com/tpexpress
Tel: (0845) 600 1671

Virgin Trains
    85 Smallbrook Queensway
    Birmingham B5 4HA
    www.virgintrains.co.uk
Tel: (0870) 789 1234
Fax: (0121) 654 7528

WAGN
    Hertford House
    1 Cranwood Street
    London EC1V 9QS
    www.wagn.co.uk
Tel: (0845) 781 8919
Fax: (0122) 345 3606

Wessex Trains
    2nd Floor, Broadwalk House
    Southernhay West, Exeter, Devon EX1 1TS
    www.wessextrains.co.uk
Tel: (0845) 600 0880
Fax: (02920) 430 214

Appendix

A SELECTION OF ONE-WAY
RAIL FARES IN BRITAIN

Deciding whether or not you should purchase a BritRail Pass becomes a matter of simple arithmetic. Plan your trip to Great Britain, decide what places you want to visit, and use the fares listed below to determine if the cost of individual rail segments exceeds the cost of a BritRail Pass. Round-trip fares are slightly less than double the one-way charge. Children five to fifteen years of age, inclusive, pay half fare. Children younger than age five travel free and do not need a ticket. All fares are applicable as of press time and subject to change without prior notice. Fares are given in U.S. dollars. To convert to pounds sterling, apply current rate of exchange. For example, at press time, the rate was approximately $1.00 = £.54

Appendix

	ONE-WAY FARES			ONE-WAY FARES	
	First Class ($)	Standard Class ($)		First Class ($)	Standard Class ($)
From London to:			**From London to:**		
Aberdeen	242.00	175.00	Oxford	28.00	22.00
Aviemore	242.00	175.00	Penzance	181.00	131.00
Ayr	253.00	183.00	Perth	242.00	175.00
Bath Spa	111.00	52.00	Plymouth	181.00	131.00
Birmingham	113.00	82.00	Portsmouth	51.00	39.00
Brighton	51.00	39.00	Salisbury	111.00	82.00
Cambridge	44.00	34.00	Sheffield	113.00	82.00
Canterbury	47.00	35.00	Southampton	51.00	39.00
Cardiff	155.00	112.00	Stratford-upon-		
Chester	139.00	101.00	Avon	93.00	69.00
Coventry	113.00	82.00	Windermere	211.00	153.00
Dover	47.00	35.00	Windsor	28.00	22.00
Dundee	242.00	175.00	York	168.00	122.00
Edinburgh	224.00	162.00			
Glasgow	253.00	183.00	**From Glasgow to:**		
Gloucester	121.00	88.00	Aberdeen	88.00	65.00
Hastings	51.00	39.00	Birmingham	187.00	136.00
Inverness	242.00	175.00	Dundee	88.00	65.00
King's Lynn	91.00	67.00	Edinburgh	32.00	25.00
Leamington Spa	93.00	69.00	Inverness	88.00	65.00
Lincoln	113.00	82.00	Manchester	146.00	106.00
Liverpool	139.00	101.00	Perth	88.00	65.00
Manchester	139.00	101.00	Sheffield	173.00	125.00
Nottingham	113.00	82.00	York	132.00	96.00

To order rail tickets prior to your departure for Britain, call RailPass.com toll-free at (877) RAILPASS (877–724–5727) at least ten business days in advance, or visit the Point-to-Point section of www.railpass.com.

PASSPORT INFORMATION
www.travel.state.gov

You can apply for a passport (in person if you are age fourteen or older and do not meet the requirements to renew a previous passport by mail) at more than 4,500 facilities in the United States, including many post offices; federal, state and probate courts; some libraries; and some municipal and county offices. Passport forms are also available for downloading from the

Internet (www.travel.state.gov) and you can enter your zip code to determine which facility is closest.

Apply several months in advance if possible. It usually takes a minimum of six weeks. The National Passport Information Center (NPIC) operates an automated information number: 1–900–225–7778 (55 cents per minute); operator-assisted calls are $1.50 per minute. Credit-card users (American Express, MasterCard, or Visa) may dial 1–888–362–8668 for a flat fee of $5.50 per call. A recorded message describes the documents you need and the application process for obtaining a passport and gives instructions on reporting the loss or theft of your passport.

If you are traveling in less than two weeks or if you need foreign visas, you can contact the closest regional office for an appointment, send an extra $60 for expedited service (usually this gets your passport to you in two weeks if you also pay extra for overnight delivery), or use one of the express passport services online, such as www.americanpassport.com or www.pass portexpress.com. Be prepared to pay *at least triple* the normal passport fees, which are normally $85 for a new passport and $55 for renewal or for those younger than age sixteen. But they guarantee they will get your passport to you in only one day after receiving the required documents.

The regional offices and their automated appointment numbers are as follows:

Boston: Thomas P. O'Neill Federal Building, 10 Causeway Street, Suite 247, Boston, MA 02222-1094; (617) 878–0900.

Chicago: Kluczynski Office Building, 230 South Dearborn Street, Suite 380, Chicago, IL 60604-1564; (312) 341–6020.

Honolulu: Prince Kuhio Federal Building, 300 Ala Moana Boulevard, Suite 1–330, Honolulu, HI 96850.

Houston: Mickey Leland Federal Building, 1919 Smith Street, Suite 1400, Houston, TX 77002-8049; (713) 751–0294.

Los Angeles: Federal Building, 11000 Wilshire Boulevard, Suite 1000, Los Angeles, CA 90024-3615; (310) 575–5700.

Miami: Claude Pepper Federal Office Building, 51 SW First Avenue, Third Floor, Miami, FL 33130-1680; (305) 539–3600.

New Orleans: One Canal Place, corner of Canal and North Peters Streets, 365 Canal Street, Suite 1300, New Orleans, LA 70130-6508; (504) 412–2600.

New York: Greater Manhattan Federal Building, 376 Hudson Street, New York, NY 10014; (212) 206–3500.

Norwalk: 50 Washington Street, Norwalk, CT 06854; (203) 299–5443.

Philadelphia: U.S. Customs House, 200 Chestnut Street, Room 103, Philadelphia, PA 19106-2970; (215) 418–5937.

San Francisco: 95 Hawthorne Street, 5th Floor, San Francisco, CA 94105-3901; (415) 538–2700.

Seattle: Federal Building, 915 Second Avenue, Suite 992, Seattle, WA 98174-1091; (206) 808–5700.

Washington, D.C.: 1111 19th Street NW, Washington, DC 20524-1705; (202) 647–0518.

Appendix

TIPS AND TRIVIA

Do not be surprised to see a 17.5 percent value-added tax (VAT) added to your bill for items purchased or services rendered. The VAT appears on just about everything, excluding bus/rail transportation.

Tipping: For luggage, generally tip £1.00 per bag; taxis, 10–15 percent, with a 50-pence minimum; for service staff in hotels, 10–20 percent if service gratuity is not included in bill.

Imports: You may import into Britain 200 cigarettes or 50 cigars, two liters of table wine plus one liter of liquor over 22% alcohol or two liters of liquor under 22% alcohol (e.g., fortified or sparkling wine). Two fluid ounces (60 ml) of perfume or nine ounces (250 ml) of toilet water may be imported and £145 worth of other goods including gifts and souvenirs. Regulations are strictly imposed on firearms, drugs, pornography, plants, fruit, and goods made from protected species.

Shops: Most shops are open from 0900 to 1730. Shops in smaller towns may close for one hour at lunchtime. In London, shops in the Knightsbridge area (Harrods, for example) remain open until 1900 on Wednesday, while those in the West End (Oxford Street, Regent Street, and Piccadilly areas) stay open until 1900 on Thursday.

Banks: Banks are usually open Monday through Friday from 0930 to 1530. Some are open on Saturday mornings. Most banks in Scotland are closed for one hour at lunchtime. The banks at London's Heathrow and Gatwick Airports are open twenty-four hours a day.

Holidays: Most banks, shops, and some museums, historic houses, and other places of interest are closed on Sundays and public holidays. Public transport services generally are reduced, especially during Christmastime. Please see the 2005 Bank and Public Holidays section.

Voltage: The standard voltage is 240v AC, 50 Hz.

CLIMATE

	Jan	Feb	Mar	Apr	May	June	July	Aug	Sept	Oct	Nov	Dec
Average Low (F)	35°	35°	37°	40°	45°	51°	55°	54°	51°	44°	39°	36°
Average High (F)	44°	45°	51°	56°	63°	69°	73°	72°	67°	58°	49°	45°
Average Rainfall (in inches)	4	3	3	2	3	3	2	3	3	3	4	4

2005 BANK AND PUBLIC HOLIDAYS

January 3	New Year's Day (date observed, U.K., Rep Ireland)*
January 4	Bank Holiday (Scotland)
March 17	St. Patrick's Day (Northern Ireland)*
March 25	Good Friday
March 28	Easter Monday (U.K., Rep Ireland)*
May 2	May Day (U.K., Rep Ireland)*
May 30	Spring Bank Holiday (U.K.)
June 4	Holiday (Rep Ireland)
July 12	Battle of the Boyne: Orangeman's Day (Northern Ireland)**
August 1	Bank Holiday (Scotland, Rep Ireland)
August 29	Summer Bank Holiday (England, Wales, Isle of Man, Northern Ireland)
October 31	Holiday (Rep Ireland)
December 25	Christmas Day (U.K., Rep Ireland)*
December 26	St. Stephen's Day (Rep Ireland)
December 26	Boxing Day (U.K.)*
December 27	Day in lieu of 25th

U.K. = England, Scotland, Wales, Northern Ireland
*Bank holidays
**Subject to proclamation by the Secretary of the State for Northern Ireland

TOLL-FREE AIRLINE NUMBERS AND WEB SITES
(Dialing from U.S.)

Aer Lingus (EI) ..(800) IRISH–AIR/223–6537
www.aerlingus.ie
Air Canada (AC)................. (888) 247–2262
www.aircanada.ca
Air France (AF) .... (800) 237–2747
www.airfrance.com
American Airlines, Inc. (AA) (800) 433–7300
www.armcorp.com
Austrian Airlines (OS) .... (800) 843–0002
www.austrianair.com
British Airways (BA)..............(800) AIRWAYS
www.britishairways.com
Continental Airlines (CO) .. (800) 231–0856
www.continental.com
CSA Czech Airlines
Airlines (OK) ....(800) 628–6107
www.csa.cz
Delta Air Lines, Inc. (DL)......(800) 241–4141
www.delta.com
Finnair (AY)........................(800) 950–5000
www.us.finnair.com
Icelandair (FI) ....(800) 223–5500
www.icelandair.com

KLM Royal Dutch
Airlines (KL) ....(800) 374–7747
www.klm.com
Lufthansa German
Airlines (LH) ....(800) 645–3880
www.lufthansa-usa.com
Northwest Airlines/KLM
Inc. (NW) ....(800) 447–4747
www.nwa.com
Olympic Airways (OA) ....(800) 223–1226
www.olympic-airways.gr
Scandinavian Airlines
System (SK) ....(800) 221–2350
www.scandinavian.net
Swissair (SR) ....(800) 221–4750
www.swissair.com
TAP Air Portugal (TO)..........(800) 221–7370
www.tap-airportugal.pt
United Airlines, Inc. (UA) ....(800) 538–2929
www.ual.com
USAirways (US) ....(800) 428–4322
www.usairways.com
Virgin Atlantic Airways
Ltd. (VS) ....(800) 862–8621
www.virgin-atlantic.com

Appendix

ENTERTAINMENT BOOKING AGENCIES

Applause Theatre & Entertainment Service
(Theater, Ballet/Opera)..........(800) 451–9930
Fax: (212) 397–3729
Internet: www.applause-tickets.com

Global Tickets
(West End, Shakespeare, Classical,
Rock, Tattoo, Festival)..........(800) 223–6108
Tel: (914) 328–2150 *Fax:* (914) 328–2752
Internet: www.globaltickets.com

Keith Prowse
(West End)..............................800–669–8687
Tel: (212) 398–1430 *Fax:* (212) 328–4438
Internet: www.keithprowse.com

Theatre Direct
(West End, Shakespeare) ....(800) 334-8457
Tel: (212) 541-8457
Internet: www.theatredirect.com

Ticketmaster
(West End)...........................(800) 775–2525
Tel: (212) 307–4100
Internet: www.ticketmaster.com

Appendix

TOLL-FREE HOTEL RESERVATION NUMBERS
(Dialing from U.S.)

B&B My Guest......................(800) 906–4232
   www.beduk.com
Barclay International
   (apartments)................(800) 845–6636
   www.barclayweb.com
Bed & Breakfast GB ....(800) 454–8704
   (in Britain) ....(011) 44 1491 578803
Best Western Hotels..............(800) 528–1234
   www.bestwestern.com
Castles, Cottages & Flats ......(800) 742–6030
   www.castlescottages-flats.com
Consort Hotels ....(800) 55CONSORT
   www.consorthotels.com
Elegant English Hotels..........(800) 270–9206
   www.eeh.co.uk
Forte Hotels..........................(800) 225–5843
   www.forte-hotels.com
Hilton Hotels ....(800) HILTONS
   www.hilton.com
In the English Manner
   (apartments/cottages) ....(800) 422–0799
   www.english-manner.co.uk

Intercontinental Hotels ....(800) 327–0200
   www.interconti.com
Keith Prowse (apartments) ..(800) 669–8687
   www.keithprowse.com
London B&B ....(800) 872–2632
   www.londonbandb.com
Moat House Hotels ....(800) 641–0300
   www.hotelbook.com
Pride of Britain ....(800) 98PRIDE
   www.prideofbritainhotels.com
Radisson Edwardian Hotels ..(800) 333–3333
   www.radisson.com
Red Carnation Hotels ....(800) 424–2862
   www.redcarnationhotels.com
Savoy Group Hotels ....(800) 63SAVOY
   www.savoy-group.co.uk
Thistle Hotels ....(800) 847–4358
   www.thistlehotels.com

SEA TRAVEL INFORMATION
(Dialing from U.S.)

Brittany Ferries ....(01144) 8703 665 333
www.brittany-ferries.co.uk

Caledonian MacBrayne (01144) 8705 650000
www.calmac.co.uk
(Scottish Islands)

Condor Ferries ....(01144) 845 345 2000
www.condorferries.co.uk
(Channel Islands)

Hoverspeed/Holyman/
Seacat ....(01144) 870 240 8070
www.hoverspeed.co.uk

Irish Ferries ....(01144) 8705 171717
www.irishferries.ie

Isle of Man Steam
Packet Company ....(01144) 8705 523523
www.steam-packet.com

Isles of Scilly Steamship
Company ....(01144) 1736 334220
www.islesofscilly-travel.co.uk

Orkney Ferries ....(01144) 1856 872044
www.orkneyferries.co.uk

P&O European Ferries (01144) 1574 872120
www.poportsmouth.com

P&O North Sea Ferries (01144) 1482 377177
www.poef.com

P&O Scottish Ferries ..(01144) 1224 589111

P&O Stena Line ....(01144) 1304 864003
www.poferries.com

Red Funnel Ferries ....(01144) 870 444 8898
www.redfunnel.co.uk
(Isle of Wight)

Sea France ....(01144) 8705 711711
www.seafrance.co.uk

Shetland Islands
Council............(01144) 1957 722259/268

Stena Line....................(01144) 8705 707070
www.stenaline.com

Swansea Cork Ferries ..(01144) 1792 456116
www.swanseacorkferries.com

Wightlink....................(01144) 8705 820202
www.wightlink.co.uk

Appendix

BRITRAIL PASSES

A BritRail consecutive-day or Flexipass allows unlimited travel on the entire British rail network spanning England, Scotland, and Wales. Prices are current as of press time, but are always subject to change without notice. To verify prices visit www.railpass.com.

> To order, call (877) RAILPASS (877–724–5727) or (614) 793–7651, or visit the RailPass.com Web site at www.railpass.com.

BritRail Classic Pass

Valid for consecutive days of rail travel throughout Britain (England, Scotland, and Wales).

	ADULT		SENIOR	YOUTH STANDARD
	1ST CLASS	STANDARD CLASS	1ST CLASS	CLASS ONLY
4 days	$279	$189	$237	$142
8 days	$405	$269	$344	$202
15 days	$599	$399	$509	$299
22 days	$765	$509	$650	$382
1 month	$909	$605	$773	$454

Senior 60+. Youth 16–25. Children 5–15, half adult fare. Children under age 5 travel free.

BritRail Family Pass

Receive one free child pass (age 5–15) of the same type when purchasing one adult or senior BritRail Classic Pass, BritRail Flexipass, BritRail Pass + Ireland, BritRail Pass 'n Drive, or BritRail Party Pass (up to 2 children may travel free per BritRail Party Pass; not to exceed total of 5 persons, including child, on the Party Pass). Children under age 5 travel free.

BritRail Flexipass

Valid for unlimited rail travel in Britain for the days chosen within a 60-day period.

	ADULT 1ST CLASS	ADULT STANDARD CLASS	SENIOR 1ST CLASS	YOUTH STANDARD CLASS ONLY
4 days in 2 months	$349	$239	$297	$179
8 days in 2 months	$515	$345	$438	$259
15 days in 2 months	$775	$519	$659	$389

Senior age 60 and older. Youth age 16–25. Children age 5–15, half adult fare. Children under age 5 travel free.

BritRail Party Pass

For parties of 3 or 4 passengers traveling together at all times, a 50% discount is offered on the third and fourth person's pass. Applies to the BritRail Classic and BritRail Flexipass (1st class only, Adult and Senior).

BritRail Pass + Ireland

Valid for travel in England, Scotland, Wales, Northern Ireland, and the Republic of Ireland.

	1ST CLASS	STANDARD CLASS
5 days within 1 month	$515	$369
10 days within 1 month	$849	$595

Children age 5–15, half adult fare; under age 5 travel free.

Round-trip Stena Sealink service is included between Holyhead and Dun Laoghaire, Fishguard and Rosslare, or Stranraer and Belfast via ship, HSS, or SeaLynx. Reservations are essential for Irish Sea services. Refunds not offered on dated or partially used passes; sea coupons are not refundable if unused.

BritRail England Pass

Unlimited rail travel in England (Scotland and Wales are not included on the England Pass).

	ADULT 1st Class	Standard Class	YOUTH 1st Class	Standard Class	SENIOR 1st Class	PARTY 1st Class 3rd & 4th Person 50% off	Standard Class 3rd & 4th Person 50% off
4 days	$225	$149	$191	$112	$191	$225	$149
8 days	$325	$215	$276	$161	$276	$325	$215
15 days	$485	$325	$412	$244	$412	$485	$325
22 days	$615	$409	$523	$307	$523	$615	$409
1 month	$725	$485	$616	$364	$616	$725	$485

Youth age 16–25; Senior 60+ years; BritRail Family Pass must be requested so each child (age 5–15) can travel free with each adult/senior pass holder. Additional children are half regular adult fare. Party passes allow 50% discount for 3rd and 4th persons traveling in a group.

BritRail England Flexipass

Unlimited four, eight, fifteen, twenty-two, or thirty days of flexible (non-consecutive) rail travel in a two-month period throughout England (Scotland and Wales not included).

Days Within 2 Months	ADULT 1st Class	Standard Class	YOUTH 1st Class	Standard Class	SENIOR 1st Class	PARTY 1st Class 3rd & 4th Person 50% off	Standard Class 3rd & 4th Person 50% off
4 days	$279	$189	$237	$142	$237	$279	$189
8 days	$409	$275	$348	$206	$348	$409	$275
15 days	$619	$415	$526	$311	$526	$619	$415

Youth age 16–25; Senior 60+ years. Family passes allow one child to travel free with each adult. Party passes alow 50% discount for the 3rd and 4th person traveling in a group.

Appendix

BritRail Days Out of London Pass
A flexipass for a large section of southern England.

	ADULT		CHILD	
	1ST CLASS	STANDARD CLASS	1ST CLASS	STANDARD CLASS
2 days within 8 days	$89	$59	$31	$21
4 days within 8 days	$145	$109	$31	$21
7 days within 15 days	$195	$145	$31	$21

Children age 5–15. Children under age 5 travel free.

Freedom of Scotland Travelpass

	STANDARD CLASS
4 days within 8 days	$145
8 days within 15 days	$189

Includes transportation on all Caledonian MacBrayne and Strathclyde ferries to the islands of Scotland. Discounts on several ferry operators and on certain CityLink bus services, plus covers Glasgow Underground. Discounts on some P&O ferry routes. Children 5–15, half adult fare. Children under age 5 travel free.

Freedom of Wales Flexi Pass

	STANDARD CLASS	
	ADULT	CHILD
4 days within 8 days	$89	$59
8 days within 15 days	$149	$105

Includes unlimited travel on main rail lines in Wales and most major bus services. Discounts on several of Wales' preserved railways, selected attractions, and some bus tours. Monday–Friday valid after 0900 only. Unrestricted travel on Saturday and Sunday.

Gatwick Express

	1ST CLASS	STANDARD CLASS
One-Way	$33	$20
Round-Trip	$65	$39

Travel by train from Gatwick Airport to London Victoria Station. Children 5–15, half adult fare.

Great British Heritage Pass
Offers entrance to more than 600 well-known public and privately owned castles, homes, gardens, and other historic properties throughout Britain. Includes colorful guidebook and map.

	ADULT
4 days	$35
7 days	$54
15 days	$75
1 month	$102

No discounts for children. The pass is nonrefundable/nonreturnable.

Heathrow Express

	1ST CLASS	STANDARD CLASS
One-Way	$38	$24
Round-Trip	$73	$45

Travel by train from Heathrow Airport to London Paddington Station. Children age 5–15, half adult fare.

London Day Tour

ADULT	CHILD
$110	$90

Includes an experienced guide, a luxury air-conditioned touring coach, pub lunch, cruise of the River Thames with afternoon tea, and all entrance fees. Operates daily. Children age 5–15.

London Pass

Entry to more than seventy major attractions, including Buckingham Palace (open August and September), St. Paul's Cathedral, and Windsor Castle, a 140-page London Pass Guide Book, commission-free currency exchange, free offers at restaurants, discounted telephone calls, and more. Available only with the purchase of another product.

	ADULT	CHILD
3 consecutive days	$86	$56
6 consecutive days	$120	$65

London Visitor Travelcard

Unlimited travel on buses, London Underground, and many mainline trains in London area; discount booklet to popular attractions. Choose All Zone Card to travel in all six zones of subway (includes Docklands Light Railway and transfer from Heathrow Airport*) or Central Zone Card to travel in only zones 1 and 2.

	ALL ZONE CARD		CENTRAL ZONE CARD	
	ADULT	CHILD	ADULT	CHILD
3 consecutive days	$35	$16	$24	$11
4 consecutive days	$46	$19	$29	$12
7 consecutive days	$69	$29	$36	$15

Children age 5–15; age 4 and under travel free.
*Not valid on Heathrow Express or Gatwick Express.

EURAIL PASSES

Eurail Passes entitle you to unlimited travel on Europe's extensive 100,000-mile rail network in 17 countries of Europe (England, Scotland, and Wales not included) as follows:

Austria • Belgium • Denmark • Finland • France • Germany • Greece
Hungary • Ireland (Republic of) • Italy • Luxembourg • Netherlands • Norway
Portugal • Spain • Sweden • Switzerland

Eurailpass

Consecutive-day travel on any or all days for the duration of the pass.

1ST CLASS		YOUTH
15 days	$588	$382
21 days	$762	$495
1 month	$946	$615
2 months	$1,338	$870
3 months	$1,654	$1,075

Children age 4–11, half adult fare; under age 4 travel free.

Eurail Saverpass

Rail travel for 2–5 people traveling together at all times. Price is per person.

	$498
	$648
	$804
	$1,138
	$1,408

Eurail Flexipass

Choose your travel days and use them within 60 days.

1ST CLASS	
10 days in 2 months	$694
15 days in 2 months	$914

Children age 4–11, half adult fare; under age 4 travel free.

Eurail Saver Flexipass

Rail travel for 2–5 people traveling together at all times. Price is per person.

	$592
	$778

Eurail Youth Pass*

2ND CLASS	
15 days	$414
21 days	$534
1 month	$664
2 months	$938
3 months	$1,160

Eurail Youth Flexipass*

2ND CLASS	
10 days in 2 months	$488
15 days in 2 months	$642

*Available for passengers age 12–25 on their first date of travel.

Eurail Selectpass

The Eurail Selectpass gives travelers the option to customize a rail pass by choosing any 3, 4, or 5 bordering Eurail countries that are connected by train or by ship. The Selectpass covers the 17 countries in the Eurailpass network, plus Romania; Slovenia/Croatia (as one country); and Bulgaria/Montenegro (as one country). Please contact RailPass .com at (877) RAILPASS (724–5727) or www.railpass.com with inquiries.

EURAIL SELECTPASS

Travel on any or all days for the duration of the pass in any 3, 4, or 5 adjoining Eurail pass countries.

EURAIL SELECTPASS			
	3 COUNTRIES	4 COUNTRIES	5 COUNTRIES
5 days in 2 months	$370	$414	$456
6 days in 2 months	$410	$454	$496
8 days in 2 months	$488	$532	$574
10 days in 2 months	$564	$608	$650
15 days in 2 months	N/A	N/A	$826

EURAIL SELECTPASS YOUTH*			
	3 COUNTRIES	4 COUNTRIES	5 COUNTRIES
5 days in 2 months	$241	$269	$296
6 days in 2 months	$267	$295	$322
8 days in 2 months	$317	$345	$372
10 days in 2 months	$367	$395	$422
15 days in 2 months	N/A	N/A	$537

*Youth price available for passengers age 12–26. Children age 4–11, half adult fare; under age 4 travel free.

EURAIL SELECTPASS SAVER

For 2 or more persons traveling together at all times. Travel on any or all days for the duration of the pass in any 3, 4, or 5 adjoining Eurailpass countries.

EURAIL SELECTPASS SAVER			
	3 COUNTRIES	4 COUNTRIES	5 COUNTRIES
5 days in 2 months	$304	$340	$374
6 days in 2 months	$336	$372	$406
8 days in 2 months	$400	$436	$470
10 days in 2 months	$460	$496	$530
15 days in 2 months	N/A	N/A	$674

Children age 4–11, half adult fare; under age 4 travel free.

COUNTRY AND REGIONAL PASSES

Austria–Slovenia/Croatia Pass

	1ST CLASS		2ND CLASS
	ADULT	ADULT PASS SAVER	YOUTH
4 days in 2 months	$230	$200	$167
5 days in 2 months	$264	$230	$191
6 days in 2 months	$298	$260	$215
7 days in 2 months	$332	$290	$239
8 days in 2 months	$366	$320	$263
9 days in 2 months	$400	$350	$287
10 days in 2 months	$434	$380	$311

Austrian Railpass

	ADULT	
	1ST CLASS	2ND CLASS
3 days in 15 days	$160	$109
Additional days (5 max)	$20	$15

Children age 6–12, half adult fare; age 5 and under travel free. Five-day maximum additional rail days. Bonuses include discounts on steamers, local trains, and bicycle rentals.

Balkan Flexipass

Valid for rail travel in Bulgaria, Greece, Montenegro, Romania, Serbia, Turkey, Yugoslavia, and the Former Yugoslav Republic of Macedonia.

	1ST CLASS		2ND CLASS
	ADULT	SENIORS**	YOUTH
5 days in 1 month	$189	$152	$112
10 days in 1 month	$330	$264	$196
15 days in 1 month	$397	$318	$238

Children age 4–12, half adult fare.
*Youth age 13–25.
**Senior age 60 and older.

Benelux Tourrail Pass

Valid for rail travel in Belgium, Luxembourg, and the Netherlands.

5 days in 1 month	1ST CLASS	2ND CLASS
Adult	$228	$163
Youth*	—	$109

*Youth age 4–25; under age 4 travel free.

Benelux Tourrail for Two

Valid for rail travel in Belgium, Luxembourg, and the Netherlands. Prices are per person based on 2 people traveling together at all times.

	1ST CLASS	2ND CLASS
5 days in 1 month	$171	$122

Czech FlexiPass

	1ST CLASS	2ND CLASS
3 days in 15 days	$68	$48
Additional days	$9	$6

Children age 4–11, half adult fare; under age 4 travel free.
Up to 5 additional days can be added.

European East Pass

Valid for rail travel in Austria, Czech Republic, Hungary, Poland, and Slovak Republic.

	1ST CLASS	2ND CLASS
5 days in 1 month	$226	$160
Additional days	$26	$19

Up to 5 additional days can be added. Children age 4–11, half adult fare; under age 4 travel free.

FinnRail Pass

Valid for any 3, 5, or 10 days of rail travel within 1 month.

	ADULT	
	1ST CLASS	2ND CLASS
3 days in 1 month	$214	$143
5 days in 1 month	$286	$191
10 days in 1 month	$387	$259

Children age 2–15, half adult fare; under age 2 travel free.

St. Petersburg "Add-on": From Helsinki to St. Petersburg on the Sibelius train round-trip. Train reservations must be made a minimum of 48 hrs in advance. Exchange vouchers at Helsinki main rail station a minimum of 24 hrs prior to departure time. **Available only in conjunction with a FinnRail Pass, ScanRail Pass, Eurailpass, or Eurail Selectpass (including Finland).**

	ADULT		CHILD*	
	1ST CLASS	2ND CLASS	1ST CLASS	2ND CLASS
Round-trip	$225	$145	$135	$85

Children age 2–15. Children under age 2 travel free. Passes must be validated within six months of issue date.

France Railpass

	ADULT		SAVERPASS*	
	1ST CLASS	2ND CLASS	1ST CLASS	2ND CLASS
4 days in 1 month	$252	$218	$215	$186
Additional days	$32	$28	$28	$24

	YOUTH		SENIOR
	1ST CLASS	2ND CLASS	(1ST CLASS ONLY)
4 days in 1 month	$189	$164	$228
Additional days	$24	$21	$29

Maximum of 6 additional days. Youth age 12–25; children age 4–11, half adult fare; under age 4 travel free. Senior age 60 and older.
*Price per person based on 2 people traveling together at all times, includes 40% companion discount.

France 'n Italy Pass

	ADULT		YOUTH*
	1ST CLASS	2ND CLASS	2ND CLASS
Any 4 days in 2 months	$309	$269	$199
Additional rail day (6 max)	$30	$27	$21

*Under the age of 26

France 'n Italy Saverpass

Unlimited travel for 2–4 persons traveling together at all times. Price per person.

	ADULT	
	1ST CLASS	2ND CLASS
Any 4 days in 2 months	$259	$229
Additional rail day (6 max)	$27	$24

Children age 4–11, half adult fare.
Bonuses include special fares for Eurostar, TGV, and others.

France 'n Spain Pass

Unlimited rail travel on national networks of France and Spain.

	ADULT		YOUTH*
	1ST CLASS	2ND CLASS	2ND CLASS
Any 4 days in 2 months	$309	$269	$199
Additional rail day (6 max)	$33	$29	$22

*Under the age of 26
Children age 4–11, half adult fare. Children under age 4 travel free.

France 'n Spain Saverpass

Price per person based on 2–4 persons traveling together at all times.

	ADULT	
	1ST CLASS	2ND CLASS
Any 4 days in 2 months	$259	$229
Additional rail day (6 max)	$29	$25

Appendix

Appendix

France 'n Switzerland Pass

	1ST CLASS ADULT	1ST CLASS ADULT SAVERPASS*	2ND CLASS YOUTH
4 days in 2 months	$299	$259	$199
Additional rail days (6 max)	$36	$30	$21

Children age 4–11, half adult fare or saver price; under age 4 travel free. Youth under age 26.
*Price per person for 2 or more people traveling together at all times.

German Railpass

DAYS WITHIN 1 MONTH	ADULT 1ST CLASS SINGLE	ADULT 2ND CLASS SINGLE	ADULT 1ST CLASS TWIN*	ADULT 2ND CLASS TWIN*	2ND CLASS YOUTH
4 days	$260	$180	$195	$135	$142
5 days	$294	$204	$221	$153	$155
6 days	$328	$228	$246	$171	$168
7 days	$362	$252	$272	$189	$181
8 days	$396	$276	$297	$207	$194
9 days	$430	$300	$323	$225	$207
10 days	$464	$324	$348	$243	$220

Children (6–11), half adult fare. Youth age 12–25. Bonuses for passholders include free travel on KD River Steamers on certain Rhine, Main, and Moselle River sections and free travel on selected bus lines operated by Deutsche Touring/Europabus.
*Price per person based on two persons traveling together at all times.

Germany–Benelux Pass

DAYS WITHIN 2 MONTHS	ADULT 1ST CLASS	ADULT 2ND CLASS	SAVERPASS 1ST CLASS	SAVERPASS 2ND CLASS	YOUTH 2ND CLASS
5 days	$328	$246	$246	$200	$199
6 days	$362	$272	$272	$218	$217
8 days	$430	$324	$324	$258	$258
10 days	$498	$374	$374	$298	$299

Germany–Denmark Pass

DAYS WITHIN 2 MONTHS	ADULT 1ST CLASS	ADULT 2ND CLASS	ADULT PASS SAVER 1ST CLASS	ADULT PASS SAVER 2ND CLASS/YOUTH
5 days	$300	$230	$230	$188
6 days	$334	$254	$254	$204
8 days	$402	$302	$302	$236
10 days	$470	$350	$350	$268

Greece 'n Italy Pass

DAYS WITHIN 2 MONTHS	ADULT 1ST CLASS	ADULT 2ND CLASS	ADULT PASS SAVER 1ST CLASS	ADULT PASS SAVER 2ND CLASS	YOUTH
4 days	$299	$239	$255	$204	$200
5 days	$329	$263	$280	$224	$220
6 days	$359	$287	$305	$244	$240
7 days	$389	$311	$330	$264	$260
8 days	$419	$335	$355	$284	$280
9 days	$449	$359	$380	$304	$300
10 days	$479	$383	$405	$324	$320

Holland Rail Pass

	ADULT	
	1ST CLASS	2ND CLASS
3 days in 1 month	$120	$80
5 days in 1 month	$171	$122

Children age 4–11, half adult fare; under age 4 travel free.

Hungary–Slovenia/Croatia Pass

	1ST CLASS ADULT	2ND CLASS ADULT PASS SAVER	YOUTH
5 days in 2 months	$200	$170	$140
6 days in 2 months	$220	$188	$159
8 days in 2 months	$260	$222	$189
10 days in 2 months	$300	$256	$209

Hungarian Flexipass

	1ST CLASS
5 days in 15 days	$76
10 days in 1 month	$95

Children age 5–14, half adult fare; under age 5 travel free.

Iberic Railpass

Valid for unlimited rail travel in Spain and Portugal.

	1ST CLASS	1ST CLASS SAVERPASS
3 days in 2 months	$249	$219
Additional days	$35	$30

Supplements required for travel on the AVE and Talgo high-speed trains. Maximum of 7 extra days may be added. Children age 4–11, half adult fare; under age 4 travel free.

Italian Trenitalia Pass

Valid for unlimited travel on the entire Italian Rail network including InterCity, Eurocity, and Rapido trains with no surcharge. Supplement required on Eurostar Italia, Artesia, and ETR trains.

DAYS WITHIN 2 MONTHS	ADULT 1ST CLASS	2ND CLASS	ADULT SAVERPASS* 1ST CLASS	2ND CLASS	YOUTH 2ND CLASS
4 days	$239	$191	$203	$163	$160
5 days	$263	$210	$223	$179	$176
6 days	$287	$229	$243	$195	$192
7 days	$311	$248	$263	$211	$208
8 days	$335	$267	$283	$227	$224
9 days	$359	$286	$303	$243	$240
10 days	$383	$305	$323	$259	$256

Youth under age 26. Children age 4–11, half adult fare; children under age 4 travel free.
*Saverpass for parties of 2–5 people traveling together at all times, price per person.

Norway Railpass

	ADULT 2ND CLASS	SENIOR 2ND CLASS	YOUTH 2ND CLASS
3 days in 1 month	$209	$151	$151
Additional rail day (5 max)	$35	$25	$25

Children age 4–15, half adult fare. Children under age 4 travel free; maximum of 2 children travel free per adult. Youth age 12–25. Senior age 60 and older. Travel on the Flam Railway Line not included. A discount of 30% offered on the Flam Line. "Signatur" Express trains run on the Southern Line and Dovreline; Bergen Line added. Supplement required, includes meals and refreshments.

Appendix

Paris Visite

	ADULT
1 day	$26
2 consecutive days	$41
3 consecutive days	$56
5 consecutive days	$67

Provides unlimited travel on all zones of the entire Paris Métro (subway), Paris bus routes, RER trains to the airports, Versailles, EuroDisney, and the funicular at the Sacré Coeur. Children age 4–11, half adult fare. Children under age 4 travel free.

Portuguese Railpass

	1ST CLASS
4 days in 15 days	$105

Children age 4–11, half adult fare; under age 4 travel free. Not valid on the Luis de Cameos train.

Prague Excursion

Valid for rail transportation from any Czech border crossing to Prague and returning within 7 days.

	ADULT		YOUTH		CHILD	
	1ST CLASS	2ND CLASS	1ST CLASS	2ND CLASS	1ST CLASS	2ND CLASS
7 days in a row	$55	$40	$45	$35	$28	$20

Youth age 12–25. Children age 4–11.

Romania–Hungary Pass

Unlimited rail travel in Romania and Hungary for five, six, eight, or ten days in two months.

	ADULT 1ST CLASS	SAVERPASS* 1ST CLASS	YOUTH 2ND CLASS
5 days in 2 months	$200	$170	$140
6 days in 2 months	$220	$188	$154
8 days in 2 months	$260	$222	$182
10 days in 2 months	$300	$256	$210

Youth under age 26.
*Price per person for 2 or more people traveling together at all times.

Romanian Railpass

	1ST CLASS
3 days in 15 days	$99
Additional rail day (12 max)	$30

Children age 4–11, half adult fare; under age 4 travel free.

ScanRail Pass

Valid for unlimited rail travel in Denmark, Finland, Norway, and Sweden.

	ADULT 2ND CLASS	SENIOR 2ND CLASS
5 days in 2 months	$291	$258
10 days in 2 months	$390	$348
21 consecutive days	$453	$400

	YOUTH 2ND CLASS
5 days in 2 months	$203
10 days in 2 months	$273
21 consecutive days	$316

Senior age 60 and older. Youth age 12–25. Children age 4–11, half adult fare; under age 4 travel free.

Spain 'n Portugal Pass

	ADULT	PASS SAVER
3 days in 2 months	$259	$229
4 days in 2 months	$294	$259
5 days in 2 months	$329	$289
6 days in 2 months	$364	$319
7 days in 2 months	$399	$349
8 days in 2 months	$434	$379
9 days in 2 months	$469	$409
10 days in 2 months	$504	$439

Spain Railpass

	1ST CLASS	2ND CLASS
3 days in 2 months	$225	$175
Additional days	$35	$30

Maximum of 10 days. The AVE and Talgo 200 require an additional supplement. Children age 4–11, half adult fare.

Swiss Card (ideal for skiers)

Valid for one round-trip rail journey plus 50% discount for additional trips (except for some mountain railroads that offer 25% discount) within a 1-month validity period.

	1ST CLASS	2ND CLASS
1 month—1 round-trip	$166	$124

Children under age 16, free with parent. Children age 6–15 not accompanied by parent, half adult fare. Children under age 6 travel free.

Swiss Pass

Valid for consecutive-day unlimited travel. Choice of 1st class or 2nd class. Free Swiss Family Card: Children under age 16 travel free when accompanied by at least 1 parent; half adult fare when not accompanied by parent. Includes travel lake steamers, transportation on 35 city systems, postal and private bus lines, and selected private railways, such as Glacier Express and Panoramic Express.

	ADULT SWISS PASS		ADULT SAVERPASS*		CHILD SWISS PASS	
	1ST CLASS	2ND CLASS	1ST CLASS	2ND CLASS	1ST CLASS	2ND CLASS
4 days	$260	$170	$221	$145	$130	$85
8 days	$360	$240	$306	$204	$180	$120
15 days	$440	$290	$374	$247	$220	$145
22 days	$500	$335	$425	$285	$250	$118
1 month	$560	$375	$476	$319	$280	$188

SWISS YOUTH PASS**	1ST CLASS	2ND CLASS
4 days	$195	$128
8 days	$270	$180
15 days	$330	$218
22 days	$375	$252
1 month	$420	$282

Appendix

| | SWISS FLEXIPASS | | SWISS SAVER FLEXIPASS* | |
	1ST CLASS	2ND CLASS	1ST CLASS	2ND CLASS
Any 3 days in 1 month	$250	$166	$213	$141
Any 4 days in 1 month	$294	$196	$250	$167
Any 5 days in 1 month	$338	$226	$287	$192
Any 6 days in 1 month	$386	$256	$328	$218
Any 8 days in 1 month	$450	$300	$383	$255

*Price per person based on 2 or more adults traveling together at all times; children under age 16 travel free when accompanied by a parent.
**For persons ages 16–25.

Swiss Transfer Ticket

Great for skiers or for those who will stay in 1 place. Provides for 1 round-trip ticket.

1ST CLASS	2ND CLASS
$128	$85

Children under age 16 travel free when accompanied by at least 1 parent; otherwise, children age 6–15, half adult fare. Children under age 6 travel free.

Railpass Protection

Entitles traveler to a 100% reimbursement on the unused portion of the rail pass if lost or stolen while traveling in Britain or Europe.
$10 per pass
See "Railpass/Rail & Drive Protection" on last page of Appendix.

RAIL/DRIVE PASSES

BritRail Pass 'n Drive

Valid for any 5 days (3 rail, 2 car) within 2 months. No additional rail days can be added. Additional car days up to 5 maximum.

| CAR CATEGORY | 2 ADULTS* | | ADD'L CAR DAY |
	1ST CLASS	STANDARD CLASS	
Mini	$359	$259	$49
Compact	$369	$269	$61
Intermed.	$379	$279	$71
Compact automatic	$395	$295	$85
Intermed. automatic	$409	$305	$95
Luxury automatic	$529	$429	$215

| CAR CATEGORY | 1 ADULT | |
	1ST CLASS	STANDARD CLASS
Mini	$415	$315
Compact	$435	$329
Intermed.	$455	$355
Compact automatic	$479	$379
Intermed. automatic	$505	$399
Luxury automatic	$729	$649

Children age 5–15: 1st class for $149.50, 2nd class for $102.50. Children under age 5 travel free. Extra car days for 1 adult are the same as for 2 adults.
*Prices are per person.

Eurail Selectpass Drive

Any 5 days (3 rail, 2 Avis or Hertz car rental) within 2 months in any of the 3, 4, or 5 bordering countries selected. Add up to 7 additional rail days and an unlimited number of car days.

CAR CATEGORY	2 ADULTS* 1ST CLASS	1 ADULT 1ST CLASS	ADD'L CAR DAY
3 countries			
Economy	$295	$339	$49
Compact	$309	$369	$65
Intermediate	$319	$395	$75
Small automatic**	$335	$435	$95
4 countries			
Economy	$329	$379	$49
Compact	$345	$405	$65
Intermediate	$355	$425	$75
Small automatic**	$369	$459	$95
5 countries			
Economy	$365	$409	$49
Compact	$375	$439	$65
Intermediate	$385	$455	$75
Small automatic**	$405	$485	$95

Extra rail days are $39 each (7 max).

*Prices per person based on 2 people traveling together. Third and fourth person sharing car $246 per person. Children age 4–11, $123, 3 countries; $141, 4 countries; $158, 5 countries. Additional raildays, $19.50 per child per day. Children under age 4 travel free. Hertz Eurail Selectpass Drive car not available in Norway, Finland, or Sweden.

**Small automatic with Hertz only in major locations.

EurailDrive Pass

Any 6 days (4 rail, 2 car) within 2 months for travel in any of the seventeen Eurail countries. Add up to 5 additional rail days and unlimited number of car days.

CAR CATEGORY	2 ADULTS* 1ST CLASS	1 ADULT 1ST CLASS	ADD'L CAR DAY
Economy	$415	$459	$49
Compact	$429	$489	$64
Intermediate	$439	$505	$75
Compact auto.**	$455	$539	$95
Add'l rail day	$45	$45	

Third and fourth person sharing car $365 per person. Children age 4–11, $182.50 for the basic package. Extra rail days, $22.50 each.

*Prices per person based on 2 people traveling together.

**Cars with automatic shift are available at selected rental locations.

France Rail 'n Drive

Any 4 days (2 rail, 2 car) within 1 month for travel in France. Add up to 3 additional rail days and car days. Third and fourth persons sharing car, $179 per person.

CAR CATEGORY	1ST CLASS 2 ADULTS*	1 ADULT	ADD'L CAR DAY
Economy	$205	$249	$39
Compact	$219	$269	$49
Intermediate	$235	$289	$55
Full size	$255	$319	$79
Minivan	$299	$439	$129
Compact auto.	$279	$379	$99
Add'l rail day	$29	$29	

Children age 4–11, $89.50; additional rail days, $14.50 per child per day.

*Price per person.

Appendix

Appendix

German Rail/Drive

Any 4 days (2 rail, 2 car) within 1 month for travel in Germany. Add up to 3 additional rail days.

CAR CATEGORY	1ST CLASS 2 ADULTS*	1 ADULT	2ND CLASS 2 ADULTS*	1 ADULT	ADD'L CAR DAY
Economy	$189	$235	$159	$205	$49
Compact	$205	$269	$179	$235	$65
Intermediate	$215	$285	$189	$255	$75
Compact auto.**	$269	$319	$199	$289	$95
Add'l rail day	$61	$61	$51	$51	

*Price per person. Children and/or third and fourth person need only purchase regular rail pass.
**Cars with automatic transmission are available at selected locations.

Italy Rail/Drive

Valid for 4 days of unlimited rail travel within 1 month and 2 days of car rental for travel in Italy. An unlimited number of car days may be added.

CAR CATEGORY	ADULT 1ST CLASS	2ND CLASS	2 ADULTS* 1ST CLASS	2ND CLASS	ADD'L CAR DAY
Compact	$375	$329	$638	$538	$65
Economy	$339	$289	$590	$490	$49
Intermediate	$389	$345	$650	$550	$75
Small auto**	$389	$345	$650	$550	$75

Third and fourth persons sharing car or children need only purchase a Trenitalia Pass.
*Total price for both adults.
**Automatic transmission available at selected locations.

Scanrail/Drive

Valid for 5 days of unlimited rail travel and 2 days of car rental to be used within 2 months in the Scandinavian countries of Denmark, Finland, Norway, and Sweden. Unlimited number of car days may be added.

CAR CATEGORY	2ND CLASS 2 ADULTS*	1 ADULT	ADD'L CAR DAY
Economy	$339	$399	$59
Compact	$359	$439	$69
Intermediate	$369	$449	$79

Third and fourth person need only purchase rail passes. Car rental not available in Finland. Automatics not available in Norway.
*Price per person.

Spain Rail/Drive

Valid for 5 days (3 rail, 2 car) within 2 months of travel in Spain. Up to 2 additional rail days and unlimited car days available.

CAR CATEGORY	2 ADULTS* 1ST CLASS	1 ADULT 1ST CLASS	ADD'L CAR DAY
Economy	$498	$289	$39
Compact	$538	$315	$49
Intermediate	$558	$329	$59
Compact auto.**	$578	$339	$59
Add'l rail day	$78	$39	

Third and fourth person sharing car need only purchase Spain FlexiPass. Need only purchase rail passes for children.
*Price for both persons.
**Automatic transmission available at selected locations.

Railpass/Rail & Drive Protection

This program entitles you to a 100 percent reimbursement on the unused portion of a rail pass or a combination Railpass/Rail & Drive program if lost or stolen while traveling in Britain or Europe.

$10 per rail pass or for the driver

$10 for each additional person

High Barnet
Totteridge & Whetstone
Woodside Park
West Finchley
Finchley Central
East Finchley
Highgate
Archway
Tufnell Park
Kentish Town
den oad

Cockfosters
Oakwood
Southgate
Arnos Grove
Bounds Green
Wood Green
Turnpike Lane
Manor House
Arsenal
Holloway Road
Caledonian Road
Caledonian Road & Barnsbury

Seven Sisters
Tottenham Hale

Blackhorse Road
Walthamstow Central

Epping
Theydon Bois
Loughton   Debden
Buckhurst Hill   Roding Valley †   Chigwell †
Woodford   Grange † Hill   Hainault
South Woodford   Fairlop
Barkingside
Snaresbrook   Redbridge   Newbury Park
Wanstead   Gants Hill
Leytonstone

Upminster
Upminster Bridge
Hornchurch
Elm Park
Dagenham East
Dagenham Heathway
Becontree
Upney
Barking
East Ham
Upton Park
Plaistow
West Ham

Finsbury Park
ross ras

Hackney Central   Hackney Wick   Leyton
Canonbury
Highbury & Islington
Dalston Kingsland   Homerton
Angel
Farringdon
Barbican
ell re
Moorgate

Old Street
Liverpool Street

Bethnal Green   Mile End
Shoreditch †
Bow Road
Bow Church ⊖ 200m
Pudding Mill Lane
Stratford

Bromley-by-Bow

St. Paul's
cery ne ★ n†
Bank
Cannon Street

Aldgate East
Whitechapel
Aldgate

Stepney Green
All Saints
Devons Road
East India
Canning Town
Bus to London City Airport ✈

Monument   Tower Hill
Fenchurch Street 150m
Tower Gateway
lackfriars
le ★
London Bridge
Bermondsey
Canada Water
Borough
Castle

Shadwell   Westferry   Poplar
Limehouse   Blackwall
Wapping   West India Quay
Rotherhithe
Canary Wharf
River Thames
Heron Quays
South Quay
Crossharbour & London Arena
Mudchute
Island Gardens
Surrey Quays

North Greenwich
West Silvertown
West Silvertown

Royal Victoria
Custom House for ExCeL
Prince Regent
Royal Albert
Beckton Park
Cyprus
Pontoon Dock
London City Airport
Silvertown
Gallions Reach
Beckton
North Woolwich   King George V

New Cross Gate   New Cross
Cutty Sark for Maritime Greenwich
Greenwich
Deptford Bridge
Elverson Road
Lewisham

○ Interchange stations
≷ Connections with National Rail
⛴ Connections with riverboat services
▭ Connection with Tramlink
✈ Airport interchange   ★ Closed Sundays
▲ Served by Piccadilly line trains early morning and late evening
† For opening times see poster journey planners. Certain stations are closed on public holidays.

i 24 hour London Travel Information
020 7222 1234

Textphone
020 7918 3015

www.tfl.gov.uk
www.tflwap.gov.uk/

LTM B/W FA(a) 04/03

UNDERGROUND

Reg. User No. 05/E/1433

There's no better way to see Europe than by rail. Our experts have years of experience in helping plan the perfect trip. Rail travel offers much more freedom than packaged tours and many advantages over renting a car.

www.EUROTRIPS.com

Let Us Help Plan the Perfect European Rail Excursion for You!

Visit www.EUROTRIPS.com to see a sample of some of our most popular self-guided rail tours, or if you are interested in having us build a special itinerary just for you, e-mail us at info@eurotrips.com.